Stepparenting

Creating and Recreating Families in America Today

Edited by

Stanley H. Cath
Moisy Shopper

7A₽ THE ANALYTIC PRESS

2001   Hillsdale, NJ   London

Published by
The Analytic Press, Inc., Publishers
Editorial Offices:
101 West Street
Hillsdale, New Jersey 07642
www.analyticpress.com

Set in Elante 10.5/12 by
Christopher Jaworski, Qualitext
qualitext@earthlink.net

Index by Leonard S. Rosenbaum

Library of Congress Cataloging-in-Publication Data

Stepparenting : creating and recreating families in America today /
edited by Stanley H. Cath, Moisy Shopper.
p.   cm.
Includes bibliographical references and index.
ISBN 0-88163-176-0
1. Stepparents—Psychology. 2. Stepparents—Psychology—Case Studies.
3. Stepchildren—Psychology. 4. Stepchildren—Psychology—Case Studies.
5. Stepfamilies—Psychological aspects. 6. Family psychotherapy—
Case Studies. I. Cath, Stanley H. II. Shopper, Moisy.

HQ759.92.S736 2001
306.874—dc21
2001041317

Printed in the United States of America
10 9 8 7 6 5 4 3 2 1

CONTENTS

Preface

Some Reflections on Shakespeare and the History of Family Life

The preponderance of the literature on divorce, adoption, and reconstituted families has focused on the experience of children rather than that of parents. Despite our best attempts to be equally considerate of both groups, the reader will find that most of our authors still pay significant attention to those who combine weakness, immaturity, and vulnerability, namely the young. In this, they follow an old pattern, for the very first pediatric text extant in English, *The Boke of Chyldren* by Thomas Phaer (ca. 1544), did exactly the same. The author's aim was "to do them good that have the moost nede, that is to say the children, and to distrybute in Englishe to them that are unlearned part of the treasure, which aught not to be secrete for lucre of a fewe."

Our original intent, inspired by previous work on fathers, had been to focus on the stepfather's adult experience in order to emphasize the opportunities to prevent further pain and pathology in the family system. Gradually, we found ourselves widening our horizons and including chapters on stepmothers and related topics. Our aim became more to illuminate the adult experience of divorce sufficiently to, share our new appreciation, not only of the complexities involved but also of the long-term opportunity for growth inherent in this increasingly pervasive phenomenon. Our efforts have been guided and enriched by the new research on the nature of human attachments derived from a modern psychoanalytic perspective. If we succeed in this undertaking it will be due in large measure to the contributions of our patients who have shared their diverse recollections on the intrapsychic and interpersonal meanings of having lived in splitting and reconstituting families. If we fail to succeed in this goal, it may reflect the uniqueness and complexities of this human experience, for each stepparent enters his or her new family with experiences and background comparable to none. This is the case with any family losing or gaining a new member, be it by divorce, remarriage, adoption, or death. All these events are colored by each person's initial and retrospective interpretation, uniquely distilled through the personal meaning of that event. When we add ethnic, religious, financial, educational, and family of origin variables, we often have as incomparable a research situation as has ever been studied. Yet, laymen and professionals alike try to ferret out some general, valid principles so as to make some sense out of chaos, to seek out some understanding in areas of seeming causality and thereby learn how to mitigate future stresses in such inherently turbulent settings.

The potentially tragic effects on subsequent generations of severe parental discord was beautifully illustrated almost 400 years ago by Shakespeare in his *A Midsummer Night's Dream*. Listen to Titania reproaching herself and her husband, King Oberon:

> Thy brawls hast disturbed our sport . . . [free love]
> As in revenge . . .
> The wind has sucked up . . . contagious fogs from the sea,
> It's raining all the time . . .
> Causing the rivers to flood the land.
> *Green corn has rotted ere his youth has attained a beard,*
> Everyone's work is lost.
> And the *seasons are unrecognizable.*
> *This progeny of evil* comes from our debate!

As clinicians, we can appreciate Shakespeare's portrayal of devastation in the natural world as a metaphor for human responses to the fluctuations of love and hate between the most powerful figures in an individual's life. For quarrelling or divorcing parents and their children, familiar seasons do become unrecognizable and contagion of anxious confusion spreads throughout the family land, especially when actual or perceived infidelity is involved.

The painful loss of security and bewilderment over failed commitment erases the conviction of "belonging" forever to people one thought one knew. Promises once made are too painful to remember and forever may become an incomprehensible if not an unacceptable expectation of the future.

Let us assume that Shakespeare's denouement of *A Midsummer Night's Dream* reveals his understanding that the need to restore intrapsychic order requires a new evaluation of external reality in order to reach a more creative and healing solution. Is this reflected in the statistic that the majority of the divorced remarry? Could they be impelled to erase Shakespeare's image of indifferent parents as "progeny of evil"?

Does Shakespeare's change-in-the-weather metaphor apply not only to the infrastructure of rupturing families but also to most fairy stories read to small children? A tornado marks the beginning of *The Wizard of Oz* as Dorothy, an orphaned child, is torn away from gray Kansas and her preoccupied aunt and uncle. Being similarly "lost in space" marks much of contemporary science fiction and is typified by the film *E.T. The Extra-Terrestrial*. It appears that Shakespeare's, Baum's, and Spielberg's familiar, fictional solutions to such developmental crises may be viewed as creative even if they contain similarly naïve, archaic formulas condensed into the fantasy that all one need do to restore the status quo is to get safely home. After all, omnipotent parents, especially royalty and happy families, are supposed to weather all storms and "live happily ever after." The Bard of Avon typically solved his tragedies either with healing marriages or "all's well" when and if the rightful king (or queen or heirs) was returned to the throne.

But, unlike literature, fairy tales, or cosmogenic myths, splitting families in real life almost always contain confused, terrified, and possibly soon to be "stepped" children and adults. Some youngsters, adults, or both will be helplessly tossed between alien and familiar residential spaces as their destinies rest in the hands of seemingly omnipotent legal systems with unpredictable if not unstable godlike powers. Facing these arbitrary, incomprehensible, and disillusioning forces, most participants feel earth-quake-shaken inside and report that a basic trust has been violated; justice has not been served, and that something deep in themselves as well as in formerly idealized loved ones has been irrevocably changed.

We hasten to add that while recognizing the seriousness of these self-altering events, in our thinking we do not preclude the potential for healthier and better-attuned coupling and parenting in the succeeding choices of partners. In fact much of our clinical material supports this.

Admittedly, stepparenting in all its vicissitudes may be more challenging than biological childrearing. Teachers tell us that in some of their classrooms about half the children come from multiple homes and have multiple caretakers. Many of these caretakers as well as early childhood educators are eager for help in understanding and intervening with these children and their families. Phyllis Cath has devoted much time and creative energy to meet that need in the San Francisco area. One consistent finding of her research is that children of divorce, like many traumatized youngsters, may have a hard time playing and using fantasy creatively. They seem burdened by the fact that rich, oedipal fantasies, reminiscent of Harry Potter's getting rid of seemingly inept and interfering parents, really came true. We do hope this volume will be of especial value to educators as well as to clinicians and parents.

Unless a deep parental hunger exists in a child (Cath, 1982), the expected quest for a father may be too conflicted to express openly. When the thirst for a male figure is intense, the reaction of the mother may be to understand and foster it or to deny its reality. It is times like these that require inordinate patience, tact, and self-other forgiveness by everyone concerned, including those who wish to teach or help.

Our "boke" on lessons learned about the highly difficult challenge posed in the processes of creating and recreating families will follow people as they try to reevaluate past misunderstandings and to reset themselves into a new context. Many will feel burdened but at the same time awakened by a deeper sensitivity to the importance of having one's own money, of making decisions autonomously. Despite consistent resolves to live in the present, divorced people find it hard not to keep reassessing the terms of and the prices paid for breaking apart, especially as they come to appreciate the fact that divorce is rarely a total break for their children. Yet, the children seem to be irrepressibly flexible and to be having an easier time of it than do the adults. Some feel "caught up in an unexpected morass," as one teenager described the experience of living in two homes. Others retain hopes for either a new resolution with greater fairness or a renewed appreciation by the nonresidential parent, "if only I could make him understand!" All of this anxiety may be transferred onto new lovers so that all parties find themselves in a suspended state. One boy said, "I am on cynical guard," fearing he might be too easily seduced into loving as mistakenly as he believed both mother and father did initially and might be doing again. Although the number of remarriages that fail exceeds the failure rate of first marriages, we need to remember that with special patience over time, many happier and more resilient compromises are reported the second time. As often as we were able, we selected clinical material to illustrate how remarriage was done successfully and, when not successful, why it failed.

Indeed, I believe the special value of this compilation of papers may lie in the clarity of clinical examples that portray the ongoing periods of creative, if slow, learning needed by parents and children, biological and step, as they test the waters of a new family system and try to elicit different and hopefully more attuned responses from each other.

We would like to have included more of the implications of "how to do it" than we have, but our legitimate concerns were that generalized advice is often not applicable in specific context or may be prematurely misapplied. We feared that any attempts to offer "advice to the perplexed" would be woefully inadequate and would lack the depth of understanding needed in specific situations. As clinicians, we still believe the soundest advocacy possible should be derived from a more prolonged study that includes an understanding of the dynamics of repetitive themes of thinking, feeling, and interactive behavior that characterizes each and every case. Naturally, as psychoanalysts we are deeply impressed by the roles of fantasy and unconscious motivation and believe past events in each individual will exert immense and determinative significance in a couple's family life. This experientially biased position has been reinforced by the research of the psychoanalytically informed, seasoned pediatrician, T. B. Brazelton. He writes (1994), "The opportunity for pediatricians [Editors' note: and others] to play a role in the prevention of failures in child [Editors' note: and adult] development is enormous!" He has identified these therapeutic opportunities as "touch points," critical moments in the life of each individual that permit life-altering interventions. Accordingly, encouraged by his example of applied psychoanalytic insight, we have cautiously compiled a few commentaries in selected chapters in an attempt to give some practical advice. We hope to highlight the detection of early signals of distress, such as when being together in the new relationship begins to imperil one partner's sense of being an autonomous individual in the very same way as happened in the first marriage. Our hope is that adults and their offspring may emerge from such inevitably ambivalent encounters with safer, stronger bonds, renewed self-esteem, and less retrenchment in old, regressive patterns. Divorced men and women need to reinforce their faith in themselves as competent and safe nurturers as they communicate with and interact with their own and especially someone else's child. From the base of our clinical experience we hold that reconstructing a family has the potential for enhancing safety in closeness, recognition as an individual, and the development of warm bonds even for those not blood related.

On the positive side, one woman (Sander, 1991), as far as I know without awareness of recent psychoanalytic thought on the healing import of being recognized, described her second marriage as the very first adult setting in which *she felt known by another person's mind.* This coupling became a beautiful example of mutually empathic and shared identification in which increased tolerance for each other's imperfections led to a most successful marriage.

Moisy Shopper and I dedicate this book both to the courageous people who have chosen to try again and whose associations fill these pages, and to the people with whom they have shared their travails, our authors.

—Stanley H. Cath

References

Brazelton, T. B. (1994), Touchpoints: Opportunities for preventing problems in the parent–child relationship. *Acta Paediatr.*, 394:36–39.

Cath, S. H. (1982), Divorce and the child: The father question hour. In: *Father and Child: Developmental and Clinical Perspectives,* ed. S. H. Cath, A. R. Gurwitt & J. M. Ross. Boston: Little Brown, pp. 467–479.

Phaer, T. (ca. 1544), *The Boke of Chyldren. New Engl. J. Med.,* February 2000.

Sander, L. (1991), Recognition process: Context and experience of being known. Presented at Conference on the Psychic Life of the Infant: Origins of Human Identity, University of Massachusetts, Amherst.

Shakespeare, W. (n.d.), A *Midsummer Night's Dream.* In: *The Annotated Shakespeare* by A. L. Rowe. Octavian Books, p. 246.

Acknowledgments

Eleven years have passed since this book was conceived. We might say there were unexpected labor pains on the way to its delivery to the publisher. For the patience needed to tolerate my obsessive inclinations toward greater inclusiveness of subject matter, I am deeply grateful to The Analytic Press, my coeditors, and the contributors to the book. I believe the delay enriched the book, and I use as an example the late arrival of Moisy Shopper's splendid chapter, "Incest: What Is It, and How Did It Come to Be?" For bearing with me during those 11 years of gestation, I especially thank you, Paul Stepansky, Managing Director of The Analytic Press, from the depths of my heart! Lenni Kobrin and Nancy Liguori of your staff have been professionally helpful and kindly in thoughtfulness.

To my coeditor Moisy, I say I have been a coeditor numerous times, but the harmonic resonance between us stands out as unique. You have been the easiest person with whom to discuss complex, sometimes irresolvable issues and on whom to lay an extra burden, such as the chapter mentioned above. In the process you became a most valued friend. I am pleased we are planning to work together again on a new project.

Lora Tessman, one of the most creative and generous minds in psychoanalysis today, worked in the early years as a coeditor with Moisy and me. No matter how disappointing, it is hardly to be wondered at that her own research and writings became so rewarding and demanding that she could not continue as coeditor. Lora, I will always wonder how much more your inordinately insightful understanding of the human family might have further enriched this book.

Brenda Moccia, you are so much more than a secretary. Not only have you become my everyday lifesaving and organizing stabilizer, but also an upbeat, valued presence, always there when needed. For years you have comanaged my office, but, on realizing how important this project was to me, you took on the correspondence as well as the collation of most of the papers. While to date my gratitude for your devotion is all you know, be assured it will be silently reinforced many times over by any reader who benefits from this book.

I have been deeply influenced by my life with Claire, my wife of 58 years, our three children, Phyllis, Alan, and Sandra, the people they love and have loved, and the children they generated. There is no word in my lexicon for what they gave and taught me. My children brought us six grandchildren, of whom two are lovingly considered "step." It is not surprising that these lived interactions inform almost every line I write.

Phyllis, you truly deserve special mention. You had six years before the others came to teach your mother and me *how* to be parents, and to be so proud to be parents that we wanted more. I thank you for your inexplicable resonance life long, and for the later gift of Eric (Gann), my virtual stepson. I have certainly benefited from his and your wise insights on the manuscripts we reviewed last summer on Cape Cod.

There are no words to describe my respect for my wife, Claire. She stepped back and like a stepparent was marginalized for long intervals. During these times she tolerated many hours of my absence-isolation, always rationalized as an imperative by preoccupied writers and artists. But when deadlines are over and publication brings its sobering realities, once again you become my first audience, my true friend. I appreciate your not only nourishing my ambition but every so often raising an eyebrow at any pretense I had of being on a special quest.

There are many others. Carol Hulsinger, a formidable tennis partner and freelance editor, helped me clarify objectives. Margorie Engel, current president of the Stepfamily Association of America, quite appropriately stressed a "more balanced larger picture."

To others I have not mentioned, I am in your debt as well.

—Stanley H. Cath

Contributors

Jerome S. Blackman, M.D. is Professor of Clinical Psychiatry and Behavioral Sciences, Eastern Virginia Medical School of Medical College of Hampton Roads, Norfolk, VA; Training and Supervising Analyst, New York Freudian Society, Washington, DC Psychoanalytic Training Program.

Rachel R. Boersma, M.S., R.N., C.A.R.N. is Senior Research Associate in Forensic Nursing, Harvard Medical School Program in Psychiatry and the Law at Massachusetts Mental Health Center; Instructor, Psychiatric Mental Health Nursing, Fitchburg State College.

Ira Brenner, M.D. is Executive Director and Training and Supervising Analyst, Philadelphia Psychoanalytic Institute; Author, *Dissociation of Trauma: Theory, Phenomenology, and Technique.*

Harold J. Bursztajn, M.D. is Codirector, Program in Psychiatry and the Law and Associate Professor of Psychiatry, Harvard Medical School; Author, *Medical Choices, Medical Chance: How Patients, Families, and Physicians Can Cope with Uncertainty.*

Stanley H. Cath, M.D. (ed.) is Lecturer, Harvard Medical School; Medical Director, Family Advisory Service and Treatment Center, Boston, MA.

Jamie L. Feldman, M.D. is in private practice in child and adult psychiatry and psychoanalysis, Cambridge, MA.

Henry J. Friedman, M.D. is Associate Clinical Professor of Psychiatry, Harvard Medical School; Teaching and Supervising Psychoanalyst, Massachusetts Institute for Psychoanalysis.

Robert M. Galatzer-Levy, M.D. is Training and Supervising and Child and Adolescent Supervising Analyst at the Chicago Institute for Psychoanalysis; Faculty, University of Chicago.

Jamie K. Keshet, Ed.D. is Clinical Director, Riverside Counseling Center, Newton, MA; Author, *Love and Power in the Stepfamily: A Practical Guide.*

Melvin R. Lansky, M.D. is Training and Supervising Analyst, and Director of Education, Los Angeles Psychoanalytic Institute; Clinical Professor of Psychiatry, UCLA School of Medicine.

Purnima Mehta, M.D. is Faculty, Michigan Psychoanalytic Institute; Adult and Child Psychoanalyst.

Steven L. Nickman, M.D. is Clinical Associate Professor of Psychiatry, Harvard Medical School; Coeditor, *Continuing Bonds: New Understandings of Grief.*

H. Gunther Perdigao, M.D. is Training and Supervising Analyst, New Orleans Psychoanalytic Institute.

Eugenio M. Rothe, M.D. is Associate Professor of Psychiatry and Pediatrics, University of Miami School of Medicine; Director, Child and Adolescent Psychiatry Clinic, Jackson Memorial Hospital.

Moisy Shopper, M.D. (ed.) is Clinical Professor of Child Psychiatry and Pediatrics, St. Louis University School of Medicine; Training and Supervising Analyst (Child and Adult), St. Louis Psychoanalytic Institute.

Martin A. Silverman, M.D. is Lecturer on Psychiatry, Harvard Medical School; Chair, Discussion Group on "Issues in Paternity" 1978–2000.

Brenda Clorfene Solomon, M.D. is Training and Supervising Analyst and Faculty, Chicago Institute for Psychoanalysis; Clinical Assistant Professor of Psychiatry, Abraham Lincoln School of Medicine, Chicago.

Lora Heims Tessman, Ph.D. is Supervising Analyst and Faculty, Massachusetts Institute for Psychoanalysis; Author, *Helping Children Cope with Parting Parents.*

Léon Wurmser, M.D. is Author, *The Power of the Inner Judge* and *Magic Transformation and Tragic Transformation.*

Introduction

Stepfathers

Varieties and Job Descriptions

Moisy Shopper

Folklore and fairy tales abound in stories of cruel stepmothers, but there are very few stories of stepfathers. Perhaps in the olden days the frequency of maternal deaths from puerperal sepsis in childbearing produced a large number of father remarriages and thus a large number of stepmothers. On the other hand, when a young father died—in battle or accident—there was an extended family system that would nurture and protect the fatherless family. In today's society the prevalence of divorce and remarriage create as great a number of stepfathers as stepmothers. While most stepmothers evoke an immediate association of neglect, rivalry, and cruelty (the stepmothers in *Cinderella, Snow White*, and *Hansel and Gretel*), the stepfather has no such automatic connotation. A 1993 Hollywood film, *This Boy's Life*, attempted to fill this void by portraying the stepfather as exceedingly cruel, unloving, and sadistic.

To label a person a "stepfather" is to accept automatically a legal and sociological framework as the primary theoretical conceptualization. We could, and when appropriate, we do use genetic, psychological, or child-oriented frames of classification. In the average family we see a *unity* of genetic, legal, sociological, psychological, and child-oriented frames of reference. However, in our current diversity of marriage/non-marriage formats and the many planned and unplanned modes of childrearing, we will have many variants of stepfathers and stepfather experiences. It is the purpose of this article to delineate these varieties and to comment on them.

It is a common assumption (including the legal system) that the husband of the woman giving birth is indeed the biological father of the child. While in most instances this is a valid belief, in other instances it is no more than an assumption. For example, when family members are tested for their compatibility to be an organ donor to their child, the resulting data has, on occasion, clearly shown that the father of the child did not contribute genetically to the child's conception. On occasion, there have been times when I have been consulted by a pediatrician as to how to handle this very sensitive and inadvertently obtained piece of information. When genetic counseling is required, a mother, often in confidence, will tell the genetic counselor that her husband is not the father of their child. The Swedish playwright August Strindberg, in his play, *The Father*, dealt explicitly with this issue when a wife repeatedly taunted her husband that he could not possibly be certain that he was the biological father of their child. The hurt and narcissistic wounding drives her husband to insanity.

These pediatric and literary instances have their counterparts in clinical practice. In my psychotherapy and psychoanalytic practice, I have had several instances in which the husband was not the child's father. One father knowingly accepted the child as his own, accepted full legal and economic responsibility, and acted very much the father to this child. When the child was four, the marriage ended in divorce; he acted similarly to other involved, caring fathers in wanting as much custodial time as possible. In another instance, a husband suspected his wife's infidelities. When their third child bore little resemblance to either himself or the other two children, he clearly discriminated against his "stepchild." While the affair was never made explicit, it seemed to the wife (my patient) that her husband knew he was not the biological father of the child and was expressing his resentment about her infidelity not directly to her, but rather against the child of her extramarital liaison. This marriage, too, ended in divorce. In the first situation, however, the father wanted a child and tolerated the narcissistic injury of his wife's premarital pregnancy by another man as the "price" of marriage and a child. The other father made the child the object of his anger, an anger displaced from his wife. Having two children already, his third child was not wanted, planned, or accepted. Both fathers were *legal* fathers of their respective children, but only one could be said to have been a *psychological* father. *Biologically,* both were stepfathers, but only one became a psychological father. In both instances, the legal issue was clear cut and identical, that is, each father bore legal responsibilities for and had legal privileges with his child.

The ties between stepfathers and their children, no matter how psychologically strong in intensity or duration, nevertheless have very little legal foundation or legal protection. The law is more likely to recognize the kinship of blood relatedness than the affectionate bonds resulting from psychological parenting. Since the relationship between a stepfather and his child is legally a very vulnerable one, this is not an academic issue for stepfathers. For example, a woman divorced her husband when their children were three-and-a-half years and one year of age. The father was alcoholic and had no interest in his two sons. The mother soon remarried and the stepfather was called "father" by his two stepsons. He was the only father with whom they had *any* contact. The stepfather was college-educated, well-read, interested in political and cultural issues, and a very involved and concerned father. The biological father was grade-school educated; preferred to live in a rural environment, and divided his time equally between farming, God, and AA. Through the latter two he became sober and married a woman similar to himself. When the mother of the two children, by that time ages 10 and 7 1/2, died after a brief but serious illness, the biological father "wanted his kin" and went to court to secure custody of his two biological children via a writ of habeas corpus. The judge did not wish to hear any psychiatric or other testimony, and summarily granted custody to the biological father, to take effect immediately. The two boys left the courtroom with their biological father, of whom they had no memory or even contact, and began immediately going to school and living in his rural community. The issues of change of schools, communities, friendships, and so on obviously were not considered. Not only did the two boys have to grieve for their recently deceased mother, but they now had to grieve for their psychologically deceased stepfather, who was not given any visiting privileges. The stepfather was able to see the two boys only during the court-approved maternal grandmother's visitations. The maternal grandmother, unlike the stepfather, was considered a party to the dispute, and was given visitation. While a different judge might have shown greater sophistication and appreciation of the children's psychological status, most judges are not taught this in their legal training, and many have not had good experiences with mental health professionals. While I am emphasizing the law's capacity for cruelty when the law is applied in an unfeeling and psychologically ignorant manner, I also want to emphasize our obligation as analysts to become involved in forensic issues. We are in a position to educate attorneys and judges about psychological matters so that their discretionary powers and legal knowledge may include other than a narrow legal approach.

I think this case also illustrates the extreme vulnerability of the stepfather–stepchild relationship. Wherever possible, a stepfather should attempt to adopt his stepchild(ren). In some instances, the biological father, even though uninterested and uninvolved, may still wish to maintain his "property rights" and will not voluntarily consent to the termination of his parental rights. However, when a more propitious legal situation prevails, a legal adoption solidifies and supports the stepchild–stepfather bond, which is often symbolized by a legal name change. This too, reinforces their bond, and confirms the child's identity as the child of that (step)father. While from a practical standpoint little may appear to change after the adoption, the intrapsychic changes in both child and stepfather may be considerable.

The Surrogate Stepfather

Surrogate stepfathers occur when the mother has a boyfriend (lover, paramour) to whom she is not married and who has significant contact with "receptive" child(ren) of the mother. "Receptive" refers to the child's psychological willingness to utilize the paramour as a surrogate stepfather. There often is an understanding between the adults that the relationship will not lead to marriage. Usually, the child knows that mother's lover is not the biological father. While the lover has no legal status in the household, he may psychologically fulfill the role and functions of a stepfather. Whether he lives in or has his own place of residence is not the crucial element. What is determinative is whether the child sees the paramour with frequency during the week, with consistency over time, and whether the relationship between the two adults seems from the child's view to be predominantly an affectionate one. If those criteria are present, to the child it will be considered a nuclear family. Another determinative factor is the degree to which the mother wishes the paramour to have a meaningful relationship with her child and to exert a "masculine" influence. For some mothers, the ability of the paramour to relate to and enjoy her child(ren) may be a condition for the continuation of her relationship with that paramour. Whether openly discussed between the two adults, there is sufficient unconscious communication between them that if the mother wishes the paramour to exert a surrogate father role, he will do so to the degree he wishes and to the degree that she permits it.

However, from the child's standpoint, many children, especially younger children, are quite eager to reconstitute a nuclear family, as well as relate to a male parent. This may be as strong in the girl as in the boy, albeit for different psychological reasons.

Clinical Example. When an infant boy's father died in a car accident, the mother, a political activist of the '60s, took up with a succession of men. When the boy was age seven, the mother (white) developed a long-lasting relationship with a (black) political activist. While not actually living in the home, he was an active participant in the boy's life. He was frequently there for weekday dinners, helped with homework, and coached the boy's football team. The boy developed into a fine athlete and joined other teams as well. When the mother and this man broke up, there was no period of mourning, but the boy "unexplainedly" dropped out of all his sports activities and for the first time was truant from school, preferring to spend his school time in pool halls. In retrospect, the mother reported that his black surrogate stepfather had a profound influence on her son, and to substantiate this, noted that her son spoke "black English" for several years, with all the slang, pronunciations, and intonations of a black ghetto child. Once in the pool halls, he was "discovered" by a pool shark and under his tutelage earned well as a reputable and skilled pool hustler.

This youngster needed a father, but could not have a stepfather at the time he so desperately needed a masculine influence in his life. After he suffered a serious but unrecognized bereavement (the black male activist), he actively sought out and found another surrogate stepfather in the pool hall. Some years later, when the boy was an adolescent, his mother married a nonpolitical, noncounterculture man. The boy ignored this legal stepfather and regarded him simply as the mother's husband but of no personal relevance to himself.

The above discussion is meant to illustrate the complexity of even defining the role and status of a stepfather, since we use different frames of reference for our definition: the legal, the social, the psychological; they may be at odds with one another in certain families and in the members of those families. To add to this complexity are the innumerable assortment of psychosocial variables, which create an almost infinite number of permutations and combinations of stepfather situations. To say that each stepfather situation is unique is both a truism and an understatement. Nevertheless, to establish some perspective, I'd like briefly to discuss the job requirements for being a stepfather.

First, the stepfather should be consciously willing and interested in being a parent. While an average expectable capacity to be a parent is often assumed, it may not always be present. A man's wish to parent a child is often ascertained by either the mother's inquiry or observation of the interactions between her child(ren) and the prospective husband. However intense her scrutiny, the man's unconscious wish to be parented by the prospective wife and her children may be missed during the courtship phase but, once married, becomes readily discernable in the more relaxed day-in/day-out interactions. The man, by marrying a woman with child(ren) from a prior marriage, acquires an "instant" family. If it is his first marriage, his naiveté and inexperience are obvious disadvantages, but on the other hand, he does not come aboard with a history of past habits, assumptions, conflicts, etc. from the prior marriage. A recent study (Roberts and Price, 1987) indicates that men seeking to marry into an instant family may be looking to be children in that family and looking for a dependable, established family for *their* own security. Their own family of origin is often one of insecurity. Ideally, the wish to parent a child should outweigh the wish to be the child themselves.

The second feature is that the stepfather needs to have the capacity and willingness to psychologically adopt his stepchild(ren) and make them his own. Simultaneously, he must recognize that they are not his own, and that their primary loyalty and love is to their biological father.[1] This factor may put certain limits and restraints on the child–stepfather relationship which may fluctuate over time. Unfortunately, these constraints are seldom clearly stated or defined, probably since they often vary over time and with different issues.

---

[1] Of course, this will vary depending on the circumstances and age of the divorce and the biological father's willingness to be a parent to his children post-divorce.

The ability to share or jointly parent a child with another man is a difficult, delicate and diplomatic task. It is difficult enough to parent jointly with a former spouse but here the stepfather is asked to co-parent with a man whom he may regard, both consciously and unconsciously, as his competitor and an ever-present intruder into the privacy of his new home. On the other hand, the biological father regards the stepfather as an intruder into his father–child relationship. Unconsciously, the stepfather may have all sorts of fantasies about his wife's former husband, his stepchild(ren)'s biological father, which may sometimes facilitate and at other times impede him in his role as a stepfather.

Third, many men, either before or during marriage, have a sense of how many children they want to parent. With experience as a parent they also develop a sense of how many children they feel capable of parenting and what sacrifices and altered lifestyle they wish to endure and for how long. As the marriage endures, original concepts may undergo considerable revision. Biological parents have an opportunity to more or less decide on the number of wished-for and wanted children. In contrast, the stepfather comes into an already established family of "N" children, which may already exceed his psychological quota, or may not leave room for the number of biological children he would like to have with his new wife. Or his current children from prior marriage(s), plus the wife's preexisting children from prior marriage(s), may exceed his ideal quota and/or his emotional and financial capacity for parenting, or leave no room for a biological child from this marriage. If there are children from the stepfather's prior marriage(s), his own loyalty conflicts may impair his ability to parent in an optimum way either set of children. In most instances, a father divorces only his wife, but maintains an active role as a parent with his children. However, when he remarries and becomes a stepfather to someone else's children, a not unexpected loyalty conflict ensues. Some men will place primary allegiance, financial support and emotional cathexis to their biological children and relegate their stepchildren to a secondary position. Idiomatic speech will often refer to something that is less than primary as a "stepchild." Obviously, this "stepchilding" of children interferes with his stepfather functions.

Clinical Example. When a man was divorced by his wife and she was awarded primary custody of their children, he unconsciously decided to seduce the children into loving him more than their mother. He visited extensively (even more than the divorce decree allowed), showered them with gifts, and promised even more. He showed little interest in his two stepchildren, both the same age and sex as his biological children. In fact, he contributed little to his current household, rationalizing that the mother worked, that it was "her house," and his current wife's child support payment from her prior marriage should take sufficient care of his stepchildren. When his second wife divorced him, the stepchildren were pleased to be rid of the "parasite." However, on a deeper level they were angry with their mother for having chosen so unwisely and for not providing them with a functioning stepfather.

Another criterion for effective stepfathering is the stepfather's capacity to relate to his new wife and stepchild(ren) as individuals in their own right, as opposed to replacements for a prior wife and child(ren) for whom he has not adequately grieved and mourned. Some divorced husbands are so overwhelmed by the divorce, and particularly by the loss of family, home, wife, and children, that a significant time is necessary for the grief and mourning work needed to cope with multiple actual and symbolic object losses. The mourning process can be short-circuited or even avoided by finding a replacement family of new wife and stepchildren. The replacement motive may be readily apparent in the short time-span between the dissolution of one marriage and the initiation of the next. However, the passage of time, in and of itself, does not guarantee that an effective mourning and resolution has taken place. In some cases the short time period does not indicate replacement at all. The mourning process may have occurred during a prolonged deterioration of the marriage, a lengthy decision-making process and drawn-out legal process, or both, during which time the man gradually and definitively grieved/mourned. Although the time period between the date of the divorce and his remarriage may be very brief, it would be better to judge the matter by the timing of the *psychological* dissolution of the marriage. It is no longer sufficient to judge solely by time intervals between legal decrees of divorce and marriage, but rather by the presence or absence of the intrapsychic mourning process. If the new family is a replacement for his previous family, this man will enter his stepfather status grafting his relationships with his biological children onto his relationship with his stepchildren. This encumbrance (called "baggage" idiomatically or "transference" technically) to the stepfather–child relationship increases the possibility and almost guarantees ensuing difficulties.

Thus far, I have discussed factors within the stepfather. However, if the stepfather role is to be successfully navigated, it needs to be facilitated and nurtured by other family members: the biological mother, the biological father, and the stepchild(ren) themselves. The biological mother must allow the stepfather to parent her children and to nurture and support her children's relationship to their stepfather. Clinically, I have observed a type of mother who, jealously guarding her children from any other love relationship, binds them to her and simultaneously demeans and denigrates her husband's role in the family. At the extreme end of this continuum are the women who dispense with and dispose of the father during the pregnancy or shortly thereafter, or remain in a so-called intact marriage of convenience. This type of woman actively interferes with the ex-husband's visitation or so actively demeans and vilifies her former husband that the child becomes alienated from the father. The mother, now being the only available love object, monopolizes her child's love and loyalty. However, given the social and financial problems of being a single parent, she may make a second try at marriage. Unless there has been significant psychological maturation in the mother, she may repeat the pattern and the new husband, now a stepfather, may again be belittled or otherwise isolated from the children. In essence, her devaluation and either her criticism or demeaning attitude create a husband almost ineligible for a positive relationship with his stepchildren. Both the mother and the stepfather have the available rationale that the children are not his biological children; thus, he needs little to do with or for them, particularly so if the children's biological father has maintained an important role in their lives. In addition, the interval between the woman's divorce and her remarriage, if lengthy, may lead her to develop the typical attitudes and techniques of a single parent who shares neither the power nor the perks of parenthood with anyone else. This established modus operandi of the single parent mother may not readily yield to the presence of a stepfather, even though the mother may consciously wish to provide her children with a "man in the house."

The mother clearly possesses the power to deny the stepfather his role. It is the mother who will define and redefine over time the stepfather's role for him and for her children. For example, it is within her power to decide whether the stepfather should help with the children's homework, as well as to whether he can insist that they finish their homework. Stepchildren who are coerced or disciplined by their stepfather into doing things that they don't wish to do may often be heard to say, "You're not my father, you can't make me do that," or "You can't talk to me like that," or "I'm going to live with my *real* father." Unless mother and stepfather are prepared to be united concerning the extent and power of the stepfather's right to discipline and otherwise parent her children, there will be no resolution of the issue and no peace in the family.

Clinical Example. A mother finally divorced her alcoholic and uninvolved husband. During the post-divorce period of being a single parent, she became accustomed to and then enjoyed having "100% responsibility" for her children. When the stepfather attempted to discipline his stepdaughter (i.e., to clean up her room, do her assigned chores, practice the piano), she ignored him. Exasperated, he threatened her with the one thing meaningful to her: he would refuse to drive her to cheerleader practice—forever. When the mother came on the scene, she chided her daughter for not doing all the things the stepfather had asked, and chided her husband for the silliness of his threat. Although none of the disputed things were done, she then drove her daughter to cheerleader practice, feeling that she had to drive her daughter since it gave *her* disciplinary leverage—that is, in the future she could now refuse to drive her daughter. She was totally unaware that she had undermined her husband's attempts at discipline by driving her daughter when the husband had threatened not to. She thus conveyed to both daughter and husband that only *her* threats were to be considered meaningful. The mother, my patient, readily understood her daughter's anger with the stepfather, but could not understand her husband's anger with her until some time and interpretations later.

What I hope to show is how the mother can either grant or deny the stepfather parental power with her child(ren). For a stepfather to assume that he has disciplinary authority simply as a result of being married to the mother, or living in the home, or providing financial support, is simply a fantasy, albeit a common one among stepfathers.

Like the mother, the child's conscious wishes and underlying dynamics can facilitate or block the new husband's assumption of the stepfather function. A child's adverse response to the stepfather can become an almost insurmountable source of conflict, intense enough to jeopardize an otherwise solid marriage. If a stepfather is to be accepted and utilized to advantage, there are several impediments that the child needs to confront and resolve. Parental divorce as experienced by the child has many aspects of passivity. Basically, the child's wish for an intact, loving, nurturing family was seemingly ignored. The child's preferences for custodial and visitation arrangements may or may not be honored by the parents, lawyers, and presiding judge. The inability of the child to control or understand the parental actions and decisions is experienced to some degree as traumatic. When a prospective stepfather appears, the child has the opportunity to become an active decision-maker, perhaps even a powerful one. While many mothers ask the child's opinion about the suitability of a prospective husband, the child's opinion is far from determinative, except perhaps in the child's fantasy. Realistically, the parental decision, although markedly affecting the child, is once again based primarily on adult needs and wishes. Whatever resentment the child may feel, past or present, it can be easily focused onto the new husband. To the extent that the child felt divorced and rejected by his father, now the child can reject the stepfather. In this way there is a delayed mastery of the earlier perceived rejection by the biological father. Contributing to the child's negative reaction to the stepfather is the real or imagined need to act as the biological father's agent in the father's fight against anyone who would replace him. A divorced father who is still emotionally attached to his former wife will invariably communicate this to the child in a variety of overt and covert ways. The mother's remarriage is experienced by the former husband as another and final reality confrontation with the actuality of the divorce. The profound narcissistic hurt is that the former wife is continuing on with her life without him. The mother's remarriage signifies that she is not only legally divorced, but also emotionally divorced from her former husband, and capable of a new relationship. For some men the remarriage of a former wife activates issues of separation and loss.[2] While they may be able to adjust to losing their former wife and perhaps even having initiated it, they now confront the new possibility that their children's affection will be channeled to the stepfather. It is as though the child(ren)'s affection is of a finite nature; whatever love they give to the stepfather comes out of their relationship to the father. A father overwhelmed by these fears may exhort his children not to have a loving relationship with their stepfather and, in fact, to do all that they can to reject him and create disharmony in the new family. Such paternal entreaties and motivations may fall on fertile ground and accentuate the child fighting the father's battle within the mother's home. Optimally, a stepfather would function best if there is a tacit agreement that the child is both permitted and encouraged to love them both and to have a positive relationship with both. This ideal, unfortunately, is difficult to attain and often exists more in the abstract than in actuality.

The child needs to overcome the resentment inherent in the introduction of a new family member, that is, the mother's new husband. The longer mother and child have functioned autonomously, the more the child's preferred status is threatened by the newcomer. The child's past experiences with newcomers entering the family form the psychological base for the multiple transferences that will be grafted onto the new husband. In the child's unconscious, the new husband is not unlike a newborn whom mother brings home and who is given an honored and beloved place in the family. Initially, both child and father are imbued with their optimistic wish-fulfilling fantasies, which are shattered quickly by the ensuing realities. The baby (stepfather) is not someone who will play with the child when the child wishes or who can play his type of games; the baby (stepfather) belongs more to mother than to him. The baby (stepfather) will often be given higher priority than he. This "baby stepfather" monopolizes mother's attention while the child feels the resentment of being a second-class citizen. When either parent asks the child to be helpful for them or for the household, his resentment is exacerbated.

Oedipal conflicts may often be regressively reactivated, especially if the male child regarded the mother's divorce as an oedipal victory. The child

---

[2]The issue is more in the nature of the loss of an oedipal competition for the same woman. While this is a common dynamic, in my experience it is more the narcissistic issues of loss and replacement that are crucial motivating forces.

will see the stepfather not only as a victorious preoedipal competitor, but also as a current oedipal victor supplanting himself. An analogous situation would be true for the girl child. The young girl's oedipal rivalries with her mother would be similarly reactivated. As a result, the girl frequently embarrasses/insults her mother, becomes sexually aroused by the overt sexuality of the mother's new relationship, and may "come on" to the stepfather either in fantasy or in actuality.

A mother, in the midst of the difficulties of single parenthood, looks for a husband who will be a good father to her child(ren). She looks primarily for fathering qualities and only secondarily for a man suitable to be her husband. While initially this may be seen as a parent who sacrifices her needs for those of her children, it is also possible that the mother is externalizing the intensity of her own needs for security onto her children. In some situations, it is the mother's need for the parent-like security of marriage. Sometimes the mother's confused identification with her children and externalization of her own needfulness onto them may impair her ability to find a man suitable for either husbanding or stepparenting.

Clinical Example. A widow assumed that her new husband's obsessional need to control everything was an indication of his concern, caring, and strength. She readily allowed her new husband to control her and her decisions, but her three children did not instantly respond to their stepfather's brand of "caring." As a result, an intrafamilial war broke out. When the stepfather emotionally abandoned the children, the mother supported the stepfather against her own children, thus compounding their earlier experience of parental abandonment when their father suddenly died. The three children banded together with an almost unnatural closeness in their opposition to the stepfather. When the mother indicated to them that her marriage was being threatened, they backed down and reconciled with the stepfather, with the realization that this husband was necessary for their mother's security. Some years later the youngest child, now in college, consulted me at the time of the December holidays. She wanted to visit with her mother but felt that she did not have a home to which she could return. While both older brothers felt similarly, they were symptom-free, being older at the time of the biological father's death, and in subsequent years were mutually supportive of one another but with the exclusion of their younger sister. While I did not speak to the stepfather, and have no objective picture of him, it is my assumption that the mother chose a husband based more on her own inner needs for security but experienced in their externalized form, as her children's needs for a family.

The child has a significant role in determining the acceptance and the quality of the stepfather–child relationship. Acceptance of a stepfather necessitates that the child has, to some degree, adequately mourned the lost first marriage, and the lost intimacy with the biological father. Even if the visitation is frequent and going well and father and child spend more quality time together than they may have during the marriage, it still does not compensate for the lost idealized intact nuclear family. In addition, the child needs some measure of trust and optimism that the new relationship and marriage with the stepfather will not suffer the fate of the first marriage. If a divorced father has not divorced and abandoned his child, the child's sense of trust is not overly damaged, although loyalty conflicts may produce significant turmoil. If the biological father has psychologically abandoned the child, or died, loyalty conflicts are somewhat reduced, but the sense of trust in the durability and permanence of relationships is severely stressed. (Loyalty conflicts are an intrapsychic issue and not wholly dependent on the actual presence of the biological father.)

Clinical Example. A boy was four when his parents divorced. The child's father quickly remarried, had several children, and became increasingly involved with his new family. When I saw the boy at age eight, he felt emotionally abandoned. The mother's first remarriage was brief, and the stepfather was uninterested. The next stepfather remained tied to his children from a previous marriage, and did not notice my patient. In his sessions with me, this eight-year-old refused to make eye contact, since it would immediately bring tears to his eyes. We found out that to see me was to tempt himself with entering into yet another relationship. With his history of disrupted and abandoning relationships it would be psychologically unwise, since experience had taught him that men cannot be trusted. He had learned that there is no permanence to man–boy relationships and that they carry the dangerous potential of a painful abandonment. I think this illustrates, although in the transference of a treatment setting, the difficulty in accepting a new relationship when the old ones were abandoning and rage and loss issues have not been adequately resolved.

The above example demonstrated how the biological father's perceived total abandonment was too great a trauma for the child to master. The abandonment was seemingly secondary to the father's cathexis of his new family and his limited ability to nurture more than a small and specific number of children. Here was a father who not only divorced his wife but the child as well, an action that mitigated against the acceptance of a stepfather or even stepfather surrogates.

On other occasions a biological father can be actively disruptive in preventing a child–stepfather relationship. I was an expert witness in a well-publicized sex abuse allegation case in Tennessee. The mother was divorced by her husband three years before because he felt she was spending too much time with their neonate; he felt his needs should be catered to first and foremost. After the divorce he immediately married a woman who was childless and had a history of multiple abortions. Three years later, when the mother announced her engagement to a well-respected prestigious professional man, the father took his three-year-old son for a week-long visitation and returned with allegations of sexual abuse and sadistic practices against his former wife's fiancé. In reviewing the data, it was my belief (and the trial court agreed) that these were created allegations of sexual abuse motivated by the father's continued anger toward his former wife and his fantasy that, in the competition with this well-respected professional man who would become his son's stepfather, he would lose the affection of his son and lose his status as the son's father. He was afraid and convinced that the stepfather would eclipse him as a father. After an extensive and highly publicized trial, the fiancé was found innocent of sexual abuse, but their marriage never occurred.

While I have focused on one child, oftentimes there are several children within the same family who are involved in a stepfather–child relationship. While all the children may share some common features, we should remember that each child has a unique relationship with the mother and the biological father. The uniqueness results from the combination of complex variables: each sibling's relationship with each parent; the allegiances and loyalties in the family; their ages and psychological maturity at the time of the divorce or death; their gender and gender identifications; the nature and duration of the period between marriages; the vicissitudes of the visitation and custodial arrangements; and the developmental stage of each child at the time of the mother's remarriage. Still other dynamics may be prominent in other family constellations and circumstances.

The ability to be an effective and competent stepfather requires certain traits and maturities within the man. Even under the best of circumstances, there may be factors beyond the control of the stepfather. When a stepfather comes into a family, there is not only the conscious and unconscious relationship between the current family members, but there is a preexisting readiness for transference contamination (from the biological father) of the current relationships. If the stepfather has been married in the past, there is usually a sense of loyalty, allegiance, and responsibility toward his own biological children, which may either (a) conflict with those of his stepchildren; (b) overwhelm him by their intensity, amount, and duration; or both.

Conclusion

It would simplify matters if we could establish a set of generalizations which would apply to all stepfather situations. I believe that each stepfather situation is so unique as to almost defy easy categorization. As a result, the average therapist needs the tolerance and patience for a lengthy and thorough exploratory process. The application of set formulas and arbitrary rules that derive from a few theoretical concepts is obviously desirable but is more likely to be simplistic or prone to error. To the extent that any parenthood is on-the-job learning, so too is that of stepfatherhood. An awareness of the history of relationships and the conflicting dynamic factors may serve to shorten some of the trial-and-error learning, but it is nonetheless an evolutionary process requiring sensitivity and love.

Reference

Roberts, T. W. & Price, S. J. (1987), Instant families. *J. Divorce*, 11:171–192.

Developmental
Considerations

Some Steppaternal Possibilities

Lora Heims Tessman

Disrupted relationships between father and child have a wrenching poignancy for both members of the dyad, and making peace with this state of affairs may be a lifelong task for the child. Hence, thinking about the role of the father and of ways of preserving something positive from that relationship for the child has often taken first and and urgent attention (including mine) when parents part. Stepfathers have gotten short shrift. Yet in my own work with children who have suffered the loss of a parent either through death or divorce, I have been impressed with the breadth of the constructive as well as potentially destructive role the stepfather can have (Tessman, this volume). I would like to sketch out some *internal* aspects of the meaning of stepfathers, and then to comment briefly on several special components of the stepfathering process. The special components I will refer to, or illustrate with clinical fragments, include (1) helping the child grieve; (2) being available as a new identification figure; (3) being part of a different parental unit; (4) being part of the new extended family, including at times being recruited to provide needed fathering to the biologic father; (5) being ringmaster—and sometimes clown—in the three-ring circus of the conflicting needs of children and stepchildren.

I now turn to the inner frame into which the stepfather steps. Like the analyst with patient, the stepfather with stepchild inevitably evokes a resurgence of the previous object relationship, as it was in fantasy or in deed, at the moment of disrupted growth. The stepfather enters a transference about the absent father, usually filled with layers of intense longings, expectations of disappointment, and a particular constellation of defenses against these painful affects. In addition, because the father always remains an (unconscious) object of unresolved longings, the child's new relationship with the stepfather, when it is good, threatens the preservation of these longings. So the stepfather teeters, like the analyst, somewhere between being experienced as the disappointing object of the past and as having possibilities for new ways of relating, to become a new object. Both the obstacles and opportunities of his role may stem from the oscillations between these two. Unlike the analytic situation in which observation and awareness of such oscillating meanings is fostered (and enactments eventually also become grist for the mill of understanding), in the stepparent–stepchild situation the relationship proceeds primarily through enactment. Unlike the analytic situation in which the analyst's vested interest in the outcome has its limits, the stepfather must live with the consequences of the relationship. Unlike the frame of the analytic dyad, the stepfather–child dyad by definition occurs in the context of the total family configuration, and his primary bond is not with the child, but with the new parental unit. However, also unlike the analytic dyad, there may be a freedom from constraints in time, love, emotional investment, and permanence. Under these conditions what fosters constructive internalization?

In the usual father–child dyad a process of internalization occurs accompanied by developmentally changing elaborations in fantasy of the inner representation of the other. I believe this happens for each member of the dyad, in the child for the first time, but in the parent as well. The parent's task in this is to move, at least partially, from his transference and self-conceived wishes and fears about the child, to reacting to the child as him-or herself. A history of father and child together, a kind of memory bank with joint account, from infancy on, fosters the process. In the absence of such developmentally shared experience, how might it occur between child and stepfather? Again, this question has parallels in the psychoanalytic endeavor, where we, as analysts, like the stepparent, are faced with a tenant on the couch whose internalizations have already been formed, where we seek a psychic space between the transference and the possibility of something new.

Stepparenting has been likened to having a strange bird dropped into one's nest (Visher and Visher, 1988); in this situation the quality of psychic nestfeathering on which the strange bird lands may be particularly important. Such qualities in the stepfather may include enduring facets of character, for example, the balance of narcissistic versus object related availability. But in addition, the psychic nestfeathering is made up of those motivating dynamics which stem from ancient and current dyadic and triadic introjects, once more evoked by the sudden intimacy with the stepchild, and once more externalized for a variety of enactments. Such enactments depend on the wider family dynamics as well. My hunch is that a stepparent's capacity to "internalize" the child, that is, his making a psychic space for her to inhabit, makes it easier for her, in turn, to begin to internalize him in a meaningful way. I believe this matters especially for children who have suffered a disruption in loving because of divorce or death of a parent.

Any child needs to evolve a reliable internal presence of a father, for fantasized interactions as well as eventual identification with qualities she values in him. With selective highlighting, aspects of the internal image of father become part of inner structure of the self, as well as a beloved. Until that happens a lot of dialogue (in words and deeds) goes on between the parent and child, and between the child and the internal presence. However, when the father is no longer steadily available, internalization or identification may happen abruptly as a defense against loss. In this process the image of father may be frozen in time, rather than being the gradual construction of an image which lends itself to ever changing elaboration in fantasy, a melding of fathering functions the child needs at that very moment in development, sifted through his actual, continued experience with him. Identification with father as a defense against loss is apt to be based on those aspects of memory which are most exquisitely laden with affective pleasure or pain, magnified by their intensity, and by distortions needed to preserve the image. In this way the internal father, frozen in time and meaning, is dissociated from the emotional growth of the rest of the child. In addition, the integrity of the image may be more vulnerable to contagion from others' views of the father. In order for the internalized father to develop along with the child, the opportunity for an active engagement with a father figure is needed. If the child is not too guilty to relate to someone new, she will externalize the inner father to incite a new engagement with appropriate or inappropriate males, as an attempt to revive its disrupted development. Such attempts may miscarry and have been referred to as "acting out" with pejorative implications. It is important to also recognize the positive developmental function of the process. The child's need to incite a dialogue of words and play *and* of actions can reopen the needed mutual influence, the two-way traffic between the father or father figure actually in sight and the father inside. The entrance of the stepfather may reawaken this needed dialogue. Because the child comes to the relationship with some wounds from disrupted loving, the stakes are very high, the pitfalls for stepfathers abound, and the stalwartness of his inner resources challenged. To summarize this issue, there may be two conditions necessary for a useful internalization involving elaboration of the inner representations of each other: (1) that the stepfather is emotionally present for the developmentally changing child; (2) that there be a thaw in the defensive aspects of the image of the father previously clung to, making it open to transformation.

Some special components, then, of the stepfather's importance include the following:

1. Help the child grieve for whatever has been lost or could not develop in the first place with the father. Often this happens when the child has enough of a relationship to the stepfather to make the conflict of loyalties urgent. It may require that the stepfather convey an attitude different from that of the mother, who inevitably has been disappointed in the former marriage and is attempting, in the face of this disappointment, to maintain her self-esteem. She may be invested in viewing the father as more at fault than herself. So the stepfather, if he is able, is in a special position to make a safe place for memories of the father as colored by the child's own ambivalence, without contaminating this with the naturally

different perceptions and different ambivalence of the mother. In helping the child grieve, the stepfather also assures the child that she does not have to make a choice between the two.

2. Be available as a new identification figure for the child, offering potential for enriching identifications. In my past work when I compared treatment of children aged 11 and under with adolescents, I found that enriching identifications with a new stepparent more often fostered the overall development of the child than not. This differed for the adolescents, who for a complex of reasons more vehemently extruded the influence of the stepparent (Tessman, 1978). However, initial obstacles in the relationship are often not subtle and may represent vivid conflicts of loyalty. For example, Daniel, two and a half years old, would not budge from his absent father's chair until he fell asleep each night, screaming if someone tried to lift him out of it. In this way he tried to use his body to keep any man from literally taking his father's place. Noah, 10 years old, first repudiated the prospective stepfather, telling me, "At first I thought of Steve as falling over a cliff everyday" but then slowly integrated him into his identifications over a period of years. Broadened possibilities for enriching identifications are helpful particularly to children whose fathers show the kinds of vulnerabilities in character that would be depleting to the child's self-esteem to identify with when there are no nurturing males as alternative.

3. Be part of the new parental unit. If the mother's love choice has been different in a second union, different aspects of her nature are evoked. The match or mismatch between spouses is not lost on the child. Herzog (1982) points to the importance of the "parental protective envelope" that is forged by a communicative alliance between the spouses and provides a safe space that "permits not only titration, expression and containment of libidinal and aggressive impulses and their derivatives, whose direct application might prove deleterious and overstimulating to a child, but also a mourning and restitutive place where prior and current mortifications, hurts, and discontents can be healed and handled" (p. 104). Because of the volatile nature of the emotional bonds at the time of marital dissolution, the "protective envelope" is unsealed and some of its contents spill or are censored. As a result the child may be imbued with a frightening amount of free-floating aggressive tension. In addition he often experiences an intensified pleasurable bond with one or both parents, who had been long frustrated in the experiencing of pleasure with a mate. In this kind of emotional context it often happens that after coping with the loss of the absent parent, the child has an additional acute sense of loss and mourning about the home parent as well, as his parent becomes involved with a new love or marriage partner. Ways of coping with this additional loss, or loss of "specialness," tends to be indicative of the soundness of the earlier relationship. Though reactions are often acute, their acuteness

does not signify lack of resilience in the child (Tessman, 1984). Consider Brian, who at age 12 was describing to me how he felt when he watched his mother relax in laughter with his stepfather, Paul. "It's a little better now," he said, "the Novocain is beginning to take." The needed analgesic in his mind was more effective than it had been the previous month. At that time, when mother had celebrated New Year's Eve by going moonlight skating with Paul, he watched them dance on the ice, and then simply lay down on the edge of the pond on his back, numbing himself with cold. The adults, involved with each other, had in fact not missed him until his 10-year-old sister told mother, "I think you ought to pay some attention to Brian."

During the first 10 years of Brian's life, a quietly unhappy marriage between his parents had left the home devoid of the forces of fresh sexuality. Brian had been the chief source of his mother's excitement and delight with frequent shared laughter, so that he had had an expectation of being special to people. Now the clarity of his sense of pain seemed to be a mirror of his previous pleasure. But where did his capacity for pleasure go? Brian (whom I had seen since his parents' divorce) and I explored his conscious effort to numb himself to his jealousy, so that we might see if the numbness was "leaking" into other areas of his life. "School is where I'm happiest now," he told me. "For the first time in my life I feel most of the kids like me, instead of having just one friend and mostly enemies." "How come?" I asked, "What's turning that around?" Brian: "I think I'm making an effort for the first time . . . figuring out how to live down being brainy . . . I take them into consideration more . . . I don't need to be perfect or lord it over them so much any more, so it's more fun to be with me."

I think his appraisal was accurate. Instead of a constricting depression or hostile rebellion in reaction to Paul, Brian had turned to some pubescent age-appropriate maneuvers—beginning to disengage from the overly exciting relationship with his mother (and the associated self-image of aspiring to be perfect enough to lord it over others, i.e., to be without rivals) and investing more fully in his peers. I believe his strength to manage that had to do with the assumption that all was not lost, that he had it in him to try again, and that both his divorced father and Paul were supportively available to him. Brian's plight included a common and poignant difficulty, which colored his sense of loss. When the child who has lived with parents in whom the forces of sexual vitality lay muted during his early development, is then faced, during pubescence, with a parent's second happier love match, then the fresh and scintillating sexuality provides him with a happier image of what life can be about. But parental sexuality is developmentally more difficult to integrate then earlier, because his own sexuality is simultaneously more easily stimulated and more urgently in need of deflection.

Hostilities between stepfather and child can easily crystallize around the evoked and denied jealousies in this kind of situation. Frequently overlooked by both stepfather and child is the extent to which the child longs for an alliance with the stepfather, from whom he feels excluded as well.

Brian vividly recalled the moment he knew that he loved his stepfather. After mother remarried, family cohesiveness had been an iffy struggle for a time. Brian had remained quite cool with the stepfather, ranging from conveying the message of "who needs you, I'm in charge of this family!" to feeling disloyal toward his own father to being ambivalently relieved that his mother seemed happier now.

On a day of blustering snow, the family car broke down and they were stranded. Plans for seeing the "Nutcracker Suite" were forfeited and complaints of the sister and stepsibs were loud. Paul and Brian trudged a long way together for emergency care, finally arriving at a gas station with a tow truck, their mission essentially accomplished. As they wearily stood side by side, waiting for the truck to pick them up, the stepfather turned to him and said, "Let's throw snowballs at the cars driving by,", which they proceeded to do jubilantly and raucously. Brian described the secure feeling of stepfather's leadership in saving the day, and his invited inclusion as accomplice. But what he *loved* was that stepfather did not put on a superior air. Instead, as Brian explained to me, he must have understood Brian's frequent frustration in the new family in order to dream up this playful vengeance on those cars that just rolled by without any struggle.

4. The extended family in the inner life of the child includes original father as well as the stepfamily. At times stepfather has a special fathering role to play in the extended family that fosters growth in the child. Unresolved issues between the biologic father and his history with his own father are apt to be visited on his own children.

Mr. B's marriage dissolved after several cycles of bipolar illness, during which he had not been able to control his outbursts at his wife or two-year-old son, Jonah. He was deeply humiliated by recurrent hospitalizations, by having to shift to a menial occupation rather than the professional position he had occupied, and by his ex-wife's relentless belittling of him (in her own therapy she tried, to no avail, to restrain her demeaning of him). He felt that his little son was now all that he had to live for. He showered the little boy with gifts, adulation, and demands for constant kisses, and he repeated that his only happiness lay in the few hours a week with his son. Jonah wanted to spend less time with his father, but felt enormously guilty about his father's depression. "A depression is more than a sniffle, you know," he told me, at age four, listing the ways that his father counted on him for cheer. When Jonah's mother was about to remarry, I met with her and the prospective stepfather. The stepfather wondered how he could be of help. "This might sound nutty to you," said

I, "but I have a hunch you'd get a lot of mileage out of spending a bit of time with Jonah's father. He assumes that you look down on him. He needs to feel respected by you, to be worth some attention from a male other than Jonah. That may make it less wrenching for him to entrust Jonah to you." "I kind of like the guy anyway except when he acts so pathetic," said Mr. H, the stepfather-to-be, and he volunteered to pick up Jonah from his father's house, where he could admire the drawings Jonah had made with his father. The initial result was a strange, but far from unholy alliance between the three males. It became a communication route less noxiously prickly than from mother to father and seemed to reduce the pressure on Jonah to fulfill his father's needs for self-worth.

5. The stepfather may resolve the conflicting pulls between his own children and stepchildren in a variety of ways. For example, Mr. C's own adolescent daughters blamed him for their parents' divorce and for taking up with another woman, while he expected them to adapt "seamlessly" to his new situation; in addition, he now expected them to prefer his new partner's cooking to their mother's and to compliment her on her appearance. He was quite intolerant of their jealousies and criticisms, and their relationship to him deteriorated. Both father and daughters felt unappreciated by each other. Mr. C sought solace in the less critical adolescent daughters of his live-in partner and favored them in obvious ways, for example, by taking the partner's daughter along on a trip to Europe, an invitation he had never made to his own daughters. This man's narcissistic vulnerability made it difficult for him to deal with ambivalence, and, forfeiting a good relationship with his own children, he remained bewildered about why they became so uncommunicative with him. Mr. C had entered treatment because of obsessional symptoms and insecurities about his new partner. When he terminated, satisfied with having completed his agenda for improvement, I found myself vaguely dissatisfied, wishing that enjoying and valuing his daughters more freely had also been among his goals.

If the stepfather can function to heal and vitalize the parental unit, having the flexibility to involve himself deeply in fathering functions while mother sustains her maternal caring, then the child is in luck.

References

Herzog, J. (1982), World beyond metaphor: Thoughts on the transmission of trauma. In: *Generations of the Holocaust,* ed. M. S. Bergmann & M. E. Jucovy. New York: Basic Books.

Tessman, L. H. (1978), *Children of Parting Parents.* Northvale, NJ: Aronson. (Reprinted as *Helping Children Cope with Parting Parents,* 1996, Northvale, NJ: Aronson.)

_____ (1984), The quest for the wanted absent parent in children of the divorced or deceased. In: *Marriage and Divorce: A Contemporary Perspective,* ed. C. Nadelson & D. Polonsky. New York: Guilford Press.

Visher, E. B. & Visher, A. S. (1988), *Old Loyalties, New Ties.* New York: Brunner/Mazel.

Some Important Contributions of the Stepfather to the Psychological Development of the Boy

Eugenio M. Rothe

There is a sparsity in the psychiatric and psychoanalytic literature with respect to stepfathers. An exhaustive review of the literature conducted by the author in 1998 revealed a number of papers addressing sexual abuse perpetrated by stepfathers toward stepdaughters but not one reference explaining the contributions of stepfathers to the psychological development of their stepchildren. Thus, in the field of mental health, the positive side of stepfathers remains a mysterious and challenging territory yet to be explored.

The dictionary defines the word "stepfather" as: "a man who occupies one's father's place by marriage to one's mother" and "step" as: "a prefix indicating a connection between members of a family by remarriage of a parent but not by blood." It adds that the prefix "step" derives from the German root "steif" meaning: "to bereave" as well as the old English verb "bestepen" signifying: "to deprive (as in children)" (*Random House Dictionary*, 1966). Highlighted in the etymology of the word "stepfather" are: (1) the absence of a filial blood bond; (2) the bereavement over the loss or absence of the biological father; and, (3) the potential for child neglect. This strikingly negative portrayal of the image of the stepfather, if taken literally, presents a serious concern to our society since recent statistics reveal that the United States has the highest divorce rate in the world, with almost half of all marriages ending in divorce.

Many spouses remarry, bringing along children of previous unions and creating "blended families" where both, the husband and the wife, assume new roles as stepparents.

Upon his arrival in the new family, the stepfather must assume a pivotal role in renegotiating and redesigning the hierarchy of attachments in the "reconstituted family." He must first gain the acceptance and support of the mother of the child who will serve as a "gatekeeper" in his relationship to the stepchildren. The stepfather and his spouse will become responsible for restructuring the nurturing and disciplining roles of the adults and for setting boundaries on the children and on each other (Ransom, Schlesinger, and Derdeyn, 1979).

The relationship between stepfather and stepchild carries an implicit, defining factor: the absence or loss of the biological father. The loss of the

27

biological father may exist as an "actual reality," such as in the case of death or abandonment by the father, or even when there may not be an actual physical loss, the child may experience this loss as a "psychic reality." In either case, there is an aspect of bereavement and mourning involved. In the child and adolescent psychiatric and psychoanalytic literature, there is some controversy regarding the child's capacity to mourn the loss of a parent. Furman (1992) believes that a child, even very young, can mourn if helped by the surviving bereaved parent. Wolfenstein (1992) has disagreed. She has explained how early object loss leads to developmental interferences and narcissistic vulnerabilities. She believed that children are developmentally "unready" to mourn and explained that the completion of the adolescent phase of development allows the adolescent to give up the infantile libidinal attachments to the parents and to complete fully the first developmentally determined mourning process. Wolfenstein regarded the adolescent process as a "necessary precondition" in the development of the capacity to mourn.

Mourning is accomplished through a gradual decathexis from the lost object. Some children are incapable of this gradual decathexis since self-constancy, which is not yet established, depends on the parental figure for external narcissistic supplies. The development of the child proceeds in harmonious attachment to the parental figures. When a parental figure is removed, development is interrupted and possibly arrested (Tyson, 1992). The loss of the parental figure signifies a threat to "self–other" constancy and enhances a fear of annihilation.

According to Wolfenstein (1992), the loss of a parent by a young child, some have described, produces a reaction of "hypercathexis" in the child. The loss is denied at a more or less conscious level causing a split to occur. At one level the child understands the loss, while at the same time, he engages in a "denial in fantasy" expecting the absent parent to return.

Major object loss in adults or children sets in motion a complex series of responses, including regression. Ambivalent feelings experienced toward the lost object may also succumb to a split. Usually the child tends to idealize the lost parent while projecting negative affects toward the self or toward the remaining parent. In the case of the stepchild, the stepfather may become the target of severe aggressive attacks from his bereaved stepson. Or, if the stepfather takes the place of the absent biological father, he may be idealized; since, for certain stepsons, it may be too dangerous to risk rejection or abandonment by yet another paternal figure. The success of the relationship between stepfather and stepson will depend on variables that sometimes pertain exclusively to the stepfather, such as his level of maturity, his readiness to parent, the integrity of his ego and super ego development and the qualities of his ego ideal.

The relationship with the stepson is likely to awaken unresolved preoedipal issues in the stepfather, such as his own early experiences of deprivation. These may elicit feelings of loss, with envy and rage directed toward whom he may perceive to be the more fortunate stepson. Oedipal issues are also likely to be present, since the stepson stands as the living representative of the wife's sexual relationship with her former husband. The stepson also represents an indestructible continuation of the wife's tie to the first husband.

Temperamental differences may also play a role in determining the "goodness of fit" between the stepfather and the stepson (Winnicott, 1965). The stepfather may carry former loyalties or obligations into his new family: the attachments to his own biological children by a former marriage, colored by the attitudes of his former wife toward the stepfather's new family. The stepson's mother will hold a key position in the relationship between stepfather and stepson; impeding or facilitating the bonding of such a relationship. The same can be said about the boy's biological father who, if present, may also facilitate or diminish the possibility of a good fit. Strong loyalty battles are likely to occur. If the biological father has died or is primarily absent, the quality of his memory is likely to be a factor, whether he exists as a "secret" or as an admired or denigrated family figure.

Many other factors are likely to influence the relationship between stepfather and stepson: The acceptance or rejection of the stepfather by the boy's siblings or extended family, as well as by the community and other individuals that form the family's social support system. Conflicts of loyalty may ensue and, in some way, never be negotiated successfully. The time lapse between the loss of the biological father and the arrival of a new stepfather may play a role; the boy's readiness to accept the stepfather as father's substitute, which may be strongly influenced by the particular developmental stage of the boy at the time of remarriage.

This chapter will use a developmental and object relations model to outline some of the most important contributions of the stepfather to the psychological development of the boy up until the completion of adolescence. Case material will also be presented to illustrate the role of the stepfather as a potential "intruder" or "redeemer" in the life of the stepson.

The Preoedipal Father and Stepfather

The positive role of the preoedipal father in psychological development had been largely ignored in the psychiatric and psychoanalytic literature until recent years, when several authors called attention to its importance (Abelin, 1975; Ross, 1979; Herzog, 1980; Greenspan, 1982; Gunsberg, 1982; Atkins, 1989; Pacella, 1989). The potential contributions of fathers to their children's stage of development can also be attributed to stepfathers and can be summarized as follows:

1. The father (or stepfather) provides a "protective covering" around the mother and child unit (Winnicott, 1965). He serves as mother's main source of support (Stoller, 1975), helping maintain the mothering dyad and making the mother's job less difficult and onerous (Muir, 1989).

2. The father (or stepfather) serves as an alternative figure to the child, as someone with whom the child plays in different ways than he plays with his mother (Mahler, Pine, and Bergman, 1975); a "second other" who will facilitate the awareness of separateness and will set the stage for "early triangulation" (Abelin, 1975).

3. As a love object (Stoller, 1975) and as a figure of attachment, he expands the child's repertoire of object relations and also allows the child to "love the father (or stepfather) when the other parent is hated" (Winnicott, 1965; Muir, 1989) protecting him from the fear of abandonment which results from his intermittent aggressive feelings directed toward the mother.

4. A figure of identification for the boy, allowing for the future development of the ego ideal (Blos, 1966, 1984).

5. As a facilitator to the process of separation-individuation: protecting the boy from the regressive pull toward symbiosis with mother (Abelin, 1975), allowing for the boy to "dis-identify" from her (Greenson, 1954); enhancing his cognitive capacities and ego structures (Prall, 1978), promoting the consolidation of his gender identity, self-esteem, and setting the stage for the oedipal period.

6. The father (or stepfather) directly modifies the behavior of the boy by reward and punishment (Stoller, 1975), containing the aggressive drive of the boy, promoting the development and internalization of superego precursors and setting the stage for the consolidation of the super ego after the oedipal stage.

7. The father (or stepfather) protects and shields the child from the extrafamilial, as well as from the intrafamilial hazards. The latter may be a mother's engulfing libidinal or aggressive drives (or drive derivatives); the former, excessive drives or demands from siblings and other family members.

Abelin (1975) made important contributions toward the understanding of the preoedipal child. His theory is based on the earlier findings of Piaget (1964, 1968), Mahler et al. (1975), and Spitz (1965). He postulates the existence of "early triangulation" as the cornerstone for the cognitive and psychosexual preoedipal development of the boy.

The role of the preoedipal father (or stepfather) consists in allowing the boy to differentiate himself from mother and helping him to consolidate his sense of self. A more detailed explanation of this process will be addressed elsewhere in this book.

In the course of a panel of psychoanalysts dealing with the topic of "early triangulation" (Prall, 1978), Abelin was quoted as stating that perhaps the reason why Freud did not address the role of the preoedipal father was because: "the pre-symbolic father" cannot be recalled in the analytic material of adult patients. This assumption can also apply to the stepfather. In recent years, this omission has been addressed and corrected by several authors (Greenspan, 1982; Gunsberg, 1982; Pacella, 1989). Since preoedipal memories are usually inaccessible to conscious awareness in most human beings, sometimes this developmental stage can be partially reconstructed by the accounts of other people involved. The role and contribution of a stepfather to the preoedipal development of a boy and his mother can be surmised from this case history obtained from the boy's mother.

Case 1

Mrs. W, a 57-year-old woman, was seen in therapy over a crisis that occurred after she discovered that her husband of 36 years had been having a sexual affair with a coworker. The affair had dissolved and the husband had apologized profusely. Mrs. W, however, was deeply hurt by the occurrence, but reacted with caution and fear, suppressing her anger and slowly trying to overcome her feelings of having been betrayed by her husband.

Mrs. W, an only child, had lost her father at an early age and had since lived with her mother. When she was 21 years old, she married her first husband, who moved into the house with Mrs. W and her mother. This living arrangement immediately led to tension and new triangulation between the couple and the mother-in-law. Mrs. W became unexpectedly pregnant as the marriage had begun to collapse. Joshua was born into these chaotic circumstances. The boy's father had become progressively more verbally and emotionally abusive toward his wife and mother-in-law, accusing the latter of undermining his authority and "castrating him." One day the husband slapped the mother-in-law in the face and the police were called. The husband left the house feeling angered, ashamed, and humiliated. Soon thereafter he filed for divorce and moved to the West coast, permanently severing ties with the three of them. Joshua was only six months old at the time. Mrs. W began to work and left Joshua in the care of the boy's grandmother. At work she met an unmarried man 10 years her senior who began to court her. Mr. W (the stepfather) had risen from humble beginnings and had overcome a multitude of obstacles in his life. He was somewhat obsessive and lacking in spontaneity, but was hard-working, serious, and successful. He was a self-proclaimed "self-made man" in whom Mrs. W saw the strengths and qualities that she longed for in a man. The couple married after a brief courtship and Mr. W moved his wife, mother-in-law, and Joshua into a new house. The boy was one and a half years old at the time. Mrs. W recalls that her husband soon became unhappy with the new arrangement. He perceived Joshua as "spoiled rotten" and overindulged by the two maternal figures. Initially, the stepfather seemed irritated and rejected the boy, chastising his wife for not providing more structure and for setting her son up "to be a failure for sure." Soon after stepfather's arrival, Joshua expressed much interest in Mr. W. Every morning he waited anxiously for his stepfather to come out of his bedroom and followed him everywhere, including into the bathroom, where Joshua became absorbed in his stepfather's daily rituals of shaving and brushing his teeth. If Mr. W ignored him, he would protest loudly and vehemently. When Mr. W arrived from work Joshua responded with visible excitement and actively sought his company. He responded dutifully when Mr. W began to redirect him and appeared anxious if it seemed he might lose the stepfather's approval. Unquestionably, Mr. W soon established himself as a strong figure in the family. One day, politely but firmly over dinner, he expounded the need for the mother-in-law to move out of the house. Indeed, he had already made arrangements for her to move to an apartment nearby. "It made sense to everybody and there seemed no point in arguing," Mrs. W explained later. Joshua survived this transition with minimal trauma, spending working hours at his grandmother's and returning to his parents' home in the evening.

When Joshua was three years old, Mr. W was mowing the lawn, and during a break Joshua tried to imitate him by taking off his shirt and attempting to push the lawn mower. Mr. W was amused and called his wife. Furtively, both quietly observed as the child unknowingly continued his impersonation of the stepfather. Mrs. W noticed a tear in her husband's eye and thought to herself, "I think they've accepted each other as father and son."

When Mrs. W came to therapy, Joshua was already an adult. Living in another state, he was described by his mother as a successful professional, married, with two young children. The oldest one was named after his stepfather. Joshua maintained a close relationship with his parents and the family visited each other often.

Mrs. W told the therapist, "How can I be angry at my husband over this affair. I owe so much to this man, he saved me and my son, he saved us both!"

As illustrated in this case material, the contributions of the stepfather may be of crucial importance to the psychological development of the preoedipal boy. Even though Joshua himself did not participate firsthand in reporting this material, it appears that at least some of his major developmental hurdles were facilitated by the relationship with his stepfather. I would venture to reconstruct that Mr. W became a strong dominant figure in the household. He functioned as a good provider as well as a guardian of the stability of family structures, looking after his wife, stepson, and mother-in-law. He was available as an alternative figure of attachment, as a love object, and as a figure of identification. This allowed the boy to imitate, admire, and partake in his masculinity. Mr. W invited Joshua to move away from the symbiotic pull toward his mother and grandmother by modifying Joshua's behaviors through reward and punishment, teaching the boy to contain aggressive drives which promoted internalization of superego precursors. Stepfather served as a facilitator as his stepson achieved dis-identification from the mother and grandmother. In my opinion this allowed the boy to consolidate his gender identity, promoted the maturation of his cognitive capacities and other ego functions, safeguarded his autonomy, and promoted his self-esteem.

The Stepfather's Role in the Oedipal Stage

In the boy, the Oedipus complex was considered resolved by taking the father as the object of the ego ideal and incorporating that ideal into the superego (Tyson and Tyson, 1990). In the process of resolution, the defensive fantasies of the boy were believed to be due to the emergence of an intrapsychic representation of the oedipal father as a tyrannical figure, capable of instilling terror of castration, someone to be feared and reckoned with.

Gerson (1989) explained that this portrayal of the father was, in some ways, supported by western culture until recent times. This unidimensional social image of the father as a disciplinarian and educator completely lacking in empathy, is being replaced by a more contemporary conception of the father as someone who shares many nurturing responsibilities with the mother, albeit maintaining his identity as a father (Pruett, 1985).

Jacobson (1992) maintained that the love of the father toward the son is more important in facilitating the resolution of the Oedipus complex, as it allows the boy to develop a self-loving ego ideal.

The stepfather and stepson have to traverse a dangerous path; they may find themselves engaged in oedipal rivalry "too real" and frightening to both participants. The stepson may stand to the stepfather as the living representative of the "other man" who once possessed his wife sexually. In turn, the boy may find difficulty coping with the intensity of ambivalent loving and hating feelings he experiences toward a man with whom he does not have a filial blood. Not only does this man not love him unconditionally but he could regard him as "mother's extra baggage," seemingly capable of either abandoning him or, if he does not observe his best behavior, casting him out. This outcome could have disastrous consequences, producing yet another loss of a male figure in the boy's life. These real or imagined fears may become heightened if, from the start, a "temperamental misattunement" arises between the stepfather and the stepson.

Michaels (1989) commented on idealization and "excessive goodness" children attribute to the nonresidential parent. This split could lead to the vilification of the stepfather. Narcissistically injured, the stepfather may personalize the boy's aggressive tirades and respond with either sadistic retaliation or defensive withdrawal. Both are, in the boy's mind, tantamount to abandonment and rejection.

The arrival of the stepfather in the single parent family threatens most stepsons with the loss of any "special position" they may have developed with mother. After being displaced by a powerful intruder a boy may feel as if he has lost both parents. The stepfather, in turn, may not have had a chance to cement his relationship with his new wife. He may find, upon his arrival in the new family, that the generational boundaries have been weakened and that triangulations and alliances occur, undermining his authority in the new family. Conflicts between stepfathers and stepchildren are sometimes "expected" and better tolerated than conflicts between the adults (Ransom et al., 1979). This places the boy at a risk of becoming the "scapegoat" or "identified patient" in the new family, assuming the burden of guilt over tensions that develop between other family members. This may be especially true if the mother identifies the boy with his biological father, projecting onto the boy the negative characteristics of the hated, devalued, or denigrated absent father.

Upon his arrival in the new family, the stepfather must bear upon himself the responsibility of negotiating new roles and loyalties and restructuring the family in terms of nurturing and disciplining roles, acting as a fair but firm arbiter of justice, imparting rewards and punishments for particular behaviors in the child. The mother, in turn, plays a key role as the gatekeeper of these negotiations. The stepfather's capacity to parent will be tested at the onset during the oedipal stage. The stepfather's capacity to nurture derives from his identification with his own mother and father as well as his projection of the "good me" self-object fantasy (Gerson, 1989). In some cases, psychological trauma, loss, or rejection experienced in the stepfather's own life may lead to an altruistic defensive resolution, enhancing the stepfather's capacity to parent and nurture, in a "reparative attempt" of his own negative life experiences (Gurwitt, 1982, 1989). The opposite may also be true. The stepfather may possess impediments in his capacity to parent. These may also derive from negative maternal or paternal identifications that have shaped his character structure, which may include (1) a fear of losing narcissistic supplies; (2) a resurgence of homosexual conflicts; (3) the conviction of having been inadequately parented; (4) inadequate separation-individuation; (5) lack of a preoedipal relationship with his own father; and (6) conflicted maternal identification, among others (Gurwitt, 1982, 1989). In certain cases, stepfathers may find it easier to parent a daughter (Benedek, 1970) in order to avoid awakening narcissistic and oedipal conflicts in themselves.

The following case will illustrate the failure of a stepfather in his role as "redeemer" of the stepson.

Case 2

Mr. D, a 42-year-old homosexual, came to therapy complaining of feelings of depression precipitated by the recent break of an eight-year relationship with his male lover. In spite of being intelligent, articulate, and well educated, Mr. D received mediocre evaluations in his work performance. He appeared to lack initiative and self-discipline, he frequently arrived late at work after staying up partying and socializing in bars during week nights. Mr. D could not understand what was "the big deal about this damn punctuality as long as I get the work done." His attitude of entitlement sometimes alienated his coworkers. Mr. D had sought out male partners who assumed a protective, parental role toward him and took over management of his financial matters. Mr. D chose to attend to housekeeping and socializing chores. From Mr. D's narrative, it became apparent that his former lover had become exasperated with Mr. D's dependency and felt that he had been assigned a heavier burden in the relationship than that of the patient.

Mr. D's father had had an affair with his secretary and left the family. Mr. D's mother became so enraged she constantly berated and denigrated her former husband in front of the boy. Simultaneously, she formed a closer relationship with Mr. D, praising him for being a "good child," sensitive and delicate, like herself and unlike his father.

Mr. D's mother remarried when Mr. D was four and a half years old. Mr. D's stepfather, a widower, was 20 years older than his new wife. He had already raised two children from a previous marriage and was cordial, if not indifferent, to Mr. D. The stepfather enjoyed social and financial prestige and led an active social life. His many professional evening engagements soon bored Mr. D's mother; she chose to stay home with her son, making him her confidant and companion. Mr. D perceived his stepfather as an absent peripheral figure. One day, Mr. D accidentally overheard the stepfather talking to a friend, "When I remarried I had done my share of parenting, I think I'm going to sit this one out." This comment deeply injured Mr. D. After this event, he narrated, "I cringed every time I heard my stepfather's footsteps coming through the door."

Mr. D's biological father had also remained detached. There were many promises he did not keep. Silently he disapproved of Mr. D's passivity and the effeminate mannerisms, which were apparent. Over time, both Mr. D and his biological father found themselves "disliking each other intensely." As an adult, Mr. D remained close to his mother and spoke to her on the phone "almost every day." He told the therapist he felt: "My mother is a wonderful and interesting woman, she is really my role model and my best friend." When Mr. D's stepfather died, the patient was surprised to find out how indifferent he felt about the event and commented, "At least the old geezer left my mother a good chunk of money."

From a psychoanalytic perspective, it is possible to reconstruct the following scenario. Mr. D had identified with his mother and quite strongly sought a sexual object choice patterned after the distant stepfather, assigned the role of family custodian. The patient's lack of autonomy and empathy had a watershed effect, impairing his initiative, his capacity for industry and possibly his generativity. His identity patterns played a role in defining his difficulties with mature and intimate relationships (Erikson, 1950). In this case, it seems Mr. D's stepfather failed to protect the boy from the symbiotic dyadic pull toward his mother, permitting intergenerational boundaries between the mother and the boy to become blurred. He failed to assume a leadership position in the new family, restructuring the disciplining and nurturing roles of both parents. The stepfather ignored Mr. D, abdicating his duties as a model of identification, a love object as well as a modulator of the boy's libidinal and aggressive drives, leading to narcissistic fixations, gender identity confusion, and difficulties in the development of the ego ideal and the superego (Lamb, 1976).

The Stepfather's Role During the Latency Stage

The latency stage is chronologically situated between the rivalous battles of the oedipal stage and the storm of adolescence. It provides an ideal, restful plateau for a much needed "honeymoon period" in the relationship between the stepfather and the stepson. Not only is the stepfather's contribution essential to the boy during latency, but the boy is more likely to acknowledge this fact by showering the stepfather with love, admiration, respect, and "good behavior" in a manner in which the stepfather will feel appreciated; because of this, the stepfather will also be more likely to become emotionally involved with his stepson. Significant cognitive maturation takes place during latency, leading to a more accurate perception of reality which sometimes may lead to disappointment in the boy's idealized perception of the figure of the parents. The child defends from this disappointment with the reparative fantasy of the "family romance" or "the imaginary friend" (Tyson and Tyson, 1990). In the case of the stepchild, the absence of the biological father renders a quality of reality to these particular fantasies.

The transition from magical to logical thinking leads to the process of "decentering," with the abatement of egocentric causality. This new achievement allows the boy to view the world through another person's eyes and thus to develop the capacity for empathy (Tyson and Tyson, 1990).

Preoedipal sexual drives continue during latency, but no new aims appear (Blos, 1966).

The stepfather becomes a crucial figure for the boy when, after the alienation produced by the rivalous oedipal battles, the boy turns back to the stepfather for guidance.

The following case illustrates how a positive relationship in latency served as an anchoring point for an otherwise turbulent lifelong relationship between a stepfather and a stepson.

Case 3

Mr. L, a 35-year-old successful Jewish architect, lost his biological father to a car accident when he was an infant. His mother remarried when the boy was five years old. Mr. L's stepfather was a child survivor of the Holocaust and was described as suffering from symptoms of severe chronic posttraumatic stress disorder. These included periods of self-isolation, depressed moods and chronic irritability. In spite of being financially successful, having overcome monumental obstacles in his life, Mr. L's stepfather was described as having a pessimistic outlook on life and very little trust in people, a constriction of his affect interfered with emotional relationships. Only Mr. L's mother was able to "connect" emotionally with her husband, being maternal and protective. This inevitably increased rivalries between the stepfather and the stepson. Mr. L felt responsible for being ignored, rejected, and pushed aside by the stepfather.

After more than two years in once-a-week psychotherapy, Mr. L told his therapist: "All my life I've been struggling toward an impossible dream, 'to be loved by my stepfather.' I know that at some level he does love me. How could he not, I've done everything he wanted me to and I've made him proud. He'll never tell me face to face, of course. I always have to find out from third parties. It's been hard, very hard, dealing with this man who sometimes appears as if he were dead inside. I grew up thinking it was always my fault I could not get his attention or ever please him. Now a part of me knows that he's incapable of more, that his human side was murdered when he was a child and what I got was only half of a person. I also struggled with guilt over any demands I placed on him. He let me know nothing in my life could compare with the hardships he went through. I think, though, that I'm slowly coming to terms with him. There were some very good times; when I was between eight and 12 years old, we were real buddies. Almost every weekend we went to Yankee Stadium together. He loved baseball and so did I. We ate hot dogs and one day they were giving out baseball bats at the stadium. Can you believe it, I still have that bat in my closet! We used to browse through *National Geographic* magazines together. He told me about Eastern Europe and used to mesmerize me with his stories. I could have listened to him forever. Then something strange happened when I became a teenager. I changed and it seems that we've been at war with each other ever since. He's a good man at heart, I surprise myself sometimes when I realize how much like him I've become. Now, when I reach out to him and feel that cold emptiness that used to upset me so much, I try to think about those baseball games, what a treat they were!"

In spite of the emotional limitations of Mr. L's stepfather, he served as a model for selective identification for his stepson. Mr. L introjected positive moral qualities, such as curiosity, a capacity for industry, and competency during latency. The stepfather provided him with mentorship and a model of masculinity. Within a framework of appropriate socialization, the game of baseball served as a metaphor through which, among other things, Mr. L's stepfather was able to transmit the sublimation of aggressive drives and their transformation into assertiveness, competitiveness, and competency. His stepfather's stories stimulated the boy's curiosity and his capacity for sublimation through fantasy, possibly enhancing creativity. The stepfather's fascinating narratives also served as a vehicle for the intergenerational transmission of information adding a new enriched image of the stepfather as a model of identification. The latency stage for Mr. L represented an "island of sanity," and a reference point in an otherwise troubled relationship with an emotionally damaged stepfather. The loss of Mr. L's biological father at an early age promoted the tenacity of egocentric causality, his self-blame. Mr. L repeatedly attempted to gain his stepfather's love as if to undo the pain of the loss of biological father, his "impossible dream."

The Stepfather in Adolescence

Adolescence is known as a period of psychic restructuring characterized by an increase in drives and a shift in ego functions. The development of abstract thinking (Piaget, 1964) allows the adolescent to grasp the complexities of reality and to begin to develop more realistic assessment of the world around him. This permits the adolescent to move away from the idealized parental conception of latency and to begin the process of dis-idealization and dis-identification. This process will set the stage for a journey which, if negotiated successfully, will culminate with the adolescent's consolidation of his own identity and a move toward a mature object choice outside of the parental family unit (Blos, 1966; Tyson and Tyson, 1990).

Adolescence is also conceptualized as a mourning process involving painful decathexis from the parental figures of childhood. The adolescent's newly acquired cognitive maturity allows him to understand the irrevocability of the passage of time and brings about longing, depressive affects and regression that are characteristic of the process of loss.

Wolfenstein (1992) not only explains adolescence as a "trial mourning" but sustains that it is a "necessary precondition for the successful completion of mourning."

In the case of most stepsons, unless the biological father is present, and even when he is present at a distance, we may assume that a previous loss or separation from the biological father has occurred. This brings about a series of complicated family dynamics which will acquire different configurations according to the variables involved. For example, (1) the age of the boy when the loss occurred, (2) the hiatus of time between the loss and the arrival of the stepfather, (3) the climate in the house before, during and after the arrival of the stepfather; as well as innumerable other possible variables.

In essence, one must take into account that, not only will the adolescent be expected to negotiate the difficulties of the particular developmental stage, but will also have to recapitulate the earlier loss of his biological father when he was "unready" to mourn. After accomplishing object constancy, an adolescent who has suffered the loss of the biological father may be prone to narcissistic fixations unless an appropriate substitute can be found. And unless the hiatus between the loss and the arrival of the paternal substitute is not prolonged (Wolfenstein, 1990).

In adults, the sudden loss and decathexis of a loved object may lead to regression and to a period of disorganization (Bowlby, 1992). In a child, where stability and continuity of self are not yet consolidated, this may be experienced as a regressive assault, and a severe discontinuity of the self, leading to acting out. Such as is illustrated in the following case.

Case 4

Carlos, a 14-year-old Hispanic adolescent, never met his biological father, who had abandoned the family when the boy was six months old. His mother remarried when the boy was five years old and the union produced two other children. Carlos became very attached to his stepfather, a carpenter who proved to be a good husband and provider and was attentive to Carlos, serving as a good role model for the boy. Carlos's stepfather and mother began experiencing severe marital difficulties and the stepfather abruptly abandoned the house and severed all contact with the family. Carlos was 13 years old at the time. Soon thereafter, the boy's behavior began to deteriorate rapidly, he became truant in school, joined a gang, began smoking marijuana, and engaged in petty theft. A year later, he was declared ungovernable by his mother and at this point, he had accumulated nine judicial charges; as a consequence of which he was being evaluated for residential placement.

Carlos presented as an irritable and despondent young man whose anger was quite visible and who possessed a self-destructive quality. When questioned about his family, he expressed deep feelings of anger and disappointment at having been abandoned by his stepfather. He blamed his mother for the stepfather's departure and explained to the examiner, "My stepfather is my real father. The other guy was just my 'sperm father.'"

Carlos's stepfather contributed to his development by providing ego and superego support to the boy in the form of guidance and mentoring and by providing a nurturing and loving relationship. The sudden loss of the loving attachment to his stepfather and of the external narcissistic supplies the stepfather provided caused a severe discontinuity in the boy's self-constancy. This led to a regression and acting out behavior in the boy, which was an attempt to self-regulate his depressive affects and to bolster his sense of faltering masculinity. Also, a reactivation of the previous loss of the biological father intensified the despair in this narcissistically vulnerable adolescent. This earlier loss reinforced omnipotent immature defenses causing Carlos's aggression to be directed inward, which may have accounted for the boy's depression and self-destructive behavior, and outward, which would explain his conduct disordered behavior.

The stepson may put his stepfather to trial more intensely during adolescence than at any other developmental stage. The adolescent may deal with the painful task of separating from the parents by reaction formation, which may lead to a barrage of hostile attacks toward the stepfather, who may be treated by the adolescent stepson with hate and contempt (Lewis and Volkmar, 1990). As a consequence, the stepfather may suffer deep narcissistic wounds, feeling unappreciated and betrayed. This may lead to sadistic retaliation, depression, or withdrawal on the part of the stepfather. In the process, feelings of rejection in the earlier part of the life of the stepfather may become reactivated, compounding the injury. The stepfather may also experience feelings of disappointment, loss, or rage when the stepson begins to individuate, defining his identity in a manner that does not conform with the "selfobject fantasy" held by the stepfather about his stepson. Also, the stepfather may experience oedipal competitiveness against the stepson. For example, the stepfather may feel envy over the boy's girlfriends, his youth or his future potential. He may be reminded of his own early experiences of deprivation and compare himself to his more fortunate stepson resulting in feelings of envy, loss, or rage. The stepson may also serve as a vehicle through which the stepfather may act out unacceptable unconscious impulses (superego lacunae), a process which may prove damaging and destructive to the stepson (Johnson and Szurek, 1952).

The following case illustrates how the stepfather's withdrawal from the life of the stepson at a crucial stage in adolescence impacted negatively on the development of the boy's adult character.

Case 5

Mr. Y, a 49-year-old man, was evaluated as a possible psychoanalytic training case. He presented the following reasons for seeking an analysis: (1) an inability to accomplish his professional potential after having changed careers three times due to feeling confused about his future and lacking fulfillment with any particular profession; (2) his inability to achieve "emotional closeness" with his wife and child and his perception of himself as "dull and not a very interesting person"; (3) he also blamed himself for being "too accommodating" with others and unable to assert himself or openly to express disagreement or hostile feelings for fear of being disapproved or rejected.

Mr. Y presented as a polite man, who spoke in a monotone and avoided any topic that carried an intense affectual component. He appeared vague and devoid of passion. His narratives were delivered in a slow drawn out style and were usually circumstantial. In observing his own countertransference, the therapist found himself feeling distracted during sessions, sometimes feeling bored, with his mind wandering off to other topics when Mr. Y spoke.

Mr. Y's biological father had died of a heart attack when the patient was nine years old. He remembers the event with indifference, experiencing an "absence of grief," explaining that his mother had to go back to work and that "other than that, it was business as usual." Mr. Y's mother remarried when the patient was 12 years old to a man she met at work. Mr. Y's stepfather was a car salesman who was also interested in collecting vintage model cars and owned several of these which he kept at home. Mr. Y recalls being fascinated by his stepfather's "T Bird" and enjoying the times when he assisted the stepfather with the mechanical and aesthetic maintenance of the car.

One day when the parents were out, Mr. Y found the keys to the "T Bird" and, without the parents' permission, "took the car for a spin." The outing culminated in a car accident from which Mr. Y emerged unharmed. He was 14 years old at the time and did not have a driver's license. Mr. Y crashed the car into a tree rendering the vehicle a complete loss. Mr. Y recalls being "terrified" by the incident and experienced difficulty narrating the events during the session "even after all these years." Mr. Y suffered a second car accident at the age of 17, while returning from a party with school friends; this time he was under the influence of alcohol, and caused serious damage to the family car. Mr. Y told the therapist that, "My stepfather personalized this, as if I had done it on purpose and he never forgave me. Even to this day, when I visit him and my mother, I feel that he is still holding a grudge and that he disapproves of me. It's strange, when I'm around him, I feel like a bad kid, as if he was silently telling me that I am a 'no-good loser who will never amount to much.'"

The death of Mr. Y's biological father at the age of nine appears to have overwhelmed the boy's ego capacities to deal with the loss. As a result, Mr. Y defended against the experience of loss through massive denial producing an "absence of grief" (Deutsch, 1992). There was a three-year hiatus between the death of the father and the arrival of the stepfather. Mr. Y's memories at this time were repressed alongside his acceptance of his father's death. The boy then transferred his feelings of love and admiration to the stepfather, who appeared to welcome the role of mentor and role model. However, a combination of positive and negative oedipal strivings as well as his admiration of the stepfather, appeared to have led the boy to take the stepfather's car (a prized phallic possession) and accidentally destroy it, causing terror in the boy. This "accidental parricide" (or castration) of the stepfather caused confusion, guilt, and anxiety in Mr. Y, leading to further acting out which culminated in a second car accident. This second event finalized the stepfather's withdrawal and rejection of the boy. Mr. Y's displays of aggression toward the stepfather appeared to have caused a deep narcissistic wound in which unresolved issues in the stepfather's early life, may have led him to reject and denigrate the boy, marking him as: "a no-good loser who will never amount to much," an image of himself which Mr. Y apparently incorporated. The loss of the biological father in latency and the two accidents caused Mr. Y to become "terrified" of his aggressive drives and aggressive potential. This interfered with the development of appropriate sublimatory defenses. Instead, Mr. Y suppressed his aggression with obsessive compulsive defenses which decreased his capacity for industry and generativity (Erikson, 1950). The loss of the biological father and later, of the stepfather, as well as his fears of his own aggression, may have interfered with his capacity for intimacy, producing a repression from consciousness of all affectual responses. This affected Mr. Y's character structure and interfered in his capacity to develop interpersonal relationships. The constriction of his affect acquired the form of a "character armour" that made others, and Mr. Y perceive himself as a "dull and uninteresting person." The patient's loss of his biological father during latency and the withdrawal and rejection by the stepfather in early adolescence, impaired Mr. Y's "second individuation process" interfering with his capacity to develop his sense of identity and self-definition (Blos, 1966). This may have accounted for Mr. Y's confusion about career choice and his lack of a clear direction in the professional arena.

This case illustrates how a promising relationship with a stepfather, who could have served as a redeemer of the boy's psychological development, served to cause regression, fixation, and a watershed effect that impaired all of Mr. Y's later psychosocial developmental stages (Erikson, 1950). The stepfather's own unresolved feelings may have caused him to suffer a deep narcissistic injury which led him to respond in a retaliatory manner that seriously affected Mr. Y.

The stepfather plays an important role in containing and preventing the possible derailment of the adolescent process of the stepson, caused by the narcissistic vulnerabilities that result from the early loss of the biological father, when the boy had not yet developed the capacity to mourn.

The stepfather's role in a blended family and his ability to negotiate successfully an appropriate relationship with the stepson's biological father, will be illustrated in the following case.

Case 6

Sean, an Irish-American boy, was 11 years old when his mother married Mr. Perez, his stepfather, a Hispanic man who was decent and successful in his profession. The stepfather had custody of two other children from his first marriage and had sought therapy in order to deal with his guilt feelings, associated with having divorced his emotionally disturbed first wife. Sean's mother and the three boys were subsequently seen in therapy as a family. The night of the wedding, shortly after returning home from the ceremony, Sean was found on the living room couch in tears and in fetal position with his face buried in one of the pillows. Sean asked to be left alone when his mother attempted to console him. His stepfather later approached him quietly and, putting a hand on his shoulder, whispered to him, "I know how hard this must be for you, but remember that your mother will always be your mother and your father will always be your father, and I promise that I'll do the best so that you and I get along."

Sean continued his usual weekend visits and vacations with his biological father and a few months later, Mr. Perez's nine- and six-year-old sons from the previous marriage came to live with the family. The stepfather bought a larger house and the family began a long process of renegotiating boundaries and limit setting with the three boys. The stepfather seemed particularly irritated when, during the family's first Christmas together, his own parents showered Sean's stepbrothers with expensive gifts, forgetting to bring Sean a present. An argument ensued in which Mr. Perez confronted his own parents indicating to them the three boys had to be treated equally or otherwise the grandparents would not be welcomed in the house. As a result of this, the stepfather emerged as a strong figure in the new family, securing his position as a firm and fair leader. Sean's mother, as well, began setting limits on her two stepchildren and on the stepfather's emotionally disturbed former wife. Sean's mother proved to be nurturing, honest, and forthright and through the efforts of both parents, order and harmony were established in the new family.

One day, the stepfather reported to the therapist that "Sean had gotten involved in a fist fight at school, in order to defend his youngest stepbrother, who was being called derogatory names for having a darker skin color than the other two boys." Mr. Perez expressed feeling proud and deeply moved by this event. The family continued to thrive through different crises, including a period of severe acting out, on the part of Sean's youngest stepbrother, who defamed and devalued the family in order to be allowed to live with his disturbed biological mother, whom he sorely missed. Sean's mother and stepfather showed tolerance and patience through the crisis, which resolved when Sean's younger stepbrother returned to the family, one month later, in a state of depression and disappointment over the experience.

Sean began excelling and obtaining academic honors in school and surprised the family when he also thrived athletically, becoming a "varsity letterman" in several sports. At the time of his high school graduation at the age of 17, Sean was selected as "king of the homecoming parade," after having excelled on his school's football team. Mr. Perez reported to the therapist that Sean had, once again, deeply moved him when he approached Mr. Perez with a special request for the day of the parade. He asked that he be allowed to sit in the back seat of the car, with his mother and biological father. He then asked the stepfather to drive the car and sit in the front seat with Sean's two stepbrothers. He concluded by telling his stepfather, "I hope you will do this for me, I know you will, you've always been there for me."

Mr. Perez's success as a stepfather and as a magnanimous leader in the new family can be attributed, in my opinion, to some of his own early life experiences. As a child, Mr. Perez had been cruelly tormented by his school peers for being overweight and for having a speech impediment. As a result, both of his parents had diligently and lovingly protected him by highlighting and supporting his abilities and strengths. His father encouraged him to participate in sports. Over the years, Mr. Perez was able to overcome many of his early difficulties and developed into an athletic, towering man, who possessed a warm and affable personality as well as an engaging sense of humor. In spite of his unremarkable academic record, Mr. Perez had risen to occupy an important managerial position, with several dozen employees under his responsibility and leadership. On rare occasions, when addressing emotionally charged issues in therapy, Mr. Perez developed a mild stutter in his speech, highlighting a vulnerable side to his otherwise imposing persona.

I would venture to speculate that Mr. Perez was able to internalize and identify with the loving and nurturing qualities of his own parents, which contributed, among other things, to consolidate his self-esteem, his superego, and ego ideal. The integrity of his psychic structures allowed him to develop an altruistic resolution by which the painful experiences he endured as a child were transformed into a paternal desire to nurture and mentor. Mr. Perez accomplished, in this way, a reparative emotional experience. His positive experience with sports probably contributed to the sublimation of aggressive drives and drive derivatives and may have been partly responsible for Mr. Perez's professional success and leadership qualities. He was able to contain the aggressive drives and drive derivatives of the different family members, setting the limits and boundaries in the new family, which included the former spouses. The integrity of Mr. Perez's ego structures also enabled him to be an effective mentor role model and a love object to his stepson and his own biological children. His capacity to form a mature, loving relationship with his wife, contributed to further stabilize the family unit. Mr. Perez's wife (Sean's mother) also played a key role in the success of the new "blended family."

The stepfather occupies the position of a love object, mentor, role model, and modulator of the aggressive drives of the adolescent boy. His role will allow the stepson to complete, in as much as possible, the developmental tasks of adolescence which include (1) the consolidation of a sense of identity; (2) the accomplishment of mastery over drives; (3) the development of a heterosexual object choice outside the parental family unit; (4) and the development of a realistic view of the world. The stepson's adolescent process will also allow the stepfather to rework many of his own unresolved developmental conflicts.

Conclusions

The mission of becoming a stepfather is a difficult one, since it begins with the encounter of a child who has already experienced the loss of another paternal figure. The stepfather's role will then not only involve the usual paternal functions that allow the boy to negotiate successfully the different developmental stages; but it will also involve a reparative and restorative element. In this process, the stepfather's ego and super ego integrity will be tested and will also allow the stepfather to rework his own unresolved issues, characteristic of each of the stepfather's own developmental stages.

The stepfather has to be able to contain, modulate, and sometimes even encourage the boy's aggressive and libidinal drives, becoming a "constant," as well as providing a degree of continuity and certainty in the boy's life. This will allow the boy to integrate the split off negative affects which resulted from the previous loss of the biological father. The stepfather will contribute to the development of a new "paternal construct" or "father imago" (Lansky, 1989) which will encompass elements of the mother, biological father, stepfather, and the self, as well as of the self as viewed in relation to the connections between all the other components.

This new parental construct will serve the boy as an anchoring point for the integration of the self, so that the resolution of mourning can take place, inasmuch as possible, during the process of adolescence in order for the boy's psychological development to proceed without interruptions.

References

Abelin, E. (1975), Some further observations and comments on the earliest role of the father. *Internat. J. Psycho-Anal.*, 56:293–302.

Atkins, R. N. (1989), Divorce and the fathers: Some intrapsychic factors affecting the outcome. In: *Fathers and Their Families*, ed. S. H. Cath, A. Gurwitt & L. Gunsberg. Hillsdale, NJ: The Analytic Press, pp. 431–458.

Benedek, T. (1970), Fatherhood and providing. In: *Parenthood*, ed. E. J. Anthony & T. Benedek. Boston: Little Brown, pp. 167–183.

Blos, P. (1966), *On Adolescence*. New York: Free Press, pp. 52–148.

——— (1984), Son and father. *J. Amer. Psychoanal. Assn.*, 32:301–324.

Bowlby, J. (1992), Pathological mourning and childhood mourning. In: *Essential Papers on Object Loss*, ed. R. V. Frankel. New York: New York University Press, pp. 185–221.

Brown, A. C., Green, R. J. & Druckman, J. (1990), A comparison of stepfamilies with and without child-focused problems. *Amer. J. Orthopsychiat.*, 60:556–566.

Bugner, M. (1985), The oedipal experience: Effects on development of an absent father. *Internat. J. Psycho-Anal.*, 66:311–320.

Cath, S. H. (1982), Divorce and the child: The father question hour. In: *Father and Child: Developmental and Clinical Perspectives*, ed. S. H. Cath, A. R. Gurwitt & J. M. Ross. Boston: Little Brown, pp. 467–479.

Deutsch, H. (1992), Absence of grief. In: *Essential Papers on Object Loss*, ed. R. V. Frankel. New York: New York University Press, pp. 223–230.

Erikson, E. H. (1950), The eight ages of man. In: *Childhood and Society*. New York: Norton, pp. 247–274.

Esman, A. H. (1982), Fathers and adolescent sons. In: *Father and Child: Developmental and Clinical Perspectives*, ed. S. H. Cath, A. R. Gurwitt & J. M. Ross. Boston: Little Brown, pp. 265–274.

Freud, S. (1897), Extracts from the Fliess papers. *Standard Edition*, 1:177–280. London: Hogarth Press, 1950.

Furman, E. (1992), Some effects of the parent's death on the child's personality development. In: *Essential Papers on Object Loss*, ed. R. V. Frankel. New York: New York University Press, pp. 382–402.

Furman, R. (1992), A child's capacity for mourning. In: *Essential Papers on Object Loss*, ed. R. V. Frankel. New York: New York University Press, pp. 376–381.

Gerson, M. J. (1989), Tomorrow's fathers: The anticipation of fatherhood. In: *Fathers and Their Families*, ed. S. H. Cath, A. Gurwitt & L. Gunsberg. Hillsdale, NJ: The Analytic Press, pp. 121–126.

Gill, H. S. (1991), Internalization of the absent father. *Internat. J. Psycho-Anal.*, 72:243–252.

Greenson, R. (1954), The struggle against identification. *J. Amer. Psychoanal. Assn.*, 2.

Greenspan, S. (1982), The second other: The role of the father in early personality formation and the dyadic-phallic phase of development. In: *Father and Child: Developmental and Clinical Perspectives*, ed. S. H. Cath, A. R. Gurwitt & J. M. Ross. Boston: Little Brown, pp. 123–138.

Greif, J. B. (1979), Fathers, children and joint custody. *Amer. J. Orthopsychiat.*, 49:311–319.

Gunsberg, L. (1982), Selected critical review of the psychological investigations of the early father–infant relationship. In: *Father and Child: Developmental and Clinical Perspectives*, ed. S. H. Cath, A. R. Gurwitt & J. M. Ross. Boston: Little Brown, pp. 65–86.

Gurwitt, A. (1982), Aspects of prospective fatherhood. In: *Father and Child: Developmental and Clinical Perspectives*, ed. S. H. Cath, A. R. Gurwitt & J. M. Ross. Boston: Little Brown, pp. 275–300.

_____ (1989), Flight from parenthood. In: *Fathers and Their Families*, ed. S. H. Cath, A. Gurwitt & L. Gunsberg. Hillsdale, NJ: The Analytic Press, pp. 167–190.

Healy, J. M., Malley, J. E. & Stewart, A. J. (1990), Children and their fathers after parental separation. *Amer. J. Orthopsychiat.*, 60:531–543.

Herzog, J. M. (1982), On father hunger: The father's role in modulating of aggressive drive and fantasy. In: *Father and Child: Developmental and Clinical Perspectives*, ed. S. H. Cath, A. R. Gurwitt & J. M. Ross. Boston: Little Brown, pp. 163–174.

Jacobson, E. (1992), Return of the lost parent. In: *Essential Papers on Object Loss*, ed. R. V. Frankel. New York: New York University Press, pp. 233–250.

Johnson, A. M. & Szurek, S. A. (1952), The genesis of antisocial acting out in children and adults. *Psychoanal. Quart.*, 21:323.

Kirshner, L. A. (1992), The absence of father. *J. Amer. Psychoanal. Assn.*, 40: 1117–1138.

Lamb, M. E. (1976), The role of the father: An overview. In: *The Role of the Father in Child Development*, ed. M. E. Lamb. New York: Wiley, pp. 1–61.

Lansky, M. R. (1989), The paternal imago. In: *Fathers and Their Families*, ed. S. H. Cath, A. Gurwitt & L. Gunsberg. Hillsdale, NJ: The Analytic Press, pp. 27–46.

Layland, W. R. (1981), In search of a loving father. *Internat. J. Psycho-Anal.*, 62:215–223.

Lewis, M. & Volkmar, F. R. (1990), *Clinical Aspects of Child and Adolescent Development*. Philadelphia, PA: Lea & Febiger, pp. 193–252.

Mahler, M., Pine, F. & Bergman, A. (1975), *The Psychological Birth of the Human Infant*. New York: Basic Books.

Michaels, C. S. (1989), So near and yet so far: The non-resident father. In: *Fathers and Their Families*, ed. S. H. Cath, A. Gurwitt & L. Gunsberg. Hillsdale, NJ: The Analytic Press, pp. 409–424.

Muir, R. (1989), Fatherhood from the perspective of object relations theory and relational systems theory. In: *Fathers and Their Families*, ed. S. H. Cath, A. Gurwitt & L. Gunsberg. Hillsdale, NJ: The Analytic Press, pp. 47–62.

Neubauer, P. B. (1989), Fathers as single parents: Object relations beyond mother. In: *Fathers and Their Families*, ed. S. H. Cath, A. Gurwitt & L. Gunsberg. Hillsdale, NJ: The Analytic Press, pp. 63–76.

Pacella, B. L. (1989), Paternal influence in early child development. In: *Fathers and Their Families*, ed. S. H. Cath, A. Gurwitt & L. Gunsberg. Hillsdale, NJ: The Analytic Press, pp. 197–224.

Piaget, J. (1964), *Six Psychological Studies*. New York: Random House.

———— & Inhelder B. (1969), *The Psychology of the Child*. New York: Basic Books.

Prall, R. C. (1978), Panel: The role of the father in the pre-oedipal years. *J. Amer. Psychoanal. Assn.*, 26:143–162.

Pruett, K. D. (1985), Oedipal configurations in young father-raised children. *The Psychoanalytic Study of the Child*, 40:435–456. New Haven, CT: Yale University Press.

Random House Dictionary of the English Language, Unabridged Edition (1966), New York: Random House.

Ransom, J. S., Schlesinger S. & Derdeyn, A. P. (1979), A stepfamily in formation. *Amer. J. Orthopsychiat.*, 49:36–44.

Ross, J. M. (1979), Fathering: A review of some psychoanalytic contributions on paternity. *Internat. J. Psycho-Anal.*, 60:317–327.

———— (1982), Mentorship in middle childhood. In: *Father and Child: Developmental and Clinical Perspectives*, ed. S. H. Cath, A. R. Gurwitt & J. M. Ross. Boston: Little Brown, pp. 243–252.

Sarnoff, C. A. (1982), The father's role in latency. In: *Father and Child: Developmental and Clinical Perspectives*, ed. S. H. Cath, A. R. Gurwitt & J. M. Ross. Boston: Little Brown, pp. 253–264.

Solnit, A. J. (1989), The non-custodial father: An application of Solomonic wisdom. In: *Fathers and Their Families*, ed. S. H. Cath, A. Gurwitt & L. Gunsberg. Hillsdale, NJ: The Analytic Press, pp. 425–430.

Spitz, R. A. (1965), *The First Year of Life: A Psychoanalytic Study of Normal and Deviant Development of Object Relations*. Madison, CT: International Universities Press.

Stoller, R. J. (1975), Healthiest parental influences on the earliest development of masculinity in baby boys. *Psychoanal. Forum*, 5:232–262.

Tyson, P. & Tyson, R. L. (1990), *Psychoanalytic Theories of Development: An Integration*. New Haven, CT: Yale University Press, pp. 57–60, 311–319.

Tyson, R. (1992), Some narcissistic consequences of object loss: A developmental view. In: *Essential Papers on Object Loss*, ed. R. V. Frankel. New York: New York University Press, pp. 152–267.

Winnicott, D. W. (1965), *The Maturational Processes and the Facilitating Environment*. New York: International Universities Press.

Wolfenstein, M. (1992), How is mourning possible? In: *Essential Papers on Object Loss*, ed. R. V. Frankel. New York: New York University Press, pp. 334–362.

Between Marriages

A Period of Dread

Stanley H. Cath

This volunteered personal reminiscence by an older woman resonates well with Dr. Solomon's example of a belated appreciation of a stepparent, and adds another level of understanding to the reasons why it sometimes requires years to earn a place of trust in a reconstructed family. In this recollection, the period between marriages was dreaded as a parade of women passed in review before the family.

"After my mother died when I was fourteen, Dad was between marriages. Ha! I just realized how much I dreaded that intermarriage phase! It took two long years for him to find someone. He was the kind of man everyone would expect to vote for life and remarry. Yet, for us in this interregnum, he held a veto power over our lives. In those years, we dreaded each and every woman he brought home, most of whom we could not stand. There was one who always turned up the heat even though we thought it was too hot already. We were so glad when she disappeared. Others seemed to be the typical gold diggers, out to feather their nests as if we were that rich. It seemed we were in limbo for two whole years.

"At 16, I met the woman who would become my stepmother. Because I liked her light-heartedness right away, I began to secretly hope Dad would pick her as his wife. But I now think my objections to her concealed my shame at thinking she was a vast improvement over my mother who was a gloomy type with a cloud over her head just like Eyor. I somehow believed if I let my father know how much I liked her, he'd get rid of her, like I fantasized he had gotten rid of my mom. He seemed like a playboy and I was convinced we just didn't like the same kind of people. But I was just a kid then.

"As the oldest, I had taken over all the cooking, cleaning, and just took care of everything that came up around the house. The family joke was that I was as good as a wife to my dad as my mother. I knew it was because I was so unlike my sloppy friends, I always wanted things just so.

"But she came in and freed me up from all that and made it easy for me to leave for college the next year. There I met my husband. Early in my marriage, I began to appreciate that my stepmother, whom I had hardly acknowledged, really had allowed me the room, time, and space to build my own life, but I tell you it took years.

"In fact as adults I found we had a lot in common. We knitted, crocheted, and often joined up to take on local projects together. She was an extremely competent woman and somehow recognized that I was a competent person too. She was smart enough not to try too hard and let me have my own head and follow my own inclinations."

Editors' Comment

Even and especially when the stepparent may be preferred, there can be a strong loyalty conflict, the mother's absence (death) notwithstanding. The stepmother not only allowed her to once again become an adolescent with her own life but also removed her from acting as though she was a better wife to her father than her dead mother had been. The oedipal overtones are subliminally implied. Father belongs to stepmother, and she too has to find another (her future husband).

Affect Tolerance

A Crucial Requirement for Substitute Parenting

Steven L. Nickman

The ability to tolerate painful affect, without resorting to primitive defenses such as denial or a flight into activity, is a mark of mature functioning. Being a parent calls for this ability, and being a parent in special circumstances may require it even more. Parents of handicapped or ill children, adoptive parents, and stepparents share the circumstance that aspects of their child's life and their life as parents are more complex, and in some ways more difficult or painful, than corresponding aspects of other families' lives. This chapter will describe certain challenges to the ability of adoptive and stepparents to maintain emotional equilibrium. (Foster parents share similar challenges, but their more limited commitment in terms of elapsed time with the child and legal responsibility may mitigate the severity of the stress they experience; foster parenting will not be referred to explicitly below, although the discussion could easily be generalized to include it.)

McDougall (1991) writes of certain analysands, "I came to realize that such patients, because of their internal fragilities, were unable to contain and work through the powerful affective states that had been stirred up by external events. They preferred to plunge into some form of action, or rather felt they had no choice but to do so" (p. 155). Some of the vicissitudes of substitute families may usefully be viewed as arising from this difficulty on the part of parents, bearing in mind that McDougall's term "action" could be seen as including a wide range of avoidant behaviors and other forms of psychic activity. (Perhaps to the point is the apocryphal remark of President Eisenhower to his peripatetic Secretary of State, John Foster Dulles: "Don't just do something, Foster, stand there!")

Stepparenting

The new stepparent comes into an established family as the husband or wife of a person with children; as a result, all the relationships in that family

---

This chapter, originally entitled "Affect Tolerance in Adoptive Parenting," appeared in *Issues in Psychoanalytic Psychology*, 21:63–76, 1999. It has been modified for the present volume and is printed with permission of the journal in which it appeared.

are altered. Likewise, unless the parent has been widowed, the relationships of the parent and children with the ex-spouse are changed. Everyone in the home may experience anxiety as familiar routines and habitual interactions need to be explained to the newcomer, while the newcomer may be acutely missing the routines that previously characterized daily life and the family members that are no longer present in his or her daily life. The pain of loss, if recent, may add to difficulties of adjustment. In addition, everyone may worry about how others perceive them and how well they are functioning in the new situation and may be anxious about feelings of physical attraction, experienced across generations, when the incest taboo has not been present as a buffer.

More detailed discussion of stepparenting in its various aspects will be found in the other chapters of this book. Of the many possible stresses that can accompany the stepparenting situation, some are illustrated by the following case example.

Cathy C, age 10, was brought by her mother and stepfather, Dora C and Jack D, for psychopharmacologic management. Cathy was the oldest of three sisters, the younger ones being Lisa and Carolyn, and she had a history of emotional difficulties dating back to age five. She had been seen in consultation and therapy by respected child psychiatrists. When she was seven, her father, a health professional, died after a protracted illness and she was badly affected by the loss. Her behavior became more demanding and she was often unreasonable and at times assaultive.

When Cathy was nine, her mother married Jack D, a former colleague of her late husband. Jack had a six-year-old son, Adam, who lived with his mother after their divorce. Adam had social difficulties and behaved in a rejecting way toward Dora C, evidently as a form of protest against his parents' divorce and the presence of another woman in his father's life. Cathy was unable to tolerate Adam's presence in the home and would throw tantrums when he came, as well as attacking him verbally. She was also quite unpleasant to her stepfather and did not respect the parental couple's boundaries, often entering their bedroom without knocking and commenting on the things she imagined they did together. She had difficulty empathizing with any family members and when things were not going her way, would occasionally throw objects. Her younger sister alternated between complaining about Cathy's behavior and imitating it. Cathy was seeing a psychotherapist twice a month; the therapist's office was in the same institution where her father had worked and she seemed to view the building as her terrain, walking familiarly into the offices of people she knew.

From the pharmacologic standpoint the diagnosis of bipolar disorder was entertained and a mood stabilizer was prescribed. Cathy tolerated only low doses and modest results were obtained. Psychological testing revealed attentional problems and a nonverbal learning disability, but more striking *who gets ejected?*

was evidence of inflated self-esteem and lack of empathy for others. A stimulant was tried for attentional problems but was poorly tolerated. Cathy had always been successful in school and had a special interest in dramatics; she frequently obtained parts in amateur productions. Until age 13 she had an adequate number of friends, but after that point her self-absorption and the superficial quality of her relationships began to take a toll on her peer relationships. School work began to suffer and school attendance became a problem. Her parents considered placement at a therapeutic residential school, but Cathy begged to be allowed to continue trying; she was taken to a new therapist who did not have familiar associations for her, so that she would not have the temptation to transgress boundaries. At the present time it is not clear how much longer Cathy will be able to continue living at home and attending her public school.

Meanwhile Jack D's ex-wife moved to another part of the country with their son Adam, an event that Jack experienced as highly stressful, and his feelings about the move were further aggravated by his ex-wife's statement that she was moving Adam away partly because of Cathy's behavior. Jack has experienced a clinical depression, which is somewhat improved with psychotherapy and medication; Jack and Dora have discussed whether or not they will have a child of their own, and this is not an easy topic for them to resolve because of the stresses they have undergone and the possible additional stress that might arise from having another child.

Clearly emerging from their joint history is the unremitting emotional stress they have both endured from a variety of sources, and the ability both have had to maintain emotional equilibrium the majority of the time. Aspects of their parenting that may have suffered as a result of problems with affect tolerance include Dora C's excessive tolerance of Cathy's behaviors over time, and a difficulty shared by Dora and Jack in constructing vacation time away from the children that might have helped them to feel rested and authoritative upon their return; it seems likely that chronic fatigue, arising from emotional stress, has led them to have problems taking this type of initiative, and their relative inability to do so may have exacerbated ongoing problems within the family to some degree.

A first-person account by Mrs. D follows:

// parallelism

"First I think it is noteworthy that there is a definite tension when Jack and I review what we have been through with Adam and Cathy. When we talk about Lisa and Carolyn this tension is notably absent. One of the first differences that occurred in the triangular parenting of Adam was when he was under my care and I needed to take Carolyn to the doctor. The nurse practitioner noticed Adam was unable to sit still, interrupted constantly and demanded the nurse's attention when Carolyn needed it. I had always found Adam to be a very needy and demanding child with a low frustration tolerance. I attributed this to his being an only child. The nurse thought it was more serious and encouraged us to seek an evaluation.

"Jack agreed, but his ex-wife Joan was reluctant and said Jack was crazy and needed to see Adam as sick. We went through with the evaluation and got Adam the help he needed. I feel Joan was very threatened with Jack's control of therapy and scared what a therapist would think of her, and we both think this contributed to her move to Georgia when Adam was eight.

"In the beginning of our relationship I felt I was often the one who tried to look out for everyone's needs. This often caused tension with Jack as he and Joan only saw Adam's needs and not those of my three girls. If there was any problem between the kids it was the girls' fault. Jack did come around to see that Adam played a role in the girls' reactions. Before Adam was on medicine he was unable to answer simple questions the girls asked. Communication was impossible with Adam for the first six months of his coming to the house every weekend. Joan added to this tension by calling Jack at work blaming the girls if Adam complained of an incident. Jack would come home angry after her calls.

"When Cathy began to lose control the tension rose to a level of angry fights between Jack and myself. He wanted greater limits to be set on Cathy. I had a higher tolerance of her outrageous behavior. The emotional part of me and my love for Cathy made all of the steps we were taking with her very painful for me as compared to Jack, who was free of this attachment. Although we are much more together with our handling of Cathy, it is still an area where emotions get hot very quickly.

"During the time when Cathy was trying to drive Jack out of the house and had made it too uncomfortable for Adam to come, there were many fights, especially when Jack came home from his Sunday visits with Adam. To this day he is angry with me that I did not let him spend more time with Adam. His ex-wife blamed him and his lack of time with Adam and said she would never have gone to Georgia if he had spent more time with Adam. Jack believed this to some extent and blames Cathy and me for Adam's move to Georgia.

"The latest struggles we've gone through have been over the idea of Adam living here, and the idea of Jack and I having a child. When Jack and I were first together I got pregnant. While I wanted the baby I did not want to have one with a man who did not want it. I still feel angry about the abortion and Jack's original promise that I could have the baby. This is a central issue for me in regard to Adam ever coming to live here. Jack would have Adam live here at any time. While we have not resolved this issue, the feelings have been discussed and we know we will never have a child together. If Adam does want to live here it would have to be looked at at the time. This issue is unresolved.

"Our present plan for Cathy is that she will attend a boarding school. We have hired an educational consultant to help us find a good match for her. Jack feels this has been a long time coming. My emotions allowed Cathy to have too many chances to act in a way that eventually made it impossible for her to remain permanently in our home. I will miss her but will welcome the quietness and the attention I will be able to give Jack, Lisa, and Carolyn. Our relationship has survived because of our desire to talk through problems. This is an ongoing process. Also, Jack and I get along famously when we do not have children around. We are forward-looking and know this will be a big portion of our relationship. If Cathy is successful at boarding school it will be a great reduction of stress for the family. I give credit to Jack for sticking out this relationship when many other men would not have stayed. I feel this speaks for the love we have for one another."

The antecedents for Dora C's inability to set firmer limits on Cathy's behavior are not well understood, particularly any elements that may arise from her own upbringing, but one aspect that has emerged clearly is that Cathy suffered greatly during her father's prolonged illness and after his death, and Dora saw her as a damaged and vulnerable child on this account. Ms. C had been unable to tolerate the discomfort of being more authoritative with her daughter; the possibility exists, however, that Cathy has a biologically driven illness that would have frustrated anyone's parenting abilities. Both Dora C and Jack D emerge as having had a great deal of resilience, including the ability to persist in the face of powerful sadness and anxiety.

Adoptive Parenting

Being an adoptive parent usually involves exposure to a variety of potentially anxiety-provoking situations. These include some that are unique to adoption, and some which differ little from corresponding situations in parenting one's own biological situations, yet have a particular adoption-related "flavor." This section will describe first a specific task of adoptive parents, disclosure of adoptive status and subsequent dialogue with the child about it, that has been viewed traditionally in terms of the child's age and readiness, but might equally be seen as depending on the ability of the parents to bear painful emotions. I will then refer to a general parenting task, that of limit-setting, in the context of adoption. Each situation will be illustrated by a case example.

Blum (1983) describes the interaction between adoptive parents and their own parents, stressing the narcissistic losses caused by infertility and the need of adoptive parents for confirmation and support from the grandparents, who may be unwilling to provide such support because of their own conviction that "blood is thicker than water" and their own need to perpetuate the biological line. "The idea that the adopted child might be returned as damaged goods within a year of the adoption . . . finds its counterpart in the adoptive parents' sense of themselves as damaged, which may also reflect the attitudes of their own parents toward them and their adopted child."

Blum proposes the idea that an internal stressor is made even more stressful by a lack of empathy by key individuals in the social surround. I believe this idea is central to the psychology of adoptive parents. Before Blum's paper appeared, Kirk (1965, 1984), a sociologist, had demonstrated covert but widespread bias against adoptive families, and from this developed his influential notion of "shared fate," involving the idea that adoptive parents can best help their children deal with their status by accepting the fact that adoptive families are seen by society as different. (This idea continues to bear fruit today, and is echoed by advice commonly given to parents adopting transracially or from abroad: "You are now a biracial (or international) family, not a majority family with a minority member.") With Lewis, I proposed (Nickman and Lewis, 1994) that adoptive families often meet with serious lack of understanding in professionals to whom they turn for help, and pointed to crises in the adoptee's adolescence (particularly when the child was placed from foster care after infancy) as the most dramatic example of adoptive families meeting with a lack of understanding and empathy.

Kirk proposed the term "role handicap" for adoptive parents in relation to their subtle stigmatization, and this continues to be a useful concept, particularly bearing in mind that when infertility, single parenthood, or other adverse life circumstances have contributed to the adoption, there is also an internal source of distress. The ability to bear painful feelings is strongly influenced by existing stresses, whether their source be intrapsychic, external or both.

Adoption-specific situations include the various stresses connected with infertility, which brings many people to adoption. Another is the stress of informing a child about his or her adopted status; related to this, in the case of a child adopted after infancy, is the need to communicate with the child about his origins and the circumstances of his adoption. Yet another group of stresses arises from the stigmatization of adoption in society and the various experiences of adoptive parents and adopted children and adolescents related to being seen as different from the norm. These include negative attitudes on the part of grandparents and extended family, unwelcome singling out of the child by her school, insensitive comments by strangers, and failure of mental health professionals to understand adoptive families, sometimes with harmful results.

Universal situations with specific characteristics in adoptive families include the instinctual and cognitive transitions that comprise normal development. Oedipal resolution is affected by a child's knowledge of adoption; as pointed out by Wieder (1978) and Schechter (1970), the knowledge that there are two sets of parents complicates renunciation of the oedipal goal and identification with the parent of the same sex. The sexual awakening of adolescence is tinged by a child's knowledge of adoption and fantasizing about his origins in his birth parents' sexual behavior, sometimes leading to a rebellious identification with birth parents and premature sexual activity, particularly when his relationship with the adoptive parents is strained.

In terms of cognition, Brodzinsky, Schechter, and Braff (1985) pointed out the transition between a relatively simple and unconflicted view of adoption held by young children, and the more complex view involving sadness about relinquishment, that often takes its place around age seven, coinciding with Piaget's stage of concrete operations. (Transient depressive reactions to the knowledge of being adopted have been seen in younger children, but one wonders whether such children may be reacting largely to the affect of their parents.)

An Adoption-Specific Situation in Early Childhood: Disclosure of Adoption, with Subsequent Dialogue

Since the modern era of agency adoption, placement workers have recommended disclosure of adoptive status to the child as early as possible; they often exact a promise to do so. Knight's (1941) recommendation to tell early is typical of an era in which adoption was often seen largely in terms of the benefit to the adoptive parents; he cautioned that if the child were not told it would result in discomfort for the parents if the child should find out accidentally. Other observers stress the possibly devastating effect of chance discovery on an older child or adolescent. The recommendation for early telling was based partly on this risk, and partly on what might be called an "immunization hypothesis" that if the child hears the word, even before she has any understanding of its meaning, and is then gradually introduced to the corresponding facts, it will cushion the blow.

Clinical experience has demonstrated that such a procedure does not prevent loss and grieving, especially after the onset of latency, but Brodzinsky's demonstration that young children have only a partial understanding of adoption has not led to a recommendation for later telling. Rather, it appears most clinicians still believe that disclosure well before age seven is wise even though the child will not understand adoption maturely—that is, that loss is involved—because the cognitive framework is in place, paving the way for the child's understanding to unfold.

The discussion in the psychoanalytic literature during the 1960s raised the question of possible harm arising from early telling. Peller (1961, 1963) argued that a child needs to know he or she is a beloved member of the family, and there is no corresponding need to know about adoptive status.

These authors and others discussed a number of cases to support the idea that later disclosure is less harmful to the child's oedipal resolution and self-esteem. The argument was somewhat convincing (though not based on controlled studies), but the recommendation was not widely followed and early disclosure continued to be the norm.

An external event then impinged on the discussion. By the end of the 1970s adoption had become more popular and the population had grown, but the number of healthy white infants available for adoption had not grown, due to increased acceptability of single parenthood and availability of contraception and adoption.[1] The result was a relative scarcity of infants. Newer forms of adoption became increasingly popular including international, transracial, and special-needs adoption; the latter term refers to children past infancy from the foster care system (who previously would have remained in foster care or group homes, or gone to residential facilities) and to children with physical, emotional and developmental disabilities.

For the increasing proportion of families adopting in nontraditional ways, the old questions about disclosure took new forms. Transracial and international adoptees placed in infancy still needed disclosure, but other elements had to be added to the discussion. Children placed in the toddler years retained some memories of prior placements, and those placed after age four had detailed memories, so that the conversations these children needed were not about the fact of placement but about the reasons for it, the adoptive parents' knowledge and attitude about the birth parents, and the child's memories and feelings about past events. The prominence of newer forms of adoption beginning in the 1970s led professionals to interest themselves in these situations and drew attention away from the older debate about when to disclose to children adopted as infants.

These newer forms, however, deepened the discussion in the media and in the adoption community about how to communicate with adopted children. Because of the universal need to establish some dialogue between parent and child in the newer forms of adoption, and the increasing value put on directness and openness with such children, secrecy or discouragement of discussion with early-placed adoptees became less acceptable. Parents of infant adoptees, to the extent that they were in contact with parents involved in newer forms of adoption, were influenced by this trend toward open communication. Another influence was the trend toward identified and open adoptions of infants, with contact between adoptive and birth parents, which also implied substantial communication with the child about the adoptive process, and sometimes direct or indirect

---

[1]It is believed at that time African-American parents were not as interested in agency adoption as Caucasian parents.

contact between child and birth parent. Thus the newer forms subtly influenced the older.

Meanwhile the personal difficulties of adoptive parents in communicating with their children also became more complex. Whereas formerly most adoptive parents had little information at their disposal beyond the fact that the birth parents were unable to care for their child and wanted to find a good home, now many parents had specific knowledge of the biological parents and of past events in their child's life, often including neglect and abuse. How much did the child want or need to know, and at what age? Parents had to weigh their protective impulses against their belief that the more children knew about their backgrounds, the more sense they could make of their lives. Many parents disclosed information gradually based on their estimate of their child's ability to assimilate certain types of information. Certain facts were commonly held back until midlatency or later, particularly criminality of birth parents, or the existence of siblings.

Contemplating disclosure of adoption to a child awakens anxiety in parents. They may feel that by this disclosure, in the child's eyes they will be abdicating as parents or abandoning the child. New distinctions are created that did not exist before: biological parents versus known parents, children who have to cope with this circumstance in their lives and children who do not. Parents may feel defensive before their child if infertility is a feature, or guilty that they have "taken" the child from his original parents; such guilt may be experienced toward the child, toward the birth parents or both. Parents also feel protective toward their child and fear she will suffer as a result of the disclosure and that their relationship will be permanently altered. Probably the most important underlying concerns for both parent and child are separation anxiety and narcissistic injury.

Case Example. The case of Arthur A illustrates a mother's inability to experience affect related to important losses in her life, and subsequently her great difficulty in parenting her adopted son and talking with him directly and empathically about his adoption.

Arthur A, age six and a half, was brought by his parents for consultation because of defiance and aggression. His mother said he had been strong-willed since he was placed with the A family at one week of age. He weighed almost eight pounds at birth and in the beginning was healthy and delightful (and even at the time of presentation his parents acknowledged that he was an affectionate child). His behavior soon became a concern. "We think he's hyperactive; I saw it when he was eight months old. He wouldn't stay in bed. He was very determined. We've classified him as a strong child with whom we must be firm. Things became worse when Arthur was four and his little sister Jennifer entered the family at the age of three months. Mrs. A said, "My life has been disrupted on a regular basis." Arthur had been hitting and biting other children in kindergarten and was expelled from summer camp. He bit an adult at church. At home he was generally better than in group situations, but there were problems at home as well, and he had rammed his sister's head against a wall. Jennifer had then banged her own head, leading the parents to worry about Arthur's influence on her self-esteem.

Both parents were in their early 40s and had been married before. Mr. A was vice-president for marketing of an insurance firm; Mrs. A said, "I work in sales and marketing; I give CEOs ideas to make their businesses grow. I had a $150,000-a-year career before me when we got Arthur. I left my career, but I haven't changed my life style." Mr. A had no children by his first marriage; Mrs. A had had a son, Warren, in her previous marriage who had been killed by a drunk driver at age 15, nine years earlier. Colleagues had advised her to seek help for depression. She remembered her therapist saying to her at the end of the first year, "The biggest part of your role is gone. If I were you I would try to have a child."

It developed that both Mr. and Mrs. A had problems with fertility, and they eventually turned to adoption. They considered an older child initially but were advised to try to get an infant. Mrs. A had several additional losses within a few years of Arthur's arrival. When he was four months old, cancer cells were found on a Pap smear of Mrs. A, and she was advised to have an immediate hysterectomy. Mrs. A's mother died when Arthur was two, and her father soon after. There was a hint that Mrs. A might have received some harsh treatment from her own parents as a child. Mr. A's job involved frequent travel, and he commented, "I wonder if my being away contributes to this. My wife still overprotects Arthur. Every time I come home we go through a weaning process."

Arthur knew of his adoption but "I don't think he understands it at all. He knew he was in someone else's tummy. It's not a big deal to him. He saw us adopt Jennifer. He hasn't shown any curiosity about his birth parents. He is interested in my son Warren, who died."

Arthur was seen twice. Due to his aggressive play, in the waiting room, an inflatable clown was broken. He chose to have his mother enter the playroom with him the first time; he settled down at the play table, but his mother wanted to convey more information, and as we stood, she told me in a low but audible voice that Arthur's father had been a drug addict. Seen alone, Arthur showed no sign of having heard his mother and he willingly played a drawing game. His first drawing was called "a mutt" and resembled a fierce rabbit; his second, "a cat," looked large and menacing. He had not been told the purpose of the meeting, and I explained that I was interested in children's troubles and problems. He said, "When Jennifer . . ." and stopped, then asked if what he said was private. Even with reassurances, he could not continue. He spoke about playing outside with friends, and playing computer games, then came back to his troubles: "My troubles are top secret." I suggested that some troubles might have started when his sister came, and he said, "You promise not to tell? Fighting with my sister is one trouble, but the first two troubles are top secret, and the fourth one's top secret."

To the second session Arthur's mother brought an inflatable clown to replace the broken one, though she had not been asked. I expressed thanks to them both. I asked Mrs. A to tell Arthur in her own words the purpose of coming. She did so rather briefly, then left Arthur with me. He said, "I don't want to talk about problems." He made several Play-doh figures saying they represented his sister, then wanted to do something else and I suggested the drawing game. His first drawing was "a piece of bread, smiling." Next was "a rhinoceros with a bird on his back, that warns rhinoceroses about hunters that want to kill them." Next was "a person sinking, a tidal wave is going to sink him"; the figure was without arms. The final drawing was "a cartoon face," evidently a pulling back from dangerous themes. Asked about his wishes, he said he'd like to be a crossing guard or a scientist. Then he noticed a tank of tropical fish and asked, "How do fish poop?" I showed him a humorous book that describes various animals and how they defecate, and he was fascinated. He said, "Hey, I've got it! Food makes poop and drink makes pee." Arthur seemed to welcome the opportunity to regress to anal and oral themes.

Meeting again with the parents, I asked about Mrs. A's remark about Arthur's birth father, and her reply was that she didn't know that Arthur had been listening. She added, "I have this inner nagging, that this birth mother picked us out to be Arthur's parents." These remarks suggested to me considerable covert hostility to the child, and I was also concerned that at the beginning of the first visit Mrs. A had allowed Arthur to kick the clown so hard that it broke. During the meeting we went over the DSM–III–R criteria for attention-deficit hyperactivity disorder and for oppositional-defiant disorder. Mrs. A fully endorsed 9 criteria for ADHD and 5 for ODD (sufficient to make the diagnoses), while her husband endorsed only 4 and 2 criteria respectively.

At that point I suggested that while an organically based attentional problem might indeed be present, together with a comorbid oppositional disorder, there appeared to be other possibilities to be looked at before a trial of medication was justified. I mentioned Arthur's guardedness and preoccupation with themes of danger and secrecy, and said that aggression is sometimes seen in children who suffer from anxiety or depression. I recommended a full battery of psychological tests to clarify the diagnosis. The parents promised to call me with their decision, but when I had not heard from them for two weeks I called Mrs. A, who told me she was dissatisfied with the consultation. "Why do we need testing? Why blame us?" she said. "Why not just treat him for ADD? These mothers all have poor prenatal care, you know." I wrote to her subsequently but she did not reply and I have had no follow-up.

Though the material is limited, I believe this case illustrates what can happen in the parenting process when a parent is unable to fully experience her own affects—in this instance, grief and depression related to the sequential losses of her first child, her fertility, and both of her parents. Although Mr. A seemed warmer and less committed to a pathological view of Arthur, his wife was the dominant person. Her past griefs, frustrations, ambivalences, and disappointments were apparently not available to her in a conscious way but were instead acted out in her interpersonal behavior, presumably on many fronts, and clearly in her relationship with her son.

Arthur's mother saw him consciously as a replacement child. Mrs. A gave him conflicting messages. Because of his "low" background (about which he was supposedly not curious), not much could be expected of him; yet if he were in any way to assuage her sadness about the dead Warren he would have had to live up to an idealized standard. The parents believed themselves to be virtuous participants in a Christian church and were not motivated to look at their own contribution to Arthur's difficulties; instead they saw his jealous act of aggression toward his sister as "endangering the safety of our house." Mr. A said, "We firmly believe the Lord gave us these children, so we want to be the best parents we can," but he was confident that his wife's approach was the correct one. It appears that they used their religious beliefs to justify their rigid view of Arthur, who therefore remained at risk within the family.

An Adoption-Influenced Situation in Latency and Adolescence: Managing Behavior and Setting Limits

Case Example. Martha B, a homemaker, sought counseling because she and her husband, a respected attorney and law professor, were worried about their adopted son Barry who was at college several hundred miles from home. He had overspent on credit cards and was doing poorly in his courses, but of even greater concern was his statement that he thought he was bisexual. The Bs also had an adopted daughter Joelle, two years younger than Barry. I agreed to see Barry to assess whether he could benefit from therapy and had several meetings with Mrs. B alone and one with Mr. and Mrs. B.

Barry, home for the summer, came for several sessions. He was intelligent and dramatic with a lively but critical sense of humor, and disparaged the therapist he had recently seen at college. He spoke of the disadvantages of homosexuality but did not appear to be very conflicted about it and had had numerous experiences. He spoke of a 42-year-old businessman in his college town who had become his protector: "He'd do anything for me, he'd kill himself for me," and of a friend whose father was an arms dealer, "he negotiates between foreign countries, and he's building a city in Africa." The histrionic, grandiose quality of these statements was characteristic of Barry. He maintained contact with me for several months but the therapeutic goal was unclear and he soon dropped out of therapy. At that point his mother decided she would like to work with me to help her adjust to her son's homosexuality and his continuing failure to respect interpersonal and generational boundaries, and to look at her own ways of reacting and responding to him. She came for weekly therapy for several years, then continued to come every two to four weeks for several years.

She was slightly below middle height, plainly but tastefully dressed, and agreeable to a fault. She expressed genuine concern for me, for example if I had a cold or cough, but this concern at times was exaggerated: if I was late to the hour, she apologized to me for having made me feel pressured to arrive on time.

Mrs. B was the youngest child of a well-to-do Jewish family in the South. Her parents were generally supportive but not insightful and she remembered incidents of being humiliated as a small child and times while in college when she did not feel understood in her choices and desires. She occasionally attended meetings of the family business. She was not employed and was quite troubled that she was not "doing anything" beyond serving as an unpaid, part-time instructor at an art museum. She had graduated from a prestigious women's college and had numerous interests including photography and poetry, but spent little time on these pursuits; instead she had amassed a large collection of newspaper clippings which she reread and organized into categories. She had a good relationship with her daughter and her husband but frequently went into what she regarded as irrational rages at him. At these times she would occasionally make a gesture as if to stab herself. Mr. B often went abroad to present at professional meetings and Mrs. B was conflicted about these; she felt resentful, as though her husband wanted to involve her in his achievements when she felt so unaccomplished herself, but she always went. Her interactions with friends and relatives were warm and they clearly valued her highly, but she had difficulty asserting herself when assertion was called for. She had particular difficulty with one female in-law whom she perceived as narcissistic and controlling. This woman had established a close relationship with Barry years before, and Mrs. B believed she encouraged Barry in his inappropriate, entitled behavior.

Mrs. B felt quite guilty because she kept fond memories of a man she had almost become engaged to over twenty years before, and fantasized about him during intercourse with her husband. After some months another sexual theme emerged. When she was eight years old a rabbi who came to the house to give her Hebrew instruction had fondled her and this was repeated six or seven times until she complained to her parents. The lessons were immediately stopped, but she felt her mother was not empathic and blamed her for not putting a stop to the behavior earlier. As she talked about this a different Mrs. B emerged, full of anger, and she regretted that the man had died so she could not expose him in his home community. This theme led to description of her feelings of being incomplete when she discovered her infertility. Mrs. B had long felt there was a connection between her molestation in childhood and her infertility. Though she saw it was not logical, she nevertheless continued to feel it. During the therapy she began attending women's groups and identifying with the women's movement.

When the Bs adopted Barry at several weeks of age they were both delighted with him. He was attractive, with a lively temperament, and they felt relief that they could be parents and give a child the benefits of their life together which they both felt to be rich and committed, both to each other and to the society in which they lived. Mrs. B in particular felt vindicated because of her past feelings of inadequacy. Barry's early development was smooth and without problems, and it became clear that he had high intelligence.

Mr. and Mrs. B differed somewhat in their parenting techniques. While both tended to be gentle and nonconfrontative, Mrs. B, in addition, suffered at times from a dissociative tendency when the situation required her to set a firm limit on Barry. (Early warning signals appeared during Barry's junior high school years when he was found to have cheated on tests and experienced social difficulties.) In therapy it became clear that Mrs. B's past anger at key events in her early life would come close to consciousness at these times, and she would dread having to express anger at him for fear that the anger would become overwhelming and some unknown, disastrous result would occur. At the same time, however, Mrs. B sometimes experienced some unacceptable activity of Barry as not too bad, and she would internally admire him for certain behavior that was overassertive, arrogant, or outrageous, though she was aware of a connection between this and her wish that she could have been more assertive in her own life. More conscious in Mrs. B was a parallel tendency to perceive Barry as a wonderful child who graced the Bs' life with his presence, for whom the Bs should be externally grateful to the birth parents, of whom Mrs. B often felt unworthy because of her own self-esteem difficulties. Occasionally she had conscious fears of losing him, and when her husband's relative showed a special interest in Barry, Mrs. B was quite upset, believing the cousin was being competitive with her and was consciously exploiting a birth parent fantasy on Barry's part. From my own standpoint I thought Mrs. B might be right about this; Barry also sought out the relative in ways that excluded Mrs. B.

Mrs. B's lack of self-assurance was communicated to Barry over the years. By his late teens he had begun regularly inserting himself into adult discussions and did not hesitate to criticize his parents (particularly his mother) and their activities and style of dress. He made clear his disappointment that his parents were not more in tune with the latest fashions in clothing and leisure activities, and found fault with their business decisions. The Bs were occasionally embarrassed by Barry's behavior when attending a family function, since he spoke to men and women in the parental generation as though they were his contemporaries and thereby indicated deficient respect both for these family members and toward his parents.

Barry is now past 30 and lives with his partner in another state. The two of them had a commitment ceremony attended by the parents of both men; they have a joint business venture and Barry still struggles with fidelity to his partner. Martha B has continued to function as a homemaker and a member of her community, and has taken great pleasure in the marriage and subsequent pregnancy of her second adopted child, Joelle. The daughter has at times been puzzled and upset because of Barry's behaviors but Mrs. B has hesitated to have a talk with Joelle to explain how difficult her brother has been for the whole family, feeling that this would be disloyal to Barry. Mrs. B suffers from intermittent low-grade depression and is helped by long-term fluoxetine. She now returns for therapeutic sessions six to eight times per year, and these often focus on some new crisis with Barry, sometimes in his personal life but more often to some new inappropriate intrusion he has made into the life of the extended family. (At one point he had business transactions with a friend whose family was said to be associated with the Mafia; his wish to involve his parents in this deal led to much conflict when they decided they wanted no involvement.) At these times it is clear that Barry has been allowed to transgress generational boundaries or limits of common courtesy and that a limit needs to be set. When I suggest this, Mrs. B is grateful but then becomes confused, asks me to repeat what I said, then proceeds to write it down.

It seems likely that the most difficult affect for Mrs. B is anger. When intruded on by a male, (her husband, her son) in a way that reminds her of her childhood molestation and her unsatisfactory dealings with her family about it, she becomes unable to function effectively and instead of realistic annoyance or anger she enters a dissociated state of mind. Unfortunately her earlier analysis and therapy did not deal successfully with this problem in time to prevent its leaving a mark on her son's character—probably because her husband's career had not reached its later level and her son was not born yet or was very young, so that the feelings of co-optation arising from the husband and son did not arise sufficiently often to be analyzed.

Discussion

Two adoptive families are described in which one or both parents' impaired tolerance of painful affect appears to have been instrumental in the origin of difficulties in the children. The writer worked briefly with the first family and in an extended way with the second, primarily with the mother. No claim is made that affect tolerance is the only psychodynamic influence involved. In the first case one could implicate maternal narcissism; in the second, "superego lacunae" in the parent, leading to character pathology in the child (Johnson and Szurek, 1952) may have been operating as a result of Mrs. B's repressed anger at her childhood experiences.

The psychoanalytic literature of the 1940s, 1950s, and 1960s about adoption contains numerous contributions that might be reread with profit today. A dominant theme in this literature is the caution that children placed in infancy should not be told too early about adoption, lest it confuse them. A close reading of these papers suggests that a major concern leading to this recommendation is the possibility that parents would overemphasize this topic with their children due to their own ambivalence or unconscious hostility. A possibility not emphasized by these writers is that the main pathogenic influence in early telling was not the factual content, but rather the state of mind of the parent when discussing adoption with the child. Thoughtful observers have long recognized that disclosure of adoption to one's child is a painful process, and before the newer forms of adoption became widespread, it was not unusual to find clinical attempts to justify never telling a child about adoption. This chapter argues that adoption disclosure is inevitably painful to both parent and child, perhaps analogous to a parent taking a child to a painful, perhaps repetitive medical or surgical procedure, but one that is necessary for health.

What permits parents to do this is the confidence that they, their child, and their relationship with the child will survive the process. When parents do not have this confidence—when they cannot tolerate the painful affect provoked by the situation—they are unable to deal with the topic in an open and confident way and to respond to their child's curiosity. In such situations adoption may be insufficiently explained with little follow-up, overstressed to the point where the child feels rejected, or brought up at moments of anger. Children cannot comfortably accept adoption as a part of themselves if they sense that their parents cannot do so. If this argument is valid, it suggests that early disclosure is reasonable after all, if the parents can find a comfortable, confident state of mind from which to do it.

A corollary from the second clinical case is that later aspects of adoptive parenting may also depend on the parents' ability to hold difficult emotions in awareness, as is indeed the case with any kind of parenting. This consideration is of particular importance, not only for the later childhood and adolescence of infant adoptees, but also for adoptees placed after infancy, whose parents may need to deal with difficult past histories and troublesome behaviors over an extended period.

Conclusion

The argument is advanced that a high level of affect tolerance is a useful attribute for people who undertake substitute parenting. Affect tolerance is a pragmatic concept derived from psychoanalytic thinking and can be thought of as depending on aspects of executive functioning, personality structure, and defensive mechanisms. Stepparenting and adoptive parenting are mentioned as two types of substitute parenting, and examples are given of stressful aspects of both, placing at a premium the capacity to tolerate strong affect, primarily anxiety and depression.

References

Blum, H. P. (1983), Adoptive parents: Generative conflict and generational continuity. *The Psychoanalytic Study of the Child*, 38:141–163. New Haven, CT: Yale University Press.

Brodzinsky, D. M., Schechter, D. E. & Braff, A. M. (1985), Children's knowledge of adoption. In: *Thinking About the Family*, ed. R. Ashmore & D. M. Brodzinsky. Hillsdale, NJ: Lawrence Erlbaum Associates.

Johnson, A. M. & Szurek, S. A. (1952), The genesis of antisocial acting out in children and adults. *Psychoanal. Quart.*, 21:323.

Kirk, H. D. (1965), *Shared Fate*. New York: Free Press.

————— (1984), *Shared Fate*, expanded ed. Port Angeles, WA: Ben-Simon.

Knight, R. P. (1941), Some problems involved in selecting and rearing adopted children. *Bull. Menn. Clin.*, 5:65–74.

McDougall, J. (1991), *Theaters of the Mind*. New York: Brunner/Mazel.

Nickman, S. L. & Lewis, R. G. (1994), Adoptive families and professionals: When the experts make things worse. *J. Amer. Acad. Child Adol. Psychiat.*, 33:753–755.

Peller, L. E. (1961), About "telling the child" of his adoption. *Bull. Phila. Assn. Psychoanal.*, 11:45–154.

————— (1963), Further comments on adoption. *Bull. Phila. Assn. Psychoanal.*, 13:1–14.

Schechter, M. D. (1970), About adoptive parents. In: *Parenthood*, ed. E. J. Anthony & T. Benedek. Boston: Little Brown, pp. 353–371.

Wieder, H. (1978), On when and whether to disclose about adoption. *J. Amer. Psychoanal. Assn.*, 26:793–811.

The "Henry VIII" Syndrome
The Mystical Biological Bond Versus a
Stepfather's "Watching Her Spoil Her Own"
Stanley H. Cath

In a courtroom waiting for a trial to begin, I sat next to a man who looked up from his reading to exclaim, "I know you from somewhere!" and then looked down again at his papers. In a few minutes, he exclaimed, "Aha!" and, much to my amazement, ignoring how many others in the court might be listening, he remembered out loud:

"Now I know. Many years ago, I consulted you about my marital problem . . . but just one time. We were getting a divorce. I'd married a woman with three small children and didn't like the way she was raising them. I'd always wanted to have children so, at first, it seemed a natural setting, from the outside that is. She was a nurse and I was a graduate student at the time, but *I couldn't stand watching her spoil them!* [I remained silent.]

"Yeah, we didn't come back because she felt we were not getting anywhere in seeing you. She said she was offended because you drank from a cup coffee during the interview.

"But I thought you acted very professionally. In fact one thing you said I still carry in my mind after all these years. Two of her children from her first marriage had been adopted before she had the third naturally. You wondered if not being able to have our own children might have something to do with the problem between us. I didn't understand it at the time. But over the years I kept thinking, how did he know? It didn't sit well with her.

"You see, I remarried the right woman the second time. I've found an incredible mystical bond as a biological father with his own child. I'm so excited about my four-year-old boy. Whatever politics were involved, I can understand Henry VIII getting rid of a wife who couldn't give him his own son. *Not having the child you want is enough to make you feel disconnected from your wife.*"

While there may be some truth in this for some men in some couplings, we need be grateful not all stepfathers feel this way. And not all people are so exhibitionistic!

The Contemporary Stepfather's Search for Legitimacy

Ira Brenner

A man does not give out cigars when he becomes a stepfather. Apparently not knowing whether congratulations or condolences are in order, the greeting card companies, holiday creators, and calendar manufacturers have not seen fit to invent Stepfather's Day. Even when the media covers the topic of stepfamilies, more attention is generally given to the stepmothers than to the stepfathers. In fact, our society has no celebration or institutionalized ritual to mark this new status. The stepfather enters this new realm silently and immediately after the marriage vows are exchanged. The children may not even be present. However, if all are fortunate, they will be there, assuming that custody schedules allow it and that the relationships are healthy enough for all to tolerate witnessing this union. So, in this inauspicious way, a new family is formed, de facto. This beginning does not do justice to what has become one of the predominant constellations in American family life. And the stepfather is a crucial but enigmatic member of this reconstituted family. With this imbalance in mind, I am happy to have the opportunity to contribute to the growing literature about stepfathers. It is a topic of both personal and professional interest.

In my individual work with men who are or become stepfathers, I am struck by the extent to which this issue can also be overlooked in treatment. Yet, in almost every case I have seen, there is dynamic importance to the meaning of his relationship with his stepchildren and or the extended cast of characters. The understanding of these complex relationships may provide an often untapped analytic opportunity. The vagueness and uncertainty of the stepfather's position, which often relates to an imbalance between responsibility and authority, although unique from case to case and family to family, invariably seems to incorporate the theme of legitimacy. As a result, it may become a repository for such issues which may conceal underlying psychopathology.

Visher and Visher (1990) observe that "the role of the stepfather is a particularly ambiguous and ill-defined one, as he struggles to accomplish a series of tests for which he has had no preparation" (p. 88). While many writers contend that stepfathers are confronted with the issues of authenticity, blending, and "how much," of a parent to be (Bernstein, 1989; Eckler, 1993; Papernow, 1993), others (Fast and Cain, 1966) doubt if any stepfather, no matter how capable, can ever be successful in this parental role. It has even been stated that there is such a prejudice regarding stepfathers that they do not matter at all (Simon, 1964).

In a long-term follow-up study comparing 144 remarried and intact families, Hetherington (1987) reported that stepfathers rated themselves to be low on expressed positive and negative emotion toward their stepchildren. They tended to be less involved in the care and disciplining than the control group of nondivorced, biological fathers. Relating more like a stranger trying to ingratiate himself, the stepfathers were described as polite but distant. After two years of remarriage, they became more intolerant of provocative behavior from their stepdaughters, especially over issues of authority and respect regarding the mother. In addition, they tried less frequently to set limits and exert control because they were less successful than the nondivorced fathers. To summarize, "it seems likely that in the early stage of remarriage, the new step-father is viewed as an intruder or competitor for the mother's affection" (p. 201). Furthermore,

> attempts by the step-father to exert control, even authoritarian control, over the child's behavior or disengagement early in the remarriage are associated with rejection of the step-father by the children and with childrens' problem behavior. A step-father who first establishes a warm relationship with the stepson and supports the mother's parenting and later moves into an authoritarian role has the greatest possibility of gaining acceptance and facilitating the adjustment to stepsons. In contrast, even when the step-father is supportive and gives appropriate responses to a stepdaughter, her acceptance is difficult to gain [pp. 203–204].

It would, therefore, appear that certain aspects of the stepfather's status depend on the gender of his stepchildren, but the timing of his arrival needs to be considered also. To look at this data psychodynamically, Freud (1933) pointed out the difficulties that girls have negotiating the oedipus complex because of the need to change libidinal objects from the mother to the father. For a young girl to negotiate this feat twice, once with her biological father and again with her stepfather, could be a factor in the increased likelihood of her having difficulties accepting him. And, for the young boy, one would not expect the developmental window of opportunity to stay open indefinitely here either, in order to meet his need for a benign rival with whom he can identify. Consequently, the stepfather can be seen to be joining a family already in progress, so to speak. Whereas the father was seen as the classical source of "the law" in the family, the internalization of which contributes to superego formation (Freud, 1939), the stepfather's entry into the family during the child's postoedipal period might seem as though he were appearing belatedly with another set of rules. Similarly, earlier developmental factors related to preoedipal and dyadic issues (Mahler, Pine, and Bergman, 1975) may also come into play as the mother's own psychic disequilibrium related to divorce and remarriage must be considered, too. And, finally, the mutual influences of both the child's development and what might be seen as the stepfather's own sense of legitimacy or entitlement, be it healthy (Apprey, 1988) or pathological (Kernberg, 1975), need to be factored into the equation also.

To illustrate these issues, I will offer a clinical vignette that has been disguised as per Clift's (1986) guidelines. And I will then comment further on the question of whether being a stepfather is yet another "impossible profession."

Case Report

Mr. G was a 35-year-old married man and stepfather of one. He presented with complaints of fatigue, depression, and great uncertainty about the future. He had recently been passed over for a long-awaited promotion, a managerial decision which greatly increased his chances of being laid off due to "downsizing" in his particular industry. Almost overnight, his career prospects went from one extreme to another. He was beset with waves of panic over several weeks accompanied by chest pain, palpitations, and night sweats. Extensive medical workup revealed that he was in fine physical health, however. The panic eventually subsided, but he was left in an enervated state which persisted months after his job security was reestablished. He was then referred for treatment after an unsuccessful round of antidepressants prescribed by his family physician convinced him that he needed to talk to somebody.

Mr. G described himself as responsible, stable, and helpful, but a little on the cautious side. In situations which required initiative or a bold stance, he generally demurred, a trait which made him a rather indecisive leader, but a very good follower. Later on in treatment, he wondered if his lack of confident assertiveness led to his not realizing his potential and being surpassed by his colleagues. For most of his life, however, he just thought of himself as an "easygoing guy." The older of two boys by four years, Mr. G described an unremarkable childhood with normal developmental milestones and an absence of traumata. His earliest memory was of seeing his mother's pregnant belly and being told that he would be getting a baby brother or sister. Having never been separated from his mother prior to her labor, during which time he was sent to an aunt's house for two weeks, Mr. G reported feeling exiled and displaced by the birth of the baby. Mr. G's mother was described as loving, gentle, and devoted, with a strong sense of "family values." She tried to ensure harmony at home and discouraged fighting between the brothers. Mr. G's father, a taciturn and hardworking manager who kept very long hours, was more of a threat than an active presence in the young boy's life. Though materially generous and thought to be fair-minded, his father was described as being somewhat limited in his expression of emotions.

Throughout elementary school and middle school, Mr. G was an average student who was recognized by his teachers as having a greater capability than he demonstrated. Though physically active, he did not enjoy or excel in team sports, often being one of the last to be chosen for the team. He preferred to play quietly with one or two friends instead. His adolescence was not turbulent nor marked by great overt interest in girls. Extremely self-conscious about acne and his hair, he avoided dances and rarely asked a girl for a date. Toward the end of high school, he did find a steady girlfriend, although he did not have sexual intercourse until his second year of college. Continuing to be somewhat hesitant about his perceived appeal to the opposite sex, he was never part of the "cool" or "in" crowd, and in reaction to keeping up with fads or trends, became somewhat stodgy. Unwilling or unable to "keep up with the times," he subtly retreated into premature maturity, taking pride in his dependability, decency, and niceness instead. His college career was essentially satisfactory but unremarkable, and he went on to graduate school, which prepared him for his chosen field. Once again, he followed a safe and predictable course, getting a job which did not unduly tax his capabilities but had some growth potential. Once "settled" in what appeared to be a company in an industry in which he could work until retirement, he reveled in the predictable nine-to-five world for several years until he realized how lonely he was.

A series of ill-fated relationships left him feeling that his "life plan" might not work out until he met a recently divorced woman through a mutual friend. The woman, rather attractive and intelligent, was somewhat depressed over the struggles of being a single parent. Mr. G could not imagine that she would have been interested in him. And, having used all her strength to extricate herself from a disastrous marriage with a vain and narcissistic man whom she romantically idealized despite his ongoing indiscretions, she was hesitant to get seriously involved again with anyone. Long on promises but short on action, the ex-husband essentially dropped out without providing support or having contact with his young son. She did not think she could ever trust a man again. And, furthermore, her first impression of Mr. G was that he was rather "square" and not her type. He, however, was not rejected outright because the woman was touched by how her son, Billy, had taken to him. Mr. G also enjoyed playing with the boy who had begun to look forward to his Sunday afternoon visits which apparently were more successful than his Saturday night dates with just the woman. And so, their courtship was essentially a reconstituted triangle centered around a lonely four-year-old boy who had lost contact with his biological father.

Mr. G married the woman about two years later, when he was in his late twenties. Mrs. G gave up her efforts to get financial support and encourage visitation for her son from her ex-husband. She rationalized his situation and tried to perpetuate a positive image of him as a father "for the boy's sake." Mr. G did not interfere with the intermittent, painful telephone calls and other correspondence between his wife and her ex-husband, quietly hoping she would just forget about him completely. He was delighted to have his stepson call him daddy and felt more like an adoptive father than a stepfather. In due course, Mrs. G became pregnant, had another son as well as a daughter, and a concerted effort was made to treat all the children "equally." While it was not a secret, per se, the subject of Billy having "another" father, or a "different" father, or a "real" father was avoided and at times almost pretended not to exist. Consequently, the younger siblings grew up with a very dim awareness, at best, that he had different parentage than they did.

Over time, a pattern emerged such that Billy's biological father would be "resurrected" during developmental milestones, such as birthdays, graduations, and religious events. Most frequently, he would be contacted by Mrs. G and reminded of his paternal obligations, in the vain hope that he would be shamed into "doing the right thing," such as sending a token birthday present. Mr. G never interfered or expressed any opinion about it, deferring to his wife's wishes but inwardly feeling crestfallen that she did not give up on him completely years ago. Later on in treatment, he came to recognize an enormous sense of jealousy, inferiority, and inadequacy that she would try to rehabilitate her ex-husband on these occasions. He had hoped that his presence in their lives would have been enough to make up for any bad experiences from the past. Afterall, he was a good provider and a "good man." But underneath it all, he felt great doubt about his self-worth. At such times, he felt that he was more of a stand-in for the biological father and that his wife had regrets over her divorce and remarriage. Since at these times Mr. G's feelings were heavily defended against, however, he was only aware of a vague sense of uneasiness and wanting to withdraw. In each of these scenarios, Billy would be enlisted by his mother into speaking to his father on the telephone, rekindling hopes of contact, presents, or some other sign of affection. Occasionally, he would receive a disappointing card long after the event in which the father wrote a meager apology and an insincere promise that he would invite the boy to visit him "next time."

Billy's hopes would be falsely elevated by his mother's inability to mourn for her own loss of the marriage. It was revealed in Mrs. G's own therapy at a later date, that not only were there separation and loss issues owing to a conflicted relationship with a dominating and irascible mother, but also due to a life-threatening illness sustained by her father while she was in latency. The father was left with physical limitations and cognitive deficits which rendered him listless and almost lifeless (Freud, 1919) at times, a situation which is most confounding for a young child (Kaplan, 1995). Unable to mourn for her still alive but "dead" father (Feigelson, 1993), Mrs. G could not reconcile her early image of him as vibrant and actively involved in her life with the later images as remote, uninvolved, and uninterested. Her continued efforts to revive him and restore him to his former state continued throughout his life and were apparently displaced onto her former husband. Therefore, it seemed that an unconscious collusion (Sander, 1989) may have existed between Mr. and Mrs. G about the role of Billy's biological father in their lives.

From Billy's perspective, Mr. G was the only father he ever really "knew." It was not until he became a feisty preadolescent that his challenges to parental authority took the provocative form of "I don't have to listen to you! You are not my real father!" This contribution to Mr. G's overall narcissistic disequilibrium was greatly overshadowed by his job woes and not appreciated until treatment was well under way.

In treatment, Mr. G's therapy evolved from a twice-a-week insight-oriented psychoanalytic psychotherapy to analysis after about six months. It became evident to him that his problems, while triggered off by substantial stress, had a deep-seated basis that influenced all realms of his life. In his characteristic fashion, he did not want to "push" himself too much, preferring the analyst to instruct, teach, and tell him what to do. Passivity, obsessional defenses, and a degree of doubt about the process pervaded the sessions. A pseudocompliant transference associated with somatic complaints made progress rather slow going and uncertain. Initially Mr. G also had a limited capacity to articulate his own affective states but did show considerable curiosity about other people's dynamics. Over time, he became preoccupied with the patients who preceded and followed him, creating elaborate fantasies about their lives and reasons for treatment. He reacted to the temperature of the couch, commenting on whether it was "warm" or not. It if was warm, then it meant that the patient who was there before him must have used it and was in analysis also. Therefore, he was not the only "sucker" using the couch. On the other hand, that also meant that he was not my "only patient" in analysis. In addition, it became important to him who had "seniority," that is, which patients had been in treatment the longest and where he fit into this carefully constructed hierarchy. At this time, the unconscious allusions to his insecurities precipitated by the reorganization at work were clear and interpretive work was tolerated at that level.

He developed a profound sense of ownership of his allotted appointment times and any deviation from the schedule on my part was met with dismay and a betrayal of his underlying apprehension that "something bad might happen." He defended against his rage over fearing he was being replaced by employing the mechanism of reaction formation.

He imagined that he was being asked to give up or move his hour for a worthy cause, be it for a less fortunate patient or some lofty humanitarian activity he thought I was participating in. Eventually, however, he began to realize that underneath this veneer were crucial feelings which took him back to the birth of his younger brother, where he felt displaced, cast aside, and permanently removed from his position as his mother's one and only.

Efforts to regain his mother's exclusive attention were foiled by not only the demands of his colicky baby brother, but also his father's insistence that he "grow up." A transient bout of enuresis was his regressive solution, which not only regained some of mother's attention away from his new rival, but was also a flight from oedipal strivings and castration anxiety associated with his father. Threatened by replacement by his brother and inadequately prepared for the oedipal quest for his mother, Mr. G tentatively retreated and had been biding his time ever since.

Interestingly, these insights and the reconstruction of his childhood did not occur until resistance pertaining to his stepfatherhood was recognized and analyzed. Mr. G seemed to be somewhat stymied in his analysis after he became mired in a defensive retreat from narcissistically tinged phallic-oedipal transference issues. Certain objects and pieces of furniture in the office became libidinized as these themes were enacted in a variety of ways. For example, the desk became a "hot" topic as he lamented that his desk was not as big as mine. He then developed a ritual of emptying all of his personal belongings from his rear pockets and placing them on a corner of the desk before he lay on the couch. Although this behavior was consciously motivated by not wanting to be uncomfortable on his back, unconsciously he was challenging me by staking his "claim" for the desk and anxiously awaited my retaliation for his impudence. When none was forthcoming, he became emboldened, emptying his belongings from his front pockets also and occupying a greater surface of the desk with his symbolic feces. In so doing, it appeared that the phallic competition of "whose desk was bigger" gave way to a rivalry, albeit with regressive anal overtones, for the coveted territory of the oedipal mother's body, as represented by the desk.

Eventually, this daily enactment became so time-consuming and outrageous that even Mr. G began to suspect he was trying to get my attention in a provocative way, and it was quite amenable to interpretation. Mr. G was also very careful not to let his coat touch mine as he hung it on the coat rack, as this action was also suffused with great meaning. Fearing it conveyed a homosexual wish that he was more interested in me than his wife, he kept his distance so our "penises" would not touch. As he vacillated between his furtive attempts to be a "pretender to the throne" and his retreat to a submissive, homosexual, negative oedipal position, Mr. G felt like an inadequate fraud. He could not feel like a man in his analyst's office and his progressively acute awareness of his plight filled him with embarrassment, shame, and rage.

Things came to a boil when I announced that my office was being relocated. Even though he would not be inconvenienced, because in fact it was actually closer to his place of work, Mr. G had an unusually strong reaction. He became dismayed, confused, and panicky, as though our little world was about to be torn apart. I was now adding insult to injury since he was already concerned that I favored other patients over him, especially one particular man whose superior progress he imagined to be taking place was "measured" by their occasional passing in the waiting area. In an uncharacteristic outburst one day, Mr. G blurted out that he even felt like a stepchild whose feelings did not matter. "Stepchild?" I inquired, repeating the word not only for emphasis, but also because it was both a metaphor and a topic that had not come up since the initial evaluation years before. Mr. G associated to his now preadolescent stepson, Billy, whose challenge to his legitimacy, "after all he had done for him," had wounded him deeply. After some exploration, he realized more deeply how Billy's own deep hurt and resentment over his biological father's neglect and disregard might be coming into play. Mr. G then began to recognize how *he* might have identified with his stepson. It was also discovered that when he first met Billy, he was the same age Mr. G had been when he was displaced by the birth of his baby brother. The lonely four-year-old in Mr. G had apparently reached out and befriended another lonely four-year-old who later became his stepson. With minimal encouragement, Mr. G then further explored the heretofore unexamined realm of his being a stepfather.

In addition to his identification with his stepson, there were several triangles whose significance became clear to the patient. There were the obvious ones including his wife and stepson (and those with each of his children), but the ones incorporating Mrs. G's ex-husband were quite surprising in their poignance. Mr. G realized, for example, that another resonance occurred similar to how he felt around the time of his brother's birth, whenever the ex-husband would get included. He began to realize that he could not reconcile that he was "second in line," a status that alluded to both his father's prior claims to his mother and to his being eclipsed by his baby brother. The seeds of this recurrent scenario were apparently sown in the beginning of his courtship and continued to grow over the years. As such, despite his best efforts, he never quite felt "legitimate," "official," or fully entitled to be Billy's stepfather. This dilemma apparently reactivated his childhood conflict over his thwarted claims for his mother. The unconscious dynamic equilibrium that he and Mrs. G put into place enabled the ex-husband's presence to be invoked at will and perpetuate his oedipal conflicts. Once recognized, Mr. G was then more in a position to work through this childhood repetition. Similarly,

Mrs. G's need to mourn further over the "death in life" of her father was also a crucial factor. When some degree of mature reconciliation of these issues was achieved, the climate in the family facilitated Billy's ability to confront his biological father with his abrogation which then enabled his own mourning for this disappointing relationship to proceed. In this way, the whole family seemed to evolve as Mr. G's inner sense of legitimacy and healthy entitlement became more solidified.

Discussion

Apprey (1988) observes that one's "sense of entitlement largely determines whether he or she will . . . fail to claim what is appropriately his or her due and suffer consequent ineffectual distress" (p. 93). Invoking Anna Freud's (1965) concept of developmental lines, he contends that the growing child's sense of ownership of his own body is the foundation of healthy entitlement. Initially, it is instinctually based and derived from those preoedipal origins which lead to the differentiation and the delineation of boundaries between the self and the nonself. Here the ego is immature and is dominated by primary process thinking and omnipotence. At this time, the child would begin to experience the transition of beginning to have a sense of ownership of his body-self and the mother would be transmitting her own sense of entitlement during this process. In the next phase, the oedipal child would need to renounce his wishes and identify with admired objects. He is to become aware of the need to negotiate for primacy with loved ones, not just to expect it. Postoedipal development would then allow for the enhancement of mutual respect in such relationships, associated with the further repression, reaction formation, and sublimation of instinctualized entitlement. As a result, the sense of entitlement would have less of an influence on the regulation of self-esteem.

Throughout puberty, adolescence, and young adulthood, progressively more stable sense of identity, with its accompanying self and object representations enables one to withstand the loosening of ties with one's parents and to make a more realistic appraisal of their limitations. A mature sense of entitlement then enables the individual to make an appropriate object choice and to relinquish more infantile narcissism. "Entitlement can now accommodate an external reality of accepting one's self as one really is and the world for what it is" (Apprey, 1988, p. 97). Such a man will have then acquired this mature sense of entitlement and the accompanying superego development (Modell, 1965) necessary to feel he has the right to live, to procreate, and to care for the lives of others. If not, certain decisions or life situations may recapitulate earlier fixations and reinforce his sense of not being worthy or deserving of what is due him.

And I would contend that contemporary stepfatherhood, with all of its inherent ambiguities and vicissitudes, is just such an example of the type of life situation that greatly challenges a man's sense of legitimacy and underlying healthy entitlement.

In the case described above, Mr. G, by many criteria, would have been seen as being in a rather ideal stepfather arrangement. His situation was not as complex as it is with others, since he was previously unmarried, had no children, and "acquired" only one stepchild at a relatively young age. Since he was financially secure, he was able to absorb the expenses of raising his stepson and indeed functioned very much like a "real" father. Yet, despite these relatively optimum conditions, Mr. G's neurotic vulnerabilities meshed with his becoming a stepfather, and it was as though he had unconsciously activated a time bomb on a long fuse when he got married. The combination of his crisis over nearly losing his job and his reaction to the insolence of his preadolescent stepson, which was magnified by his unconscious rage at his wife for not being able to let go of her ex-husband, appeared to precipitate his unremitting symptoms. In order to rectify the situation, both husband and wife entered treatment. With the help of his analysis, Mr. G then became able to appreciate how his marital situation was an unconscious replication of his oedipal dilemma which was complicated by the birth of his brother. From then on there were always two rivals in his life, a problem which was perpetuated by marrying a woman with a son and an ex-husband, even though his presence was more psychological than real. It is important to point out, however, that his being a stepfather was an "incidental finding" to his initial presentation and might have been overlooked or not fully appreciated in therapy. It may be that my own experience as a stepfather heightened my sensitivity to these issues.

In families which are more complex than Mr. G's, such as those in which the stepfather has his own children, a relationship with his own ex-spouse (which, by definition, would need to be disturbed also), joint custody issues on both sides, financial stress, and considerable ambivalence between the generations, it does indeed raise the question of whether we are dealing with another "impossible profession." The pitfalls may seem endless. Perhaps part of the problem lies in the disparity between today's realities and the original meaning of the prefix *step-*, which, according to the dictionary (*New Shorter Oxford English Dictionary*, 1993), is derived from the Old English word for "bereaved." The original connotation, therefore, was that a stepfather would be a man who married not a divorced woman but a bereaved woman, that is, a widow with a child or children. Under these conditions, there was no other father alive anywhere, so the contemporary problems just outlined above would not have existed or needed to be contended with. I wonder, therefore, if part of the problem is that unrealistic expectations may accompany becoming a stepfather, and whether something as basic as a name change might be a small but useful external "step," as it were, in the direction of clarifying things.

In closing, I will offer a vignette based on my own personal experience. Because it is about my lovely teenage stepdaughter, it cannot be disguised, so it will, therefore, be brief. We have known each other for many years, and during this time, I have been seen as everything from an uninvited guest who never left, to a helpful, but mildly annoying presence who is summoned only to change a light bulb or kill a bug for her. But, she has come to love me, almost in spite of herself, although she has been loathe to express directly her feelings. It is as though she were to put herself in a loyalty conflict with regard to her actively involved father with whom she also lives as part of the joint custody arrangement. Yet, anytime she has ever been with us and has become ill or worried about any kind of medical problem, she has always called for me. (I might add that she does not have to be delirious with fever for this to happen!) It seems that being sick somehow "legitimizes" my involvement in her life and lowers an inhibition to reach out to me. I have long recognized the extraordinary difficulty a child in her situation might encounter and have tried to be available "when needed," but not pushy. This is a delicate balancing act, however, that I am sure I have not been able to achieve at all times. And, as we physicians are prone to do, I find myself thinking in medical analogies when trying to understand or explain a phenomenon. With regard to my stepdaughter, it became evident to me early on that I was not wanted or needed to become a father to her—she already had one!

At times, however, she did want and need *something* from me, and it was imperative for her mother and me to figure out what it was. I, meanwhile, had conceptualized myself as being a bit of a consultant—a consultant in paternal caretaking as it were, but this is a rather cumbersome expression, so I doubt it will catch on. I hope a more creative individual will come up with a better name. So, in my nameless role as her "consultant," I could be requested to do a variety of things, ranging from nothing at all to insect extermination, furniture repair, or medical care. Over time, I then became entitled to participate in the delicate matters of discipline and "fathering" activities, especially those which promoted her individuation (Mahler et al., 1975). My efforts were generally most appreciated in advocating for her autonomy, independence, and growth. In this way, I could see that by being mindful of my limited authority and responsibility, I could be most useful by supporting her development. My inner sense of value, therefore, could be maintained by finding a niche for myself in my stepdaughter,s life. To put it simply, I learned that the best way to build a foundation with my stepdaughter was to be as available as possible when she needed me. Often she would say to her mother, "Call Ira!" But when she began to call for me directly, I knew I was finally on the right track leading to that long road to becoming a "legitimate" stepfather.

References

Apprey, M. (1988), Concluding remarks: From an inchoate sense of entitlement to a mature attitude of entitlement. In: *Attitudes of Entitlement,* ed. V. Volkan & T. C. Rogers. Charlottesville: University Press of Virginia, pp. 93–97.

Bernstein, A. C. (1989), *Yours, Mine, and Ours.* New York: Scribner's.

Clift, M. (1986), Writing about psychiatric patients. *Bull. Menn. Clin.,* 50:511–524.

Eckler, J. D. (1993), I'm just a stepfather. In: *Step-by-Step-Parenting.* Cincinnati, OH: Betterway Books, pp. 99–110.

Fast, I. & Cain, A. C. (1966), The stepparent role: Potential for disturbances in family functioning. *Amer. J. Orthopsychiat.,* 36:485–491.

Feigelson, C. (1993), Personality death, object loss, and the uncanny. *Internat. J. Psycho-Anal.,* 74:331–346.

Freud, A. (1965), *Normality and Pathology in Childhood: Assessments of Development.* New York: International Universities Press.

Freud, S. (1919), The "uncanny." *Standard Edition,* 17:219–256. London: Hogarth Press, 1955.

_____ (1933), New introductory lectures on psychoanalysis: Femininity. *Standard Edition,* 22:119. London: Hogarth Press, 1964.

_____ (1939), Moses and monotheism: Three essays. *Standard Edition,* 23: 7–137. London: Hogarth Press, 1964.

Hetherington, E. M. (1987), Family relations six years after divorce. In: *Remarriage and Stepparenting: Current Research and Theory,* ed. K. Pasley & M. Hinger-Tallman. New York: Guilford Press.

Kaplan, L. J. (1995), *No Voice Is Ever Wholly Lost.* New York: Simon & Schuster.

Kernberg, O. (1975), *Borderline Conditions and Pathological Narcissism.* New York: Aronson.

Mahler, M., Pine, F. & Bergman, A. (1975), *The Psychological Birth of the Human Infant.* New York: Basic Books.

Modell, A. (1965), Right to a life: An aspect of the superego's development. *Internat. J. Psycho-Anal.,* 46:323–331.

New Shorter Oxford English Dictionary (1993), Oxford, England: Clarendon Press.

Papernow, P. L. (1993), Stage 6: Contact, intimacy, and authenticity in step relationships. In: *Becoming a Stepfamily.* San Francisco: Jossey-Bass, pp. 198–211.

Sander, F. (1989), Marital conflict and psychoanalytic theory in the middle years. In: *The Middle Years: New Psychoanalytic Perspectives,* ed. Oldam & Lebert. New Haven, CT: Yale University Press, pp. 160–176.

Simon, A. W. (1964), *Stepchild in the Family: A View of Children in Remarriage.* New York: Odyssey Press.

Visher, E. B. & Visher, J. S. (1990), *Step-Families: Myths and Realities.* New York: Citadel Press.

Fear of Maternal Aspects of a Stepmother

A Homage to My Stepmother, a Woman Who Transcended Living with an Adolescent Stepdaughter

Brenda Clorfene Solomon

All theory is personal. As an analyst who has reared two adolescents, I can now appreciate the complex tasks of parenting one's own children, biological or adopted. In a newly blended family that includes a headstrong adolescent daughter, however, a stepmother may face complexities beyond her worst nightmares. From my current vantage point of a mutually loving and respectful relationship, I think back on the time when I was such an "impossible" stepdaughter. Parenting an "almost" adult child, let alone an "almost" adult stepchild, is a subject on which there is little research. I hope my story and my ideas, although personal and contextually specific, may help others to understand blended families that include a late adolescent daughter and a stepmother in midlife.

Unexpectedly my mother died of an unusual brain tumor when I had been away at college for just a few weeks. I was seventeen. Because I was an only child who had always been closer to my father, his shock and disarray about the death led me to worry about his well-being. My concern convinced me to drop out of school for the semester and return home to take care of him. At that time, I did not recognize that my concern about him was also an externalization of my own overwhelmed state. During the next two years, I attended a commuter's college and did what mourning work an adolescent, ambivalent about her mother, could do. Additionally, I enjoyed the oedipal "pleasures" of being my father's only "woman." Two years later, my father, then 51 years old, having sufficiently worked through his grief, married a beautiful, 44-year-old widow. (Three years before she married my father, her husband had died at age 47 from a myocardial infarction.) She had one young adolescent son at home and an older daughter who lived away at college. In my pseudomaturity, I had convinced myself that I should live with a friend in my dead mother's home while my father moved in with his new wife, Hilda, and her son. To my dismay, Hilda insisted that if we were ever going to be able to blend into one integrated family, we should all live together in her place. My father agreed. I was horrified but did not wish to upset my father so I complied with their wishes. For two extremely painful years, we all lived together.

Decades later Hilda told me how often I hurt her, how she sought my father for solace and turned her other cheek to me with maturity and a firm self that many a stepmother might emulate.

Some personal anecdotes from those two years will set the stage for the theoretical material that follows. During the semester I dropped out of school, a friend's mother became concerned with my lack of structure and asked her (and my mother's) psychologist friend to "create" a tabulation job for me. Although then I did not appreciate my informal "therapeutic connection" to this male psychologist, he certainly encouraged me to talk to him about my mother's death and my plans to continue my lifelong plan to become a doctor. Regrettably he also predicted that I would become depressed if and when I became a mother. Today, as an analyst I fully appreciate how grandiose rendered negative predictions are counter-therapeutic. His prediction haunted me until my motherhood experiences proved him wrong.

My father was intellectually gifted but not psychologically sophisticated. His pleasure and pride in me had always been expressed nonverbally. This reflected both his wish to dampen the adolescent tension between my mother and me as well as not wanting me to get a "big" head. As an adult, I learned how he had bragged about me to his friends. His characterologic style was to be strong and silent. At the moment of my mother's death, he embraced me and said what I took to be a command, "We must be brave!" For me, this meant, "Do not talk about your pain."

When I first met Hilda, she seemed unbelievably sweet, verbally expressive, and accepting of me. I was cool and polite but knew I felt threatened by her confidence and beauty. What would this new woman in my father's life mean for my relationship with him? Because she came from a distant part of the city, the idea of moving to her apartment seemed to me a move to a foreign culture. I had never lived outside my insular community except for those brief weeks at college in another Midwestern state. In order to master my anxiety about this move, I became totally invested in my boyfriend, focusing on plans to marry as soon as possible. Then came my father's and Hilda's wedding. As is her style to this day, she insisted that everyone make speeches celebrating the new union. I was unfamiliar with any adult expressing so much affect, let alone so much positive, flowery "stuff." I wondered, "Was it sincere?" To top it off, she publicly acknowledged the continuing psychological presence of the two dead parents. She insisted that all those gathered at the wedding should continue to feel free to speak of the love and losses we had all sustained. To her continuing credit she has embraced the extended families of my mother and her own first husband and woven them into the fabric of all our lives, a fabric she calls "her tapestry."

Since I had to move into her space, I also had to disassemble my mother and father's home. As a late adolescent, I "hated" my own mother's taste in antiques and china . . . much too "old fashioned" for the modern woman I wanted to be. I offered them to my father, if he wanted to take them to his bride. Hilda, unbeknownst to me, told my dad to sequester these heirlooms away until I was older, because she guessed that I would probably change my mind. After I married, she presented them to me. Now, I treasure Hilda's extraordinary prescience along with my mother's bequests.

As I recall how I argued against any opinion my stepmother expressed at the dinner table, whether political or psychological, I now marvel that I did not provoke her retaliation or hostility. Clearly I thought I was being subtle, but of course my hostility was blatant to her. My hostility was slightly tempered, however, by my affection for my new stepbrother. Since I had never had a sibling, I enjoyed his admiration of me and our alliance against the new older generation. A 14-year-old, in early adolescence, he was quieter in his responses to his new stepfather, choosing to absent himself as much as possible. Retrospectively, my stepbrother ambivalently experienced relief at relinquishing his fantasied role as his mother's only "man." (There is no such phenomenon as an oedipal victory.)

One paradigmatic scene I recall involved my buying a new spring coat. I was accustomed to choosing my own clothes within my mother's strict budgetary frame. When my stepmother heard me discussing my uncertainty about a coat that I had seen, she suggested she accompany me to the store. Trying to be polite in front of my father, I reluctantly agreed. I expected a replay of the struggles with my mother (my transference) whom I experienced as reining in my expansiveness in spending or other activities. At the shop, Hilda watched as I tried on the coat I favored. She then suggested I try one that she selected, a cost considerably more expensive than I ever would buy. I remember twirling admiringly as I modeled her choice. Dizzy, I was thrown into a moment of insight. She was not as I expected.

Hilda was a master at accentuating the positive. My mother had always expressed her anxieties about my ambition and enthusiasms: Although she was progressive in her belief that women should have the capacity to be self-supporting financially, she tried to limit my professional aspirations, insisting I should be a nurse rather than a doctor. When I would not acquiesce in her idea, in my senior year of high school she arranged to have her psychologist acquaintance test me for career counseling. Much to my mother's dismay, the psychologist said I had the requisite capacities to pursue medical school, claiming it was only a matter of my being able to work hard and sustain my motivation. Hilda, on the other hand, broadcast publicly, with admiration, my premedical studies and future plans. I felt confused about my mixed responses of anger, embarrassment, and pleasure. In those years I experienced everything about her to be diametrically opposed to my mother's ways: her relaxed housekeeping, charitable organization work, and pleasure in learning to play golf with my father. (My mother abhorred golf.)

My slowly accepting a more positive relationship with Hilda may appear to parallel a mourning process for my mother. However capable I was of mourning, the process would remain incomplete until my first analysis some 10 years later. Hilda seems to have offered a new opportunity without a simultaneous giving up of the old. Moisy Shopper (personal communication) suggests that I had a developmental reversal. I was accepting a stepmother during an adolescent process which usually requires distancing from the mother and competing with the father's spouse.

Competing with Hilda for my father was a complex arena. My father had suddenly become sexualized for me as I could not ignore his open demonstration of physical affection to Hilda. I hated seeing it! When my mother was alive, I was able to fantasize that my dad had a latency-aged developmental arrest. His sexuality seemed hidden in his sublimations with golf, music, and the law. I had managed to disavow his sexuality (and my mother's). Living in my stepmother's apartment, I arranged to stay as far away from their bedroom as possible, but I could not blind myself to their love. His "new" sexuality, however, freed me to explore my own. This became an environmental advantage. For adolescents younger than I was, similar blatant sexualization of the parent may produce a precocious entrance into sexual involvement with boyfriends, precocious because oftentimes it may go against the girl's wishes or her developmental readiness.

In a newly blended family, the stepparent should recognize that the first few years of ambivalence and anger must be tolerated in order for a long-term positive engagement to evolve. Short-term pain can lead to long-term gain. This process is an enormously challenging task for a middle-aged stepmother. She, as is the case with many other women at midlife, struggles with narcissistic issues of lost youth, menopause, reading glasses, and wrinkles. They cannot always keep their young surfaces. Formanek (1986) puns, "They must learn their lines" (p. 139). Others have written about some mothers' envy of their adolescent daughters, who have their lives all in front of them. When these midlife tasks are complicated by the loss of a spouse, a new marriage, and a hostile stepdaughter, the scene is set for the potential disaster eternally captured by Snow White and her stepmother. There can be significant interplay between the psychological development of late adolescence and the psychological development or disturbance of their parents or stepparents. Galatzer-Levy observed, "It has occurred frequently in my experience that major crises in previously well-functioning late adolescents and young adults may follow on the heels of crises in their parents' lives such as divorce [or remarriage] in middle age" (p. 29). Death and remarriage constitute such crises. There is a significant intertwining of the psychological development of late

adolescent and young adult individuals with the psychological development or disturbance of their parents. On a more positive note, Benedek
(1959) described the phenomenon in which the development of a child
allowed the parent a "second chance" to work through the developmental
phases that had not been completed or resolved by the parent in his or her
own life before the child appeared.

I will review some relevant ideas concerning late adolescent development. Next I will reconstruct my father's and stepmother's capacities as
exemplars of continuing adult development in midlife.

Reflecting on how disrespectful an adolescent I was, the following
theories are relevant. I hypothesize that my stepmother was the recipient
of my deidealization of my mother, stepmother and all adult women. I find
Marohn's theories, edited by Marohn, Doctors, and Leider (1998), most
relevant:

> Ideas about narcissistic bonding are more useful in understanding
> the struggles of the adolescent to separate from infantile attach-
> ments to parents than is the usual emphasis on libidinal incestuous
> attachments. As young people mature, they separate psychologically
> from the parents of childhood by achieving a different sense of the
> relationship: Parents are no longer slavishly idolized or adored, but
> may remain as respected, important, valued human beings in one's
> life (Marohn, 1984). Adolescents defend against their childhood
> attachments by de-idealization and disparagement, by negating mir-
> roring, and by stimulating disgust. They displace their needs for
> narcissistic bonds onto peers or onto other adults and thus develop
> crushes, infatuations, and other varieties of self–selfobject connec-
> tion [p. 10].
>
> Adolescence brings with it a reworking of the internal experience
> of the relationship between the self and its selfobjects—not that this
> is the first revision since the oedipal age, for fundamental to the
> self–selfobject model is the recognition that the dyad is continually
> moving toward redefinition. However, adolescence is a phase of
> marked and dramatic transformation. The healthy self modifies and
> adjusts the nature and meaning of the relationship between itself
> and its selfobjects consistent with ongoing physiological and cogni-
> tive development [p. 11].

As Palombo (1987) stressed, the adolescent's needs for selfobjects
are quite different from those of previous developmental stages.
They are certainly not a simple recapitulation of earlier needs.

> Adolescents arrive at this phase with specific developmental
> needs for particular responses from their caretakers. The na-
> ture of the selfobject functions required at this stage is different
> from those of prior stages. . . . While adolescents may bring with

them unresolved issues or selfobject deficits from prior developmental stages, these only serve to render more complex the
task of the traversal of this phase. These deficits, or the regressions to prior modes of functioning, do not constitute the
essence of the phase appropriate struggle. Rather the comple-
menting of the self by new selfobject functions is central to the
negotiation of this phase [p. 12].

Coming from a different theoretical model, Blos considers the multiple
factors that contribute to the adolescent developmental process. Blos
(1998) maintains,

I have no quarrel with the view that the external environment plays
a crucial role in the growth of the individual. But my experience
suggests that the internal environment and psychic motivation play
an equally important role. It is the interrelationship and interplay
between the inner needs, desires, and tensions of the individual with
those of the outer world that make and shape a person [p. 330].

All theories of adolescent developmental consider the impact of the
environment. In my case the environment was the newly blended family.
My inner world was unstabilized and reorganizing.
    At times of transition, as in a newly blended family, Thelen and Smith's
(1994) nonlinear dynamic systems approach applies: "Self-oganization in
natural systems can only occur when these systems are both complex and
open to flux with the environment" (p. 55). Small changes in the environment can create large reorganizations. Within a dynamic systems perspective, adolescence may be considered a period of reorganization in the
context of greater complexity. Jaffe (2000), employing this dynamic system
approach, argues that

the classic dichotomies or erratic qualities of adolescent behavior are
not by definition indications of alienation from superego and ego-
ideal with the reappearance of infantile narcissism, nor are they
indications of loss of self-cohesion attendant to deidealization of
stabilizing self objects. Instead, they are evidence of a person in
active reorganization. In a systems perspective, self-organization is
not separable from relations.

Jaffe suggests that phases of development are macroscopic observations, a "view from above." He argues for a more complex, microscopic
examination of the individual as "the view from below." This later view
shows development (including adolescence) as

asynchronous, meaning that not all components change at the same rate. It is also nonlinear, meaning that it may occur with regressions, spurts, and plateaus. The overall view of progression is a function of the cohesiveness, resilience, and flexibility of the human system as it is active in assembly within parameters of context and task. There is equifinality, with many possible subsystem configurations yielding the same overall manifest adaptive responses. Patterns that emerge may change as conditions change.

Conditions in my life changed because I was mourning the death of my mother as well as adjusting to my newly blended family. Garber (1984) noted that we do not know how adolescents mourn. Their mourning is quite diverse and does not follow any prescribed pattern. Garber proposes, "The postloss adapatation of the child is in large measure determined by the reactions of the important adults in his life. It is indeed possible that these postloss responses of significant adults shape the child's stability as well as his psychopathology (p. 184). The adolescents whose parent has died are depicted as exceptionally sensitive, perceptive,and empathic to the adults. The adolescent is seen as more empathic to the surviving parent's distress than other adults are. In assuming that position, the adolescent may become idealized and be viewed as a more worthy competitor for the surviving parent's affections. That the adolescent is seen as wise and sensitive beyond her years emphasizes the notions of hypermaturity and role reversal. Often the parent's sexual needs and longings are hinted at but never made explicit. If the widowed parent remarries, triangular elements become accentuated. Some stepchildren who are in such blended families attempt to divide the newly married couple in order to conquer the oedipal parent.
Blos's observations are relevant here:

When an adolescent faces a significant recombination in her life through her parent's death or divorce followed by a new marriage, prolonged adolescence may result. In fact, an adolescent crisis may be adhered to with persistence, desperation and anxiousness. . . . The fervent clinging to the unsettledness of all of life's issues renders any progression to adulthood an achievement which is hardly worth the price. This dilemma leads to the contrivance of ingenious ways to combine childhood gratifications with adult prerogatives.

Slow or paused passage through adolescence does not necessarily signal pathology. Consideration of recent developmental contributions (including self psychology, dynamic systems, etc.) indicate that total separation and full independence from the parent is not the goal.

Using classical theory, Rocah (1984) writing on fixation in late adolescent women observed, "True detachment from parental authority (Freud, 1905) is achieved through the internalization of a set of guiding principles and ideals derived from resolution of conflicts of ambivalence pertaining to actual idealized parents" (p. 81). Using a developmental model to understand resistance in analysis, Rocah notes, "When self and object distinctions leading to object recognition and constancy are established, the anxiety mobilized in response to environmental impingments has been termed by me the fear of maternal influence" (p. 86). The impingement for me was a stepmother:

> This aspect of bedrock resistance is derived from an attempt to preserve the primitive self organization made up of personal aims against any new influence. The reaction to impingement is negativism. The negativism is both a reaction to impingement and at the same time can be the outcome of identification with an aggressive mother [pp. 86–87].

This negativism was certainly true of me.

When an adolescent child is living with a new stepparent, she may be continually stimulated by her parent's new romantic relationship and her fantasies about their sexual lives. Therefore, an even greater than expectable accumulation of negativism and aversion can enter the adolescent's behavior and sexual fantasies.

Using a more global concept, Bohannan (1984) considers identification as a central issue for most adolescents.

> For the child of a remarried parent, the identifications are even more complex:
> 1. If the identification with a stepparent threatens the identification with a parent, the child will probably resist the new identification.
> 2. Identification with the remarried parent must be altered because the remarried parent seems to be a different person . . . the parent herself/himself has a whole new set of identifications. Identifying with one's mother as one's father's wife is somewhat different from identifying with some "stranger" as father's wife.[1]
> 3. The age specific processes of psychological growth occurring at the time a child must do all this new work obviously affect the processes of identification [p. 211].

---

[1] The Vishers say that, based on their clinical evidence and their wide experience in conducting workshops for stepfamilies, the most difficult relationship in the stepfamily is that of stepmother–stepdaughter.

With these transitional dynamics in mind, the tasks of becoming an optimal stepparent of an adolescent might be analogized to the tasks of becoming a usable therapist for an adolescent. As Jaffe (2000) suggests,

Adolescent psychotherapy is messy. The lived experience of this developmental disjuncture is reflected in messy descriptions of adolescent treatment as a stepchild of psychoanalysis, in the difficulty defining analyzability in adolescence, and in the pragmatic approach of adolescent psychotherapists, who have proceeded by doing what works.

The stepparent, as must the therapist, should provide an environment in which growth can occur. "Variability, then, is an indicator of a system in flux, and an important aspect of transitions to new overall forms of behavior. During times of transition, when subsystems are not strongly cohesive, small changes in the environment or the organism can create large reorganization." Also helpful in this time of reorganization is a realistic valuing of the importance of the relationship as well as imagining the process having an eventual positive outcome. "Clinically there is cohesion between therapy and development because the processes of therapy are the processes of development itself" (Jaffe, 2000).

The requirements of the initial relationship from the stepparent's perspective includes clarity and an acceptable frame such as "house rules" and responsibilities, interest, respect, and a goal to become empathic with the adolescent. Since most stepparents are not mental health professionals, they cannot conduct conceptually sophisticated psychological assessments of "their" individual adolescent. The special characteristics of each child's history, strengths, and derailments that she brings to a newly blended family are intuitively assessed by the stepparent in a lived experience day by day. The specific characteristics of the stepparent, as with a therapist, will determine the ultimate goodness of "fit." Her values, affective availability, cohesiveness of self, capacity to tolerate uncertainty and flexibility, will make each intersubjective relationship unique.

The stepparent, as the psychotherapist, will be the recipient of negative as well as positive transferences. However, the stepparent does not necessarily interpret these transferences. She must live with them, ideally tolerate these distortions, and not minimize the adolescent's experience.

Elson (1984) suggests,

As the child matures, the responsive mirroring, echoing, confirming, guiding function of parents as selfobjects is uniquely transmuted by the child into psychic structure, but it is a two-way process in which parental psychic structure also undergoes transformation. . . . Applying the theory of self psychology to parenthood permits an enlarged understanding of the process [p. 298].

Elson continues,

> Parents may indeed experience with each child a reactivation of deficits or distortion in any phase of their development, but maturer forms of narcissism—as increased empathy with childhood needs, increased wisdom and creativity, and specifically the ability to respond to the child as a center of perception and initiative—now permit the parents to perform their caretaking functions without unempathic intrusion of their own conflicts. The parental self may be sorely taxed by intrapsychic or interpersonal events [pp. 298–299].

Elson concludes,

> It is part of maturing parental empathy, wisdom, and acceptance of human transience to be able to do so while moving toward a less central position in the lives of their children. Mirroring, confirming, and guiding continue as parental functions but without confining closeness which fails to recognize the increasing need of separateness, the validity and strength of self perception and initiative in the younger generation [p. 312].

For the stepparent coping with a recent death and remarriage, this maturity in functioning may seem to be an impossible hurdle.

What factors may have been significant in my stepmother's ability to glide over this hurdle? Lieberman (1993) reminds us that the way in which the individual functioned prior to the loss is an important predictor of later adaptation (p. 78). To appreciate the complexity of reaction to spousal bereavement, information is needed on the person prior to the loss. The fact that Hilda had already had a good marriage, reared her own adolescent daughter, was well-educated, curious about worlds unexplored, and had in her own character unusual flexibility and resiliency, contributed mightily. Her own capacity to transform herself, reaching out to meet a new partner, offers proof of her resiliency. I suspect that Hilda's widowhood in her mid-40s accelerated what Gould (1993) characterized as an "awareness of death somewhere in the future, and this thought is never again far off the screen of consciousness" (p. 24). How time is spent becomes a matter of great importance. Gould suggests that in this phase of life one gives up the illusion of absolute safety. "But at times we have choices. We catch ourselves in the act of re-creation" (p. 68). It is Gould's concept of the transformational task that should be the organizing unit and vital center of adult experience.

Hilda's transformational task was enhanced by her healthy functioning before the loss of her first husband, but becoming a "good enough" stepmother also depended on the nature of the new marital relationship and its strength in creating a parenting alliance. Cohen and Weissman (1984) "suspect some of the pathology attributed to adolescents, such as splitting the parents, may stem from the absence of such a parenting alliance" (p. 38). The stepparent and natural parent in the blended family must form a new parenting alliance:

> As a concept the parenting alliance is a paradigmatic self–selfobject relationship vital to the evolving parenthood experience and other adult tasks. It encompasses interactions between spouses which pertain to child rearing, with the provision that these behaviors are appropriate to the developmental needs of children [p. 33].

This is where the function of the natural parent, in this case, my father, was pivotal. His empathic capacity for his new wife in her difficult stepmother role allowed her to value this new parenting alliance. Hilda intuitively realized that the father–daughter closeness might threaten her marriage and that stepmother–stepdaughter friction would also adversely affect her relationship to her new husband. This was a delicate line that needed to be maintained without too much wavering and vacillation.

The relationship which operates between the parental partners is the fulcrum about which the new family process evolves. This alliance plays a critical role in the continuous unfolding of the parenthood experience. It can perform a sustaining function for the individual partners as each responds continuously to the developmental progression of the child.

Cohen and Weissman (1984) explain:

> The parenting alliance is that component of a marital relationship which is distinct from the libidinal object needs of the spouses for each other. However it clearly involves the issues of self-esteem and its vicissitudes which can endanger the adult's feeling of competence, effectiveness, and well-being. The alliance consists of the capacity of a spouse to acknowledge, respect, and value the parenting roles and tasks of the partner. Ideally, this capacity should be both firm and resilient to permit the alliance to endure when one or both partners experience stress in the parenting sphere or in other pertinent aspects of life [p. 35].

Paul Bohannan (1984) states,

> Stepfamilies must throw off images of the nuclear family and redefine who is in and out of the new organization. The main problem

for the stepparent is identification with the children of the new spouse. Many who enter stepfamilies are unprepared for the combination of sameness and differentness. As a social group, the stepfamily is immensely more complex than the nuclear family. When the stepfamily blends because each parent has lost a spouse to death rather than divorce, the blending may be less complicated [p. 205].

Bohannan (1984) recalls that "Emily and John Visher (1979) have pointed out that all stepfamilies are built on loss. Not only have the protagonists experienced a series of losses of object relationships, but also a series of shifts and losses in the identifications that are an important dimension of the ego and superego, and of the self" (p. 208). "Severing one's identification with the exspouse is probably never complete, if for no other reason . . . the children are constant reminders" (p. 210). Therefore, Hilda's insistence that all of us could discuss how we missed those who died and openly make references to them was a crucial ingredient in our blendings.

Bohannan considers that the remarried parent in a stepfamily must reorder identifications.

Identification with a new spouse may not be a problem—indeed, it may seem to be an experience of finally discovering your "real" self in the new lover. However, for some, the identification with the exspouse seems seriously to interfere with, or at least color, the new relationship. . . . But the most difficult part is that there is almost no identification at all with the children of the new spouse. That has to be consciously built [p. 210].

Hilda was able to do that with the active participation of my father.

If a stepparent is able to build this identificatory fabric, the tapestry woven may provide a splendid cloth, especially if there are grandchildren. After 12 years, Hilda once again became a widow and has been my children's only surviving grandparent. For their entire lives, my sons have considered her grandmother Hilda, not stepgrandmother. She has enriched their lives and mine. I thank her.

References

Benedek, T. (1959), Parenthood as a developmental phase: A contribution to libido theory. J. Amer. Psychoanal. Assn., 7:389–417.

Blos, P. (1998), Book Review: Adolescent Development, Psychopathology, and Treatment, by H. Spencer Bloch. J. Amer. Psychoanal. Assn., 46:326–330.

Bohannan, P. (1984), Stepparenthood: A new and old experience. In: Parenthood: A Psychodyamic Perspective, ed. B. Cohen & S. Weissman. New York: Guilford Press, pp. 204–219.

Cohen, R. & Weissman, S. (1984), The parenting alliance. In: *Parenthood: A Psychodyamic Perspective,* ed. B. Cohen & S. Weissman. New York: Guilford Press, pp. 33–63.

Elson, M. (1984), Parenthood and the transformation of narcissism. In: *Parenthood: A Psychodyamic Perspective,* ed. B. Cohen & S. Weissman. New York: Guilford Press, pp. 297–314.

Formanek, R. (1986), Learning the lines: Women's aging and self-esteem. In: *Psychoanalysis and Women: Contemporary Reappraisals,* ed. J. Alpert. Hillsdale, NJ: The Analytic Press, pp. 139–160.

Freud, S. (1905), Three essays on the theory of sexuality. *Standard Edition,* 7:125–243. London: Hogarth Press, 1953.

Galatzer-Levy, R. M. (1984), Adolescent breakdown and middle-age crises. In: *Late Adolescence: Psychoanalytic Studies,* ed. D. D. Brockman. New York: International Universities Press, pp. 29–52.

Garber, B. (1984), Parenting responses in divorce and bereavement of a spouse. In: *Parenthood: A Psychodyamic Perspective,* ed. B. Cohen & S. Weissman. New York: Guilford Press, pp. 183–203.

Gould, R. (1993), Transformational tasks in adulthood. In: *The Course of Life: Vol. 6. Late Adulthood,* ed. G. Pollock & S. Greenspan. New York: International Universities Press, pp. 23–68.

Jaffe, C. (2000), Organizing adolescents (adolescence): A dynamic systems perspective on adolescent development and psychotherapy. *Adolescent Psychiatry,* 25:17–43. Hillsdale, NJ: The Analytic Press.

Lieberman, M. (1993), A reexamination of adult life crises: Spousal loss in mid- and late-life. In: *The Course of Life: Vol. 6. Late Adulthood,* ed. G. Pollock & S. Greenspan. New York: International Universities Press, pp. 69–110.

Marohn, R. (1984), Disappointing and deviant youth and the rage of the elders. *Child. & Youth Serv. Rev.,* 6:367–373.

———— Doctors, S. & Leider, R. J. (1998), A reexamination of Peter Blos's concept of prolonged adolescence. *Adolescent Psychiatry,* 23:3–19. Hillsdale, NJ: The Analytic Press.

Palombo, J. (1987), Adolescent development: A view from self psychology. *Child & Adol. Soc. Work J.,* 5:171–186.

Rocah, B. (1984), Fixation in late adolescent women: Negative Oedipus complex, fear of being influenced, and resistance to change. In: *Late Adolescence: Psychoanalytic Studies,* ed. D. D. Brockman. New York: International Universities Press, pp. 53–92.

Thelen, E. & Smith, L. (1994), *A Dynamic Systems Approach to the Development of Cognition and Action.* Cambridge, MA: MIT Press.

Visher, E. & Visher, J. S. (1979), *Stepfamilies: A Guide to Working with Stepparents and Stepchildren.* New York: Brunner/Mazel.

The Challenge of Maintaining the Fathering Role After Divorce

Overcoming Shame

Eugenio M. Rothe

The father's diminishing contact and progressive emotional disengagement from his children is a frequent outcome of divorce which has been amply documented. Wallerstein and Kelly (1980) report that most fathers lose at least some contact with their children in the five years following a decisive marital separation and that 90 percent of the children ultimately find themselves in sole maternal custody. Wallerstein (1991) also reported that, in spite of regular visitation over the 10 years following divorce, the intensity of the father's relationship with his children diminished in most cases, and that the richness of their emotional relationship also decreased. Furstenberg and Nord (1985) reported even more dramatic findings: 23 percent of the divorced fathers had had no contact with their sons or daughters in the previous five years, and 20 percent had not seen their children during the entire preceding year. These researchers concluded that, in the majority of families, marital disruption effectively destroys the ongoing relationship between children and their biological parent living outside the home.

In spite of these findings, relatively little attention has been paid to the psychological states of fathers after divorce. Fathers are more often viewed as responsible for causing the divorce (Atkins, 1989). According to many, the complexities of coupling and marriage may include a search for a regressive fusion with a component part of the ego ideal. This quest may lead to a vulnerable dependence on the person chosen, who, unconsciously to be sure, is needed to regulate self-esteem. When the "self" depends too much on eternal objects for self-esteem regulation, any failure to maintain the idealized merger with the chosen object results in humiliating shame.

This realization may lead to states of passivity that may engender covertly more shame and an overall conviction-reflection of being unlovable. The primary source of narcissistic injury may well be the loss of object, and to need someone, particularly a despised someone, may be experienced as especially humiliating. In this scenario, among the more "immature defenses" (Vaillant, 1988) projection deserves particular attention. Nathanson (1987) has described how shame may be defended against by projection, which engenders a feeling of "contempt" toward the other.

The unconscious attempts to relocate shame from within the self onto the other person through projective identification.

In other scenarios "acting out" can also function to defend against shame, as when ego responds by actively turning against the environment, for example, in the form of rage and envy. Rage serves to expunge shame from the self by directing aggression at the "offending object," "offending" because the object may have failed to mirror the individual, failed to accept his idealization, or rejected him as a desired object of attachment. Rage is a common defense against narcissistic injury in general but may also be reinforced by helplessness to attune the environment to personal needs. Envy may contain a malignant form of hatred toward a previously considered good object. The accompanying rage attempts to control, destroy, and render useless the good object. Shame may be transformed into "shamelessness" and acquire an exhibitionistic character, reinforcing feelings of agency, assertiveness, and independence; thus, triumphantly overcoming negative aspects of shame.[1]

Humiliation represents an interpersonal form of shame in which there is an actual or an internalized "humiliator" (usually a highly cathected object) who perpetrates the humiliating act against the self. The dictionary defines humiliation as an act that "lowers one's pride or dignity" or that "mortifies," which, in turn, means "to make dead" (*Random House Dictionary*, 1966).

Morrison (1986, 1987, 1989) cautions that depression frequently masks underlying feelings of shame and that often times, it is only the depression which is treated. He suggests that the therapist should be guided by his own feelings of shame and failed aspirations, elicited in the countertransference with these patients, in order to more accurately diagnose and treat these patients.

Whatever the complexities involved, divorced fathers are nine times more likely to be hospitalized for acute mental illness, a rate that is three times higher than their married counterparts (Bloom, Asher, and White, 1978). A father deprived of his "average expectable contact with his children" is more than likely to suffer considerable emotional pain, whether acknowledged by him or others or not. His failure may be highlighted and possibly exacerbated by a vengeful wife, whether justified or not. It is also true that diminished emotional contact with children may be strategy used by some fathers to get even wit former wives. In a group of fathers seen in psychotherapy by Atkins (1989) following divorce, feelings of anxiety, depression, loneliness, grief, anger, and despair were commonly reported. Wallerstein and Corbin (1996) observed diminished capacity to parent as an expectable short-term consequence of most divorces. A variety of

---

[1]Editor's note: probably operative in so-called deadbeat dads.

conscious and unconscious fantasies of abandoning the young have been reported. In some fathers, this fantasy may be coped with by "sudden flight" or an unexpected total rejection of a child or children from a failed marriage. Paradoxically, the fantasy to abandon the child may be partially neutralized intrapsychically by an increased need for closeness/contact with the child. In many cases this leads to the father's treating he child as a peer, thereby blurring intergenerational boundaries.

Since shame is considered such a powerful negative emotion, especially in men, it is frequently defended against by concealment. Morrison (1986, 1987, 1989) and others (Nathanson, 1987, 1990; Broucek, 1991) reaffirm shame is usually ignored as an important psychodynamic precipitant in a variety of human situations. The following clinical vignette will highlight the role of shame as a concealed factor in a divorced father's struggle with impulses to withdrawn from his children. It will also point to the implications of shame as an obstacle for stepfathers in assuming their parenting role in a blended family. Case material will illustrate the origins, psychodynamic theories, treatment, and recovery from shame in a divorcing father.

The Case of Mr. Spiegel

Mr. Spiegel was a successful attorney in his middle 40s, who had recently been elected to the bench as a circuit court judge, the same office that his father had held years before. He was married, with two children, a boy and a girl, ages seven and four years. I first met Mr. Spiegel when asked to see the son, Ted, to rule out attention deficit disorder. Ted, however, appeared to be suffering more from great anxiety over the daily loud verbal confrontations between his parents. "They scream so loud that all the neighbors can hear them," he blurted out with embarrassment. Mr. Spiegel and his wife reprimanded the children over minor transgressions by screaming at them as well. Both children were scared of their father, even though no physical abuse was ever reported. The wife, in turn, appeared to bear some responsibility in provoking Mr. Spiegel and in vicariously enjoying his loss of control. Although I recommended a combination of individual therapy for the children as well as family therapy, the family dropped out of treatment.

Two years later I received an urgent telephone call from Mr. Spiegel, asking to meet with me "individually as soon as possible." When a frazzled, cigarette-smoking Mr. Spiegel dropped onto my sofa, he sank into silence and then exploded, "Doctor, I don't know where to hide, I can't face anybody, I've never felt so humiliated in my entire life," he exploded. "It's a big massive shanda (a Yiddish word used to describe a shameful event). As far as I'm concerned, my wife, Judy, is dead. I have to cover all the mirrors, she's dead but I still want to kill her with my bare hands."

Since the last time we met, the couple had agreed to a trial marital separation, during which Mr. Spiegel had moved out of the house and into an apartment. One day, as he returned to the house unannounced, he surprised his wife in bed with a woman. "I wanted to die then and there before I could turn around and kill them both," he said, puffing energetically on his cigarette. Mr. Spiegel explained that the event was followed by several loud confrontations, after which his wife had admitted her homosexual orientation. She had been suppressing this since early adolescence, she said, but had finally to come to terms with it.

I began seeing Mr. Spiegel in therapy twice a week. He was experiencing considerable difficulty concentrating at work, had increased his cigarette consumption to three or more packs a day, and was losing weight. At night, unable to sleep, he spend hours obsessing angrily about a multitude of ways in which he would exact revenge on his wife and her female lover. Mr. Spiegel refused my recommendation to begin treatment with antidepressant medications, accepting only a mild benzodiazepine to help him sleep. We began exploring his life and his marriage as he attempted to "keep it together, one day at a time."

Mr. Spiegel was the adopted and only child of a conservative Jewish couple who lived only a few blocks away from his current home. His father had been a prominent man in his professional community. He described his mother as "your average traditional housewife, a sweet woman, everybody who knows her loves her." He was very close to both of his parents and very proud of his father, "even though for years I resented having to live up to his name and reputation." Mr. Spiegel had had a privileged childhood but, at around age nine discovered, due to a malicious indiscretion by a male cousin, his adoptive origins. Neither Mr. Spiegel nor his parents knew anything about his biological parents, since this had been part of the agreement with the adoption agency. Even though he always felt loved by his adoptive parents, Mr. Spiegel felt rejected and demeaned by his extended family, especially an uncle and aunt and their three children. The uncle, his father's brother, had never achieved the same amount of professional success as Mr. Spiegel's father. Envy was built in. "During the Jewish holidays," he painfully remembered, "my aunt, my uncle, and my cousins would insist that in order to be Jewish, you had to be born a Jew. They did this on purpose, to rub it in my face, to make me feel like an outsider." During adolescence, Mr. Spiegel manifested "conduct problems" and went through a period of drug use and acting out behavior. Expelled from several private schools, finally graduating from a military academy located outside the state, adding, "My cousins and my aunt and uncle really ate this up." In college he had an unremarkable academic record, "basically screwing around and having a good time." After college, still using marijuana daily, Mr. Spiegel went on several trips abroad and held a series of odd jobs, which he considered beneath his talents. He resented his parents silent disapproval and what he experienced to be his extended family's "joy at the fact I was working very hard at becoming a failure." Mr. Spiegel explained, "One day I realized I was only living for my next high because something was eating away at my insides." With the support of his parents, Mr. Spiegel began treatment as an outpatient in a drug rehabilitation program continuing with individual therapy and attending Narcotics Anonymous meetings for the next three years. As a result of the therapy, he embarked in an unsuccessful attempt to locate his biological parents but this failure led to a profound feeling of depression. "I slowly discovered that my (adoptive) parents were really great people, that they loved me and that that's all that really mattered." Through his father's connections, Mr. Spiegel was accepted into professional school, where "I discovered I was smart and it came easily to me." While attending school, Mr. Spiegel met Judy, an attractive, hip graduate student everybody was after but nobody seemed to be able to conquer." Judy became a "challenge" and Mr. Spiegel courted her aggressively for over a year before they began living together. Judy seemed to enjoy the fact that Mr. Spiegel was older and more experienced than her previous suitors and admired his optimism, drive, and ambition. They married after graduation and Mr. Spiegel began spending long hours at work, as the couple proceeded to settle into family life and to have two children. "I felt grounded, complete, my life finally had a purpose and the children really brought my parents and me closer together for the first time in many years," he added with deeply felt emotion. This newfound closeness with his parents propelled him to attain the same laurels as his father. Mr. Spiegel's father "ran the entire 'campaign,' he felt so proud of me that he seemed to be getting younger by the minute, it was as if he was living his life again through me. I have to say that those were some of the best years of my life, and for my father too, I think!"

Mr. Spiegel reported that after the success of his campaign, his wife complained of having been "left out" and became jealous, saying, "Ever since you're a superstar, people don't even notice I exist." He added, "I felt it wasn't fair. It was the first time in my life that I really liked myself and Judy was trying to ruin everything." He added that she had tried to embarrass him in public by highlighting negative events from his past and by "flirting with other men right in front of my face, and now this shanda!"

In the months that followed, Mr. Spiegel complained about how "the gossip about this scandal has spread like wildfire; I even feel embarrassed to go out on the street." He obsessed for hours about how these events would affect his career and fantasized about the negative comments that others would make about him. Slowly, over a period of several weeks, his attention began to shift away from himself and toward his children. "How will this affect them?" he asked repeatedly, demanding from me concrete answers and obsessing over strategies to "minimize the damage." Mr.

Spiegel began connecting his own feelings of shame over being adopted with the shame that his children would have to face as a consequence of their mother's homosexuality.

At this point an important shift in therapy took place. Mr. Spiegel embarked on a mission to try to protect his children. He began spending more time with them and negotiating new living arrangements with his wife and her lover. Judy and the children moved into the home of Mary, her female lover, along with Mary's six year old daughter from a previous marriage.

Mary's ex-husband had been out of touch for some time. When Mr. Spiegel moved back into his house alone, a profound feeling of depression triggered a process of mourning: "There's such emptiness and desolation!, I couldn't survive if it weren't for my parents. They're really supportive and sometimes we talk all night into the morning." To his surprise, "The neighbors have been very nice. They come up to me as if to offer condolences. They seem to feel sorry for me, I still don't know how to feel about all this. What I do know is that every time I face someone I imagine my aunt and uncle and my cousins deriving joy from my misfortune."

Subsequently, Mr. Spiegel submerged himself in his work, spending his free time visiting with his two children and including Mary's daughter in their outings. "I feel so bad for the little girl, she looks at me puzzled, as if trying to figure out how I fit into the picture." Over the following year, Mr. Spiegel and Judy finalized their divorce and they slowly allowed themselves to be seen publicly with Mary and the three children. "It's a weird family. I guess we're the soap opera version of the Addams family," he said chuckling with difficulty. He reported feeling very happy as to how the little girl had become attached to him and as to how enthusiastically he was always received by his two children, adding, "I'm slowly beginning to forgive Judy and Mary for what they did. They make me feel very needed—it's as if I'm the father of all five of them." Mr. Spiegel continued to thrive professionally. He began cutting back on the psychotherapy visits to an "as-needed basis" and during his last visit he reported, "I'm doing okay, but I really can't date anybody yet, because the wound is still too fresh." Mr. Spiegel added, "It's ironic, but people I know come up to me and tell me how well I've handled this whole situation and how much they respect me. Frankly, it would have been preferable if it had never happened, but given the circumstances, it turned out the best it could."

Discussion

Mr. Spiegel can be considered to be an individual with a relatively well-integrated sense of self. Unlike more narcissistically vulnerable individuals, the experience of shame does not occupy a central role in Mr. Spiegel's life. Shame began playing a prominent part after he learned about his adoption. This disruption also affected his self-esteem and led to confusion regarding his professional goals, temporarily affecting his capacity for generativity. Mr. Spiegel's substance abuse possibly served the purpose of self-medicating his depression as well as his underlying feelings of shame. His acting-out behavior, on the other hand, may have played a role in defending against shame through reaction formation, turning passive into active by appearing to others and to himself as a "shameless" individual. The support and consistency offered by Mr. Spiegel's parents throughout his years of turmoil may have provided the necessary holding environment, which contributed to Mr. Spiegel's decision to finally seek professional help. During the therapeutic process he was able to rediscover his adoptive father, identify more with him, and project onto the father his own narcissistic aspirations. The father, in turn, welcomed the idealizations and derived rejuvenating energies by identifying with his son. This highlight provided Mr. Spiegel with a reparative emotional experience, which helped to promote his capacity for industry and generativity, to consolidate his sense of identity and, through the mechanism of identification, to turn his envy of his father into ambition and pleasure in success.

Mr. Spiegel's shame was reactivated in a rather brutal fashion by his wife's double betrayal, her infidelity and homosexuality. This humiliation mobilized a series of defense mechanisms that ranged from avoidance (to hide and conceal) to more obsessive defense.

Mr. Spiegel was able to call on good internalized objects of his past and to mobilize his capacity for empathy and compassion. He compared his own painful childhood experiences of shame to those of his own children and to those of Mary's daughter. This led to an altruistic resolution by which he was able to overcome shame by becoming a protective father and surrogate stepfather to Mary's daughter and a paternal figure to his ex-wife and her lover. Even though it was clear that some aspects of Mr. Spiegel's mourning process remained to be worked through, his altruistic resolution allowed him to gain the admiration and respect of the members of his community. This helped him overcome his shame and allowed him to repair and consolidate his self-esteem. It is important for clinicians to recognize and correctly diagnose and treat issues of shame in divorcing fathers, in order to best protect the father–child relationship following divorce.

References

Atkins, R. N. (1989), Divorce and the fathers: Some intrapsychic factors affecting the outcome. In: *Fathers and Their Families*, ed. S. H. Cath, A. Gurwitt & L. Gunsberg. Hillsdale, NJ: The Analytic Press, pp. 431–458.

Bloom, B. L., Asher, S. J. & White, S. W. (1978), Marital disruption as a stressor: A review and analysis. *Psychol. Bull.*, 85:867–894.

Broucek, F. J. (1991), *Shame and the Self.* New York: Guilford Press.

Furstenberg, F. F. & Nord, C. W. (1985), Parenting apart. *J. Marriage & Family*, 47:893–904.

Morrison, A. P. (1986), Shame, ideal self and narcissism. In: *Essential Papers on Narcissism*, ed. A. P. Morrison. New York: New York University Press, pp. 348–371.

_____ (1987), The eye turned inward: Shame and the self. In: *The Many Faces of Shame*, ed. D. L. Nathanson. New York: Guilford Press.

_____ (1989), *The Underside of Narcissism.* Hillsdale, NJ: The Analytic Press.

Nathanson, D. L., ed. (1987), *The Many Faces of Shame.* New York: Guilford Press.

_____ (1990), *Shame and Pride: Affect, Sex, and the Birth of the Self.* New York: Norton.

Random House Dictionary of the English Language, Unabridged Edition (1966), New York: Random House.

Vaillant, G. E. (1988), Defense mechanisms. In: *The New Harvard Guide to Psychiatry*, ed. A. N. Nicholi. Cambridge, MA: Harvard University Press.

Wallerstein, J. S. (1991), The long-term effects of divorce on children: A review. *J. Amer. Acad. Child Adol. Psychiat.*, 30:349–360.

_____ & Corbin, S. B. (1996), The child and the vicissitudes of divorce. In: *Child and Adolescent Psychiatry: A Comprehensive Textbook*, ed. M. Lewis. Baltimore, MD: Williams & Wilkins.

_____ & Kelly, J. B. (1980), *Surviving the Breakup.* New York Basic Books.

The Stepfather in a Reconstituted Family

H. Gunther Perdigao

I found no papers on stepfatherhood in my search of the psychoanalytic literature. It is a puzzling omission, considering that more than 50 percent of marriages end in divorce and that a large number of divorced parents remarry and have stepchildren. Based on data from the 1990 U.S. Census, the Stepfamily Association of America (SAA; Lincoln, NE) estimated in 1998 that 52 to 62 percent of all first marriages would eventually end in divorce, that 75 percent of divorced persons would eventually remarry, and that about 65 percent of remarriages would involve children from prior marriages and thus would form stepfamilies. The SAA (1998) states that the estimated rate of divorce for remarriages is 60 percent. Additionally, one in three Americans is now a stepparent, a stepchild, a stepsibling, or some other member of a stepfamily. More than half of all Americans today have been, are now, or will eventually be in one or more step situations. Stepfathering is a complex and challenging responsibility. There are more stepfathers now than ever, and it appears that the majority of them have a positive influence on their stepchildren's lives.

Parenthetically, as far as the law is concerned, the stepfather remains in a peculiar form of legal limbo. He cannot sign a consent sheet for surgery for his stepchildren, nor is he held legally responsible for them. The only time the law concerns itself with him is when criminal charges are involved. Remarriages in which one or more sets of children are involved have been quite stressful and from the clinical perspective require a lot of work to be ongoing. Life during the courtship period is often characterized by unrealistic, quite magical fantasies. When everybody begins to live together, these illusions are put to the test and soon dispelled. A marriage ceremony does not automatically blend preestablished families. To a significant degree, the success or failure of remarriage may depend on how the stepfather conceives of, structures, and conducts the relationship with his new wife's children. Friends and relatives, especially if they have had the experience, tend to discourage someone considering such a complex, highly charged task. In that his new wife married him not just as a partner, but also to varying degree, as a parent, fathering may become an indeterminate part of the silently agreed to husbanding contract.

Thus, while there are many issues to be resolved when a stepfamily is newly formed, I know of no formal outline or description in the psychoanalytic literature of the kinds of conflicts and emotional rewards that will confront a stepfather. Children will relate to the stepfather in the light of their past experiences with men or father(s), but their responses will also be influenced by current needs set in the context of highly ambivalent images of trust and safe attachments. Stepfathers, in turn, will respond to their stepchildren's concerns guided by their own memories, mental representations and deeply set characteristics formed in past family settings also informed by more immediate expectations.

Phases of the New Relationship

Broadly speaking, then, the new relationships may be divided into three phases. The first is the *courtship phase,* in which both adults are likely to be on their best behavior and the future stepfather tries hard to get the children to like him in order to earn entrance into an established family.

Vignette. Susie was eight years old when her parents divorced. A few months later her mother starting dating a man who took a great interest in Susie. She basked in his attention and enjoyed his open affection. Then suddenly without apparent reason, her mother broke off the relationship. This now was Susie's second loss. After that she kept a safe distance from her mother's suitors. Later, when the mother had a serious relationship and remarried, Susie never allowed herself to be involved with her stepfather. In spite of his entreaties and sincere efforts to have a relationship with her, she rebuffed him at every turn.

This courtship phase may be terminated by the ceremony of marriage, which initiates an *early marital phase* characterized by testing of the waters. Once a fun-loving friend of mother moves in and begins acting like a serious second parent, restructuring of all relationships follows.

Vignette. Tommy was 12 years old when his mother remarried. During the courtship phase, he had gotten along well with his future stepfather but when the latter moved in and began to set some rules, Tommy became very resentful. He felt that this man was usurping his father's role and often called his father to complain about the new man in the house. Feeling abandoned by his mother, he actively tried to pit father and stepfather against each other. In her loneliness following the divorce, mother had made the boy her confidant and failed to set boundaries to his behavior. During the courtship phase the future stepfather sensed the depth of the attachment to mother and tried to woo Tommy by indulging him, taking him to baseball games, and buying him fancy computer games. This gave Tommy a false feeling that all the attention would continue to be showered on him and no demands placed on his behavior. Following the marriage, he was expected to follow new rules, became resentful, and felt he had been duped.

Vignette. Bob was 14 years old when his mother remarried. Very quickly the new marriage became strained. The stepfather made Bob his confidant and would go into his stepson's room to complain to the teenager how unreasonable his mother had been. After a marital argument he would sleep in the extra bed in Bob's room. Bob, meanwhile, felt he was betraying his mother and became very anxious. All along he reported that he sympathized with his stepfather's point of view.

If the new arrangements can be reasonably integrated, a *long-term marital phase* evolves. These phases require special readjustments to frustrations balanced by new gratifications for all the participants if the marriage is to continue to be stable.

Vignette. Ricky's father traveled a great deal. When at home, he was not very interested in his children. He had a distant impersonal relationship with his son. When Ricky was 10 his mother remarried. His stepfather, a surgeon, had children by a previous marriage and even during that time felt guilty he had neglected them because of his work. Despite Ricky's earlier caution during the courtship phase, he and his new stepfather hit it off well. The latter was more ready and able to be the father to Ricky that he had never been to his biological children, and Ricky responded warmly to the good will and interest shown in him.

As noted above, unrealistic expectations about the stepfamily's future may color the idealized future even of a second marriage. Friends have been heard to opine, "It's a triumph of hope over experience." The meshing of the gears of various generations is not always easy in a traditional family, but it is especially problematic in the reconstituted one when some are grieving for an absent father and others are trying to break free of familial bonds. The tolerance for and management of the everyday diversity of lifestyles, gradually exposed in day-to-day interactions between a stepparent and newly "adopted" children, presents an ongoing challenge for everyone involved. The stepfather does not have the advantage of a common family history and the stepchildren lack the comfort and compatibility of marital love to soften the impact of contrasting pulls, rivalries, and traits between the participants.

Some Reactions to a New Stepfather

The resistance to and nature of the bonding to the stepfather, then, depends on multiple variables, some of which affect how quickly a close or warm attachment may take place. One of these will be the individual child's receptivity to a new stepfather. This "readiness" may be influenced by how long the mother has lived as a single parent, the nature of her "single" relationship with her child or children, and the circumstances under which the present rearrangement took place, be it abandonment, divorce, or widowhood. Each of these painful circumstances, or a combination of several, may create a unique constellation that affects the children's willingness to enter a new relationship. From the clinicians' point of view a new, happy rearrangement is rare. An acrimonious divorce associated with much "family anxiety" about future relationships with men may have led to highly cautious inertia on one extreme to violent aversion on the other. Abandonment by father or mother may leave in its wake extreme reluctance "to be as vulnerable again." Death of a parent may lead to guilt and/or retrospective idealization. All of these external events intertwine with internal stepfamily dynamics to become a great challenge to maturational forces.

Whatever the reason, when the biological father is no longer a daily member of the immediate family, intensified bonding by the children to the remaining, residential parent usually takes place. In such circumstances the mother and one or more of the children may be drawn much closer together than before, seemingly in the service of security, support, and survival. They may have learned to depend on each other to provide nurture and each fulfills some of the roles held previously by the missing parent.

The mother, especially if she must enter the work force, may come to depend on the children to take specific responsibilities, such as helping more around the house. When the biological father remains an active, if nonresidential, presence in his children's lives, they often may be forced to "choose sides." Active comparisons between the characteristics of the father and stepfather may become a constant annoyance in the family's collective minds.

Clinically we encounter various types of responses on the part of the children we see. A rare few express eager anticipation and excitement at having a man in the house. This reaction is probably accentuated by a need to separate from someone perceived as an engulfing, overcontrolling mother. Magical expectations, built up during the courtship period when the child received "treats" or was taken places by the mother's suitor, play a pivotal role here. Oedipal-age children may welcome the arrival of a man, especially when a boy suffers from an identificatory hunger for a male or the girl finds the stepfather a safe vehicle through whom to work out some aspects of her oedipal fantasies. Children, especially of "a single parent," may not have had an ongoing or remembered relationship with a male. The void may be filled by imagining what it would be like to have a Daddy who will pay more attention to them as witnessed in some traditional families.

A complex aspect of these reactions may involve loyalty conflicts. A child may fear that, if he becomes attached to a stepfather, he will have to abandon or betray his biological parent. Another child may be especially concerned about how his father will react to mother's remarriage, that this event will end his potentialities for a meaningful relationship between them forever. Indeed, it occasionally does. In order to deal with these fears, some children reject all kindly overtures of the stepfather. Some not only maintain their distance, older ones move away, but younger ones behave in extremely provocative ways to annoy the stepfather. In so doing they communicate their distress to mother as well, if she is listening. Another group of children may try to sabotage and destroy the new marriage in order to assuage guilt over the sensed betrayal of their biological father.

Some mothers date repeatedly. In some families, hopes for a new father are awakened only to have them dashed by an admired male quickly disappearing from the scene. Certain children develop very strong defenses against another disappointment; to ward off another painful loss, initially at least, they frustrate the stepfather's efforts at building a relationship. A seemingly endless period of provocative testing may be intended to determine if the stepfather really means to stick around. This insight may be made a part of our attempts at psychoeducational intervention.

Enhanced ambivalence may occur when, following father's departure, a selected child becomes mother's best friend and begins to sleep in the same bed with her. A new stepfather would become an obvious obstacle to this now highly charged, habituated relationship with mother and her warmth. The new couple may even "lock the bedroom door to boot," so that this evicted child becomes convinced that he has lost another parent.

Lastly there is the scenario in which children retain strong fantasies of an eventual reunion of their biological parents. Some of these children may have blamed themselves for the divorce and harbored secret fantasies of being the mediators of reconciliation. With actual remarriage, such romantics are confronted by their powerlessness and unconscious rage. Yet these fantasies have persisted dynamically so that some guilty children cannot tolerate unmodulated fun or joy within the reconstituted family. They may act out by repeatedly sabotaging the new family's happiness at shared events like holidays or picnics.

To be sure, before and during divorce, many children have had to adapt to multiple changes in all kinds of circumstances over which they have had no input and little control. Mother and stepfather may feel free to make serious family changes without even consulting their young. But these unexpected changes in parental priorities, values, interests, geographical settings and outside relations greatly affect children and pose one developmental challenge after another.

Against this shifting, insecure backdrop, unknown, unique aspects of a stepfather's ways of being and doing gradually unfold and may create various degrees of apprehension because the child (or spouse) may find them alien or strange. Less able to predict the new father's responses, it is not surprising that it takes so much time and effort to understand each other and to become "familiar" again. Ideally, some few stepfathers will be empathic enough to tolerate a period of testing and exile and skilled enough interpersonally to wait and eventually earn the place of a trusted ally.

This tolerance for postponed gratification is inordinately important when dealing with teenagers, who, by their very nature, are self-preoccupied and less considerate of others. Burdened with their own age-specific challenges, they tend to be less disposed to accept readily the daily presence of a stepfather in their lives, and particularly prone to test limits as they go "out." Often, they displace onto the "new father" their own preexisting, disavowed conflicts, supplemented and colored by traumas connected with the inevitably ambivalent phenomenon surrounding parents who divorce and remarry. In remarrying, mother has certainly communicated, especially to the adolescent, that she too has different kinds of attachment needs, which, although quite resonant with her child's, precludes him. Possibly stimulated but also "insulted" by a parent's "independent decision" to transfer her emotional needs and dependency wishes to others, some teens place even more importance on outside connections and accelerate their object finding. Developmentally impelled toward separating from an incestuous but now "contemptible" love object, he or she may prematurely attach to another parental figure. Some teenagers seem less constrained by the usual intergenerational demarcations of age and seek for others of their parent's generation. Lack of understanding of this "normal" maturational search by all generations may lead to what for the moment seems like disastrous results as increasing turmoil contaminates all familial relationships.

The Stepfather's Reaction to the Children

So far we have discussed primarily the child's reaction to the stepfather. Let us focus on some of the other ways a stepfather may try to relate to his new children. As noted above, he is initially prone to curry favor with his future wife by romancing one or more of the selected children. This may be complicated when a particular adolescent, probably a female, becomes an ally or confidante. This may work for a time as long as the unreality mirrors the adult mirage of a stepfamily as a happy paradise. Such seductions are usually temporary and ultimately fade or lead to painful disappointments both in the adults and in the teenager.

At this point, an additional pitfall is the temptation of some stepfathers to compete with the biological father's often-idealized imago by trying to show the children that he can "out-father" their father. This also usually ends in disappointment, as loyalty, especially to a deceased father, will ultimately prevail.

At the other extreme of seduction is yet another scenario. A stepfather's behavior may quickly reveal that his primary or only interest is in his new wife. As interactions during crises soon reveal an avoidance of any unnecessary intercourse with his stepchildren or little time for or patience with their struggles, everyone apprehends where his priorities lie. A hostile or detached attitude is particularly perplexing to those whose secretly held, albeit ambivalent wish is "to let stepfather in." Yet, his manifest attitude impoverishes any remnants of the seemingly indestructible, longed-for intimacy with an understanding and supportive father. Children in this setting quickly perceive that they are an unwanted addition and may have great difficulty managing the hostility generated by their being considered an impediment or burden to the stepfather's conceit of a new family setting. As mothers come to realize the seriousness of this rejection, stepparental relationships may cool or dissolve completely. Many such stepfathers, unable to accept the ultimate primacy of attachments of mothers to their children, may flee from their second marriages as they did from their first, and for similar reasons.

One of the greatest challenges for a stepfather, then, is to establish credibility as a fair, reliable, interested, and ongoing presence in the family's lives. Trust can grow only if the children develop the convictions "we can count on him" and "we are *all* safe in his presence." But these convictions of trust may be needed by some stepfathers as well, and both parties can come to trust each other only as a result of the more intimate as well as ordinary daily interactions between all members of the recreated family.

A particular problem often arises in the reconstituted family when the stepfather feels family patterns are too disorganized for his comfort or the children seem terribly spoiled to him. Compelled to introduce more control, he may institute what he considers essential parenting routines in the best interest of the family. In military fashion, some stepfathers expect the new household to adopt immediately his new rules and march to his personal tune. Stepping like this into an established family with what may seem like inflexible standards rarely succeeds. The children often resent the intruder assuming an authoritarian role he has not earned. His ideas implicitly or explicitly criticize mother's way of being with her children and how she has been or is presently doing things. They are likely to let him know he does not truly belong in the established hierarchical system of power. Forceful methods almost invariably create increased resistance. A man with strong narcissistic needs that demand quick approval of his ways will likely find that approval not forthcoming. In time he may regress into a sadomasochistic mode of interacting with the new family.

Vignette. A widower in late midlife had lost his depressed, alcoholic wife to suicide decades before. His mourning was deep and complicated by the distance his children seemed to need to avoid a confrontation about his role in their mother's demise. By his 60s, still vital, working and lonely, he consciously decided he had learned his lesson enough from years in therapy to "choose" to set his own needs aside in the interest of reestablishing a family. Maybe a second time would be different! Indeed, it was all sunshine and roses during the courtship phase. But after marriage, he found himself feeling increasingly neglected and enraged. It seems his working wife took him at his word and devoted herself almost exclusively to the children's needs as soon as she came home from work. Although he became more critical of their not participating in keeping the house clean, he tolerated these arrangements until he retired and wanted more of his wife during the day or on vacations. His hostility escalated even more when she said in no uncertain terms, "My kids come first," and refused to travel with him. Within a few months, after several such confrontations, his wife felt obligated to choose between the two competing parties. To him, her adamant devotion to the children had had a progressively corrosive effect on the fabric of the marriage he expected. Divorce was followed by a serious depression in both partners. Within the next year the wife developed a fatal cancer. The stepfather and the children were driven permanently apart even though on several occasions they met when simultaneously visiting the mother's grave on Memorial Day. Somehow, they conveyed to him that they held him responsible for their mother's death.

As in the case just cited, many men who marry into established families secretly may have been and are still intolerant of children and their needs. Incredulous when one or more of the children sense this, stepfathers are understandably reluctant to enter quickly into an easy relationship. Frequently their dilemma is compounded when his stepchildren have already had an obviously poor relationship with their biological father and are still suffering from his abuse, neglect, or abandonment following divorce. Their hostile, hesitant, prolonged provocation may revive the stepfather's memories of bad experiences with his own father or stepfather. Some stepfathers may dimly recognize in the stepchild's defenses a mirroring of their own adaptive maneuvers in sharing a loved one. Such caution on the part of the child may be experienced by the stepfather as a guilt-laden reflection of his rejection of a parent or of his poor judgment in entering the situation at all. In some circumstances, it may lead either to a counterphobic overinvolvement on the one hand or an angry distancing on the other. Some will "wash their hands" of the most reluctant child and select a favorite one. Other stepfathers shrug off rejection by rationalizing that this of that particular child is "not mine anyway."

Another difficulty may arise in the early marital phase. It is common for some children to test to see how far they can stretch the rules before a new stepfather takes action or asserts the need for more respect. Obviously, the nature of his response will set the tone of the relationship more or less firmly. Working parents often come home tired, compete for their child's affection, and sometimes snap at each other over the issue of "how to handle the problems of a growing child." If overly harsh with their criticism, conflicts around aggression may be aggravated. This is especially likely if these interactions coincide with a maturational period in which a small child is struggling with impulse control. The mother's response to the stepfather's reactions, or what she may see as interference, especially if she has not asked for it, may become a crucial variable.

When there are two sets of children in a reconstructed family, the issue of fairness over the distribution of resources may become the prime concern. Adults and children both wonder, will all the children to be treated the same? Who will become the favorite(s)? Will there be two or more sets of rules, one for him, one for her, and one for a new child of the reconstituted marriage? Should a new set of variables be introduced for a child of the new union?

By cultural consensus, and bolstered by statistics and the media, stepchildren need to be secure from inappropriate sexual interest by stepfathers. Where family members are not related by blood, the incest barrier is not built in automatically nor does it seem to operate as efficiently. Adolescent stepdaughters may need to test the waters to be sure there is no danger of displaced affection and the stepfather will not cross boundaries and exploit them. Children will quickly notice how much interest a stepfather takes in their own or a sib's private lives. Everyone wonders how much he will respect their need for time, distance, and privacy and not invade their space inappropriately. Testing may include being committed enough to chauffeur, go to school functions, dance recitals, or ball games? But even if he *does* all these things acceptably, the question remains, will he be *attuned* to age-appropriate narcissistic excitements and respond empathetically when children need support in containing their own passions? A stepfather attuned to these issues may well earn the deep respect and affection of his stepchildren and his new wife.

Vignette. Colleen was 14 years old when her mother remarried. She was very suspicious of her stepfather and wanted nothing to do with him. She acted as if he were a rapist and throughout her adolescence kept her distance. Realizing that the stepchild felt threatened by the relationship and was sophisticated enough to suspect that her own (incestuous) urges toward her biological father were at the base of her insecurity, the stepfather kept a safe distance and was careful never to overstep any bounds. The relationship between them remained strained until Colleen married.

After that she was able to show her stepfather the affection she had developed silently and express her appreciation that he had treated her with respect throughout her adolescence.

Vignette. Ellen was 13 when her mother remarried. She had developed early and was physically quite mature. Her stepfather resented her sloppy ways and would often come into her room to scold her without knocking on the door. At times he would become playful, hugging and tickling her. As time wore on the relationship degenerated into a sadomasochistic struggle as the stepfather tried to impose discipline on her whenever the tickling sessions grew too intense for him. Ellen complained bitterly that he did not respect her space and felt confused about the boundaries between them. The stepfather claimed she did not appreciate his efforts to help her become more organized, and that he as a parent had the right to enforce rules as he saw fit.

The Marital Relationship

This leads us to the last area to be discussed in this chapter. All new marital partners do form a unique alliance, which begins by restructuring their relationship as it pertains to each other as a couple parenting stepchildren. Blending two families takes even more time and effort than the first time a baby enters an ordinary family. Each spouse has his own quite altered-by-experience set of expectations and defensive styles of parenting. How will each react to the other's way of handling different situations as they arise? To an indeterminate degree, the mother may want her new husband involved in the parenting of her children. Yet most divorced women have been traumatized and feel a need to adopt a protective, gatekeeper role in determining just how much she will permit him to do and become. Difficulties arise should the wife be unwilling to let the new husband "parent" her children (or vice versa), only under the condition he proceed exactly as she demands. Few spouses function comfortably if they are turned into a psychological extension of the other's idealized fantasies or fearsome, reparative desires. Even when she remains reluctant to let the new husband share direct parenting responsibilities, a mother may accuse him of not being sufficiently involved.

Conclusion

Reconstituted marriages are most complex with many sources of tension. Initially there is the adaptation to each other's ways compounded by moving in and remarriage to the demands of the children. In the new family each member is required to make unwanted sacrifices. Should a wife perceive or believe the stepfather does not like the child she especially loves, or finds her children "do not like the man she loved enough to bring home," she may feel "caught in the middle." A stepfather must be attuned both to his wife's dilemmas and to the needs of children of various ages, and must expect to be disappointed in himself. He has entered a situation in which he may be viewed as an intruder or a savior. As all these demands are placed on him, he may need to balance his loyalties to the children of his first marriage with his obligations toward those of his second. What if his new wife cannot stand his child or children? How do he and all the participants achieve a balance between past and new lives?

All of this only touches on some of the challenges a stepfather experiences when he steps into a new but established family's life. In a situation requiring sensitivity and tolerance, much depends on his emotional capacity to make concessions and work out compromises. Some men do it again and again, marrying more than twice and having several sets of stepchildren. Some seem able to maintain the ongoing relationship these multiple constellations demand from within and without. How will each new wife and each new set of stepchildren place themselves, respond to past allegiances, and present demands for new attachments and future entanglements? We have much to learn!

References

Current Population Reports (1995a), Series P20-514. Washington, DC: U.S. Government Printing Office.

_____ (1995b), Series P23-180. Washington, DC: U.S. Government Printing Office.

Countertransferences
Stepfathers in Midlife and Beyond
Stanley H. Cath

A Failed Father and Stepfather

I offer here a more complex reconstruction of the deeper meanings to men of many seemingly rejuvenating but often misleading and disappointing adventures in coupling in the last half of their lives. While not gender specific, there are major differences between men and women in coping with age-specific depletion and disintegration anxieties and realities. As with divorce, a better understanding of the additional complexities involved in late-life infidelities or remarriages in both sexes, all endemic in today's world, may make life easier for patients, their families, and their therapists, especially as regards countertransferences in the latter two.

Initially, "affairs" are most often regarded by the rest of the family as "stupid" or "just a fling," even when the timing and context of this anxiety-laden and pressured search for a more perfect match is intellectually acknowledged as having something to do with the mysterious, midlife crisis. In midlife and beyond, there are many contradictions between manifest and covert behavior.

Every therapist has a conscious and unconscious set of values about his own and his patients' personal deviations from theoretical norms. Whatever conceptual framework has been added by clinicians in training, it seems common to take a more tolerant stance with patients than with family or more intimate friends. Whatever the case, strong protective affects are usually activated in therapists listening to sometimes lurid or bizarre accounts of war between the sexes and the tendency is to take sides when confronted by seemingly self-destructive or liberating infidelities. I think we have been often misguided in thinking we understand divorcing people in general by monitoring clinical cases. At other times we overestimate just what we can do to be helpful and have to shift our preset, preconscious expectations of what benefit patients derived from our therapy.

To enhance real empathic identification, in my opinion, may require us to resist premature closure on what is operative and approachable. I hope to set the stage for a broader appreciation of the significance of some of the factors related to the passage of time in step-relationships. In this wider context, midlife poses many challenges due to depleting processes of living long (Cath, 1966) as they merge almost imperceptibly into uniquely programmed, subtly ominous messages of senescence. Visible and invisible threats to external and internal integrity create a particular kind of sub-conscious somatic-psychic anxiety, which I have described elsewhere as "depletion anxiety" (Cath, 1966). Most often, this time-specific sense of impending dissolution, disorganization, and disintegration, all heralding impending death, is experienced as a form of low-grade panic. It may be compounded by living through such factors as the declinations of one's progenitors, the more sensitive awareness of fluctuations in one's own reserves, or diminished resiliency under stress. While often viewed conde-scendingly by observers as a midlife crisis, subjectively this transition may include a desperate, self-serving, last chance for restitution-appreciation, spiced with real or fantasy retribution for what life and significant others have failed to gratify.

Coping with intense affects arising from this inner perception of unrealized dreams and accumulating flaws may be quite varied, ranging from compulsive reenergizing of work, deeper immersion into personal pleasures or sports, to a completely new beginning in other arenas. Some of these efforts border on delusions of everyday life marked by magical searches for virtual fountains of youthful health. Particularly "object needy" men or women may abandon some or all established attachments for a new, seemingly less demanding and less ambivalent relationship. We find this pattern richly represented in literature. Aging protagonists often seek and sexualize an idealized child-person such as Lolita (in Nabokov's novel of the same name) or Tadzeo (in Thomas Mann's *Death in Venice*). Mrs. Robinson may find her "graduate." Others move in the opposite time frame and seek a "mature," powerful mother–father imago settled in a home with children with whom they may vicariously identify or compete as illustrated below by "Peter." Still others seem destined to spiral downhill, so well illustrated by Arthur Miller's Willy Loman or several of the cases Lansky described in *Fathers Who Fail* (1982).

Guided by this broader perspective, it is possible to take a more empathic look at the intrapsychic landscape of one middle-aged man who kept struggling to make things right, to become "number one," and who, *mirabile dictu*, compulsively chose the path of a "lesson-teaching" stepfather.

Peter

Peter reported he had been deeply bruised by two divorces and still dreamed of finding a relationship in which he could feel he was "number one." I realized later that his positive transference to me over decades of interrupted sessions was the closest he had ever come to realizing the illusion of a favored status. My unconscious countertransference may have mirrored his dream and simultaneously encouraged his quest. The am-bivalent, suggestive way he described the uniqueness of our relationship was, "You're one helluva friend, but Lollobrigida you're not!"

At 60 years of age, having "failed in two marriages," he began dating. Peter had several unsatisfactory affairs and seemed worried about "getting hitched to some old crock who will need to be cared for for the rest of her life." Unfortunately, this was a projection of his feared self-destiny in that such "high living" demanded more energy than he could muster and was further limited by highly consistent messages of failing tissue integrity, namely, mild diabetes and impotency. He also had lost several childhood friends to cancer. Adding to his emotional isolation was the fact that his two sons had hardly anything to do with him although he claimed he had many friends "to fill the gap."

Peter's struggle not to become depressed by this series of traumatic disappointments must have been conveyed to me and were consonant with my own concerns. Like many men, he found it especially painful to shelve his favorite sport of golf because of "my balance and peripheral neuropathy." He watched the progressive shaking of his hands sensing correctly he might have early-stage Parkinson's disease. He knew something about many of these age-specific declinations, for he had witnessed the depletion, diseases, aging, and deaths of his wife, grandparents, parents, father-in-law, and a host of golfing partners. One other disaster he never could forget was the death of his inebriated, youngest brother in a single-car accident.

A gregarious and successful salesman, Peter also mourned the loss of habitually being number one at work. For the first time he became somewhat phobic, hating being alone at home at night. The oldest child of an alcoholic mother and abusive father, he had always wanted "to get away from home and all those 12 f—ing kids!" Driving at 3 A.M. had always been a passion. We talked about real dangers as well as possible identification with his brother's vehicular "escape from this G-D world." But, although he enjoying talking to me "without interruptions," such introspective therapy was "hard" on him and I learned to respect his sense of vulnerability.

I know I was also taken in by his high personal coefficient of charm, his level of activity in his condition and at his age, as well as by his smiling good humor. This hypomanic presentation changed quickly after he received news his second wife had committed suicide. He could not believe she could be so desperate and not turn to him. Then there were additional insults such as the stroke of a treasured, in-law cousin who had accompanied him on golf tours and occasional binges. He deeply missed his mother-in-law (from his first marriage) as a weekly drinking partner. In his loneliness, he took to dating on the web, but "nothing took."

As a golfer and traveling salesman, his country club had been a second home. It had become a source of women and he was known as a self-confident lothario. But inwardly Peter was quite concerned about an inner unsteadiness due to his progressive nerve degeneration. More panicked than ever, he began an earnest quest for someone he laughingly described as having to accompany him "into the valley of death."

I lost track of him for several months. He returned excitedly, "engaged to Alice." "The only rub is two of her three daughters are divorced and live at home." I hoped he had returned to explore second thoughts but that was not to be. He did wonder what would happen if Alice's daughters didn't like him or took up too much of her time . . . or what if *her* diabetes acted up . . . who would go first?

He hesitated enough to observe, "I've pulled myself together and started looking again cause I knew I deserve a better deal!" But in a few months, "liking the way we treat each other," he decided Alice was "Mrs. Right" and the daughters were no threat. Within three more months he realized he had miscalculated the depth of the girls' resentment as they resisted his attempts to charm and buy them. Soon, he asked if he could bring Alice into a couple's session. But she resisted this and asked to talk to me alone. Not surprisingly, she knew her husband "could not tolerate being in second place to my daughters, much less anyone else! And they do come first! What did I ever see in him? I think he drinks too much. This marriage is over!" Despite my efforts to open up his way of defeating himself by demanding to be first when others clearly had priority, Peter was soon ejected from the house never to return.

Alice died of cancer within a year of their divorce. On the anniversary of her death, one of the saddest moments in his life occurred. Visiting Alice's grave on a cold, gray Sunday morning, he "bumped into the three girls . . . they just turned away from me . . . just as my kids did . . . I could have killed them!" Unable to thaw their coldness, he said, "I felt utterly alone, without a soul who cared whether I lived or died! It's so humiliating!"

Despite this highly charged atmosphere of defeat, shame, and aloneness, begging, I thought, for self-exploration, the trauma was soon brushed aside, as was any guilt over Peter's murderous wishes toward his stepchildren. "Those women got rid of me just like they did their father!" In his intolerance for the affect of shame, he reminded me of the protagonist in Woody Allen's film *Crimes and Misdemeanors* and of Willy Loman in *Death of a Salesman*. All through this limited therapy, I had to deal with the feelings of watching an aging man, unable to tolerate frustration and terrified of being abandoned, unable to assume responsibility and persistently ending up in a cul-de-sac. In my mind I knew socially I would have shunned this man for his naked braggadocio, his self-preoccupation, and interpersonal scotomata. He rarely listened to anyone. I consoled myself with the thought that his courage in venturing into a new relationship attested to the positive life-sustaining power of being dyadically alive even if triadically doomed to failure. From a simplistic point of view, he failed to deal with the intensity of unresolved competitiveness with children.

When losing, he would experience paranoid regressions with the final consequence, that is, of living and dying alone.

After his third divorce, we met sporadically and superficially on his terms as "good friends." No longer megalomanic, Peter, looking and feeling much older, lived alone for several depressive years until cardiovascular complications took their toll. His last attempt at being number one involved a nursing aide from a home-care agency. His two sons could not understand his attachment to a motherly caretaker except as an "affair," and they were furious when she was left a small gift of money in his will.

Discussion

Almost every chapter in this volume documents how complex the process of becoming a "step" may be, but usually without considering the progressive limitations inherent in the aging process. Roth found that the prefix *step* derives from an Old German verb, *bestepen*, "to bereave." To this definition, I would add the concept that the failure to recognize and modulate sufficient aggression toward sibs may last a lifetime and lead to serious interpersonal problems, especially in stepfathers when maternal resources are strained. Add alcoholism to the mix and the prognosis is poor.

Beyond midlife we need consider the impact of inevitable biological depletion and psychological insults in those whose concerted efforts at adult restitution have been limited and self-defeating. The thesaurus does not emphasize the heartbreaking realization that when an elder "steps" into an established family, he may be still preoccupied by deep and long-held wishes of how life was supposed to have been lived and what he still thinks he deserves. For many unconscious reasons, Peter failed to heed the warnings of his past and once again could not permit overlapping triads to work. While many stepfathers suffer their reactions to established gratification–discipline patterns in silence, others, like my patient, become critics of the "spoiled" alliances. With the shame-inducing rejection of their best efforts, they transform themselves into the stereotypical "evil" stepfather. When the rivalry for mother became overt and Peter was exposed as "jealous and petty," he responded with, "If accused, why not be it? . . . They don't deserve any better."

It may well be that, under such circumstances, some men become physically abusive, as I feared he might do. It was as if he were trying to force his new wife and her offspring to recognize his brute power, his rightness, rather than be dismissed as insignificant or placed in second place again. Another stepfather described this situation as "better bad than dead."

References

Cath, S. (1966), Beyond depression: The depleted state. *Can. Psychiat. Assn. J.*, 11:329–339.

Lansky, M. (1992), *Fathers Who Fail: Shame and Psychopathology in the Family System*. Hillsdale, NJ: The Analytic Press.

The Vantage Points of
Two Stepsisters in Midlife

Stanley H. Cath

An old maxim is that every child has a different parent. Sometimes stepchildren have very different mothers and fathers or combinations thereof. One of my analysands, Ann, gave the following account of an unusual family constellation. Her parents had "checked out on each other" (divorced) when Ann was in the eighth grade. Her father soon remarried a widow with a four-year-old daughter, her "stepsister," Louise. Growing up in two separate remarried households, it was easy to play at seeming affectionate but still remain distant and uninvolved. Ann described this as "sidestepping, a special kind of pas-de-deux choreographed for stepkids only."

A few years later, a series of unfortunate circumstances led to Louise's moving into Ann's minifamily. As teens, they seemed to share the idealized image of Ann's mother as a generous, loving, engaging, and encompassing person. The step-relationship between them had been unusually well tolerated, as both girls tended to be affectionate and tried very hard not to offend. Both fathers and stepfathers had been relatively distant, professionally preoccupied, figures. While the transitions between families had been difficult, they were not recalled as especially traumatic.

Some 20 years after her second, seemingly better marriage, however, Ann's mother died of cancer. As fate decreed, by midlife both stepsisters had married, all the parents had died, and both had children. When they found they were living in the same small community, they were delighted. But over several years their visits dwindled to sporadic. Both expressed regrets that their children, who seemed to play so well together in the past, now rarely had contact. Ann, by now 44 years of age, reflected on the state of affairs:

"When we do hang out, I feel such an anxious dread. On one level, I feel Louise is my closest living relative. For many, many years, though not biologically related we shared a common past, in part a common family. Why should she make me feel so uncomfortable; I've nothing to feel guilty about. It's a new sensation, like I stand alone, and feel scared. I find myself thinking about it obsessively. Then I realized it has something to do with her new take on my mother. I don't remember her feeling that way before! Could we have lived in the same house? Did we really have the same mother for 20 years?

"I felt so weird until last Christmas when my cousin told me she found being with Louise had become nerve-racking because her hostility to my mom spills all over and seems inappropriate. She wondered how could I be so dense as not to see it? I said either I had blinders on or it has something to do with her having teenage kids, but we all have that . . . maybe it's a midlife change. Oh my God, we sure remember a different mom. Louise has developed a strange compulsion to let everyone know that she had been the teenage stepchild who wasn't wanted.

"That was not the way I remembered it nor did my cousin who remembered my mother as never withholding anything from anyone. Naturally, Louise had to have a very different mom from me, and a stepmother, okay, but it never seemed a big issue then. I just always knew and accepted she envied my closeness with my mom . . . and with my stepfather, her dad as well. You know I envied myself! I know I just didn't feel cheated, whereas she did. But, why do I feel so put off now? I could take it then. When she bounces all this off me now I feel shaken up, bewildered . . . and I feel cheated . . . as if she succeeded in making me feel like she did.

"Oh, there is one thing she doesn't tell people. Before she came to us, her mom had been battling with brain cancer for years and was really unable to give her much. I had never thought of it as related but she was hit twice by the same whammy, two moms with cancer. I didn't think of that, and whatever her mom did give . . . Louise never gives her credit for it. She paints my mother with the same brush as hers, as not caring for her . . . so she feels deprived both by her birth mother and her stepmom. Oh, and by me! I feel as if she is reproaching me and is critical of my kids."

After a long pause, as if gathering all this together, Ann said softly, "and she is about the same age as when her mother got cancer." Some time later, she reported:

"I finally confronted Louise and told her that is not the way I remember how my mom was with me or her, and neither did my cousin. She didn't seem to hear it . . . at first . . . and I sensed she still wanted to punish me by convincing me of my mother's inability to give. She gave as an example that mom never helped her with her dancing lessons. I told her that's not what I remember because mom had been a dance teacher and that is what she did for both of us. I said the difference in our ages must have made a big difference because in the two years before she died, mom lost a lot of strength. Then I blurted out, 'Mom checked out on us because she had to, not because she wanted to . . . and we shouldn't check out on each other!' She said she understood that but still seemed hurt. I said I didn't know where all the hurt was coming from and changed the subject to how we are all anxious about growing older and what might happen to us like it did to our parents . . . that I was worried about breast cancer too! Was she worried about brain cancer? Will we pass the gene on to our kids? I think she heard that and it got easier.

"I know it was unfair now . . . maybe there are other things too. Louise was left alone with mother when mom was in so much pain. Maybe we did take things for granted. It is all so sad . . . [tears]; I was trying to hold on to the good times, they have been so important to me. I can't see my parents as negatively as she does, or for that matter as most of my friends do. God knows I tried to be the best daughter when mom was sick, but I had to finish college. . . . I told myself it was what she wanted. Funny thing about school . . . I remember doing things so grudgingly . . . but I got through. When the time came to take SATs, I didn't do well and had to take a summer course. . . . Mom was horrified. Just not working hard enough, she said . . . maybe I was angrier than I realized about that at the time. I guess what I did was fairly normal . . . I was still a kid and had other things on my mind. I think now maybe what I did to make up for my lack of attention to Mom was to try to be a good big sister to Louise, 'cause when she became a teenager she needed a lot of looking after. We wrote a lot. It was an unconscious exchange. I took her on as my responsibility and kind of hoped she would take on mom, and she did. It made for some kind of bond between us, but it never was verbalized very much."

I noted how difficult it is to take care of a sick parent and how differently adults respond to the demands for changing their life course. It all reminded me of Robert Lincoln's situation. After his father's assassination, he found himself responsible for a highly disturbed mother he felt had to be committed to an asylum. If we can judge from his later refusal to be buried with the rest of the family in their crypt in Springfield, Ohio, he probably harbored deep resentments about being chosen by fate to fulfill this role.

Ann listened carefully and responded, "Maybe that's why I see myself as standing alone, especially when my sister is angry with mom. Something makes me uncomfortable because I have always felt best when I fill in the blanks for people. I provide, care, nurture, and give information, whatever people need . . . I try to fill in the blanks. My husband often asks me, 'Ann, why can't you stop acting like that? You don't have to be on hand for everyone.' He calls me the Earth Mother. I tell him he's jealous, but I think he's on to something."

I asked, "Did you notice you called Louise your sister? Could you have promoted her because even an Earth Mother may need someone to lessen her fears of standing alone? Can it be your discomfort represents some uncertainties of what to feel if people are not in a pas-de-deux and sometimes felt angry and cheated?"

Ann answered, "I know that's right. When I was working on our taxes the other night, I thought to myself, I am a decent person. I don't want to cheat. But I did think about it. All of a sudden I felt down in the dumps. I remembered how my stepfather had been angry when Mom got cancer, because she no longer was able to do his taxes. Another blank space I tried to fill. I took an accounting course. We all were feeling angry and cheated and took some of it out on each other. I still don't think I feel as betrayed as my stepsister or so much out of the circle that she thinks everyone else was in, but part of me now wonders why I could not have seen where she was coming from? That mom couldn't be there for us meant we had to do it ourselves . . . she couldn't help it . . . no one could!"

The Death of a Stepfather

A Funeral That Cuts All Ties

Stanley H. Cath

David, my 40-year-old patient, lost his stepfather John just three years after the latter's third marriage to Mae. In contrast to the widow, David had known John for almost half of his life and was the logical person chosen to speak at the funeral. Reflecting on this event, he said, "My new stepmother was only that in name. There was little affection between us. Given a choice we both would keep away from each other. Still, it is my lot to make up a list of all John's relatives including her family, 'the steps' as I listed them, and all the friends from both sides. I also have to make the actual funeral arrangements."

Then he observed poignantly, "I'm really tired of throwing dirt on one of my parents. David was only my stepfather but he meant a lot to me. The only one left to be a grandmother for my kids is an oddball stepmother come lately, one I don't like, can't tolerate, or feel any emotional attachment to."

Laughing sardonically, he added, "I still slept okay last night, but I had a dream that I was in a funeral parlor in front of a casket. It turned into a boxing ring with Mae in the corner and my stepsister [Mae's teenage daughter] in the other corner and somehow I enjoyed it. I think they both deserve each other because all they ever do is box and fight and now that he is gone they can really get at each other. Fathers, oh I mean stepfathers too, do dilute things, don't you know? Then I had to go to the halfway house and tell my crazy sister our stepfather was no more. She insisted our mom and dad were not dead! Despite heavy meds, she really fluctuates in and out of reality. The problem is when should I insist? And I still haven't solved the problem of explaining her situation, not just being psychotic but what it means to have such a screwed-up family, that is, to my kids. Despite whatever I've told them, they look scared when they visit her. But so am I!

"At the moment I'm so tired of lawyers too. I just finished two years with my mother's estate and now my stepfather's . . . it's too much, just more dirt! Speaking of dirt, I had a vision in the cemetery after everyone had left. I imagined shoving Mae into the coffin and shoveling dirt on her. Hah! Not so tired of shoveling dirt after all. I'm really tired of being diplomatic, so kind and understanding to people I don't feel connected to. It reminds me of a week before I had a similar fantasy of bumping off one of my aunts. I guess I can be mean, but I just try not to show it. Yet, I wasn't mean to my stepdad . . . I was there for him as he got old and weak. Maybe it was because he didn't need to be institutionalized like my mother and sister. He really was there for me for so many years. But in the end he did his own strange things. Suddenly he became religious on me although he had nothing to do with religion all his life. His will says cremation but his new wife wants him buried . . . she got him into her church. . . . So how should he be buried? There is so much I cannot say and cannot express, there is so much I cannot respect him for. People think he was a good grandfather, but I really knew how he felt about some of his grandchildren. I try to focus on our relationship but to be executor of my stepfather's estate on top of my father's estate is too much, to deal with all these people most of whom I hardly know. I thought it was the worst thing my father could have done . . . to make me the executor of his will with my screwed-up sister. I always feel caught up in other peoples lives . . . I wish I could be doing something for someone whose life was more together, more respectable rather than so mixed up . . . someone to follow in the future. What can you expect from steps like these . . . after the funeral . . . outside of the will . . . death cuts all ties."

Clinical Dimensions

Stepfathers

Clinical Explorations

Robert M. Galatzer-Levy

Contemporary rhetoric favors the idea that stepfamilies, and many other variations on family structure, should be readily accepted and valued in the same fashion as nuclear families. Unfortunately, this rhetoric does not tell us how this is to be accomplished psychologically, particularly by members of these "new" families. Standard narratives of development, whether embodied in psychoanalytic theory, conscious and unconscious personal stories, creative works, or the mass media, describe complex paternal roles. By definition, in such narratives, the stepfather is an anomaly, a new figure whose place in the psychological world is largely defined in relationship to the absent father. The very existence of a stepfather marks the father's absence.

It is no wonder, then, that children, stepfathers, and other family members are challenged to find an appropriate psychological and interpersonal place for the stepfather. In this complex situation we expect solutions to reflect issues such as the ongoing intrapsychic dynamics of the child and stepfather, the reasons for the presence of a stepfather, the family dynamics of the old and newly constructed family, and community expectations about the stepfather's role (Coleman, 1994; Kurdek, 1994; Popenoe, 1996).

The idea that a child could ordinarily expect to reach majority in the care of two biological parents is new (Mason, 1994). Limited life expectancies well into the 20th century meant that it was common for a child to lose a parent to death before the end of adolescence with the result that many children had the experience of being raised in families from which one of the biological parents was absent. Perhaps because it is so new the normative narrative of the nuclear family is extremely powerful among Americans, so that members of families trying to psychologically integrate their family structure are often left with limited guidelines. Thus stepfathers and stepchildren commonly find themselves in a position of attempting to create new, satisfactory stories about how families will operate. Studies of populations of stepfamilies show that this effort commonly fails, especially when stepfamilies are formed after children enter school and more especially when the children are adolescent (Hetherington and Jodl, 1994). On the other hand, many stepfamilies function well psychologically.

By looking in depth at the psychology of three boys, each of whom responded differently to his stepfather, I intend to suggest a hypothesis regarding the psychological freedom that allowed two youngsters to benefit from the experience of having a stepfather, while a third youngster seems to have been impacted negatively by the experience.

In this essay I briefly describe analytic experiences with three adolescent boys for whom stepfathers played a central developmental role. All three boys experienced their parents' divorce and for all three the divorce and its aftermath played major roles in their subsequent psychological development (Wallerstein and Johnston, 1990). While each of the boys was deeply interested in the father and a relationship with the father, and each formed paternal transferences which were the subject of analysis, the very different meanings of their current image of their fathers and stepfathers produced strikingly different transference configurations and relations within the family. Though not providing systematic data on the impact of divorce and stepfathering these cases do give another means to examine observations derived from more superficial but more systematic study (Amato, 1994; Zill, 1994). They also provide a means of enriching the emerging picture of the psychological role of fathers in normal and disturbed development (Greenacre, 1963; Leonard, 1966; Hurn, 1969; Mitscherlich, 1969; Levi, Stierlin, and Savard, 1973; Brody and Brody, 1978; Parke, 1981; Cath, Gurwitt, and Ross, 1982; Herzog, 1982; Ross, 1982a, b; Blos, 1984; Lincoln, 1984; Lohr et al., 1989).

Case 1

Jay, whose parents' marriage ended when he was four, sought treatment as a college student because pervasive obsessional thinking interfered with feeling authentically engaged in school, play, or relationships. The haunting question of whether his actions reflected his wishes or an attempt to be a "good boy," acting as someone in his life position should, led to endless, tense ruminations.

Despite doing well academically and being attractive to both women and men Jay rarely experienced pleasure. The beginnings of pleasure were often experienced as signs of danger that would tempt him to act inauthentically. Whenever he began to enjoy something, he feared later realizing that he had been tricked into doing something he did not want. When others, be they teachers, friends, or girls who became interested in him, attempted to interest Jay in things that might reasonably anticipate would provide him pleasure Jay became tense, angry, and felt exploited. Whether it be an academic subject, a companionable activity, or sexual intercourse Jay superficially complied with what he experienced as demands while resenting what he experienced as efforts to make him untrue to himself.

Analysis seemed to Jay to be a pointless task, a continuation of his unending and destructive self questioning. However, Jay stayed with it, all the while seeing his compliance with the implicit analytic expectation that he continue as another example of his giving way to a dishonest force that harmed him while ostensibly offering him help. The analyst was experienced as ineffective and helpless in the face of the patient's neurosis, much as Jay felt himself to be helpless and ineffective in the face of felt demands. Indeed, as every interpretation was treated as wrong, obvious or ill-timed, the analyst felt increasingly helpless and angry. The treatment felt like a Sisyphian task. The analyst often wondered whether Jay should not be encouraged to make good on his threat to quit, but even tentative confrontations about the dissonance between Jay's opinion of the analysis and his very regular attendance met with clear indications of Jay's intention to stay and his anger at the analyst who forced him to do so.

When, after an extended period of analysis, Jay asked to try medication, the analyst prescribed fluoxitine, which, though it seemed to the analyst to decrease Jay's agitation, was reported by Jay to have little subjective effect. Soon the medication became something that the analyst had seduced Jay into taking. The decreased agitation was taken as evidence that the analyst was trying to help Jay settle for a second-rate life and side effects of delayed ejaculation and weight gain as proof that the analyst was willing to "destroy" him.

Jay's theory of his own neurosis was that he was filled with pent-up rage and pain over the loss of his father. This loss resulted when his parents separated and his mother began living with another man who shortly became his stepfather. Jay variously believed that his cure would lie in being allowed to fully express the feelings that he associated with that time, or in finding a substitute for his lost father. Yet the concrete expression of both of these longings seemed impossible—the former, because he would need to become violent and destructive in the office; the latter, because it was associated with frightened sexual fantasies about the male analyst in which the analyst would, by anally penetrating Jay, make him aware of the analyst's manliness and share that manliness with Jay.

A prolonged negative therapeutic reaction emerged. The patient believed that because the analyst had interpreted and encouraged the expression of these fantasies, the analyst wanted sexually to seduce him, and to "ruin my life" by arranging for ever more severe suffering for Jay. For example, the analyst's interpretations were often regarded as efforts to force Jay to "think," a painful and futile process that left Jay more confused and upset than he had been before the interpretation.

References to Jay's desires for food, elimination, or sexual gratification were similarly seen as attempts either to confuse him or to force him into activities about which he was uncertain as to whether he wanted to do them or not. Sometimes Jay would come to sessions hungry or feeling an urge to urinate. When the analyst responded to Jay's statements that these feelings were so strong that he could think of nothing else by wondering if Jay might prefer to get a snack from the vending machine in the building's lobby or to use the wash room, Jay became enraged at these attempts to "confuse" him. Even comments on Jay's most direct and explicit statements of homoerotic interests were understood as attempts to make him gay.

Jay insisted that what he needed from the analyst was straightforward and elementary and often demanded that the analyst admit that he was incompetent so that Jay could get on with his life in some other way. At the same time, indications that the analyst was uncertain or questioned his own capacity to help Jay led to terrified clinging to the analytic situation and increased fantasies of sexually submitting to the analyst. On three occasions in response to the analyst's vacations, Jay "quit" the analysis, only to return after a few weeks angry at himself and the analyst who enslaved him in this futile effort. The enslavement was based on Jay's desperate need for help and his wish to "believe in" the analyst.

In the countertransference the analyst felt variously sorry for Jay, for himself as incompetent and inadequate and helpless to do very much. While the historical constructions discussed further on supported the analyst's belief that Jay's difficulties in analysis did not originate completely from the analyst's ineptitude, the analyst often felt profoundly uncomfortable, worrying that perhaps Jay's claim that the analyst was using the idea of transference as an excuse for the analyst's ineptitude might be true. The analyst usually waited longer to make interpretations than he ordinarily would have in other analyses, until the material seemed to him absolutely blatant, primarily as a means to reassure himself that he was not behaving in the way Jay accused him. Jay, sensing that the analyst had ideas that he did not share, took this behavior as evidence that the analyst was lazy and unwilling to put forward the necessary effort to make the analysis successful. The analyst often felt guilty, as though he were, in fact, harming the young man.

Jay's vivid recollections of his stepfather supported the idea that he was engaged in a transference in which the analyst was experienced as like the stepfather. Manifestly, the stepfather was deeply concerned for Jay's welfare and education. He remained involved with Jay after he and Jay's mother divorced when Jay was a young adolescent. He had strong opinions about how Jay should be raised, what educational measures would benefit the boy's well being, and how Jay should conduct himself as an older adolescent.

The stepfather's attitude toward Jay's father was particularly troubling to Jay. He thought it was appropriate that the boy be upset by the end of visits with his father, but set strict limits on the duration of this upset, forbidding Jay to cry after an hour following the separation. Similarly, he believed it useful for the boy's development that he should engage in numerous tasks that the boy found tedious. Protests were met with stern lectures about how the tasks were good for the youngster. Jay responded to his stepfather not so much with rebellion as disgust. A minor physical defect of the stepfather's preoccupied Jay and made his "skin crawl."

The work ethic values with which the stepfather attempted to inculcate Jay were not simply onerous but had specific meaning for the youngster. They sharply contrasted with his father's values, which focused on being true to one's self even at the expense of economic stability. Though not clearly formulated by Jay until the matter was discussed in the analysis, Jay had a theory of his parents' divorce that seemed quite plausible. He thought that his mother had abandoned his father because of the fear that his father's focus on self-realization would make him economically irresponsible and leave the family destitute.

The divorce of his stepfather and mother both relieved and distressed Jay who, at the same time, was glad to be rid of his nemesis, appalled that his mother was involved with an even more unsatisfactory man from his point of view and, more subtly, was left with an intense, uncomfortable feeling that was gradually formulated during the analysis as distress at the idea that no man could "conquer" his mother.

As this transference was further explored and related to his experience of his stepfather, the theme of disappointed rage as opposed to competition with the stepfather emerged with increasing clarity. The boy did not so much want to compete with and beat the analyst-stepfather, as to admire him but felt enraged that the analyst failed to provide him with an opportunity for idealization. Further exploration of these ideas suggested that both the transference to the analyst and feelings about the stepfather related to disappointment with Jay's father, whom Jay saw as having given up or acted foolishly in the conduct of his life. Shaping his contempt for all important men—stepfathers, analyst, and himself—was the image of the weak, inept father unable to maintain a relationship with Jay's mother or to provide for her needs.

Jay's parents' separation and Jay's mother's choice of his career-oriented stepfather seemed to have been precipitated by the father's exploring the idea of leaving a stable, remunerative job to take up a career in the arts, a career which had never taken off. Jay increasingly noticed that this failure was, in large part, the result of father's characterologic difficulties, manifest as a process of unending training and preparation for pursuing a career rather than actual pursuit of that career. Jay's conscious image of his father shifted from seeing him as an absolutely wonderful and sympathetic figure to viewing him as unsympathetic and impotent. At the same time, Jay's increasingly intense, almost hypochrondriacal fears about himself emerged with clarity. In particular, he was convinced that his penis was very small, even though in his very limited sexual experiences, two girls with whom he had been involved had chosen to comment on its large size. While consciously the patient grew more angry and disparaging with the analyst, he became increasingly sensitive to interruptions in the analytic work. Weekends, and even more, longer vacations seemed nearly intolerable to him. He often left messages on the analyst's voice mail to inform the analyst of how painful his life was and asked for help only to return to the Monday hour thinking of quitting the "useless" analysis. Longer interruptions often precipitated strong desires and plans to quit the analysis altogether. Attempts at interpersonal relationships were dominated by shame as he believed that if he were to present himself honestly, people would be repelled by him, but that putting up an adequate social front required such strenuous effort that interactions with other people involved excruciating effort.

This feeling was closely linked to the compliance that had been so clearly manifest early in the analysis. Metaphors about toilet training and the equation of authentic expression with the freedom to defecate when and where one chose now came together with ideas of being tortured by the analyst and the equation of all potentially pleasurable activities with painful, forced evacuation, to suggest a history in which images of toileting were central. The analyst "forced ideas" out of Jay's mind; ejaculation could only occur when Jay strained to force semen out of him; aspects of the patient's family history made it appear extremely likely that his toilet training was actually completed at a time when his mother was under very great pressure to accomplish it. While mother's current personality strongly suggested that she would likely have been very uncomfortable with the messiness of babies and diapers, images suggestive of toilet training became a central metaphor for the patient's sense of a depleted self. In order to maintain a relationship to others, he must put aside his own will and desire entirely and painfully comply with their demands. Within this context, fathers failed him in two ways. Being too weak to stand up to the mother, they were neither allies nor models in solving the dilemma of maintaining relationships while being one's own self. Additionally, the stepfather became a displacement figure for the demanding mother of toilet training.

Developmentally, Jay's difficulties could be traced to his early relationship with his profoundly anxious self-preoccupied mother who desperately needed to control the boy lest she feel overwhelmed. The ordinary processes by which an infant's experience of himself, his own affects and desires, emerges through interaction with his caretakers (Stern, 1977, 1985, 1988, 1989a, b) had been profoundly distorted so that Jay's sense of his own wishes and desires was permeated with doubt about their origins.

The role of Jay's stepfather in the boy's development was, thus, highly complex and very negatively toned. Jay's later development was significantly shaped by his tendency to form stepfather transferences to virtually anyone, including his analyst, who might seek to influence him. His unconscious vision of his stepfather was as an amalgam of that which was destructive of his own will, destructive of his idealized relationship to his father, an oedipal competitor. The image of the stepfather appears to have arisen in part as a defense against hostile feelings toward each of his parents associated with both narcissistic rage at his mother who failed to support his early development and made intolerable demands of him, oedipal competition with his father, and rage about his father's departure. Thus the stepfather came to embody all that was wrong with the world in Jay's eyes. Perceiving any "new" figure in his life as another edition of the stepfather Jay experienced virtually all contacts that called for emotional investment of any kind as contact with this destructive elemental force in his life.

Case 2

At 15, Jim was as successful as a youngster could be. Intellectually gifted, he was an outstanding student; athletically talented, he starred on varsity teams; socially graceful, he was well liked by peers and adults; amorously able, his precocious relationship with his girlfriend was admired by his fellow students.

While maintaining many of these capacities, most of the pleasure in exercising his abilities seem to disappear abruptly following a schoolyard fight in which Jim, having easily bested the other boy, saw the fear in this youngster's eyes and felt deeply anxious himself.[1] Jim ended his relationship with the girl despite continuing to feel tender toward her, found it difficult to be aggressive in athletics, continued to perform exceptionally in school, but found the work uninteresting and, while continuing to be much liked by those with whom he interacted, felt little pleasure in the interactions.

In Jim's family, referral to a psychoanalyst seemed "natural" in the situation. Jim had grown up in a world of brilliant people many of whom had positive experiences with analysts and analysis. Both his father and stepfather were internationally renowned intellectuals, and though his mother had not continued her formal education beyond college, in Jim's opinion, she was brighter than either of her husbands. Jim's parents' marriage had ended as the result of his father's compulsive promiscuity and preoccupation with pornography, which was regarded by the rest of the family as a "tragic illness." Mother and stepfather were both in treatment with psychoanalysts, as was a stepsibling, so that the endorsement

---

[1]This episode occurred at a time when such fighting was not unusual and not the subject of adult intervention that would occur today.

and admiration of psychoanalysis within the family was extraordinary, except by the boy's father.

The father, who had managed in some ways to be extraordinarily successful despite a profoundly traumatic adolescence, was anticipated by the mother to be unsupportive of the analysis. Neither manifestly in favor of, or opposed to it, but certainly unwilling to support it financially. Whatever the father's actual attitude in this matter (there was substantial evidence to suggest the correctness of mother's perceptions about it), mother saw little point in challenging father's statement that he did not have the wherewithal to support all but a fraction of the cost of the analysis. Similarly, she said, that despite his stepfather's extensive engagement in Jim's life, it was not the stepfather's responsibility to pay for the analysis. The bottom line was that if the analyst wished to work analytically with her son, he would have to accept a substantially reduced fee, which he did. Thus, in the very setup of the analytic situation, a major configuration of the boy's life was repeated in which it was arranged that he have a significant relationship with a man, but that the boundaries and nature of that relationship remain imperfectly defined.

Jim's relationship to both his father and stepfather was rich and complex. The boy greatly admired and enjoyed involvement in his father's professional activities, and the father reciprocated by finding ways to involve Jim in them. However, in other areas, the father was startlingly unavailable. He responded to any conversation that hinted at addressing emotional issues by becoming somnolent, often literally falling asleep in mid-sentence. It was not uncommon when father took the boy to dinner, that his son would have to wake him up at the completion of the meal.

In contrast, the stepfather was a bundle of "psychoanalytically informed" affectivity who would angrily and explosively tell his sons and stepsons as he retired to the bedroom with Jim's mother, that he knew they wanted to kill him and have the mother for their own pleasure, but that he was the one who now had power. Not surprisingly, angry competitive interchanges were the bread and butter of Jim's interaction with his stepfather. Yet, though rarely vowed, their mutual affection and respect was evident even as the patient recounted rageful conversations that parodied Greek drama and psychoanalytic text.

As usual, the central transferences of Jim's analysis involved paternal figures. The problem was, which paternal figure? Was the angry, competitive father manifest in the transference representative of the boy's oedipal fantasies when his parents were separated, experiences and fantasies involving his manifestly competitive stepfather, or representative of awareness of the analyst's sense of having been placed in a position where the boy displayed his prowess to the analyst who felt taken advantage of? The situation was not simply that transference configurations were overdetermined and that each of these factors contributed to the manifest transference, though this was certainly the case. Instead, it became apparent that the image of the tripartate father served a defensive function in which as the boy clarified feelings toward one male figure, he immediately diluted the insight by switching the fantasy to involve a different father. He seemed to come supplied with an ever ready displacement for feelings that he might have toward any of three paternal figures, and this ever available displacement partly stood in the way of working out what he felt toward each of them (in this he differed from the previous patient who used a similar configuration to support splitting defenses).

As this situation was clarified, the use of such displacement became less extensive and internal images of the two fathers emerged with increased clarity. Additionally, the person of the analyst emerged as an important figure for identification. Images of his two fathers served different and complementary functions in Jim's psychological life. Jim's biological father remained a figure around whom struggles concerning ambivalent idealization were played out. After some struggle, for example, the patient chose to follow a career similar to his father's with which were mixed certain features of his analyst's interests. At the same time, the patient felt angry contempt for his father's impoverished interpersonal life and, in particular, for his incapacity to enter into a satisfactory marriage. Competitive feelings were largely directed at the stepfather and worked in relationship to him so that, for example, the patient felt interest in choosing a career that would allow him to become wealthier than the stepfather, primarily to demonstrate that he could do so.

Ultimately, Jim developed relationships with his father, stepfather, and analyst in ways that had great depth and served Jim well. Despite the divorce of his mother and stepfather, Jim maintained a close relationship with his troubled but psychologically rich stepfather in a manner that included deep mutual care and respect. Similarly, despite his father's limitations Jim was able to engage the father on an intellectual level that both men found pleasurable. After terminating his analysis in his early 20s, Jim remained in contact with his analyst, returning periodically for periods of therapy as he faced various crises. Despite great talent and substantial success in his career, finding a definitive professional identity was difficult for Jim. Remarkably, in his 30s he was able to find a career path that was very well suited to his talents and interests that combined elements of the ideals of his father, his stepfather, and his analyst.

An interesting feature of Jim's personality emerged in his early 20s after the termination of his analysis. Jim had an unusual capacity to involve himself with mentors. Based partly on his very substantial talents Jim was unusually able to attract and engage in sustained, mutually rewarding relationships with male mentors. These relationships appear to have been deeper and less ambivalent from both sides than such relationships ordinarily are (Hanson, 1984; Irvine, 1985; Brefach, 1986; Walker, 1986; Fagenson, 1988; Bushardt, 1991).

Despite the problematic nature of some of his relationship with his stepfather and his use of relationships to multiple father figures as a means to defend against full engagement in some conflictual elements of his relationship with each of these figures, Jim seems ultimately, with the help of analysis, to have used the several relationships with father figures to promote and enrich his own development. Rather than losing a father, he seems to have gained additional fathers through his parents' divorce and, by virtue of having worked through the complexities of relationships to paternal figures, to have developed an unusual capacity to enrich his life through deep relationships with such figures.

Case 3

John began his analysis at age 13 when his parents were divorcing. Always a talented, but somewhat inhibited boy whose "sweet nature" had made him a favorite with adults, John's inhibitions intensified in response to his parents' breakup. He felt depressed and lost interest in school and extra-curricular activities. Friendships and the beginning of heterosexual interests waned. He responded to his parents' separation passively and attempted to avoid difficulty. He tried to make the limited time he spent with his much-loved father into pleasant, stressless outings; he left the room whenever he saw indications that his mother might become mani-festly upset and retreated into the bathroom whenever his older sister gave him "a hard time."

Both because of his substantial distress and his compliant character, John readily entered analysis. What limited resistance there was to begin-ning treatment was manifest in the parents, though this resistance resulted from John's actions in not informing them of the profound level of distress that caused him to want analysis. This process was, once recognized, readily and effectively interpretable to John. This analysis, which I have described elsewhere (Galatzer-Levy, 1985), proceeded unusually smoothly, with particular clear delineations and working through of character issues of passivity and compliance, identification with his mother, who was perceived as masochistic, and anxiety about competitive wishes that centered around images of the father as particularly vulnerable.

During the third year of John's analysis, his mother met and became engaged to a man who had many of the father's virtues but was superfi-cially more aggressive and outgoing. At the time, John had not only maintained a good relationship with his father, but their relationship had been greatly enriched as John became less fearful of his own aggressivity and increasingly recognized that his father was a more effective and psychologically potent individual than he had thought him to be. Though in certain ways limited because John spent little time with his father except as a visitor, John's relationship with his father appeared to have been richer following the divorce than when his father resided at home.

John's relationship to his stepfather was characterized by an enjoyable idealization. There was indeed much to admire in this effective, intellectually gifted, and civic-minded man. In addition, the stepfather in several superficial ways resembled the analyst. As termination was considered from time to time, John would reassure himself that he could tolerate the loss of the analyst because the father might in some way substitute for him. In particular, John had often contrasted the analyst's Jewish affectivity with his father's Anglo-Saxon reserve. Now the stepfather was seen as another source for Jewish humor and emotionality. In fact, the stepfather, who was a skillful raconteur was seen as having these good qualities to an even greater extent than the analyst.

Uncertain about the depth of commitment of both his stepfather and himself, John sometimes debated the extent to which he wanted to engage with his stepfather. He sometimes worried that he was attempting to take a place with his stepfather that went beyond the bounds of their expectable relationship. For example, he was concerned that direct expression of his warm admiration for his stepfather might be seen as inappropriate or awkward because their relationship was so brief and they had, in a sense, been thrown together without choosing each other. John met this difficulty in a manner that was new for him, while still integrating his characterological avoidance of confrontation. With great social grace he not only spoke of his admiration and wish for involvement with his stepfather but at the same time acknowledged that his stepfather could reasonably not welcome the full intensity of his feeling. Far from reflecting neurotic anxiety, this concern addressed what appeared to be a realistic ambiguity in their relationship in a fashion that promised to lead to its resolution. John was able to understand and tolerate that his stepfather, a very busy man with several children by a previous marriage might have little emotional space in which to engage with a stepson. Fortunately, the stepfather welcomed John's overtures and the relationship developed.

John recognized that the relationship with his stepfather reflected important psychological needs and processes including displacements from the analytic process, ideas that the relationship might substitute for limitations in his relationship with his father, fantasies of competition with his father, identification with his mother, and aspects of ordinary adolescent idealization of mentors. Yet, in addition to these dimensions of the relationship, it seemed that John and his stepfather created a new sort of bond that did not fit neatly into preexisting categories but rather reflected a vision that they cocreated. This new relationship apparently enriched and pleased them both. It seemed to support, rather than interfere, with John's relationship to both his father and his analyst.

The new relationship that John and his stepfather formed is consistent with an idea that Bertram Cohler and I (Galatzer-Levy and Cohler, 1993) develop. We argue that normal development is *not* characterized by a diminished need for external supports for the self. Instead, the apparent diminution in this need results from an increased capacity to find multiple sources of support from individuals, institutions, and cultural constructions. As a result the loss of any particular support has less impact and there is greater potential for the enrichment that comes through multiple important relationships. I believe John and his stepfather were engaged in this type of activity with the additional feature that they were creating a new form of relationship specific to their own needs and situation.

Discussion

Our three case vignettes confirm an impression that the experience of having a stepfather is highly contingent on the situation and the psychology of those involved. Stepfathers may seem to be, as Jay said, "the devil living in my house"; or function, as John experienced his stepfather, as benign presences who facilitate youngsters' development; or their significance may lie any where between these extremes.

Popular writing and psychoanalytic study tend to focus primarily difficulties with stepfathers, a focus which may not be unreasonable considering the findings from a population sample of children's adjustments to stepfamilies. Yet, as the cases presented here suggest, for some children, even children in sufficient psychological difficulty to be in need of analysis, experiences with stepfathers may facilitate and enrich development.

Naturally the child's experience will be determined in part by the stepfather's behavior. Stepfathers are no more immune than any other group from interferences in relating to children. More important, the development of a relationship with a child is commonly a secondary and ambivalent motive for the stepfather's involvement with the youngster. Stepfathers may approach the relationship with images concerning the child that include such negative fantasies as the child is competitor, the child is a symbol of mother's past relationship, the child is a burden, the child is indicator of the stepfather's infertility, the child is the object of correction, or the child is an opportunity for narcissistic gratification through shaping the youngster. Though various forms of attachment commonly bond the stepchild and stepfather, the ambivalent nature of the relationship, the lack of positive social role models for it, the relative absence of satisfactory social supports for it, the impingement of other, more significant, relationships into it, explicit and implicit threats of its disruption, and the fragmentary nature of the relationship all combine commonly to limit the stepfather's actual engagement. For purposes of this discussion, it is sufficient to note that the child forming a relationship with a stepfather has a significant likelihood of encountering complex, ambivalent, and unclear responses that are both in and outside of awareness. At the same time, it is equally clear that many men have the capacity to function well as stepfathers and that given sufficient opportunity without undue strain, they may grow into the role.[2]

The child's capacity for discovering new possibilities is at least as important as the stepfather's contribution to the new relationship. Jim and John despite evident neurotic aspects of their personalities had good capacities to find and use appropriate developmental objects. Though Jim's stepfather was a difficult individual with an explosive temper who actively created conflict in the family, Jim had the capacity to use even this difficult man to promote his development. This capacity increased with Jim's analysis during adolescence because the analysis helped Jim to work through his side of the competitive interaction with his stepfather. Similarly, when John's stepfather became available during the course of the boy's analysis, this youngster's already well-developed ability to use new individuals in his life to promote his development, significantly enhanced as a result of analytic work on the resistance to forming and recognizing a transference to the analyst, allowed him to benefit greatly from interaction with his stepfather. Both boys had excellent support from their fathers, who were not threatened by their son's new relationship with a paternal figure because of their continued strong involvement and clear importance to their sons. In contrast, Jay's stepfather appears to have served little positive developmental role in the boy's life. Though limitations in the stepfather's personality certainly contributed to this failure, Jay's already existing intense pathology was the primary force that transformed the relationship into one in which the stepfather was seen as the center of all that was evil and controlling in Jay's experience.

Thus, the experience of the stepfather and the role of the stepfather in development, while influenced by many factors, is likely to be strongly shaped by the child's readiness to enter into a new, useful relationship. Many of the children who have the opportunity to enter a new relationship

---

[2]George Eliot's *Silas Marner* provides a fictional account of how the developing capacity for parenthood emerges in an individual whose psychopathology would seem to have precluded it within the context of caring for a child over a long period of time. This is consistent with Benedek's (1959) formulation that the challenges provided by caring for a child normally result in psychological development in the parent. A similar process is likely to be put into action through stepparenting. However, for the stepparent, lack of social support and even social interference, are likely to limit the opportunity for intense immersion in the relationship to the child that appears to be central to the transformative impact of that relationship on the parent.

with stepfathers have already been traumatized by loss of a parent through death or divorce. They are likely to have had experiences of being raised by depressed caregivers or individuals whose character pathology interfered with the maintenance of a sustained relationship with a spouse. The population findings regarding stepfathers need to be looked at from the viewpoint that difficulties manifest in relation to the stepfather need not reflect an inherent problem in the relationship. In fact, as two of the cases presented here suggest, when the child is in a psychological state that permits using the stepfather as a new object and external factors promote this use, the experience of the stepfather may enrich and compliment experiences with the father and other developmental experiences.

References

Amato, P. (1994), The implications of research findings on children in stepfamilies. In: *Stepfamilies: Who Benefits? Who Does Not?* ed. A. Booth & J. Dunn. Hillsdale, NJ: Lawrence Erlbaum Associates, pp. 81–88.

Benedek, T. (1959), Parenthood as a developmental phase. In: *Psychoanalytic Investigations*. New York: Quadrangle, pp. 378–401.

Blos, P. (1984), Son and father. *J. Amer. Psychoanal. Assn.*, 32:301–324.

Brefach, S. M. (1986), The mentor experience: Influences of female/male mentors on the personal and professional growth of female psychologists. *Dissertation Abstracts International*, 47(1-A):123.

Brody, S. & Brody, A. S. (1978), *Mothers, Fathers and Children*. New York: International Universities Press.

Bushardt, S. C. (1991), The mentor/protégé relationship—A biological perspective. *Human Relations*, 44:619–639.

Cath, S. H., Gurwitt, A. R. & Ross, J. M., eds. (1982), *Father and Child: Developmental and Clinical Perspectives*. Boston: Little Brown.

Coleman, M. (1994), Stepfamilies in the United States: Challenging biased assumptions. In: *Stepfamilies: Who Benefits? Who Does Not?* ed. A. Booth & J. Dunn. Hillsdale, NJ: Lawrence Erlbaum Associates, pp. 29–36.

Fagenson, E. A. (1988), The power of a mentor: Protégés' and nonprotégés' perceptions of their own power in organizations. *Group & Organization Studies*, 13:182–194.

Galatzer-Levy, R. (1985), The analysis of an adolescent boy. *Adol. Psychiat.*, 12:336–360.

———— & Cohler, B. (1993), *The Essential Other: A Developmental Psychology of the Self*. New York: Basic Books.

Greenacre, P. (1963), *The Quest for the Father*. New York: International Universities Press.

Hanson, P. A. (1984), Protégé perceptions of the mentor–protégé relationship: Its complementary nature and developmental tasks. *Dissertation Abstracts International*, 44(11-B):3509.

Herzog, J. (1982), On father hunger: The father's role in the modulation of aggressive drive and fantasy. In: *Father and Child: Developmental and Clincial Perspectives*, ed. R. J. Cath. Boston: Little Brown.

Hetherington, E. & Jodl, K. (1994), Stepfamilies as settings for child development. In: *Stepfamilies: Who Benefits? Who Does Not?* ed. A. Booth & J. Dunn. Hillsdale, NJ: Lawrence Erlbaum Associates.

Hurn, H. T. (1969), Synergic relations between the processes of fatherhood and psychoanalysis. *J. Amer. Psychoanal. Assn.*, 17:437–451.

Irvine, J. J. (1985), The master teacher as mentor: Role perceptions of beginning and master teachers. *Education*, 106:123–130.

Kurdek, L. (1994), Remarriages and stepfamilies are not inherently problematic. In: *Stepfamilies: Who Benefits? Who Does Not?* ed. A. Booth & J. Dunn. Hillsdale, NJ: Lawrence Erlbaum Associates, pp. 37–44.

Leonard, M. R. (1966), Fathers and daughters: The significance of "fathering" in the psychosexual development of the girl. *Internat. J. Psycho-Anal.*, 47:325–334.

Levi, L., Stierlin, H. & Savard, R. (1973), Fathers and sons: The interlocking crisis of integrity and identity. *Psychiatry*, 35:48–56.

Lincoln, L. M. (1984), Fathering and the separation-individuation process. *Maternal–Child Nursing J.*, 13:103–112.

Lohr, R., Legg, C., Mendell, A. E. & Riemer, B. S. (1989), Clinical observations on interferences of early father absence in the achievement of femininity. *Clin. Soc. Work J.*, 17:351–365.

Mason, M. (1994), *From Father's Property to Children's Rights: The History of Child Custody in the United States.* New York: Columbia University Press.

Mitscherlich, A. (1969), *Society Without the Father.* New York: Shocken.

Parke, R. D. (1981), *Fathers.* Cambridge, MA: Harvard University Press.

Popenoe, D. (1996), *Life Without Father.* New York: Free Press.

Ross, J. M. (1982a), The roots of fatherhood: Excursions into a lost literature. In: *Father and Child: Developmental and Clinical Perspectives*, ed. S. H. Cath, A. R. Gurwit & J. M. Ross. Boston: Little Brown, pp. 3–21.

———— (1982b), In search of fathering: A review. In: *Father and Child: Developmental and Clinical Perspectives*, ed. S. H. Cath, A. R. Gurwit & J. M. Ross. Boston: Little Brown, pp. 21–32.

Stern, D. (1977), *The First Relationship of Infant and Mother.* Cambridge, MA: Harvard University Press.

———— (1985), *The Interpersonal World of the Infant.* New York: Basic Books.

———— (1988), Affect in the context of the infant's lived experience: Some considerations. *Internat. J. Psychoanal. Assn.*, 69(Pt. 2):233–238.

———— (1989a), The representation of relational patterns: Developmental considerations. In: *Relationship Disturbances in Early Childhood: A Developmental Approach*, ed. A. Sameroff & R. Emde. New York: Basic Books, pp. 52–68.

———— (1989b), Developmental prerequisites for the sense of a narrated self. In: *Psychoanalysis: Toward the Second Century*, ed. O. K. Cooper & E. P. A. Cooper. New Haven, CT: Yale University Press, pp. 168–180.

Walker, W. B. (1986), Mentor/protégé relationships of male and female elementary and middle school principals. *Dissertation Abstracts International*, 46(9-A):2515.

Wallerstein, J. S. & Johnston, J. R. (1990), Children of divorce: Recent findings regarding long-term effects and recent studies of joint and sole custody. *Pediatr. Rev.*, 11(7):197–204.

Zill, N. (1994), Understanding why children in stepfamilies have more learning and behavior problems than children in nuclear families. In: *Stepfamilies: Who Benefits? Who Does Not?* ed. A. Booth & J. Dunn. Hillsdale, NJ: Lawrence Erlbaum Associates, pp. 97–106.

The Ready Acceptance of a Stepfather
"I Learned to Love Him Very Slowly"
Stanley H. Cath

"Lest the Helpless Fall Through the Cracks and Become Street People"

At this point it seems appropriate to ask, under what circumstances might a stepfather be more readily welcomed into a family? I have heard many generalizations but they are rarely as complex as when revealed under a psychoanalytic lens.

In her middle years, a highly conscientious woman found herself feeling quite burdened by the care of a chronically ill brother. In her analysis, Alice had explored the strange admixture of gratification and obligation derived from the inordinate amount of energy compulsively devoted to this "lost cause" rather than to immediate family needs. But her two children were "adjusting wonderfully" and she felt "so lucky to be married to an understanding husband." While she tried hard "to balance between the two men in her life," she recognized her husband had an extra burden to carry, namely her deep worry about, and attachment to, her younger brother. While she wondered about the possible role of guilt, she was more inclined to attribute her constant, protective devotion to her inheritance of a clear sense of herself as someone chosen to be a caretaking, loving "survivor" of a tumultuous divorce. By contrast, her brother had inherited "a vulnerability to mental disease, although maybe from our maternal side" and he had remained "nonfunctional most of his life." Yet, she often wondered where her energy and integrity came from and why she had escaped his curse. Confusion and guilt over just whom she was "neglecting most" led her to seek analysis.

"Almost from the beginning everyone in the family had known there was something different" about her younger brother, Tim. From Alice's description of growing up together, it was likely Tim had had many of the soft signs we now think herald schizophrenia. After a most "awkward adolescence," he withdrew from almost all contact with peers. In an extreme reaction to the son's ineptitude and lack of ambition, his father had withdrawn and developed a special closeness with Alice. As she watched her father's hostility and disappointment spread to his mother, wife, sisters, and son, she could only marvel at her own escape. She was surprised she never had as much adolescent turmoil as her friends. But, sensing her father's insecurities, Alice also shielded him from the retaliation of others. It is not surprising that Alice became depressed intermittently and secretly considered that she had failed in the compelling task of pacifying and protecting everyone.

By his 20s, Tim had been through all kinds of therapies without avail. Several suicidal attempts were associated with "humiliating hospitalizations." She realized how closely she identified with him by remembering "a secret dread of growing up and finding out I was a schiz too, that I could end up in a mental hospital just as he did." After her marriage to a similarly considerate man, together they monitored their two boys for the familiar, telltale signs of developmental problems.

Promises Made and Kept

A turning point in her life soon became the focus of much of our work together. On her father's deathbed, when my patient was in her teens, her long-divorced but still very much involved father extracted a promise from her to care for her brother in her father's place. While it seemed consonant with what she had already undertaken as a responsibility, she gradually appreciated, even if the promise was true to her best self, how much she had sacrificed. On the other hand, she rationalized, "our relationship had always been so special I had to keep my word."

When her mother remarried several years later, Alice readily accepted her stepfather. "It was my way of keeping peace, and, his being there for my mother made my going away to college so much easier." Beside this sense of gratitude for her freedom, she added, "I learned to love him very slowly, very cautiously . . . not the same as my father, but almost." Despite college providing some respite, even from considerable distance, my patient continued to be the conscientious, articulate, pacifying adult in a chaotic, constantly shifting, visitation-laden, two-family scene.

She remembered one Christmas vacation at home, playing a game in the living room at her stepfather's home. Her brother was "on pass." The younger kids (bio and step) were asked what they would do when they grew up. Her brother rambled on in his loose-jointed, nonsensical way. She tried "to rescue him by reminding him of his skill with wood." Stepfather erupted and made no secret of his contemptuous wish to be rid of "this crazy boy who did not know what he was good for!" Everyone was stunned by his callous rage and the seeming expendability of a disappointing stepson. It was remembered as an overt demonstration of her stepfather's "willingness to discard . . . how could someone be this way?" But used to a father's callousness, Alice secretly interpreted this event as a call to reinforce her earlier promise to her biological father. "The message was my brother still needed my help and I could and would continue to protect him! But my stepfather was my ticket to freedom and I needed him as well. What a way to trap a kid!"

Until her analysis, no one, including her husband, had ever realized how much an anxious dread of abandonment underlay her calm, always smiling and seemingly flexible exterior. She connected her inner terror of her world falling apart due to something she had done or not done to the fear of being as expendable as her brother should she lose her calm. Further analytic work soon revealed these anxieties had predated his arrival on the scene and probably reflected her anxious, insecure attachment to the mother.

While the reconstructed families included two half-brothers, they remained somewhat idealized and distant strangers. She never took them on in the same way as mother took on strangers; they were not *her* responsibility. The two stepbrothers appreciated her steady resourcefulness but could not help teasing her about being "Daddy's little girl" or "teacher's pet." She began to explore her pattern of attachment and her readiness to accept some people and not others.

We also tried to understand why in times of stress she was so ready to turn to men and away from women. This trend had been recreated with father, brother, stepfather, and in the transference. A female therapist had referred her after a nonproductive year. We came to think of this tendency as an unconscious pact of safety reached with men in that her associations consistently revealed a greater basic comfort level with males and distrust of females. Yet, she had idolized her beautiful and seemingly serene mother even as she detested the social world the mother inhabited so far removed from the rest of the family. While Alice consciously deprecated mother's life style as superficial, a deep longing for this ephemeral woman provided the underpinnings for another highly ambivalent aspect of her character. She had never been able to work for another woman in authority. She found it hard to be sympathetic to young women whereas she could be quite understanding of the elderly. We came to understand this as derivative of the fusion of longing for and yet anxious about trusting competent, mother-like people. While she volunteered to comfort the abandoned and the sick, we found an anxious denial of identification with them, just as she had done with her brother prior to her analysis.

But to turn the clock back once again. Several years after her second marriage, things took a turn for the worse with Alice's mother. A pillar of respect in their suburban community, mother was visibly deteriorating. Sequentially, she lost her sense of appropriate social timing and then her control of selected groups of muscles, and finally became incontinent. After a series of puzzling falls, a diagnosis of multiple sclerosis was made. Because my caretaking patient seemed so adaptive, resilient, and blessed with a fine sense of humor, she became even more the focus of stability for her original as well as her reconstituted family. While never actually verbalized in situ, in analysis my patient articulated the usually silent question asked by most families who have parted and reconstituted when biological elders deteriorate:

> Whose responsibility is she, anyway? For Alice the answer was too clear. As with brother there seemed "no one else." But this time it was different and not so easy. Stepfather increasingly resented the limitations of his new wife's illness and the occasional contact with the flawed son of her first marriage. As my patient's responsibilities increased logarithmically, she uncovered a truly basic fear. Her anxiety was rooted in, "Lest the helpless fall through the cracks and become street people!" Another secret promise to prevent such an outcome had been wordlessly made.

With mother's increasing infirmity, stepfather looked to Alice more as the woman of the house, even seeking her advice about the two stepsons. While nothing explicit had ever happened between them, she found herself surprisingly relieved to get back to college. Still, she would return home most weekends. Home aides were relied on to fill the gap. She wondered if her secret but new sense of alienation from her stepfather was perhaps because he seemed either too grateful or too free with embraces whenever they met. Or, she asked, was it "just my Oedipus complex coming alive?"

While very different men, both fathers had been made welcome in Alice's heart and seemed to facilitate her separation-individuation from a distant mother preoccupied much like Alice herself with the needs of ailing people. It is my impression that her ready acceptance of her stepfather was to a considerable degree a replica of the alliance she had made earlier with her father, maintaining her balance through her mother's deteriorating illness and keeping at bay her deeper longing for a more attuned mother.

Stepdaughters and Stepfathers
Living Together in a Haunted House
Martin A. Silverman

> As I was going up the stair
> I met a man who wasn't there.
> He wasn't there again today.
> I wish, I wish he'd stay away.
> —Hughes Mearns

To understand the problems faced by stepdaughters and stepfathers, it is necessary to delve into the psychology of loss and abandonment. Parents are supposed to be there for their children, looking after them, taking care of them, providing love and affection, meeting their material needs, protecting them from harm. They are not supposed to leave. They are not supposed to die. They are supposed to *be there*—where they are needed.

But sometimes they do leave. Sometimes they do die. Even though they're not supposed to. And the children they leave behind tend to feel bereft, betrayed, abandoned—and enraged! They do not necessarily know that this is what they feel, for in the egocentric, preoperational thinking of the young child (and, via regression, of the Unconscious of the older child and adult), in which temporal simultaneity connotes causality (Piaget, 1954; Silverman, 1971), to have been abandoned is to have deserved to be abandoned—to have brought it upon oneself. The rage at the abandoning parent is not allowed to be conscious. It tends to be repressed, in the service of Cinderella-like idealization of the lost parent, with whom there is hope of one day being reunited. Since the rage cannot exist in a detached, free floating state, it tends to be redirected toward the parent who is there, in the form of ambivalence, and toward the self, in the form of guilt—conscious, unconscious, or both.

A. Albert, a Boy Who Responded to Loss by Searching Among the Stars

The above is exemplified by the plight of little Albert, whom I met when he was just three years of age. Albert's mother had all but given up hope of ever falling in love, getting married, and raising a family when she met

147

Albert's father. After a brief, whirlwind romance, they married and conceived a child. When Albert was born, everything seemed perfect. Life could not have been more full. Albert's parents loved each other fiercely—and they doted on the child who was the embodiment of their union. Then Fate intervened. When Albert was only a toddler, his father came down with a mysterious illness. After extensive evaluation, he was diagnosed as having a rare but invariably fatal disease.

Albert's mother was distraught, but she pulled herself together and threw herself into joining with her husband and child in extracting as much happiness as could be obtained from whatever time remained for them to be together. When her husband died, however, there was nothing left. It was as though making a lifetime out of a year and a half had used her up. Depression and despair swept over her. She began to spend the days in bed. The will to live drained out of her. She could not help thinking—and saying: "If someone had to go, why couldn't it have been the baby? We could have made another baby." She largely withdrew from interaction with her child. Albert made it apparent in multiple ways that he felt bad for being alive while his father was not. He teased and provoked in such a way that he incurred ostracism and punishment.

Albert was dazed by the loss of his beloved father, followed soon thereafter by the emotional loss of his mother as well. Separation from home became difficult for him. He took to bringing in one stuffed animal after another to school with him each day, and he carried a string around with him everywhere he went. This gradually gave way to an obsessive preoccupation with the Beatles. This emerged after he saw the film *The Yellow Submarine,* with its story line centering around the search to find the lost members of the Sgt. Pepper's Lonely Hearts Club Band and unfreeze them from the state of deathlike, suspended animation into which they had been placed by evil magic. This in turn yielded to an obsessive interest in the television series *Star Trek,* which, upon exploration, turned out to be connected with the wish to search in the heavens for his father—so that he could kill him!

B. Bella, a Woman Whose Father Abandoned Her Only to Return as an Intolerable "Stepfather"

I did not meet Bella until she was a middle-aged adult. Her father, a self-centered, grandiose, self-proclaimed religious scholar, apparently could not tolerate her mother's diversion of interest away from him to the baby when she became pregnant with Bella. He developed the delusional conviction that Bella's mother had deceived him and that the baby was not his. After a succession of increasingly stormy rages he walked out, leaving his wife and unborn child in desperate circumstances.

Bella's mother applied for welfare. She moved in with her married sister and continued to reside there for many years as a humiliated, dependent, poor relation. A little while after Bella's birth, her mother began to work as a domestic, cleaning people's homes. She never ceased being beholden to her sister for having rescued her and remained subservient to her in all ways. She reminded Bella repeatedly that she was not as good as the daughter of her successfully married sister, and she never let her forget that it was she who, by her birth, had destroyed her mother's marriage and wrecked her life. Bella, who had started out as a bright-eyed, inquisitive, energetic infant and toddler, increasingly evolved into a quiet, shy, inhibited little girl and adolescent. She seethed in silence over the condescension with which her cousin treated her. She responded to her aunt meekly and deferentially. She could not even look at her uncle, let alone talk to him. Unhappy and browbeaten, she never could concentrate on her school work. She barely eked by in school despite good native intelligence.

To make things worse, the father who had disowned her, who had abandoned her and her mother, and who had never paid a penny of support, relegating them to a life of poverty, reappeared when Bella was five years old and began to demand visitation with his daughter. His friends apparently had pushed him to do so. Bella's mother could not bring herself to raise an objection. She told Bella that it was her duty to grant her father's request for visits with him. After all, he was her father, and the ten commandments demanded filial devotion to both parents—no matter what.

Bella was forced to accept periodic visits from this man, without demurral and without protest. She had to submit to his kisses, although they filled her with revulsion. His very touch made her shudder. Sitting next to him in a movie theater and seeing him smile down at her·from time to time evoked waves of nausea, and there were times when she had to rush out to the bathroom to throw up. It was bad enough having him as a father, she said. After an initial absence of five years, he had suddenly become a "terrible stepfather" as well, she told me.

Bella came into treatment because life, which seemingly had dealt her one blow after another, had become a masochistic and miserable torment. A pretty girl with an eye for fashion and color, she had attracted the attention of a very eligible young man who stood to take over eventually a very successful family business from his father. He married her despite the disapproval of his parents, who considered her beneath them because of her lowly origins. They did not consider her, the relatively uneducated daughter of a penniless, abandoned woman who cleaned houses for a living, a suitable match for the scion of their family fortune. She never received acceptance from her parents-in-law, and her young husband was unable to stand up to his irascible, intimidating father on her behalf.

Bella was reasonably happy nevertheless. She had her husband and her children to love and to be loved by. And even if her in-laws treated her coldly, distantly, and disdainfully, there were plenty of others who recognized her worth. After a while, her father-in-law seemed to take to her. Impressed with her looks and with her fashion sense, he warmed to her considerably. Finally, there was a father figure in her life with whom she could feel comfortable.

Then things began to unravel. One night her husband had a seizure. Then he had another one. He turned out to have a cerebral aneurysm. She single-mindedly nursed him through a series of operations, but he only grew worse and worse. She all but abandoned her children to devote herself to his care. Finally, after a long, tortuous siege, he died.

Her in-laws were wealthy. She was the mother of their grandchildren. Surely she and they would be well looked after. She was so wrong. Her father-in-law smilingly passed her papers to sign. She signed them without looking at them. As she soon discovered, she had signed away her interest in the business. Then she learned that the beneficiary of her husband's life insurance had been that family business. With this, her father-in-law broke off ties with her. Her father-in-law (and eventually her mother-in-law as well) had nothing more to do with her or with her children. History had repeated itself. She and her children were left destitute. Not only had she lost the man she had depended on to take care of her and her family—the father of her children—but she also found herself abused and abandoned by her *father*-in-law, a certain kind of step*father*.

Like her mother in the past, she went to work to take care of herself and her family. Unlike her mother, however, she worked herself up rapidly to a position of authority. And in the course of her work, she met a man who appeared to fall in love with her. When he proposed marriage to her after a brief courtship, she readily accepted. Finally, she would be loved, appreciated, and looked after properly.

After they were married, however, things changed. As she gradually became aware, he had married her not out of love but in the quest for a housekeeper and a nanny to take care of his young daughter from his first marriage (his first wife had died). He doted on his daughter and treated *her* children like the "stepchildren" in classic Gothic tales. He also revealed to her something he had previously hidden from her: he had a chronic, progressive illness that one day would require that she nurse him and physically take care of him—"push him in a wheelchair"—the way she had had to do with her first husband. The love and affection he had lavished on her during the courtship faded and disappeared. After a while, the sexual aspect of their relationship ceased to exist, rationalized as the consequence of his physical illness and the depressive effect of a number of business reversals.

As in the past, in relation to her father-stepfather, she was miserable with her husband but could not break off the connection with him. She blamed herself for the way he treated her, and kept doubling and redoubling her efforts to win his approval, approbation, affection, and love. She relived her experience with her cousin, in her aunt and uncle's house, by sacrificing her own children as she ardently wooed her husband's daughter from his first marriage, even though her stepdaughter increasingly insulted and mistreated her and her children. As she eventually came to understand, she was desperately trying to be a good stepmother to her second husband's daughter in the hope that he would respond by adopting her and her children and take as good care of them as she was taking of his daughter. The effort, of course, was fruitless. The more she catered to him and his daughter the more both of them expected it; and they never reciprocated. It was not until her own daughter grew up and ran off with a ne'er-do-well who used and abused her that she became aware of the irrationality of what she was doing and sought psychiatric assistance for herself.

C. Cindy, a Girl Whose Gift for Storytelling Illuminated the Meaning of Adoption

Every stepchild, in one sense, is *an adopted child,* whether adoption proceedings have been carried out legally or it is merely de facto and implicit in the structure of the child's life. Parental loss and abandonment are the unavoidable legacy of adopted children. Reaction to having been abandoned by parents is an integral part of the experience of children who have been adopted. It is necessary, therefore, in considering relationships between stepchildren and stepparents to take a slight detour into examination of the psychology of adoption.

To have been abandoned constitutes a major narcissistic injury. Hurt and anger inevitably are central features of the attitude an adopted child maintains toward the parents who have been lost. This is exemplified in what was expressed to me by a nine-year-old girl, adopted at birth, who was brought for treatment because of unhappiness that was interfering with her performance in school despite excellent native intelligence and a lively, creative mind. One day, Cindy was playing with little plastic animals in my playroom. She was toying with what appeared to be a father and mother tiger and a father and mother lion. She picked up a little cub and mused over it doubtfully. "What's the problem?" I asked. She shook her head. "I don't know whether it belongs in the tiger family or the lion family," she said. I looked at her and said softly, "*You* know how that little cub feels." Her eyes opened wide. She looked up at me and asked, "Do you know what it's like to look into the mirror, and not see the face that *should* be there?"

Then she offered a story: Once upon a time there was a young couple that wanted *so much* to have a baby. They waited and waited, but no baby came. Finally, after years of wanting and waiting, the woman became pregnant. They were very excited and very happy. The day came when she was close to delivering. But then her husband told her he had to go away on a business trip. "You can't go now," she exclaimed. "I'm going to deliver the baby any time now. We need you *here!*" his wife declared. His whole career was at stake, however, and he told her that he *had* to go. So he left on the trip. While he was away, she went into labor. She telephoned him at his hotel. "You have to come home—right away!" He hopped on the next flight. The plane crashed and he was killed. Meanwhile, his wife had given birth to the baby. It was a girl. The new mother was very happy, but then she got the telegram informing her that her husband had been killed. She was so shocked that she had a heart attack and died. Now the baby had no parents and had to be placed for adoption.

This was quite a story she had put together. The baby was orphaned and had to be adopted because her parents died. And *she* was the cause of their deaths. *She* had killed them. With the remarkable talent with which she had been endowed, Cindy had put into literary form a more or less universal theory among adopted children as to their origins. Adopted children, understandably, feel rage toward the biological parents who have given them away. They yearn to be wanted, however, and idealize their biological parents in order to maintain their narcissistic well-being. They feel guilty, therefore, for being murderously angry at them. Cindy, as illustrated in her story, transformed her rage at her abandoning biological parents into responsibility for their disappearance from the scene. *They* had not abandoned her. *They* had not sent her away. *She* had sent *them* away. She had murdered them, in fact.

Through our delving together into the meaningfulness of this story, Cindy and I came to understand some important aspects of the distance and apartness she had been feeling from her parents. They loved her and doted on her, and she loved them. Nevertheless, she had been maintaining a degree of aloofness from them that pained not only them but her as well. We became able to recognize that her aloofness related to pain that they were not her *original* parents. With her guilt over her rage at her biological parents for abandoning her which she had transferred to her adoptive ones, she also was afraid of hurting her parents if she allowed herself to get too close to them.

When Cindy was a little older, her storytelling interest took a turn toward science fiction, and, in particular, toward space travel as a theme. At first, she connected it generically with her having been adopted: "*All* adopted children come from outer space. You didn't know that? We're aliens." When we looked further into the details of the stories she was writing, however, we found a component that was identical to something contained in little Albert's preoccupation with space travel, namely, the search for the lost, abandoning parents—so that they could be executed. Working through the rage psychotherapeutically (around expressions of disappointment and anger at me, coupled with threats to leave me) enabled her later on to initiate, together with her adoptive parents, a search for her biological progenitors so that she could fill gaps in her self-esteem and self-image and feel less like an "alien." In her mind, Cindy had viewed her adoptive parents as stepparents who had taken over from her original parents who had been lost to her but had not eliminated them from her life.

D. John Irving's Literary Creation of Dr. Daruwalla and His Alter Ego, Dhar

Another gifted writer who has employed his talent in the service of expressing the hurt and rage felt by children whose parents have abandoned them, and the effect it has on their relationships with the parental figures who take their place, is John Irving, who lost his own father at a very early age. The pain and puzzlement of abandoned children are a pervasive theme in his popular and very moving novels. His 1994 novel, *A Son of the Circus*, is an extraordinary literary expression of this constellation. The book contains a long, meandering story, within which several subplots emerge, unfold, intertwine, and coalesce. On the surface, it is a murder mystery, but much more salient is the impact upon the reader of the overlapping themes of parental abandonment, narcissistic injury, yearning to be reunited with lost parental objects, intense ambivalence that reaches the proportion of incestuous striving countered by and interwoven with murderous rage, and the enormous problems these themes impose on abandoned children and the parental figures who step into their lives and take the place of the parent(s) whom they have lost. Operating on a wrenching emotional level, Irving drags his readers into the world of unrelievable pain and volcanically destructive love–hate that can make life unbearable for stepchild–stepparent pairs. These stepchild–stepparent duos, without conscious awareness of what is taking place, so often find themselves bewilderingly unable to obtain the satisfying, mutually fulfilling relationships for which each of them yearns but neither can have because of imprisonment in the effects of the past.

As the book opens, we meet Dr. Farrokh Daruwalla, an orthopedic surgeon who has left the land of his birth and has become a citizen of another country. He does not feel truly at home in either of them, however. He has lost his fatherland, but he has not been able to attach himself to the new land that has embraced him as one of its own. He is a man without a country to which he can feel he belongs. He travels back and forth between India, where he was born, and Canada, which has accepted him but of which he does not truly feel a part. (Later on in the novel we hear about mistreatment he endures in his new country at the hands of a small group of home-born Canadians who resent his arrival there from foreign parts to join them as a stepbrother in their nation.) He is distant from the citizens of the land of his birth and *also* of his new home. We are told, in connection with this, that Farrokh feels "vaguely guilty that he knew very little about either his native or his adopted country" (p. 34).

He is a man with a dual quest. On the one hand, he is searching to find his identity. On the other, he is carrying on the work of his orthopedist father, whom he idealizes and idolizes as a saint who contributed unstintingly to the welfare of children. He is doing so in a very strange fashion, however, devoting himself to hounding achondroplastic dwarfs in the circus (which we are made to see stands symbolically for his native land) in order to collect blood from them in a pitiful, hopeless attempt to solve the mystery of what they have received genetically from their parents that consigns them to a life of stunted, crippled torture. Along the way, he rescues abandoned, parentless children and obtains a home for them in the circus, where they are fed and cared for but where, in their new life as acrobats, they are put at serious risk to life and limb.

Farrokh reveres the memory of his father, and spends as much time as he can dreamily sipping beer at the club in which he has inherited membership from his father. He *loves* the club at which his father had been a member. It is, we are told, "the only place (other than the circus) where Dr. Daruwalla felt at home" (p. 64). He thinks resentfully while he is there about the foolhardy way in which his father had alienated and angered a group within the Indian culture, which led to his having been assassinated, rendering Dr. Daruwalla fatherless.

We learn that Farrokh has in effect made himself the stepparent of a young man who had been abandoned by his parents at birth. He has also has become a screenwriter and has created a film identity for his stepson, "Police Inspector Dhar," that is elegant and illustrious but at the same time has made him a target of hatred and murderous rage directed at him from one group after another within the Indian populace. His stepson has become so identified with his film persona that he imagines himself to be a gifted detective able to solve crimes in real life.

In the midst of Daruwalla's musings over these matters, an old man at the club is mysteriously murdered in an eruption of sudden, inexplicable violence. The murder appears to be connected with death threats against Dhar. These triple killings—past, present, and future—form the nidus of a strange and exotic murder mystery.

Farrokh is entranced with circus life in India, in no small measure related to the circus practice of taking in orphaned or abandoned children and training them to be performers, especially to be acrobats. He not only is addicted to attendance at the performances, sitting in a front row seat that puts him as close as possible to what is taking place at the circus, but he particularly enjoys attending the practice sessions, where he mingles with the performers in their tents. These are "the privileges that made Farrokh feel he'd been adopted. At times, he wished he were a real son of the circus; instead, Farrokh supposed, he was merely a guest of honor" (p. 27).

The children who actually are adopted by the circus have been saved from squalor, starvation, and despair. Their training as acrobats gives them a hazardous life indeed, however: "The doctor's children and grandchildren thought that the risks taken by the child performers were especially 'harsh,' yet Farrokh felt that these acrobatic children were the lucky ones—they'd been rescued" (p. 27).

The plot that unfolds revolves in part around a pair of twin brothers born to self-indulgent, self-absorbed, destructive, and self-destructive actors who care little for their progeny, or for anyone else. When the parents leave India, they leave one of the twins behind. Farrokh Daruwalla becomes the de facto stepfather of the abandoned child, whose racial origins are ambiguous but whose mother in essence is the land of India. Farrokh becomes a screenplay writer, and gives his stepson an identity, within the entertainment world, that is so powerful that it tends repeatedly to take over as his seemingly real identity. Farrokh writes the scripts that define the police inspector role that makes his stepson rich and famous but at the same time so hated that he is the object of repeated threats of castration and of death.

The search for the murderer of the old man at the club leads to the eventual discovery of a bitter, murderously enraged, transsexual serial killer who, abandoned by his parents, had been raised by an adoptive mother/stepmother who seductively used and abused him and with whom he had become *ambivalently* identified. The twins are reunited in the course of the hunting down of the killer—and along the way the abandoning birth parents are done away with by the author of the book.

The cast of characters is replete with repetitive sets of twinlike doubles and alter egos that exemplify the mirror image dualities of love and hate toward the birth parent *and* toward the adoptive parent or stepparent with which adopted children and stepchildren so often are burdened. The experience of abandonment, the yearning for reunion with those who have been lost, and the murderous rage at the abandoning parents, transferred in part on to the rescuing, new parent of the abandoned child, are expressed over and over and in manifold ways in the story. Similarly, the ambivalence of the adoptive parent and stepparent toward the child, who is the ongoing, daily reminder that he or she is not the "real," preferred parent of the child is expressed in the story in multiple ways.

John Irving deftly has "Police Inspector Dhar" look different from the Indian movie audiences who view him on the screen, rendering them puzzled and suspicious about his origins. Adopted children and stepchildren do not often resemble their adoptive and/or stepparents. This is a continual reminder to the child and to the parent of the lack of consanguinity that signifies the gulf between them. "There was no credible explanation for his all-white appearance," we are told, "which fueled the rumor that Dhar was the child of Farrokh's brother, who'd married an Austrian; and since it was well known that Farrokh was married to this European's sister, it was also rumored that Dhar was the doctor's child" (p. 37).

The oedipal problems created for adoptive parents and stepparents and their children by the lack of a biological incest taboo are dramatically represented over and over in A Son of the Circus. Farrokh rescues a nubile teenage orphan girl from an older man who has turned her into a sex slave and prostitute. He spends the night with her en route to a circus he has persuaded to take her in and is severely tested by her seductive overtures. (She eventually leaves the circus, returns to the older man from whom Farrokh had rescued her, and marries him!) The reader is subjected to a flashback of Dhar's mother seducing his twin brother's roommate at school, whereupon the young man commits suicide. A child is sexually seduced (in a startlingly novel manner) by a stepparent and not only goes on to become a serial killer but also to become impotent and bizarrely disoriented and confused about his sexual identity. Dhar and his twin brother end up powerfully inhibited in their ability to function sexually. Sexual confusion, disturbance, and malfunctioning fill the pages of the novel.

Irving has brilliantly captured the dilemmas and the inner torments experienced by so many children who have lost parents and either have been placed for adoption or have been provided with stepparents (who very often then formally adopt the child). He also has been able to give literary form, very sensitively, to the dilemmas and the torments of the new parents who have filled the void created by that loss. He has illustrated in his stories, in a wrenchingly moving fashion, the way in which displacement of the rage at the lost, abandoning parent to the new one who takes the lost parent's place places an at times insurmountable wedge between the child and the stepparent or adoptive parent. He has used his skill as a storyteller to call these matters graphically and startlingly to our attention, in a way that rivets the attention of the reader.

"Running through John Irving's novels," as Mel Gussow (1998) has reported, "is the theme of lost children and absent parents: from the unknown father in The World According to Garp to The Cider House Rules, in which 'all the parents are missing.' In Mr. Irving's new novel, A Widow for One Year, a mother, severely depressed by the accidental death of her two sons, disappears for 37 years. A pivotal line in Irving's latest book reads, 'The grief of lost children never dies'" (Gussow, 1998, p. E1).

Irving's mother and father divorced before he was born, and he never met his biological father, who apparently totally abandoned him. His father never reached out to him, nor has Irving ever made an attempt to make contact with him, although he used some information about him as a war hero, which his mother made available to him in 1981 (when his own first marriage ended), in creating one of the key characters in *The Cider House Rules*. Irving's mother remarried when he was six years old; his stepfather adopted him and gave him a new middle and last name.

It is only now that Irving has begun to speak publicly about his early life. Interestingly, according to Gussow, when Irving composes his novels, he does not start them at the beginning. Unlike most writers, he begins at the end of the book instead. "As a book progresses, he may change his mind about the beginning." Gussow's next line is, "For Mr. Irving, rewriting is a compulsive act." It would appear that Irving's feelings about his own beginnings have made a contribution to his putting together his novels in such a way that he affords himself the opportunity to rewrite his story and change its beginning.

E. Elizabeth, a Woman Who Needed a Father to Tell Her That She Was Beautiful but Could Not Let Her Stepfather Do So

I met Elizabeth when she was at the midpoint of her life. A beautiful and engaging woman, she nevertheless suffered from such low self-esteem, poor self-image, and lack of confidence that she avoided public appearance and lived in terror of being exposed as flawed and inadequate. She slavishly attached herself to women who were not nearly so capable and competent as she was but were utterly sure of themselves and commanded both attention and acceptance of their taking command of things. She hated herself for not being able either to stand up to them or to free herself from her dependence upon them.

As with John Irving, Elizabeth's parents parted company at the beginning of her life, and her mother went on to remarry when she was six years old. It pained Elizabeth that she had no or almost no recollection of her biological father. Consciously at least, Elizabeth was not aware of being "devastated" by (her) father's "rejection and abandonment" of her "because it's an abstract rejection—I don't have a face to attach to it." Her father died before she was six, and she did not even have a snapshot of him until her mother gave her a few pictures of him after she had already become an adult.

Elizabeth stated that her parents were divorced some time between her birth and her first birthday. Her father, she had been told, was a very good looking, vain, self-centered man who was disappointed that she was a girl. She alternated between stating that she resembled her father and indicating that she looked like her mother. She stated that she was unhappy when she visited her father. Her mother stopped the visitations when she was two years of age, and interfered with attempts by her paternal grandparents to see her. She wished, she said, that her mother had not cut her off from her father's family. "I have no one but my mother," she said.

From the time she was two until when she turned six, she and her mother lived with her maternal grandmother. Her mother and grandmother both worked, and Elizabeth was in all-day daycare. She liked her maternal uncle, but he was away in military service. After his return, he lived with them for a short time. He was tall, handsome, *and he liked her.* She was angry when he got married, and she did not like his bride.

Her mother remarried when Elizabeth was six years old. Her mother's new husband loved her as well as her mother and he legally adopted her after the marriage. Elizabeth indicated that he was not a physically demonstrative man (or did he give up when she recoiled from his shows of affection?). He provided well for her and was eager to teach her things and to help her with her homework. She shrank away from him and his ministrations, however, and resisted his offers of assistance with her schoolwork to such an extent that she was totally unable to learn anything from him. She was uncomfortable in his presence. When there was tension between her mother and stepfather or when they quarreled, she cringed and was miserable.

Elizabeth was a chronically unhappy child, both at home and at school. She overate to appease her emotional hunger and to push away her sadness. She would eat the lunch she carried to school before she ever got there. Being overweight added further to her misery. As an adult, she still was "always eating"—or shopping. She exercised vigorously to maintain her figure, but her masochistic use of eating as a child carried over into adulthood in the form of repeatedly neglecting her teeth and gums until extensive, painful dental work or periodontic scrapings were required. As an adult, she dissolved into sobbing whenever she saw a television commercial or a news story about a happy family or about a happy mother–child relationship.

Elizabeth blossomed into a beauty in her teens. When she was in high school, the sight of her in a bathing suit entranced the good-looking young man who was eventually to become her husband. She was overjoyed that he "liked" her, "admired" her, "wanted" her, and "took pleasure in" her. He became "the love of [her] life." She adored him. When he went away to college, he broke off their relationship, in part. because of discomfiture with her emotionality and the intensity of her yearning for closeness. She was devastated, but she did not give up. She continued to reach out to him in various ways.

She had no difficulty attracting young men, and soon she began to see someone else (who was heading toward the same profession her stepfather had been in) on a regular basis. She managed to let the two of them know about each other and skillfully played one against the other until the boyfriend she really wanted told her to send the new one packing. They resumed going steady, but after a while *she broke off with him*. After an on-again, off-again relationship in which she tested his lasting devotion to her, he proposed marriage and she readily assented. It is of interest that whenever later in life she met the man who had been the "other" boyfriend, she felt very uncomfortable.

The marriage was a happy one. She loved and admired her self-assured, successful husband, but she could not help feeling irritated by his extreme self-confidence and his delight in competitively showing off his achievements and his impressive home and material possessions. She envied his close relationship with his mother, to whom he was the prodigal son, and never felt capable of matching her in beauty or elegance. Whenever she felt herself moving toward a good relationship with her mother-in-law, she felt guilty, as though she were rejecting her mother.

She felt torn between defending her mother, with resentment against her husband for complaining about her, and dreading her mother's visits. In the early years of her marriage, she was so close to and affected by her mother that her husband used to joke that he always knew when she had spoken with her because she was sounding just like her. Now she dreaded becoming like her. She found herself increasingly ashamed of and angry at her mother as the years passed, although this made her feel enormously guilty. Consciously, she connected this with rather superficial things, including her mother's "selfish" sense of entitlement that she be taken care of and her contentious personality, but it became increasingly apparent that the more fundamental, underlying reasons related to her mother's having deprived her of a father by first leaving him and then contentiously blocking him from seeing her.

Her anger at her mother alternated with guiltily blaming herself for having wrecked her parents' marriage. The stamp of her early experiences of loss and abandonment, of the residual ambivalences and guilty self-blame that emanated from them, of her (ambivalent) idealization of her biological father, and of her inability to transfer her love and devotion from her biological father to her stepfather were evident in every aspect of her life. Unconsciously, Elizabeth had never given up her relationship to her original father. She remained tied to him as the idealized, loved and loving father she needed to make her feel valued, wanted, and loved. She needed him too much to turn away from him or even to be angry at him. She remained connected to him by splitting off her rage at him and redirecting it toward her stepfather, which also helped to relieve the guilt she felt about her anger at her mother for not holding on to her original father. Her stepfather felt hurt and rejected. He could not summon up the enormous effort it would have taken to overcome his stepdaughter's protecting her image of her idealized, original father by redirecting it at him. The tense distance that existed between them also helped to protect them from oedipal anxieties they experienced. All of this was expressed in the therapeutic transference–countertransference that emerged in the course of her treatment.

F. Francine, a Girl Whose Self-Loathing Made It Impossible for Her to Love Her Stepfather or, in Fact, to Love Any Man

Francine's parents brought her for help when she was in her early teens. She was bright, attractive, personable, and talented, but she was extremely unhappy. She attended an excellent school, but felt out of place and could not feel a connection with any of the other youngsters there. At home, she was hypersensitive and irritable. She clung to her mother as though they were twins (which her mother appeared subtly to foster, despite her conscious disavowal of it). She vigorously repulsed her stepfather's affectionate or even friendly overtures and she intensely opposed her mother's efforts to encourage her to give her stepfather a chance.

Francine appreciated why her mother had remarried a couple of years earlier, after years of loneliness and very straitened circumstances following her parents' divorce when she was little, to a man who admittedly was kind, loyal, and generous. Her mother deserved a chance at a complete life, and she could understand that her mother wanted the two of them to have a complete family. She and her mother had had each other, but it was not the same as families in which there were two parents.

The only problem was that she could not share her mother's feelings for her stepfather. She shuddered when her stepfather touched her and could not tolerate even being in the same room with him. She recognized that it hurt his feelings when she recoiled from him, and that it pained him when she rejected the material things he offered her and repulsed the efforts he made to be helpful to her in various ways. It was not that he was a terrible person, although he could get huffy or grumpy at times. In fact, he was rather nice, and everyone seemed to like him, but she just could not warm up to him. She could come up with seemingly plausible reasons for her aversion to him, but their flimsiness was apparent even to her.

Francine did not really know why she was so put off by her stepfather. He complained that she was ruining his life, and maybe he was justified in that complaint. Maybe he was right, too, when he accused her of being responsible for the growing friction that existed between her mother and stepfather, but she could not help the way she felt. Anyway, he had married her mother; he hadn't married her. Her mother had to like him. She didn't have to like him. Why didn't he just leave her alone?

She did not even like her father, especially when her mother had been telling her terrible things about him for years. She felt bad about her father's having moved far away and about his failure to visit her or keep in touch with her after some early, feeble attempts, but, on the other hand, her mother had been so down on him that maybe she should not blame him for staying away. Still, she wondered what he was like now and what he was doing.

At first, Francine welcomed the opportunity to have someone she could talk to about her feelings. She had felt so alone for so long that it was good to have someone with whom she could share the pain she felt. Increasingly, however, she felt uncomfortable talking about herself and, as it became increasingly apparent, she felt uncomfortable being with someone who was compassionate and wanted to help her. She insisted that she did not want help and had not asked for help. It had not been her idea to come for treatment. It had been her mother's idea, not hers. Her unhappiness was her own private affair and she could deal with it on her own.

In fact, she indicated, she did not deserve to be helped. Her stepfather complained about how she was affecting him, and her mother was beginning to lose patience with her sullen behavior and accusing her of selfishly creating dissension in the household and contributing to her own depression. This was reminiscent of the periodic allusions her mother had made in the past to the part Francine's birth had played in the failure of the marriage between her and her biological father. According to her mother, he had not really wanted to have children. He had not felt ready for the responsibilities that came with children. If she had not been born, the marriage might not have ended. She did not ask to be born, but it certainly did not help that she came into the world when she did.

Francine could see intellectually that she had not been responsible for the failure of her mother's marriage to her biological father. It did not prevent her, however, from *feeling* that way. The fact that she looked like her father also did not help. The seething rage that her mother had felt toward him for leaving her seemed to wash over at times onto Francine, despite her mother's efforts to prevent it. It dawned on Francine that her clinging to her mother was in part a reaction to anger at her.

It made her guilty, however, to find herself angry at her mother. After all, her mother had been her sole parent for a long time, her *everything*. And in a way *she* had been responsible for her mother's hardships. Among other things, it is not easy for a woman with a young child to attract a man. It was not easy to get her to see that her anger at her mother, *and at her stepfather*, had been displaced from her absent, first father.

Francine grew increasingly depressed, withdrawn, and isolated. She began to have thoughts of cutting herself. She listened as it was pointed out to her that she was turning her frustration, her pain, and her anger back onto herself and that she apparently had been doing so for a long time. She wrestled with her ambivalent feelings about her biological father. She could see that her stepfather was an easy target for the angry feelings she had needed to deflect away from her biological father over the years so that she could cling to the hope that her parents would one day be happily reunited.

She could see that she felt so guilty about being enraged at her mother for not holding on to her first father, especially because her mother had reminded her from time to time how much she had sacrificed to provide for her while they had been alone together, that she had to punish herself. She could see that her guilt about having accepted enrollment in an expensive private school from her stepfather at the same time that she was treating him so badly had been responsible for her inability to feel at home there and to enjoy it.

Francine tried to accept assistance from me, but it conflicted so much with her need to be punished that it was extremely difficult for her to do so. She grew increasingly resistant to participating in her treatment, and found one seemingly plausible reason after another to miss sessions. She alternated between expressing appreciation for my efforts on her behalf and insisting that I was not helping her and that she wanted to stop the treatment. When she finally began to insist that she could not work with a man and wanted to try seeing a woman, her parents, exhausted and desperate, pressed for my assistance in effecting such a change. Francine indicated that I might be right that she was enacting something with me that related to intense, deepset feelings about her biological father having left her and her mother for another woman. She could see that she was doing to me what he had done to them. Nevertheless, she said, she wanted to make the change. The intense, negative transference that had developed from her stepfather, and ultimately from her original father, was so powerful that it could not be overcome through interpretation and understanding. A change was effected to a female therapist, with whom, predictably, she underwent a stormy course of further treatment.

Conclusions

Stepdaughters and stepfathers are faced with the at times insuperable task of overcoming the specter of the past. They are haunted by the ghost of the father who *should* be there but is not. As Edith Jacobson (1965) has pointed out, it is extremely difficult for children to tolerate abandonment. They tend to react with intense hurt, anger, and disbelief. They tend to deny the permanence of the loss, to idealize the lost parent, and to support their denial and idealization by splitting off the rage they feel and redirecting it toward the one who *is there*. They redirect it in part toward the parent who remains and then toward the stepparent who takes the abandoning parent's place. They also redirect it in part toward themselves.

Lewin (1937) called attention to the tendency of children who have lost a parent to glorify the lost parent and to hold on to the unconscious belief that one day he will return, like the father in *The Little Princess*. He noted their tendency to split off the anger they feel toward him onto the parent who still is there, making for highly ambivalent feelings toward that parent.

Substitute teachers know all too well what it is like to be the target of the wrath of children toward the teacher who has not come in that day. Substitute parents have to feel it for a lot longer.

The need of a stepdaughter to push away at first from her stepfather derives not only from the need to preserve the idealization of the lost parent that is necessary for her narcissistic well-being (Jacobson, 1965), but from two other sources as well. One is the resentment that is felt, whether the girl is aware of it or not, at the newcomer who not only has the audacity to take her father's place but also is taking her place with her mother, with whom she has had a very special, albeit more or less ambivalent, relationship as her one and only parent for some time. The other is the oedipal conflict into which she is inclined to be thrust by the arrival into her life of a man who fills the need she has felt for a father, but who lacks the blood tie that ordinarily helps to protect against the oedipal pull that exists between a girl and her father.

A stepfather generally has a lot of work to do to overcome the tendency of his stepdaughter to push away from him. He has to be extremely patient, resilient, and persistent if he is to succeed in establishing a warm, loving relationship with her. This is especially so, paradoxically, if a lot of time has passed since the original loss and if there has been a large degree of hurt and anger toward the first father within her, her mother, or both. He has to be able to deal successfully with his hurt and anger at being initially rebuffed and rejected. He has to struggle successfully with his own oedipal stirrings that are not only inevitable in every parent but which tend to be accentuated by the absence of the blood relation that reinforces the intrafamilial incest taboo that prevails in more ordinary circumstances. It is no mean feat that he is called upon to accomplish. And a male therapist who accepts the challenge of working with a female patient whose conflicts include those of stepdaughter–stepfather interaction is destined to experience all of this in the transference–countertransference constellations that will emerge in the course of the treatment.

That in the vast majority of instances stepdaughters and stepfathers manage to work out the problems that confront them, so that they *can* establish the relationship which both of them need to have with one another, does not diminish the enormity of the task that confronts them. It is a testimonial to the human spirit and to human resilience and ingenuity that most of the time they are able to do so. The case histories which I have cited represent extreme examples of the problems which stepdaughters and stepfathers must resolve if their lives together are to be good ones, but it is from the extreme that we often learn about what is more subtle and less visible in the ordinary.

References

Gussow, M. (1998), A novelist builds out from fact to reach the truth. John Irving begins with his memories. *The New York Times,* April 26, pp. E1, E3.

Irving, J. (1994), *A Son of the Circus.* New York: Ballantine Books.

Jacobson, E. (1965), The return of the lost parent. In: *Drives, Affects, Behavior, Vol. 2,* ed. M. Schur. New York: International Universities Press, pp. 193–211.

Lewin, B. D. (1937), A type of neurotic hypomanic reaction. *Arch. Neurol. & Psychiat.,* 37:868–873.

Piaget, J. (1954), *The Construction of Reality in the Child.* New York: Basic Books.

Silverman, M. A. (1971), The growth of logical thinking: Piaget's contribution to ego psychology. *Psychoanal. Quart.,* 40:317–341.

A Parade of Pseudostepfathers

Altruism and Gratification in a
Surrogate Stepfather

Stanley H. Cath

As a medical consultant to the Appeals Division of the Social Security System, I have scanned and evaluated the records of more than a thousand families living in various forms of connectedness. My role is to assist administrative law judges to determine if the appellants qualify for disability under existing psychiatric listings.

One of the most poignant and bizarre of cases involved a 45-year-old woman, Emma, who had four children by four different fathers. Living with a fifth man, even though not legally married, Emma described the relationship "as husband and wife." Indeed, "Big Jim" had accompanied his "wife" to the hearing, and, when asked by the judge to identify himself, replied, "Gloria's stepfather." This turned out to be less inappropriate than might be supposed in that the issue before the court was Gloria's dangerousness, and he seemed to be protecting her in an altruistic way. Her mother, the primary care physician, and the local mental health clinic had all diagnosed an "Oppositional and Defiant Behavior Disorder." My ears pricked up at Big Jim's unique self-identification as a psychological stepfather. History soon revealed that Gloria had been relegated to the role of "bad child" by mother, even before her birth. Over the years mother's negative image of Gloria colored the quality of all subsequent interactions with friends.

In the courtroom, this very obese, intimidating woman had her day. Although entitled to legal representation, Emma had insisted on being her own lawyer. According to the reports of her behavior by school faculty, counselors, and mental health workers, she generally intimidated most of the many professionals involved in this mini-pseudo-family system. The psychiatric records also revealed that Emma "had no clue" as to why *she* antagonized people or why she projected her own unreasonable qualities onto her daughter.

When interrogated by the sophisticated and sensitive judge, Gloria emerged as an aggressive adolescent who simultaneously felt helpless, ashamed, and completely bewildered, especially by her mother's inordinate suspiciousness. She talked of the series of equally helpless men who had "paraded" through her life before Jim. She never once identified her mother's live-in boy friend as any kind of father nor expressed gratitude for his being there. Yet I had the impression as an outside observer that it

165

was clear she liked, trusted, and depended on him. Being a stepfather was clearly on his conscious agenda, and he seemed gratified. The two had joined forces against a common foe.

The most striking reason for citing this case, however, is Big Jim's unique presentation as a man taking care of and protecting other men's children (and himself) from an obviously powerful but irrational woman. In his mind Gloria's rages were not her most meaningful characteristics and, in contrast to mother, he downplayed their dangerousness. Whatever other problems there might be, he stressed her need for his affection. In his words, "I don't have much trouble with her. She always hangs over me when I come in . . . as if she wants something. I am not her biological father . . . I'm not even a real stepfather, though I do regard them all as my kids. Whatever happens I am always there for them when they need me." As he spoke, he rarely looked at the judge but glared at the back of the mother sitting in front of him as if he was having a dialogue with her alone.

But we also learned from the records that over the years, several of the men who had paraded in and out had molested one or more of her four children. This family setting had always had a highly charged and over-stimulating atmosphere. "Hanging all over" him, I pondered, surely had seductive overtones. Yet, I wondered if such a bond held the only probable affection Gloria and her sibs knew. Certainly, there was no mention of grandparents or close friends. It seemed to me children in such a family system would yearn for comfort and seek warmth from whoever might, kindly in some instances, parade through this house.

It turned out Big Jim had been married before. His wife had moved away, taking their three children with her. I thought to myself that Jim was as much in need of a replacement of lost affection as all the children in this family were.

As more details emerged, it became clear that Gloria's mother had been chronically paranoid and delusional most of her adult life. Some men in the parade might well have been surrogate, reasonably sane parent-like figures, much as Big Jim appeared to be at the hearing. It seemed to me Gloria's anger and seductive behavior might be conceived of, in part at least, as a result of a number of ingredients often found in welfare families: overall neglect; a Kafkaesque sense of being accused of crimes never clearly defined; many of the ingredients of soul murder (Shengold, 1989); a deep hunger for emotional recognition; and possibly the resentment of an eldest child left to deal with a psychotic mother and, in addition, to fill in periodically for her deficiencies with the other children.

Furthermore, mother provoked many enemies wherever they had lived. Emma literally prohibited the children from grieving for the many lost "pseudo-stepfathers," sabotaging any sense of past authentic connections held by Gloria or her other children. I thought it was a breeding ground for oppositional and defiant behavior and for *turning to strangers for affection and self-redefinition.*

In the first half of the 20th century, Emma might well have spent her life in a mental institution. With adequate social services and adoption possibilities, her children might have had different destinies. Then I imagined this family of six might not be involved in this complex pathological system in which the only warmth is currently provided by a self-appointed, equally deprived, pseudo-stepfather. When Gloria's mother was asked if she was married, she replied, "I'm separated." Under his breath, the "stepfather" muttered, "I'm with my wife and kids anyway." It seemed Big Jim was given little credit for the important father-like figure he wished to be and actually had become. His efforts at restituting a family no matter how imperfect or delusional were belittled by Emma in the same way she failed to recognize the good things Gloria might have to offer. Apparently, however, Gloria could elicit a protective and affectionate response from Big Jim.

References

Kafka, F. (1937), *The Trial.* New York: Schocken Books, 1998.
Shengold, L. (1989), *Soul Murder.* New Haven, CT: Yale University Press.

On Childless Stepparents

Jerome S. Blackman

At the millennium, adults seeking psychological treatment are often not only parents, but stepparents. The incidence of blended families has grown, owing in part to the high rates of divorce and remarriage and in part to the virtual evaporation of the female virginity taboo.

Over the past 10 years, I have had the opportunity to consult with and treat a number of people who had entered into relationships where only they or their spouses had already had children. These living situations presented certain conflicts, both interpersonally and intrapsychically, for each spouse. Perhaps the most typical problem for new stepparents was the "instant" parental status they achieved (Roberts and Price, 1987), even if they had been friendly with their future stepchildren before the marriage.

In this contribution, I describe some dynamics that complicated or disturbed new marital relationships where only one spouse had children previously. It is hoped that these dynamics, though not necessarily universal, can be extrapolated to other patients, with the caveat that each human being also experiences unique unconscious conflicts, unique behavioral idiosyncrasies, and unique psychopathology.

Theoretical Considerations

Although there have been a considerable number of publications on stepparents' problems, few examine the problems psychoanalytically. Many studies examine the interpersonal problems of blended families (Keshet, 1988; Levin, 1997). Previous experience as parents, good relationships with other family members, similarity in values (parenting ideas) between parents, and inclusion of stepparents in some disciplinary activities have been cited as factors leading to stepparent satisfaction (Everett, 1998). Others have collected data suggesting that harmonious stepfamily adaptation depends more on variables in the children (Peretti et al., 1992). Successful "adjustment" has also been tied to resolution of the previous marital relation and the stability of the new parental relationship (Morrison and Stollman, 1996).

For the most part, psychoanalytic assessment or intervention has been sidestepped in favor of psychoeducational and informational counseling (Wolf and Mast, 1987; Bray and Harvey, 1995). One statistical study of 246 female and 33 male remarried adults found that remarried mothers were more focused on the child–stepfather relationship than on themselves (Visher and Visher, 1988), suggesting unconscious projective defenses. However, the concerns of remarried mothers apparently have some reality basis as well, since stepfather–daughter sexual abuse has been found to be 15 times greater than father–daughter incest (3.7 vs. 0.2 percent; Sariola, 1996).

Viewing stepparents' difficulties as interpersonal "role strain" (Saint-Jacques, 1996), as helping the child adjust (Jacobson, 1995), or as reality reactions to the new stepchildren (Filinson, 1986; Bernstein, 1989) has led many authors to recommend supportive and educational approaches (Miller, 1985; Stanton, 1986; Sager, 1987; Bielenberg, 1992). Roberts and Price (1987) and Lipsitz (1997) touch on childless stepparents' problems generated by the advent of the "instant family."

Much psychoanalytic material on stepparents, including articles that give case examples of stepparents, pertains to the parental dynamics involved in adoption (Blum, 1969, 1983; Feder, 1974; Wieder, 1977; Nickman, 1985; Sharpe and Rosenblatt, 1994). Gitelson (1945) warns that the stepparent will be seen as "a trespasser." Bohannon (1984) advises that the stepparent needs to "identify" with the stepchildren for a successful relationship. A psychodynamic approach to various pathological developments in adoptive and stepparents has been described by Visher and Visher (1988). The role of the mother in orienting the father to childrearing is stressed in the research of Lamb and Oppenheim (1989).

Psychoanalytic theory and experience have much to contribute to the understanding of stepparents, including cases where the stepparent has not previously had children.

First, from the standpoint of self-esteem regulation, a new spouse may become hurt if stepchildren reject him. Some rejection by stepchildren is predictable, since many children handle grief and anger over the loss of a biological parent by defensively identifying with the aggressor. The children will then do to the new parent what was done to them (e.g., rejection). A stepparent's disappointment (narcissistic injury) often leads to anger at the child, which may be displaced onto the spouse, causing marital arguments. When the stepparent feels guilty ("I have no right . . . ") about critical feelings toward the child, the criticism may be unconsciously turned on the self, causing the new stepparent to become depressed during the "honeymoon period" with the new family.

Modern psychoanalytic object relations theory has also added to our understanding of how people establish emotional closeness versus distance in relationships. Establishing "optimal distance" (Akhtar, 1992) with a stepchild can be a bit of a chore for the new stepparent, particularly if the stepchild is rejecting. On the other hand, the affectionate child who desires emotional closeness may unwittingly cause conflict in the new stepparent. If the stepparent has been greatly irritated by the noncustodial biological parent, closeness with the child may provoke guilt. That guilt can act as a stimulus for defenses (Freud, 1926; Arlow and Brenner, 1964), and the defenses may be pathological. For example, stepparents may withdraw from the affectionate child to punish themselves (to relieve guilt). Commonly, guilt may also cause defensive passivity.

Further, closeness with an adolescent stepdaughter may stimulate some sexual thoughts even in a relatively normal stepfather, who may then avoid the child, regress, or become overly restrictive toward her socializing (due to unconscious projection onto her of his own impermissible sexual impulses).

In some cases, the stepparent may experience guilt over competitive (oedipally based) feelings toward the spouse's ex. Renée (see case 2), for example, was conflicted about having a child by her husband. Part of the dynamics of her inhibition involved such guilt.

Not to be forgotten is the importance of unconscious transferences that may develop between stepparents and members of the new family. In particular, the oral demands of stepchildren—for attention, attunement, and soothing—may cause a drain for which the stepparent is unprepared (as are many new parents). The drain often produces negative reactions toward the children augmented by displaced frustrations from the step-parent's own childhood.

The competition of the child for the parents' time may easily be experienced as an oedipal intrusion, causing regressive competitive atti-tudes to surface toward the child. Sibling rivalry-type of verbal sparring may also be provoked by the child. Usually, biological parents' competitive and dependent transferences toward their children are attenuated as the parents attune themselves, through empathy and observation, to the reality of the child's mental state through different phases of development.

Another advantage the biological parent enjoys is the ability, over time, to develop heightened frustration tolerance and delay of gratification. My impression is that, because of their children, average-expectable parents improve in such ego strengths over time, much as an adolescent does—through gradual exposure to increasing quantities of affect-provoking and impulse-inflaming experiences (Kestenberg, 1975). The enhanced capaci-ties of normal parents must be augmented even further in the training of child psychoanalysts, who must handle the regressive tugs of highly disturbed children (Marcus, 1980; Abrams, 1991). The new stepparent has not had the longitudinal experience with the child that helps the parent to develop *parental-level ego strength* in impulse control, frustration toler-ance, and resistance to regression, for example (Marcus, 1973; Parens, 1975).

Finally, the important information regarding child development that has been discovered and collected over the past three decades (e.g., Blos, 1962; Mahler, Pine, and Bergman, 1975; Galenson and Roiphe, 1976, 1980; Lerner, 1976; Parens, 1988, 1991, 1992) can be of immeasurable educational value to parents and stepparents. For new stepparents especially, who have not been witness to the psychosexual and psychoaggressive phase development of the child, the recent lay-oriented psychoanalytic literature can be illuminating (Cath, Gurwitt, and Ross, 1982; Cath, Gurwitt, and Gunsberg, 1989; Greenspan and Salmon, 1993, 1995; Colarusso, 1994).

The following case examples attempt to illustrate certain aspects of the new stepparent situation. Although they are not necessarily "standard," the cases present an opportunity to view certain dynamics in stepfamilies.

Case 1: Mara

This 30-year-old married female attorney consulted me because of depression associated with moderate obesity and intense marital dissatisfactions.

Her current three-year-old marriage to John, a 26-year-old middle management businessman, her third and his first, was fraught with discord. Aside from their petty arguments and his sexual difficulties, a good part of her conflicts about him stemmed from criticisms and disagreements over the management of Wendy, her mildly overweight 12-year-old daughter (from her first marriage).

Mara felt consciously conflicted. She did not want a third divorce, partly because of her daughter's need for stability. Nevertheless, her daughter got into "brother–sister" style arguments with John. Wendy responded to his criticisms by becoming irritable, isolated, and resistant to Mara's attempts to calm her. Nevertheless, because of her work schedule, Mara had found it helpful that John assumed much of the verbal discipline of Wendy. When I questioned if John's involvement was so necessary, Mara associated that she had grown weary of her daughter's preadolescent volatility and negativism, so his acceptance of the role of primary disciplinarian was also a relief to her. Moreover, we could then see that some of Mara's attitude unconsciously expressed her wish to control John. During once-a-week therapy, we were able to figure out that Mara's "control" of John defended her against expression of any impulses, hostile or otherwise. Mara joked that she preferred being the "controll-er" and not the "controll-ee."

When I explored any connections of control with prior relationships, she thought she had been sensitized to control by both her previous husbands. She purposely married her first husband to get out of her house. She was 18 and pregnant by him at the time. After they were married, however, he dropped out of college against her wishes. Further in disagreement with her, he began dealing marijuana. When Wendy was born, Mara wanted no more to do with marijuana, and had constant anxiety about his dealing it. But she could not convince him to stop his criminal activity.

After she finished college, feeling she could not exert any meaningful control over his behavior, she divorced him and never heard from him again.

Her second husband, 17 years her senior, had been one of her professors in college. They had an enjoyable relationship, but he "drove [her] crazy" with his perfectionism and neatness. She gave many examples of his criticism of her and his demands that she do things his way, all of which had led her to feel a lack of control. Although she divorced him after a couple of years, he had remained devoted to her and still offered to return to her. They stayed "friends," and he continued his involvement as a father of sorts to her daughter.

In time, Mara revealed that she felt her first two husbands, as well as several boyfriends, had been "too" sexually interested in her, which she at first said she only vaguely understood. When she met John, she was relieved that he was not "controlling" or pushy about sexual activity.

Mara's concern over her own sexual urges was exacerbated in her teens when she realized boys were attracted to her "big boobs" (see Almansi, 1960). Her anxiety about sexuality was aggravated further by her out-of-wedlock pregnancy at 18 (which caused her to marry her first husband) and by an unwanted pregnancy by a different man (which required an abortion), before she met her second husband. Her recent obesity was understood by us as a protection from men and her own impulses. Following this interpretive work, she began a diet that was eventually quite successful.

We returned to examining why she tolerated John's overly critical attitude toward her daughter. She made allowances for him, since he had never had children of his own, but her tolerance turned out to be partly a rationalization. She became aware that her reluctance to discipline her daughter derived from an unconscious disidentification from her own intrusive/controlling mother. To further complicate the picture, when John disciplined her daughter, Mara leveled at him the criticisms she always felt toward her mother.

John's sexual difficulties, we learned, unconsciously relieved Mara's fear that Wendy's sexuality could get out of hand, as had her own. Later in therapy, Mara admitted she had never found John attractive. Her further associations to feeling unfairly treated by her first two husbands led us to conclude that John's suffering gratified unrequited revengeful wishes she unconsciously still harbored toward the first two husbands.

In addition, since John was "immature" (four years her junior), she viewed him unconsciously as a substitute son—relieving grief and guilt over aborting the son between marriages one and two. She treated John as though he were her daughter's brother. She would reprimand him, criticize his attitude, and encourage him to be "nicer" to Wendy, much as she might have done with a son.

Mara disliked John's criticism of her daughter for laziness and overeating. Part of John's problems seemed to be lack of experience with a 12-year-old girl, who predictably would act somewhat cantankerous and independent. But part of his problem seemed also to be anger over having such duties delegated to him.

Mara was consciously aware of wanting a more consistent father for Wendy than Mara had had. Mara gave numerous examples of her mother's inappropriate, unrealistic, and manipulative behavior that coerced Mara and her father to take care of her. (The mother would swoon and lie in bed for days.) Mara theorized that her father had left the house in order to escape the mother's control, when Mara was in ninth grade.

Moreover, when Mara inveigled John into disciplining Wendy, Mara had not counted on John's competing with Wendy for her attention. John felt deprived of Mara's interest, complaining that she was too preoccupied with her daughter's problems. To a certain extent, Mara admitted she deprived her husband, but she complained he did not understand the emotional traumas Wendy had suffered.

Specifically, John objected to Wendy's visiting with Mara's second husband. But Mara argued that he was the only consistent father her daughter knew. Mara could not convince John of this, and he felt outboxed, invaded, and jealous.

As Mara responded to treatment by taking over more of the parenting activity, she found herself even less interested in John. Six months after terminating her 18 months of treatment, she returned for a follow-up visit, and was hardly recognizable. She had lost 60 pounds, had left John, and was dating a businessman she had met in a chat room on the Internet to whom she was very attracted. Since he had a son by a previous marriage, he seemed more understanding about the various problems she had with her daughter. She came back to see me because of some anxiety over loss of control in this relationship with an apparently healthier man. He, for example, studiously avoided any disciplinary role with Wendy, and Mara was now aware enough of her motivations not to manipulate him into it.

Discussion

Mara's disidentification from her mother led her to discipline her daughter insufficiently. However, she rationalized her withdrawal from that aspect of parenting by focusing on the child's traumatization by the two previous divorces. She preconsciously managed to get John to take over the discipline, which Wendy mostly rejected.

Unbeknownst to John, he was the victim of "gaslighting" (Calef and Weinshel, 1981); he seemed to have introjected his wife's wish for her own superego to be external. Then he became the superego figure to Wendy.

John was not experienced enough as a parent of a 12-year-old to demur regarding disciplinary activity. He had not recognized his "newness" to the child. According to Mara, he did not seem to grasp the complexity of the mother–child relationship prior to his arrival, and he became involved in an "oedipal sibling triangle" (Sharpe and Rosenblatt, 1994) with Wendy and Mara. That triangle was further complicated by Mara's perpetuation of her relationship with her second husband.

In addition, John's apparent passivity, as a defense against loss of the object, led him to do Mara's bidding. She herself theorized that he yelled at Wendy after Mara had frustrated him.

Case 2: Renée

A 34-year-old married female accountant presented with a heart-wrenching dilemma. She had recently developed a fervent though ambivalent wish to become pregnant by her 49-year-old physician husband. When they had married 12 years earlier, however, she had agreed to his condition that they have no children together because he had three children from his previous marriage. When they married, her husband was still paying alimony and child support and preferred not to contend with more expense and more emotional drain.

Renée had not mentioned her recent stirrings to him. She worried that his prior children, now out of college, would probably disapprove of his fathering more offspring and would reject her for competing with their mother. She described her interactions with his children as warm and friendly when they visited during their childhood, and even moreso recently. Her fear of their disapproval turned out to be, in part, an externalization of her guilt over having allowed the courtship and sexual activity to have secretly begun before their father was legally divorced from their mother. Although I suspected much of the guilt had oedipal phase origins, that aspect did not turn out to be analyzable in once-a-week analytic psychotherapy. The five months she worked with me allowed us to understand related dynamics, however, and the insights she gained seemed sufficient for her to resolve the conflict she had initially presented.

Renée wished to understand her motivations for wanting to have a baby before she brought the subject up with her husband, and I agreed that such an approach was prudent. To begin with, we could see that two factors were now influencing her that had not entered into her thinking at the time of the "no-child agreement" with her husband. First, she was now acutely aware that her biological clock was winding down and that her childlessness would eventually be permanent. Second, she was finding her work less gratifying than she had a decade earlier. She had risen to a high level of competence, had made partner, and the challenge had diminished. The novelty had also worn off. And she now had to contend with political problems in the office that were time-consuming and, to her thinking, petty.

We learned that her current ambivalence over wanting a baby, associated with guilt over changing the "agreement," was connected to her conscious suspicion that part of her desire to have children derived from thoughts of escaping the aggression and problems in the workplace. She imagined that gratifying the demands of her own child would be more pleasurable than gratifying the demands of clients and senior partners. In fact, as she described the situation at work, I could better understand the reality of the frustrations she was feeling there.

More exploration led us to conclude that, rather than escaping work, she had initially suppressed wishes to have a child and "escaped" by working hard; then, as she grew dissatisfied at work, her yearning for children resurfaced, and she could no longer rationalize away those wishes by thinking her work could be her life.

In addition, her fantasy of oral gratification (being taken care of by her husband, not having to work) if she stopped working to become a home-maker/mother had led her to feel aggravated shame, since she loved her husband and did not want to "burden" him with extra financial responsibility. That shame led her to use staying at work as a defense. Renée also externalized the guilt: she imagined her husband would disapprove of her for being lazy. Father-transference to her husband (which I interpreted later, see below) had also led her to expect criticism from him for her orally tinged wishes.

In addition to the above-clarified dynamics, I interpreted her need to stay working to be an unconscious punishment/deprivation as well as a disidentification from her mother (who had not worked outside the home). I added some reality confrontation regarding child-rearing's not being much of an escape—since it also involved much work and frequent emotional drain. That confrontation seemed to diminish her minimization of the strife and deprivations of motherhood and decrease her guilt.

We did not sidestep the controversial question of whether being a full-time mother was necessary for children to develop in a mentally healthy way. In response to some of her factual questions to me on the issue, I discussed some of Margaret Mahler's findings about the first three to four years of life. I also explained that the exact requirements for minimally sufficient quality mothering are not clearly known.

The issues of motherhood's being draining and of the vicissitudes of sufficient quality mothering became relevant to Renée's treatment in other ways. Renée now admitted that her ambivalence about having children was also due to a lifetime conscious belief that she would be a bad mother. Specifically, she felt she could not "tolerate" a child. This belief was one factor that had led her to agree not to have children to begin with.

As we discussed the experiences she had had with her own mother, we could better understand the basis for Renée's belief in her own inadequacy. She felt her mother was constantly overwhelmed by the five children in the family. Her mother also did not protect Renée from her critical father, who spanked her periodically. He also acted as the children's parsimonious banker for their allowance, and Renée hated having to beg him for her money.

Her identification with her mother, which had led Renée to feel she could not cope with parenthood, was understood to shield her from experiencing rage toward mother. Renée's distaste for discussing her wishes to have a baby with her husband was connected to a transference expectation that he would be like her father, where she would have to beg and humiliate herself. As she clarified the reality of her husband's personality, she recounted her admiration for his parenting abilities. He was very unlike her father. She also realized her husband did not become easily overwhelmed, as her mother had.

Furthermore, her fear that she could not adequately care for a child was based on a preconscious expectation that, like her mother, she would often be alone, without help from her busy husband. That expectation of abandonment was analyzed as a fantasy of punishment that would relieve guilt caused by her competitive wishes toward her husband's ex-wife.

Those competitive wishes had been exacerbated during the period when her husband shared custody with his ex-wife. When his children visited, they often disliked leaving and would openly express their wish that Renée could have been their primary caregiver.

Lastly, Renée felt guilty that the wish for a child was not mutual. But after we clarified that her wish for a child was more specific to her husband than generalized, she felt less guilty.

She then spoke to him about her wish to have a child by him, and he surprised her by expressing enthusiasm. He even suggested that he should cut back his hours and do less hospital-based practice to diminish call so that he would have more time to spend with her and the child. She decided to stop treatment at that point.

A year later, she telephoned with a request to stop by my office to introduce me to her newborn son. She had, in agreement with her husband, stopped working, and was enjoying her role as a full-time mom with very little guilt. About two years later, I received a birth announcement for her second son.

Discussion

Aside from identification with her inadequate mother, Renée's avoidance of having a child derived from guilt over unconscious oedipal competition with her husband's ex-wife. That conflict was exacerbated by his children's preference for Renée. She also experienced negative father transference to her husband. Lastly, she lacked information about childhood development. Her unconscious transference to me as an accepting father who allowed her to procreate, and her transference wish to please me with her baby were not interpreted in this brief treatment, nor did those interpretations seem warranted or necessary.

Case 3: Skip

This 48-year-old newly remarried businessman consulted me for psychoanalytic treatment because of chronic problems with severe procrastination that had already cost him many customers, quite a bit of money, and the respect of others in the industry. He also suffered with intermittent sexual dysfunction. The personality problems associated with these complaints included mild grandiosity tempered by social ability, obsessional doubting and delay, and tendencies to withdraw from close interactions with his second wife. He had not fathered children. His current (second) wife had two daughters by her previous marriage, ages 21 and 18, neither of whom lived with the couple. But he had known them both during his two-year courtship with his wife.

His personal psychoanalysis lasted several years, and addressed the many character problems with which he had presented. During his treatment, he at first spoke of the disturbance between himself and his stepdaughters in a normalizing fashion. He was surprised when I initially pointed out that, when he was around his wife and her daughters, his penchant to "leave them alone" was a type of emotional withdrawal. When he had thought they needed time for "a mother–daughter chat," he would go to a movie alone. He did not immediately agree that he was withdrawing, but then recalled that both daughters had sought out his advice on a number of matters. He had actually distorted the reality of their interactions with him, he realized, since he usually felt they were not interested and that he had "nothing to contribute." We could see that he took a common form of courtesy toward the daughters and used this to rationalize his pathological withdrawal from them.

He voiced feelings that he did not know how to be a father. He argued that the girls already had a father with whom they communicated—albeit not a trustworthy fellow. He felt his wife was more skilled at discussing things with them. His associations about fathers led to the understanding that he was disidentifying from his father, who had been invasive, opinionated, and critical. His parents had not even attended his graduation from business school because they disagreed with his decision to marry his first wife.

These interpersonal dynamics were complicated by a lifelong fantasy of himself as the king in *The King and I*. He loved that musical, especially the sequences where Anna, the vivacious young teacher of the children, is able to loosen up the strict, humorless king of Siam. In particular, analysis revealed Skip's wish to be approached by an Anna-like figure with the invitation, "Shall We Dance?" as Anna had entreated the king. This passive mother-transference wish had led him to feel that he would pay attention to his wife's daughters only if they implored him to speak to them.

On one occasion, when his wife's younger daughter approached him to discuss her problems with a boyfriend, he became virtually speechless, although secretly flattered. Skip's next associations were to crying spontaneously while watching a TV commercial where there were baby ducks walking across the screen. The contiguity of those thoughts led me to interpret to Skip that he withdrew from the daughter to defend against grief over never having had his own children. He then recalled that his first wife had had an abortion before they divorced; she informed him of this after the fact, which hurt him. At this point, he reported "a tear in my eye," recognized he was avoiding grief, and saw that he might obtain some emotional gratification from interacting with his current wife's daughters.

He related his frustration over how his father had browbeaten his younger sister, leading her to develop serious emotional problems. He had not been able to help his sister avoid the destructive interactions with his father, and this fact contributed to his relief at not having become a father—he felt he would have been ineffectual, as he had been in protecting his sister.

The futility of his concern about his sister, which he had isolated and suppressed since early adulthood, had led him to withdraw defensively from most close personal interactions that involved intense emotion. These isolation mechanisms diminished acutely, however, when Mickey Mantle died. At that time, his sister, with whom he had not spoken in over a decade, mailed him a note of condolence, in recognition of Skip's childhood idolization of Mantle. Skip was surprised by his sister's action, and saddened about their distance.

Skip's response to this bit of analytic work included a new interest in helping others. However, after some months, his descriptions of these new interactions indicated that, through an alteration of defenses (Brenner, 1975), he had started "adopting" young women in his work. He inappropriately advised them; he tolerated their substandard performance on work important to the business (he knew about the problems, but could not "confront" the women); he became overly sympathetic on hearing of their personal problems; and he even made a couple of secretaries small loans they never repaid. In other words, he became interested in their "needs" even if they did not initiate *asking him to dance,* metaphorically speaking.

Although his new adoption behavior had pathological elements, such as eventually bringing suffering on himself (which needed further analysis), he had moved away from avoiding close contact with other human beings. He began to enjoy engaging in more meaningful discussions with his stepdaughters. More important, he became much more interactive with their mother regarding the daughters' problems, and he stopped avoiding more profound and previously neglected matters between his wife and himself.

Discussion

Skip's lack of history with his stepdaughters and his lack of experience in parenting had seemed to contribute to his withdrawal from them. However, he also had developed unconscious transference expectations that affected his behavior: he had anticipated painful sadness and inadequacy, reactions he displaced from the frustrating and depressing situation regarding his father and his sister.

Summary

Stepparents who have not previously raised their own children are at risk to have internal and interpersonal conflicts in their new marriages. Sometimes the conflicts develop between the stepparent and the stepchildren, sometimes the conflicts erupt between the stepparent and the "childed" spouse, and at other times the stepparent's conflicts are more intrapsychic, but may lead to withdrawal.

The therapist must be aware with all patients of the intertwining of interpersonal and intrapsychic factors. Certain prototypical constellations, however, may present themselves, as they are complicated by each person's personal history and dynamics.

References

Abrams, D. (1991), Looking at and looking away—Etiology of preoedipal splitting in a deaf girl. *The Psychoanalytic Study of the Child,* 46:277–304. New Haven, CT: Yale University Press.

Akhtar, S. (1992), Tethers, orbits, and invisible fences: Clinical, developmental, sociocultural, and technical aspects of optimal distance. In: *When the Body Speaks: Psychological Meanings in Kinetic Cues,* ed. S. Kramer & S. Akhtar. Northvale, NJ: Aronson.

Almansi, R. (1960), The face–breast equation. *J. Amer. Psychoanal. Assn.*, 8:43–70.

Arlow, J. & Brenner, C. (1964), *Psychoanalytic Concepts and the Structural Theory.* New York: International Universities Press.

Bernstein, A. (1989), *Yours, Mine, and Ours: How Families Change When Remarried Parents Have a Child Together.* New York: Scribner's.

Bielenberg, L. (1992), A task-centered preventive group approach to create cohesion in the new stepfamily: A preliminary evaluation. *Res. Soc. Work Prac.*, 1:416–433.

Blos, P. (1962), *On Adolescence: A Psychoanalytic Interpretation.* New York: Free Press of Glencoe.

Blum, H. (1969), A psychoanalytic view of *Who's Afraid of Virginia Woolf? J. Amer. Psychoanal. Assn.*, 17:888–903.

_____ (1983), Adoptive parents: Generative conflict and generational continuity. *The Psychoanalytic Study of the Child*, 38:141–163. New Haven, CT: Yale University Press.

Bohannon, P. (1984), Stepparenthood: A new and old experience. In: *Parenthood: A Psychodynamic Perspective*, ed. R. Cohen, B. Cohler & S. Weissman. New York: Guilford Press.

Bray, J. & Harvey, D. (1995), Adolescents in stepfamilies: Developmental family interventions. *Psychotherapy*, 32:122–130.

Brenner, C. (1975), Alterations in defenses during psychoanalysis. In: *Monograph II, New York Psychoanalytic Institute Kris Study Group.* New York: International Universities Press.

Calef, V. & Weinshel, E. (1981), Some clinical consequences of introjection: Gaslighting. *Psychoanal. Quart.*, 50:44–66.

Cath, S. H., Gurwitt, A. & Gunsberg, L., eds. (1982), *Fathers and Their Families.* Hillsdale, NJ: The Analytic Press.

_____ _____ & Ross, J. M., eds. (1989), *Father and Child.* Boston: Little Brown.

Colarusso, C. (1994), *Fulfillment in Adulthood.* New York: Plenum Press.

Everett, L. W. (1998), Factors that contribute to satisfaction or dissatisfaction in stepfather–stepchild relationships. *Persp. Psychiat. Care*, 34:25–35.

Feder, L. (1974), Adoption trauma: Oedipus myth/clinical reality. *Internat. J. Psycho-Anal.*, 55:491–493.

Filinson, R. (1986), Relationship in stepfamilies: An examination of alliances. *J. Compar. Fam. Stud.*, 17:43–61.

Freud, S. (1926), Inhibitions, symptoms and anxiety. *Standard Edition*, 20:87–175. London: Hogarth Press, 1959.

Galenson, E. & Roiphe, H. (1976), Some suggested revisions concerning early female development. *J. Amer. Psychoanal. Assn.*, 24:29–58.

_____ & _____ (1980), The preoedipal development of the boy. *J. Amer. Psychoanal. Assn.*, 28:805-827.

Gitelson, M. (1945), Psychological problems of stepchildren. *Psychoanal. Quart.*, 19:413.

Greenspan, S. & Salmon, J. (1993), *Playground Politics: Understanding the Emotional Life of the School-Age Child.* Reading, MA: Perseus Books.

_____ & _____ (1995), *The Challenging Child.* Reading, MA: Perseus Books.

Jacobson, D. (1995), Critical interactive events and child adjustment in the stepfamily: A linked family system. In: *Understanding Stepfamilies: Implications for Assessment and Treatment.* Alexandria, VA: American Counseling Association.

Keshet, J. (1988), The remarried couple: Stresses and successes. In: *Relative Strangers: Studies of Stepfamily Processes,* ed. W. Beer et al. Totowa, NJ: Rowman & Littlefield.

Kestenberg, J. (1975), The effect on parents of the child's transition into and out of latency. In: *Children and Parents: Psychoanalytic Studies in Development.* New York: Aronson.

Lamb, M. & Oppenheim, D. (1989), Fatherhood and father–child relationships: Five years of research. In: *Fathers and Their Families,* ed. S. H. Cath, A. Gurwitt & L. Gunsberg. Hillsdale, NJ: The Analytic Press.

Lerner, H. (1976), Parental mislabeling of female genitals: A determinant of penis envy. *J. Amer. Psychoanal. Assn.,* 24:269–284.

Levin, I. (1997), Stepfamily as project. *Marriage & Fam. Rev.,* 26:123–133.

Lipsitz, D. (1997), The effects of parental stress and parental acceptance upon first time parenting stepfathers with resident pre-adolescent children. *Dissertation Abstracts International,* 55(6-A):1706, 1994.

Mahler, M., Pine, F. & Bergman, A. (1975), *The Psychological Birth of the Human Infant.* New York: Basic Books.

Marcus, I. M. (1973), Panel: Separation-individuation. *J. Amer. Psychoanal. Assn.,* 21:155–167.

————— (1980), Countertransference and the psychoanalytic process with children and adolescents. *The Psychoanalytic Study of the Child,* 35:285–298. New Haven, CT: Yale University Press.

Miller, A. (1985), Guidelines for stepparenting. *Psychother. Priv. Prac.,* 3:99–109.

Morrison, K. & Stollman, W. (1996), Stepfamily assessment: An integrated model. *J. Divorce & Remarriage,* 24:163–182.

Nickman, S. (1985), Issues in adoption: The need for dialogue. *The Psychoanalytic Study of the Child,* 40:365–398. New Haven, CT: Yale University Press.

Parens, H. (1975), Panel: Parenthood as a developmental phase. *J. Amer. Psychoanal. Assn.,* 23:154–165.

————— (1988), Siblings in early childhood: Some direct observational findings. *Psychoanal. Inq.,* 8:31–50.

————— (1991), A view of the development of hostility in early life. *J. Amer. Psychoanal. Assn.,* 39(Suppl):75–108.

————— (1992), Review of *The Emergence of Morality in Children. J. Amer. Psychoanal. Assn.,* 40:261–267.

Peretti, P., Miller, P. & Martin, V. (1992), Enduring negative psychological characteristics of male and female step-children toward the stepparent. *Acta Psychiatr. Belg.,* 92:209–217.

Roberts, T. & Price, S. (1987), Instant families: Divorced mothers marry never-married men. *J. Divorce,* 11:71–92.

Sager, C. (1987), The more marriage is, the more it's not what grandma and grandpa knew. In: *Frontiers of Dynamic Psychotherapy: Essays in Honor of Arlene and Lewis R. Wolberg,* ed. P. Buirski et al. New York: Brunner/Mazel.

Saint-Jacques, M. (1995), Role strain prediction in stepfamilies. *J. Divorce & Remarriage,* 24:51–72.

Sariola, H. (1996), The prevalence and context of incest abuse in Finland. *Child Abuse & Neglect*, 20:843–850.

Sharpe, S. & Rosenblatt, A. (1994), Oedipal sibling triangles. *J. Amer. Psychoanal. Assn.*, 42:491–524.

Stanton, G. (1986), Preventive intervention with stepfamilies. *Soc. Work*, 31:201–206.

Visher, E. & Visher, J. (1988), *Old Loyalties, New Ties: Therapeutic Strategies*. New York: Brunner/Mazel.

Wieder, H. (1977), On being told of adoption. *Psychoanal. Quart.*, 46:1–21.

Wolf, P. & Mast, E. (1987), Counseling issues in adoptions by stepparents. *Soc. Work*, 32:69–74.

Naiveté

Love and Hate Factors in the Outcome of Stepfatherhood

Henry J. Friedman and Jamie L. Feldman

What does a stepfather want? Perhaps a more complete version of this question should ask what a stepfather can allow himself to want, if he expects the experience to be a good and productive one for both him and his stepchildren. There is little question that the guidelines for successful stepparenting are far from established. The predominance of feeling that few stepfathers have an easy time of it, and that most will be unsuccessful in establishing a good relationship with the children, has been most commonly related to the innate difficulty for the children involved in accepting a stepfather into their family and their emotional lives. Of course, there are plenty of examples of children who seem to react negatively to a stepfather who enters their life through the marriage to their mother even though the stepfather is eager to make a good relationship to them. The assumption of resentment of the stepfather seems almost axiomatic to those in the world of psychological ideas and concepts. Little effort has been concentrated upon what the role of the stepfather has been in generating an atmosphere of distress and despair in the family constellation. As is the case in divorce, there is a problem that revolves around the absence of best case examples which demonstrates a model of how well such an event can go if the condition of the participants is such that all parties involved can be conceived of as operating at a mature level of integration and in particular have a capacity for empathy, intuition, and concern for the feelings of others around them. When these criteria are met it isn't difficult to achieve a new experience for all parties involved in a recombined family unit. The factors that so frequently interrupt such a smooth transition and experience are the subject of this chapter.

Naiveté is seldom considered as an important and ubiquitous character trait that affects many life situations and personal interactions. Like the closely related character concept of conventionality, naiveté is often a stubborn character trait that defies the voice of reason even when it is delivered in a psychotherapy. When a naive position has become part of the structure of an individual's narcissism it is then particularly difficult to influence. That people will become estranged over issues of small narcissistic differences is relevant to the whole concept of naiveté as a destructive force in the interpersonal sphere. The expectations that individuals bring to a new situation—such as the one involved in a man living with a woman and her children from another marriage—are of great importance in determining the likelihood of conflict and failure in the result. Ironically, it is often standard, conventional expectations rather than unusual or unconventional ones that lead to difficulty. These expectations can come from the stepfather himself but more often they are the result of a collaboration between the mother and the new husband in her life. Either or both parties may bring naive expectations to the situation; not uncommonly the mother may have influenced her new husband to share her view that the stepfather is part of a new family unit in which he is to be seen, treated, and loved as the father of the household. Or the stepfather himself may hold this expectation in a stubborn and ultimately enraged fashion, recruiting his wife to share this position, enforced by both her shared naive assumption that this could be the case and her fear that her husband's disappointment with the children's response to him will defeat her attempts at a happy marriage.

Such a quandary can frequently be observed in the psychotherapy of a man who is in a relationship with a divorced woman with one, two, or more children. Even though the relationship is quite strong, both individuals hesitate to introduce the man to the children. (The reverse is certainly also true with many men who have children, and the new woman, postdivorce, has none.) In these circumstances, if a therapist probes about this, the usual response has to do with protecting the children from knowledge of parental sexuality and romance. It is frequently assumed that children will be traumatized by the awareness of a new man in their divorced or widowed mother's life. The idea that frankness with children even of young age might be helpful is frequently resisted; the idea that introducing a man to the children will be harmful if the relationship fails to work out is another major reason put forward for avoiding an introduction. It is this reasoning that is important to focus on because it reveals basic assumptions about young children and their vulnerability to attachment and loss of a new object (in this case a potential stepfather). Such individuals seldom consider projection as the basis for their concern about the impact of failure of the parental relationship upon the children. That both the potential stepfather and mother may themselves be banking heavily upon the desire to have the children show their love for the mother by investing their primary father love in the stepfather is seldom acknowledged but may well be the basis for the concern for the children's feelings of disappointment should the relationship fail to yield a "new father."

Both narcissistic grandiosity and vulnerability are crucial in the fate of the stepparent. In this case, reference is made to the stepfather, but the dynamics described in this chapter apply equally well in the case of stepmothers. The type of mature narcissism which is required to withstand the potential disappointments (with resultant depression and rage) is, unfortunately, not widely distributed in the adult population. In general, to our disadvantage, we often assume that it is, hence it is possible to shift the responsibility to the children and their inability, due to their immaturity, to accept the stepparent into the situation. It is all too easy to assume that the appearance of turbulence in the children in relation to the stepparent results from their reluctance to accept the parental divorce. Particularly in situations where the children have a good, developed relationship with their father and the children are described as resentful or unresponsive to the stepfather, it is assumed that the primary motivation comes from the children's desire to reconstitute the parental couple. This perception is increased by the antidivorce literature that has escalated in intensity in recent years. Such a perspective stems from a narcissitic stance of authors who decry the social change involved in divorce by citing incorrectly the ease with which people currently divorce. This emphasis, which denies the enormous emotional and financial pressures that work against divorce in all situations, makes it appear that current divorcing couples with children are made up of immature, gratification-seeking, selfish individuals. They are further accused of not recognizing the impact of such a selfish action upon their children. If the influence of the antidivorce literature is acknowledged, then it is a small step to concluding that the difficulty in stepfamily formation is a natural consequence of the impact of divorce upon the children. In this regard it is essential to be aware that the conclusion of such a reseacher as Wallerstein (1980), despite the apparent basis in data, is nonetheless more emotionally driven than the data reveal. Wallerstein's strongly felt, emotional conclusion about the inexorable damage of divorce to children, particularly, on their inability to value marriage because they have never seen a good one that survived, is a striking example of a researcher failing to remain even minimally objective about her subject. Wallerstein, in her strong resistance to social change, fails to acknowledge her lack of a control group which would provide her with a comparison group of couples who stayed together, one group with successful couples therapy and one without, where the impact upon the children could be evaluated. Wallerstein's prejudice seems apparent in her failure to acknowledge what any psychotherapeutically experienced individual knows, namely that adult patients raised in homes with no divorce but a persistently unloving atmosphere have an intense distrust of marriage which certainly competes with any seen in individuals where divorce had occurred.

Nonetheless, the frequent failure of stepfamilies to survive (or at least to be judged as happy by both the parents and children) has to be acknowledged. The role of parental aspirations regarding the children needs to be given fuller appreciation than it has been; the high frequency of failure in second marriages may otherwise simply be attributed to the neurotic component of the adults' relationship in marriage. In many second marriages the role of the children in the fantasies of both parents needs to be considered. There are circumstances of stepfathering where narcissistic fantasies are easily actualized. When a divorce has occurred with a child or children under two years of age and the father in effect abandons the role of father, it is possible for the stepfather to enact his fantasy of being the father to this child or children. In so far as the father is absent this may be an entirely reciprocal and synergistic arrangement. Furthermore, the experience of the stepfather as father may be gratifying to the mother who has experienced the father's lack of involvement with the children as a profound, personal rejection. Divorces of this sort, where the divorcing parents are hostile to each other and the father either abandons the children or as a result of the mother's rejection ceases to pursue his role as father are far from rare. Stepfathering in such a situation may still have the perils of hate and dislike that occur with the child's cognitive awareness, inevitable in almost all circumstances, that the stepfather isn't the real father; the real father even when totally absent from the picture is a known entity which will be dealt with by the child in accordance with their emotional position toward the mother and stepfather.

In most situations, the stepfather has not entered into such a clear, absent-father situation. Rather, one finds fathers of varying intensity, involvement, and competition. Not infrequently the stepfather feels inclined to enter into a competition to prove his superior motivation for "the good of the child." This position is often presented as a moral one. The divorcing father really has abandoned the well-being of the wife and children. He is perceived in unflattering or hostile terms in relationship to the newly formed couple. He is depicted openly or covertly as having the wrong values for child raising; this can range from issues of wealth, as in too much or too little, either of which is equated with having a corrupting effect on the children. Winning this competition is seen as essential by such a stepfather in regard to two relationships. The child is seen as the enemy if his or her preference for the father remains clear and apparent. It is deemed acceptable if the preference is driven underground. Out of sight, out of mind is the rule here. The second relationship is to the wife; should the children remain loyal to their father, the stepfather may well feel that he has betrayed and disappointed his wife. He may perceive her as having married him to achieve a new equilibrium with her ex-husband. The children, in their shift of affection and role status are then seen as confirming the view that nothing has been lost to the mother in her divorce. In essence, a meaningless man has been deleted from her life; his value is entirely lacking and can't even be seen in his functioning in a way that is helpful and important to their children.

For many women, the persistent interest and desire of their former husbands to remain involved as fathers, is an unwelcome blow to their narcissism. It underlines the specific rejection by the husband, particularly in divorces initiated by the man around his involvement with another woman, or his desire, openly expressed, for a different, more responsive spouse. The stepfather in such instances may eventually succumb to the pressure he perceives in his wife to join her in villifying the ex-husband. This may develop despite the fact that he has begun the role of stepfather with a much more receptive, even friendly idea of his relationship to the father. The narcissistic issues in such a stepfather's response involves a fusion with his wife's narcissistic injury and desire to triumph. The following example illustrates the existence and unfolding of these dynamics in a case where all of the principals involved were highly educated and alert to the issues of psychotherapy. It is an example of the triumph of narcissistic issues over rationality. The inclusion of this example illustrates a suboptimal outcome in a stepfamily related to several of the dynamics already mentioned.

Two 33-year-old professionals divorced after nine years of marriage; there was one child, aged two at the time. The marriage, which had been troubled by marked differences in personalities and preference for lifestyles, had nonetheless been intensive and to a certain extent produced considerable personal and professional success for both husband and wife. The divorce was based upon the wife's intolerance for social contact for which she had an aversion of longstanding and unexplained nature. The couple had struggled to find a way of dealing with their differences through individual analyses. A decision had been made, despite the admitted difficulty and unhappiness in the relationship, to have a child. This was a considered decision known to both parties, based on the inability to give up on the relationship the future of which at some times appeared better than at others. Neither member of the couple were willing to forego the experience of having a child. Following the birth of a son the marriage deteriorated. The nature of this deterioration was difficult to gauge; the wife was increasingly annoyed and angry. She felt that the husband's economic concerns and activities directed at achieving economic security were unnecessary. She had little concern for material security. Instead she wanted a man who saw helping her with mothering and being more "around" as important to her. In addition, her intense dislike of the company of others (always exclusive of the desire to be alone with her husband) led to a permanent break in their relationship.

In the ensuing several months following the breakup, the couple continued to share the responsibility for child care. They divided the time each of them spent taking care of the child. However, since the work schedule of the wife was less demanding it was she who managed the majority of the child care. This arrangement continued for the better part of a year following the separation. The wife, at several junctures, became more convinced that she would like to reconcile, that she could change her social patterns and accept her husband's definition of his role as provider. For his part, the husband felt a strong desire to reconcile but believed that his wife's promise to enjoy a social life was a promise made under duress and would never be honored by her in the day-to-day life that they ordinarily lived. At this point the wife began to date others, and the terms of a divorce, with generous economic arrangements for the wife and child, were agreed upon. The wife soon met a man, became involved and quickly remarried. He was also a professional whose previous marriage had ended in divorce; he was childless. By this point the wife was furious with her ex-husband and unrelenting in her conviction that it would be in the "best interest of the child" for her second husband to function as the psychological father of the child. Initially, it appeared that her second husband was unable to see the first husband as the villain she projected. However, when this led to fighting, he quickly retreated from any position of supporting the first husband in any of his efforts to see the child.

Both the mother and her second husband then turned their aggression on the father. They were mutually allied in their belief that the stepfather should be the psychologically important parent. They wanted the father to see the correctness of their position; this should include continued economic support accompanied by his willingness to absent himself from their family life. To this end, they agreed that the father should have to limit his visits to periods during the work day; they felt that he should leave them and their child alone during evenings and weekends when they should have uninterrupted family life. The father strongly resisted their position; this resistance required legal intervention. Large amounts of time and money were spent in pursuit of this difference. The mother and her second husband began to pursue the child, who was now five, insisting that he call the stepfather dad and call his father by his first name. They persisted with this stance in a seemingly immovable way until the child became overtly distressed, screaming at them that he couldn't call his stepfather daddy because that would mean that his father was dead. (This was in fact a version of the father's communication to his son that a stepfather wasn't called daddy when his father was still alive and involved.) This dramatic encounter did stop the mother and stepfather from pursuing the child further in this matter. The tension, however, continued. Curiously, it was far from two-sided. The mother and her second husband continued to view the father as an intruder upon their narcissistic scheme which was designed to buttress their own relationship by identifying them as the "good" people with the "right" values about life and their son. Their attitude toward the father continued to be both taunting and devaluing.

The outcome in this case was far from devastating or tragic. The hostility toward the father continued indefinitely. Curiously, it was the developing child who placed a limit upon criticism of the father by refusing to talk with either set of parents (the father also remarried) about life in either family. One might even say that the child who developed in this atmosphere developed unusual capacities to avoid hopelessly conflicted situations. His insightfulness can be illustrated by his ability to explain, at a much later date, that he was aware that his experience of each parent was different from what they had experienced with each other. In the polarization of two parents the child had escaped a negative charac- terization by either of the participants in a chronic and irresolvable conflict. On the other hand, the relationship with the stepfather was clearly less good than it would have been had the mother's narcissism not required that he attempt to replace the father. The second husband, in this case, brought problems of his own to the role of stepfather; the implication that it was the mother alone who determined the problems is misleading. First, his reaction formation against awareness of his resent- ment of stepparenting was a factor. Second, his competitiveness with the father appeared to be about the child but really involved his belief that his wife had never really given up her preference for her first husband. The impact on the child was in the range of observable but within normal limits. Increasingly, he could be observed to ignore differences between the two parental groups; his observing capacities about the complexities of relationships between people of his parent's generation were very reduced.

The purpose of this chapter is to focus on the role of parental character problems on the formation of a stepparenting relationship as part of establishing a recombined, functional family unit. The case presented serves well to illustrate the intensity of naive positions in determining a negative outcome. All of the parental figures in the case example had years of therapy and analysis; none was particularly pathological to the clinical eye; yet it was nearly impossible to break the impasse that evolved between the mother and her second husband's conviction that the stepfather in this situation should be the psychological father. This was true despite the father's very active interest in his son as well as his availability to see the child on weekends and evenings. While it is necessary to consider deeper motivations based upon competitive hatred and retaliatory destructive- ness, there is no question that naive assumptions on the part of the mother and her second husband played a role in their belief that it was possible for their fantasy about his stepfathering replacing the role of the father played a part in what they attempted to enact. The assumption on the part of the mother and her second husband that the stepfather should be the psychological father had been reinforced by their familiarity with Goldstein, Freud, and Solnit's (1980) *Beyond the Best Interest of the Child*. In the book, these authorities declare that the child's inability to form a strong relationship with more than one figure makes it important in situations of conflict for there to be one stable parental figure. By casting the problem in these terms, they unfortunately provided many people both within and outside the profession with a rationalization for their narcissistically determined position on how to deal with children in a postdivorce situation. This book has had an enormous influence in both legal and psychoanalytic circles because of both the certainty of the authors and their great authority within child psychoanalysis. Their naiveté is a striking factor in what they conclude if one considers the role of parental narcissism in determining attitudes as to what will be best for the child.

We are raising the question of how a healthy response to stepparenting is achieved, and what factors need to be mobilized in an individual who chooses to attempt the difficult role of stepfather, in this instance, although most of the considerations might apply to stepmothering as well. The differences with stepmothering in a postdivorce, mother alive, active and well situation are considerable. The bond to the mother is not only usually stronger on a psychobiological basis but social and personal respect for the mother–child bond is so much greater that this needs to be taken into account. There are situations in which the father has from early in infancy played a greater role in the caretaking of the children; this will be reflected in the child's greater bond to the father in the preoedipal phases of development. In such instances the stepmother may almost seem naturally more important to the children, the children responding to the father's positive involvement with his new wife, because of their primary attachment to the divorced father as the nuturing parent. The role of maturity in the stepparent cannot be overestimated. Maturity is a concept that is generally underutilized in psychoanalytic circles. It can be seen as a counterbalance to the naiveté involved in the assumptions of love in the stepfather and the resultant sense of disappointment and hate that follow the failure to have these expectations met.

The challenges for a stepfather that do not relate to the child's difficulties involve accepting a role with the children that is not assumed to be primary. A stepfather who can accept that he is not able to be the receipient of an intense love from his stepchildren is, ironically, better positioned to have a successful relationship with his stepchild(ren). In the case example that follows, the success of the adjustment within the new mother–second husband dyad and the relationship to an older (11-year-old) child depends upon the stepfather's willingness to expect only a peripheral role in the life of the child. This unusually open situation depended as well on the mother's acceptance that such a relationship was good enough for her as well. Both the stepfather and mother were, in this case, aware of desires for something more intense, more romantic as a possible outcome of their marriage. However, in this instance both were able to give up on the fantasy, accepting instead the reality of a harmonious relationship between the two of them not involving closeness with her daughter.

This case resembles the previously described one in that the participants were professionals in training and exposed to psychoanalysis and

aware of emotional issues and events. However, several factors differentiate the approach of this couple; in particular, there is a clear way in which
the second husband in this instance resisted an initial inclination to expect
the daughter in this case to love him in a significant relationship justifying
fashion. Dr. J was involved with and intent upon marrying a woman who
in addition to having a child was somewhat older and more experienced
professionally than he was. His life experience was such that marrying a
woman with children seemed a risky endeavor. Initially, he approached
this with the idea that his emotional involvement with his fiancée's
daughter would justify his not marrying a woman who like him would be
in her 30s and unencumbered by a child. The daughter, on her part, was
a pleasant and attractive child who, while reasonably receptive to her
mother's personal life, was nonetheless rather indifferent to the man in
her mother's life. She had a strong relationship with her father and saw
her mother's choice as fairly irrelevant to her life. This presented an
immediate challenge to Dr. J's fantasy of an immediate daughter in his
life. Initially, he felt disappointed and contemplated either pushing the
relationship with the daughter or breaking off the relationship with her
mother. The difficulty in accepting a kind of benign neglect from the
daughter was interpreted by Dr. J as a narcissistic injury. In discussions
with his fiancée it became clear that she didn't expect or require that Dr.
J enter into a close or competitive relationship with her daughter. She was
well aware that her daughter was very much fathered by her ex-husband;
any competitive venture with that relationship would be destructive in her
view. It was important to her that Dr. J understand that her need was for
a relationship with him. There was an opportunity to have a child together
on their own. While she felt that a new family would be formed she was
convinced that it couldn't include her daughter in the sense that Dr. J
initially felt was possible. What mattered to her was that her daughter be
allowed to participate in a fashion that pleased her. In essence, she wanted
to be sure that her daughter felt free to enter into their life as a family in
any style in which she felt comfortable.

  Dr. J attributes his ability to rethink his feelings about his stepdaughter
to both work in his psychoanalysis and the supportive, educational clarifi-
cations of his fiancée. Equipped with a new insight, he was able to take a
new position with his new stepdaughter. They became something akin to
friends who have been drawn together because each were attached in
separate important friendships with the same person. They both wanted
to see the mother-wife achieve a kind of happiness that had eluded her;
this alliance increasingly made them comrades in arms. The daughter
appreciated that Dr. J created no conflicts of loyalty with her father; on
the other hand she appreciated the differences between her father and
her stepfather. The former operated in a much more low-key fashion
about most aspects of life. Her stepfather was more expansive and more

comfortable with his exhibitionistic side. Limited identification was possible for the daughter whom Dr. J encouraged to be more active and risk-taking in her choices, although this was always done in a respectful and indirect fashion. For instance, her father didn't feel it was important for a woman to be ambitious in work; her stepfather by encouraging her mother and by his own example encouraged her to aim high in her aspirations and to follow through in achieving them.

Dr. J was aware of recurrent pressure on his emotional state related to his status with his stepdaughter. Periodically, he would start to register resentment at being somewhat outside the dyadic relationship between his wife and her daughter. The daughter, as she became more involved with her friendship for him, felt increasingly comfortable asking for advice about presents for her mother's birthday and other celebratory occasions. At such times Dr. J would begin to feel some resentment about "giving" so much without receiving enough in return. Self-analysis would return him to an understanding of the greater complexity of a stepfather–daughter relationship and an acceptance of this outcome—an outcome which certainly disappointed his naive expectations about this relationship. Resentment could be transcended. A growing appreciation that his stepdaughter, while not fulfilling his hoped-for aspirations, was nevertheless a real ally in his life. Furthermore, he came to appreciate her independence of spirit and style. He often found himself reflecting positively on her good character and solid achievements. She was, as a developing young woman, surprisingly self-contained and disinclined to burden her mother with problems or demands upon her time. While he never did develop a parental "feel" to his relationship with his stepdaughter, both of them felt that they had a good relationship. He particularly enjoyed visits from his stepdaughter, even at times remarking to himself that he was less conflicted about her than her mother who often, though pleased with her daughter in general, felt a gap between herself and her daughter.

Overall, the outcome in this second case is far more positive than in the first case. The factors involved in determining this outcome reside mainly in character differences in the two sets of mother–stepfather combinations. The role of the child in determining the outcome could be seen as crucial if one chose to study the dynamics exclusively from the point of view of the child. In the first case the child, by insisting that he couldn't call his stepfather dad because that "would kill his father" played a crucial role in frustrating the mother–stepfather position. One can image many instances in which the child would comply with the parental constellation and abandon its father. In such an instance the narcissistic position of the mother, which was accommodated by her second husband, would triumph. The naive position would have found expression in reality. The child would have been drawn into a collaboration with the mother–stepfather alliance that would have created a pseudo happy family entity.

Happiness would have been achieved at the cost of sacrificing a good relationship with the father. The mother's moralistic position was expressed as the unstated belief that if you leave me it means that you have abandoned your child, or that you are not a person who is deserving of maintaining the status of father. The mother–stepfather dyad in the first case was so caught up in their idea of the stepfather being compensated for marrying a woman with a child by taking over the benefits of the father's emotional position with the child that they were ultimately driven by hate for the father generated by dissapointment of this fixed fantasy.

In the second case, it was precisely the ability of the stepfather-to-be to consider that his desire to be the father of his 10-year-old stepdaughter wasn't legitimate in its motivation. His narcissism might desire it but his sense of decency and propriety wouldn't allow him to indulge this desire. This situation was enhanced by a mother who understood her fiancé's desire but doubted that it could ever be fulfilled with her daughter. She knew that her daughter was attached to her father even though, in her view, he had many unattractive characteristics. However, she saw no need to replace the father with her second husband, even though she did see him as a more desirable example of an adult man. Ultimately, this resulted in a friendship between her daughter and her second husband, which was based upon what had actually evolved between them rather than what either had hoped would happen.

The conditions of a reconstituted family will vary greatly from situation to situation. The approach in this chapter has ignored those situations in which the father has abandoned any interest in the children. Wallerstein (1980), in her initial report on divorced couples with children in Marin County, reported what for her was an unexplainable phenomenon. Many fathers, who had been reported in their preseparation period to be actively involved, activity-oriented, failed after separation to see very much if any of their children. Wallerstein expressed her confusion at this finding, but explained it in terms of the demands of a busy life in modern society or some aspect of shame at the divorce. She did not consider that these men had functioned as good fathers as defined by their wives in what were for them unsatisfactory marriages. Wallerstein seemed not to have considered that divorces are rarely casually evolved events; her impression that this may be the case, that divorce is as easy as a walk to the court house or to your attorney's office, may be a product of her lack of empathy for men. The men in question in her report may have complied with the demands of their wives that they function as childcare sharers, a status which they resented and for them was part of a troubled marriage. In such an instance, when they are able to break free, their response may be to treat the wife and children as a unit from which they now are free. They are able to pursue life on their own terms in the period following the divorce. As such these fathers are better not being seen as abandoning their children. It would be better in such situations not to assume that a stepfather should step into the void created by the father's seeming lack of interest in his children. Over time it is possible that such a father will find his own way with his children; a pattern of involvement may emerge, if time is given for this to occur, that represents, for the first time, a sincere emotional involvement of the father with his children. Hence, a distinction has to be made between a truly abandoning father and a seemingly abandoning father who, if given time, will find a real connection to his or her father.

Even where abandonment is real and absolute it is unclear that the stepfather has an open field in which to develop a stepfather relationship. For instance, even children without a father to relate to may in fantasy have ideas of loyalty to the abandoning father; these may include strong fantasies of ultimate reunion. There is in addition, a potential problem in stepfathering that comes from the possibility of the stepfather accepting too rapidly the children's rejection of their father. In a previous publication (Friedman, 1980), one of us described cases in which the fusion between two children, in this case daughters and their mother resulted in banishment of a father, who in his own words was far from a great father but who nonetheless continued to feel connection and yearning for these daughters. This father made multiple efforts to make contact with his daughters who were aged 14 and 16 at the time of the separation and divorce. As far as one could tell, no friend or relative responded to this man's request for help in making contact with his daughters. Shortly after the divorce the mother began a relationship with a man who she was ultimately to remarry. Curiously, the second husband was in the mental health field, which led to an assumption that he might see the importance of advocating that his stepdaughters at least explain why they would not meet with their father. This never did occur; instead it appeared that he accepted the idea that this mother and her two daughters were justified in forming a projective image of the father as a monster. In their combined sensibilities it was justifiable to shun the father. The stepfather collaborated in this position. Unfortunately, there was no data available from this man as to how he saw the situation.

Adaptation to the status of stepfather appears from reported experience to be demanding on the maturity and sensibility aspects of personality functioning. One might say that the less neurotic the adults involved, the better the chances of a good adaptation. More precisely, the nature of the narcissism of both the mother and the stepfather is crucial to the outcome in stepparenting. It isn't sufficient to underline the role of disordered narcissism in generating conflict between the stepfather and father. The nature of that disordered narcissism is best conceptualized at the borderline level of psychopathology. This is true despite the fact that the individuals involved would often not be seen as overtly borderline by those around them. However, the nature of their intent, the content of their narcissistic fantasies, of their essential goodness, and the evil of the other can best be seen as the operant result of the borderline level of function. Maturity as a character state can be taught in psychotherapy to those individuals who do not have a deeper link to a pathological narcissistic position. The purpose of the case examples provided in this chapter is to demonstrate this fact. Its importance is of great significance to those involved in providing psychotherapy for individuals facing the transition to stepfather status. It is our belief that many psychotherapists are unaware of the issues we have outlined regarding the maturity of the parental figures involved in these constellations. If the therapist focuses entirely on the child it is likely that the contribution of the parents' dynamics both as individuals and as a couple will be overlooked. This may particularly prove to be the case when the individual in treatment is insistently desirous that their narcissistic wishes with regard to the stepparental role be accepted as realistic and commonsensical. The ability to risk asking that a couple in which the wife-mother and stepfather believe that the stepfather should be the main father figure, to reconsider their ideas on this matter is an important quality for therapists involved in such clinical situations. It is easy to avoid the psychological murder of the father and accept the rationalizations of the couple. These may run along the line that the father really isn't interested or capable, that he is unable to set limits in a way that the new couple sees as absolutely necesssary for the child to turn out correctly.

Furthermore, the father may be seen as too involved with a new woman or series of women to be consider a reasonable father. While these assertions are not automatically to be considered false, anything of this nature should alert the therapist to question such assertions. A focus on the quality of affect noted in either the mother or stepfather is helpful in making this assessment. If either of them is too angry at the father and unwilling to see it as desirable that the father be kept active as a parent, then a wise therapist will consider that the dynamics described in this chapter may well be present. It then becomes a question of whether or not the therapist is able to find some flexibility in the narcissism of either the mother or stepfather. Surprisingly, the stepfather may often demonstrate a greater willingness to be flexible. In those instances where the mother-new wife of the situation is insistently dominant about her view of the situation, she has often chosen a new partner whom she is able to dominate. In such situations it may be unlikely that a couples or individual therapist can do much to alter the situation. It is wise to keep in mind that when such dynamics dominate, even the reported excellent outcome of the stepfather relationship with the children involved may be more apparent than real. Such couples are usually satisfied with a public relations type of view of their new family constellation. They insist that the narcissistically demanded success of the recombined family unit is real.

They are often superficially successful at achieving a public image of an excellent relationship between the children and their stepfather. Upon more than superficial examination this proves to be far from the case.

The purpose of this chapter has been to bring our clinical experience to bear in considering the factors that lead to success or failure of the stepfather experience. What the clinician allows himself or herself to see will vary with the degree of alertness to the issues involved in stepparenting. The idea that conventional (naive) thinking may be a dominant factor in how individuals approach the role of stepparenting has definitely impressed us as we have studied individual men attempting to step into this challenging position. Our conclusion includes the not immediately apparent idea that for a man to be a good stepfather he has to operate within the limits of a mature character. This includes the strength to be somewhat neutral about the fate of his stepparenting. This means an ability to accept that the role may involve little to no gratifying emotional experience for him. It is necessary to contemplate one's essential unlovableness in relationship to this role.

A stepfather may provide a great deal of fathering without the emotional rewards that would clearly come to an individual who had fathered a child and behaved similiarly. Perhaps, we are in the arena (to use the old jargon) of male masochism. We could restate this to mean male behavior that is not self-centered and demanding but rather takes into account the complexity of a stepfather situation and responds to it rather than to the wishes of the self. We believe that the increase in the divorce rate, particularly of individuals with young children, makes it imperative that clinical study of recombining families and observations of the actual responses to stepfathers and by stepfathers is of great importance. Individuals struggling with this dilemma will increasingly come to us for help; as therapists we need to have a template in mind of the good stepfather, the good recombinant result. We need to know the difference between a sophisticated set of workable assumptions about the possibilites of stepfathering and the conventional, naive, and wish-dominated set of aspirations. We believe that in using our clinical observations we have made a step in the direction of providing such a template.

References

Friedman, H. J. (1980), The father's parenting experience in divorce. *Amer. J. Psychiat.*, 37:1177–1182.

Goldstein, J., Freud, A. & Solnit, A. J. (1980), *Beyond the Best Interest of the Child.* Burnett Books.

Wallerstein, J. S. (1980), *Surviving the Breakup.* New York: Basic Books.

Small Step, Giant Step
A Stepfather
Lora Heims Tessman

I focus in this chapter on some internal steps as they unfolded in the analysis of a man who was beginning the process of becoming a stepfather.

"Mom said I take after *you*, 'cause we both have an eye for hidden treasures," six-year-old Jill told Dr. Scott K, taking a small step toward a sense of kinship with the man who was likely to become her stepfather. Big and small steps in tandem, they loped toward the fantastic shapes of driftwood each had sighted. Dr. K thought about how confident she seemed in her physicality, while his own strides at her age were in brain power but not physical prowess. His way of being with Jill now evoked the image of his own father's coming home from work. "Dad, Dad, teach me to bike!" Mother: "Don't pester." Father: "C'mon, Scotty, it's okay." Father's hand was firm under the bicycle seat until Scotty could balance himself. He now spoke of experiencing the analyst as offering "support till I'm ready to take off on my own." I commented that father is much in his mind when he tells me of Jill. Dr. K: "He's a *presence* in my stepfathering, for some reason more than in my fathering. But then there are a lot of changed presences since analysis."

Yesterday Jill drew a picture of his friendly bearded face, but with little houses for eyes. She looked for her room in the houses. "Jill wants to find a home in your eyes," said I, "perhaps like the hidden treasure." I wondered to myself about who they are becoming in each other's eyes, in the external world between them, in the internal world of his psyche. Why was his father more of a presence in his relation to Jill than with his own children? I believe that his freedom to invoke the internal father was related to his own changed position in a now oedipal drama in which further acts are still to come. In addition, as the meanings of "creating" became less gender-linked, he added leeway to his generative leanings.

In relation to Jill, he has been generous with imagination and caring, but careful to wait for her readiness. She has become more forward with him, sending a picture with many hearts, another with her own hand

---

I wish to express my appreciation to "Dr. Scott K," who, seven years after the end of his analysis, collaborated by reviewing, with helpful comments, the material about himself, and consented to its presentation in this book.

wearing a ring, a decorated paper plate saying, "God is great," and so on. He deals with the nuances of her requests sensitively, with an eye to the family to be. She confessed to her mother that what she most wants for her birthday is to have him take her to see *101 Dalmatians*. "Do you want to bring your friend Carol, too?" he asks. "No, because she would want to hold your hand, and so will I." He: "Well, could Mommy come with us? You could hold her hand and mine at the same time!" "Okay!"

I am impressed with the quality of the dialogue between the three, a readiness to reply seriously to questions without answers. She: "Maybe I could have Pam and Beth [his grown children] as my real sisters, and then I'd *have* to have you as my real dad." He: "Yeah, well, then what about your real dad?" She: "He could still be my dad too. But then I would have to tell people you're just my stepdad, and I don't want to." He: "You can decide what you want to tell people, but let's think about what you are telling yourself." She seems mystified by the irony of "What *is* a real dad?" when her potential stepfather has already been the more real. Her mother supports the entrance of the stepfather into the family as they openly share Jill's anguish about her difficult, abusive real father and each help her to grieve.

Meanwhile her presence in the man's psyche is subtle. He speaks of wishing to reduce his working hours, to "spend more time enjoying permanent relations, the three of us around the kitchen table, rather than the kind with clients. I feel a good shift in me to relationships where I experience more than I observe, where I don't distance myself by observing." He expects to veer friendship to include couples with children his stepdaughter's age. He comments: "I find her delightful and interesting in herself, I like her. She's an incredibly important part of Meg's life and I look forward to that, am not jealous of it. But my full love for her will come after we've been in a crisis with each other—I mean I don't know if adolescence will be fun—but I'll be there." As it developed, neither crises nor love were postponed until adolescence.

As I had the good fortune to be privy to how Dr. K evolved during his psychoanalysis, I will review the work we did together prior to the events in his life that led to becoming a stepfather.

I will select material from the analysis to trace the dynamics of those conflicts and identifications which bear on the difference he reports in his experience of being father and stepfather. These involve a progressive relinquishing of his need to be both mother and father in his attempt to invent the kind of mothering presence he wished for. As his terror of being passive and deprived in relation to mother began to abate, a vigorous enjoyment of his identity as male gathered momentum, piquantly connected to the bond with his father. I will also explore Dr. K's relation to his own creativity, often a crucial dimension in the repressed fantasies of the male parent. The meanings of feeling self-created, the creation of children and creativity cycling in tandem with denial all emerged on the landscape of Dr. K's parenting, and were part of the ever-shifting analytic scene—and part of why it ever shifted! The material quoted is intended to elaborate the issues discussed, but is not a balanced case presentation: important characters and happenings have been omitted for simplicity and confidentiality. I quote from the first two years of analysis and the initial six months of relationship to Jill (except for his thoughts about a family tree, quoted at the end of this chaper, which occur later). For her the sustaining initial bond to the stepfather was preparatory to having to confront her image of her own father, and, of course, did not take its place.

After brief comments about the opening phase, six subsequent themes are chosen as related to a shift from the more maternal nurturance toward his own children, to being the father in a different triad in his stepparenting. They are:

1. The unicorn.
2. The couch is a lap.
3. To create in the gap.
4. My penis, my self . . . and . . . goodbye, pouch.
5. Gloria, Gloria, I want to sleep with Queen Victoria.
6. In a family tree (a new triad).

Pictures from an Analysis
(He Finds Words Insufficient)

He came to analysis at age 54. A gifted, creative, appealing man, he had two Ph.D.'s and two careers, first in literature, then in human relations. Born in England in 1935, his childhood exuded both trauma and resilience. Father, a truck driver who had left school in the seventh grade, was the more supportive, playful, and emotionally available, while mother was sharp-witted, sharp-tongued, and quick to blame. Words between mother and son seemed to be both weapons and transitional phenomena for him. A difficult birth, he was a "failure-to-thrive" baby until surgical intervention loosened the adhesion of his tongue. Severe asthma began at age two and a half in a context of no effective medication. He recalled the war years, being in the bomb shelters and wearing the gas masks that were apt to precipitate asthma attacks. He suffered fears of suffocation, of dying, of drowning, and he tended to hold his breath in rage. He was claustrophobic in certain situations at the time of analysis. Scott was made to feel that his "asthma attacks" were his own fault—the result of getting excited or eating the wrong foods. He described himself as "an early observer, with a use of reading and words to protect my inner world." When he was taunted by other children for being "a walking dictionary" at about age eight, Mother berated him for being an embarrassment to her. When he then told her he felt like killing himself over this, she handed him the kitchen knife.

"For a long time, I thought I was the only child who ever wanted to kill himself. I thought of cutting my wrists." At age 10, he was "dry-humped" by a man, which was soon followed by an incident in a hut, where a group of slightly older girls "took down my pants and did things to me" while a night watchman seemed to egg them on. A scholarship to a private school at the end of latency was a mixed blessing of intellectual inspiration with a continued sense of not fitting in because of his working-class background. His high intelligence did not dull the sense of painful exclusion and inadequacy. "It was fit in or take a lot of abuse for my vocabulary, manners, clothing." In adolescence, an admired teacher in literature took him under his wing, and often home to his family, becoming an important model to him and a mentor for his first career. In his mid-20s, he married and had two daughters. He was the "better mother" in nurturing his children, but both parents drank too much and practiced a 1960s style of open marriage which became untenable and led to divorce. In his early 40s, he had a two-and-a-half-year psychotherapy with an analytic candidate and describes this treatment as "too detached and intellectual," that what "didn't happen is the connections between images, feelings, and memories. I think many of my feelings didn't find their way to the right words." Since that time, he thought that perhaps he needed analysis. Given his traumatizing childhood, I pondered about the advisability of analysis, but eventually felt reassured enough about his reintegrative capacity to proceed. Noticeably, in the evaluation he seemed to find his affects more rather than less bearable, when the communicative and adaptive aspects of his material were a first focus.

During the opening phase of the analysis terrifying images of being trapped or endangered in various ways by mother figures, falling beds, asthma, and so forth emerged, while he "soldiered" bravely through his childhood. In childhood, he had tried "jumping up beyond a wall. I could jump in the air and stay up for a while, and felt I could extend the time up there, to control that because it sure was dangerous *down there*." I was struck by the degree to which those fears that might be expectable in a country at war were linked to the comfortless perceptions of mother. He spelled this out: "I remember the endless game we played of drawing Hitler's face on the flagstone and then scribbling him out with our feet to get rid of it. And the connection with flagstone is my mother: step on a crack, break your mother's back. My mother and Hitler somehow got wound together in my head." Fortunately, there were positive introjects as well: a warm paternal great aunt with whom he could laugh, a teacher, and Father. Father was seen as so belittled by mother, however, that Dr. K described him to others as being literally a dwarf. I acknowledged early his need for egress when anxious about either closeness to me, or associations to being confined or helpless, passively surrounded, or not in control. A panic attack, which caused him to leave a scheduled MRI exam because he feared he would go crazy when immobilized, crystallized some of these issues. He veered between being astounded at feeling understood, competitive about my having any of the words (which are his domain), vigilant about possible criticism, and articulate in his seeking of me when he felt he lost connection.

Vivid, picturesque associations helped locate his transference experience. He depicted the nature of analysis, the couch, and my role in ever-changing ways. He was aware of allowing me into his world only slowly. During the second month, he said of the couch, "At the moment, this place is my childhood bed." He pictured me sitting right outside his bedroom door, allowed to listen but not to come in.

After a session in which I asked if his image of watching raindrops rolling down outside his childhood window might be his attempt to observe his tears, his sadness, rather than being in it, he wept and then placed me mentally inside the room. Cautiously, he began to become intensely attached.

The following week he brought a dream image: "I have a yellow penis with a core of black spider eggs and little black spiders—and my association was that Mum doesn't like my penis because she doesn't like spiders." In other material, the unconscious fantasy of having eggs in his scrotum as well as a penis emerges. As a child in the bathtub, he would sometimes hide his penis between his legs, pretending it was gone. He now sometimes can hardly see his penis because of his big potbelly. He said, "The change in me that I notice now, I can talk about pain. Sometimes pain is so big it will swallow you up and drown—but maybe I can swim. As a child I was always alone with my pain. It never occurred to me that another person could be with me in that. You are here, you are definitely in this room now."

During the early months, the couch appeared variously as a changing table, a kitchen table, an operating table. He associates from *couch* to *Prufrock*: "Let us go then, you and I, / When the evening is spread out against the sky / Like a patient etherized upon a table." His vasectomy 12 years earlier comes to mind: "I can't quite get the word . . ." he laughs at himself, "I want to say hysterectomy." The attending nurse

just stood there, burly, like a prison guard. I asked, "Do you have a function here?" She: "No." I: "Would you please leave then? You are making me nervous." She looked at the surgeon, nodded, and left. Somehow I associate her with my Mum, thinking of the times she saw other kids taunting me and she made that her own business, her embarrassment, instead of leaving it mine—using it to shame me more.

Now you are in the room with me and I am on the changing table and it has to be decided if I'm going to have any more babies. I feel like I'm here to give birth to me and my legs are crossed and I'd like to be able to open them at some point. Felt like I had a baby yesterday. [Tells incident in which he suggests to a parent to try to look for the good points in her dyslexic son, and she started beaming and saying, "He can do such and such."] I knew it was about myself. There is the question of what did I do wrong as a child; I thought I just "be'd" wrong. I was wrong. When my teacher wrote about me, "He must keep pegging away," I read, "He must keep pigging away." I felt like the too grubby kid.

He associates to a friend who told him he'd grown up feeling odd and ugly, and was surprised women could like him.

He: That moves me to tears now—because of loneliness. As I look at my lonely childhood, I feel it more. You taught me the word *loneliness*, and at the moment I'm cursing you.
I: For stirring up loneliness?
He: Yeah. [He notes that Ariel, in *The Tempest*, says he was taught language, and his profit on it was that he learned to curse.]

Later that hour:

He: Now I know who you are! When my daughter was born, Nurse Ross was our midwife, short, dark-haired, German fun person— who took me through the vocabulary of birth in German—and you are giving me another vocabulary here at this birth, another chance.
I: Any word in particular that Nurse Ross gave you?
He: "Placenta" is *Mutterkuchen*, and *Kindspech* means "child's pitch," a word for the first bowel movement the infant makes. A nice warm cake associated with mother even when the child is dirty. So you are the midwife, a wife, mother—and that's a really scary thought because how could I trust you as a mother? I tried to be a good parent to my kids, to be there, to tune in, to back off when necessary. I was more actively there; Joan just let things happen to them.

We began to learn more about the roots of Dr. K's robust creativity, which was part of his resilience. Producing what mothers produce (eggs and babies), he would have all resources in himself; he would not be trapped in the twinning of needing her and being hurt. Unlike her, he would and did take pleasure in what he made, appreciating and nurturing his children.

1. The Unicorn

We learned from the unicorn session about Dr. K's opposing theories of birth of self-awareness, of coming into being in the analysis, a kind of self-creation, but in connection with a parent.

He had been talking about feeling like dancing, a view of mutual attunement. "I remember another dancer who was incredibly light and so good at anticipating that if I was leading it felt as though as soon as I thought of doing something, she was—we were doing it." Driving to his sessions, he had a habit now of "dancing" his fingers on the steering wheel. He wondered about the meaning of moving freely and recalled a German essay by Kleist about "gracefulness is not itself conscious."

He: William Tell curses because the tyrant has made him conscious of what he does. When he shoots the apple off his son's head, he curses because he has to become aware. You asked me once what I liked about Kafka. In "The Metamorphosis," I interpret "the father throwing at the son an apple that festers" as one of Kafka's puns. There has been some kind of self-knowledge that festers in me—the knowledge that you are hated by a parent, that you are unclean. [He contrasts this to a Rilke poem about the *Einhorn*, the "unicorn," the "animal that names itself, could name itself, because people believed in his potential."]

. I: You describe self-awareness forced by the knowledge of hatred of the parent as painful, resented knowledge through shame, your grubbiness, the humiliation in the hut—when what you wish is to know yourself like the *Einhorn*, which defines itself with freedom of motion, your fingers on the steering wheel, a gracefulness from inner thrust . . .

He: I think in analysis up to now I've been testing you and testing me—I've been putting out things that could be material for shame, and I notice that you are not shaming me, not once. I'm putting the painful things up here, and it feels like they are stripping away when you don't shame me. About *Das Einhorn*, they didn't know but loved it anyway, from the way it wandered round, the way it held itself. They fed it on no grain, only always on the possibility that it existed, and this gave such strength to the animal. *Das es aus sich ein Stirnhorn Trieb* must be the same way that Freud used *Trieb* ["drive"], and it names itself *Einhorn, und war* ["and it was"] and could be seen in the silver mirror of the virgin in the tapestry. The virgin gently captures the unicorn in the mirror—no, *capturing* is not the right word. If the unicorn sees its own reflection, it is captured, it comes into being.

Oh, that's analysis and who you are, and I'm opening up with two observers, you and me. Analysis even up to now is a kind of intimacy I've never experienced, even with myself. I'm all excited by this.

2. The Couch Is a Lap

It is about a year later.

In the analysis he is more direct in speaking for himself, less through literature. A change took place in his intimate life: he had separated from a seven-year alliance with Ellen, who made it increasingly clear that she did not want a sexual life with him or anyone. Much material about his fathering had emerged around his having supplied the tenderness which he associated with a feminine side of himself and which had felt in short supply with his own mother—for example, "watching Pam being born, and hoping she was a girl. Why? Because then I could be as soft and gentle with her as I wanted to."

The material symbolized around laps seemed pivotal as an initial layer in his struggle with wishes and fears about the "surrounding" woman, complicated not only by experiencing his mother as destructive to him, but also by the bomb shelter, the asthma, the incident in the hut, and so on, which confirmed his sense of pained helplessness. His fantasies of rageful vengeance complicated his wishes further. The theme begins with his association of sensuality and "little girlness."

He: I'm trying to acknowledge my sensuality, angry that I'm leading a nonsexual existence. Is that appropriate to my age? Masturbating as an adolescent was not sensual, just counting how many times I could do it in a day. I think of Beth as a toddler, you could tell she was enjoying her body by the way she walked.

I: Interesting that you mention Beth enjoying her sensuality as a little girl and the question of your age. Over the past few days "sensuous" came up here after you brought in the image of the little girl at the meeting, sitting in her sister's lap, contentedly sucking her thumb and my comment that perhaps you wanted a lap. You began further associations to that, but quickly traded them in . . .

He: While you talk about that, the image is: Not comfortable on Mum's lap, my bottom is too bony. Actually she isn't comfortable. Gotta be careful not to put my leg on her varicose veins. Lady, you could have let me ride side-saddle! . . . and careful not to touch her neck and what never gets mentioned are her breasts. What comes into mind is it wasn't a safe place.

My Dad played "Hoppe Hoppe Reite," this is the way the gentlemen ride, this is the way the ladies ride.

I'm now constantly seeing myself sliding off my Mum's lap, getting off, hearing "Mind my legs."

It might be neat to sit on someone's lap and suck my thumb and curl my hair between my fingers and feel comfortable. Trying to figure out what age the person would be whose lap I could sit on at 56. I like people sitting on my lap, children. Now I'm shrinking myself down to size so that I can sit on your lap.

I have gray socks on with light blue bands so I must already be at private school and you are asking me how it went at school and you really want to hear . . .

If I turn over on this couch I would fall out the window and my check to you would fall out too, it's in my pocket.

I: You would fall off the lap, and there is a falling out about money. Perhaps you feel if I took care of you right you wouldn't need to give me money.

He: I want a peeled tomato dipped in sugar on a fork [a treat his mother sometimes gave him]. Damm it, I wanted to get on that lap, it was the only one around. I see myself as a little child being really angry about her lap, kicking and being told "Don't kick" and not having the words to say "I'm angry" or "I hate you." I see mother reacting with horror to the words "I hate you." Her mouth is pursed and horrified, and then I turn it into "I love you."

I: Was the "I love you" when "I hate you" horrified her, so you *had* to say, "I love you"? Or was "I love you" underneath like "I hate you *because* I love you and you won't be close"?

He: Underneath [tearful], and then she sent me to my room and I say, "It isn't fair"—it's the cold green room and I'm alone.

The following session:

He: Have been trying to climb on your lap since yesterday. It's really hard to stay on the lap. I slide off careful not to hit my mother's legs. I have a real hard time imagining leaning against her peacefully with her arm around me. . . . If I make myself imagine it, I have a frightening association, to Mrs. Blade. [At age five, because of his asthma, he had been sent to live with Mrs. Blade in the country for some months. He was frightened by watching her slaughter sick chickens and by her brusque impatience with him. Father visited, but mother did not.]

I: Mrs. Blade wielded a pitchfork and threw sick chickens to the pigs when you felt like a sick chicken too. . . . So comfort on the lap is interrupted fast with danger.

He: My Mum won't like it. I have smelly diapers, and the varicose veins were painful. I'm also responsible because she got them from carrying children, I thought. But she didn't carry me that much. I could be on my father's lap because the lap I wanted was angry.

I: You were angry too. So you not only had to be careful of varicose veins—what was out there—but careful of what was in there, in you.

He: To keep from kicking them—not only step on a crack, break your mother's back. But I remember kicking the crack. I see moss between the cracks. I kicked it and then would try to put it back.

I: Any more about the moss?

He: Pubic hair. I was afraid it would work—that I had killed her. Just as I was nervous when I brought mother die [a flower he would pick in the field and bring home].

I have a linguistic association to lap of luxury and Ellen withholding the money. Money would be a certain amount of comfort now. My anger about that is really destructive. I can imagine cutting her guts out. My association was cutting out the front of her. Vagina? No, that's between the legs, cutting out the lower part of her, including that part.

I: The whole lap?

He: Did I have to protect my Mum and me? I'm aware my anger at Ellen is my ripping anger at Mum.

I keep dragging myself back to the lap—I know what's wrong—I keep trying to climb on, and I put my knee in the wrong place. Where is she, dammit, why do I have to do all of it myself?

I: You wanted welcoming arms to be ready to lift.

He: The woman on the bench [in a woodcut he has described] has a casual touch with the kids. She keeps in touch not just the lap, it's the arms too. "There we go, whoopsie daisy," and that wouldn't be Mum, that would be Dad. "Don't, Joe, you'll get him excited." My dad as a grandfather played a game with my children—banging your fist on the high chair and saying, "Who's the master in this house?" Child power that says, "You're powerful, and its safe."

Now . . . there's a pair of hands, a body and arms picking me up and saying, "C'mon, c'mon, love," and putting me on a lap.

I think I just solved the lap problem. There have to be two people involved, and then I could get on a lap in my imagination—but whose lap? Your face comes to mind, I see your face—oh [long silence], the couch is a lap!

The frame of the lap remained central to the analysis for a time. In the transference, it included his fantasies of free bodily access to me, followed by fears of his then becoming a "dummy" under my control, followed by more directly phallic imagery. It was an intense period in the analysis, exhausting in its pressure simultaneously to maintain and flex ego boundaries.

He: Thinking about climbing on laps all weekend. Did things with Mum get sexualized? I've been farting a lot and wonder if it's connected.

I imagine myself sitting on an adult lap, and we are both naked. The problem is the adult is smaller than I—I hope I'm not putting too much pressure on your legs. And yes, I think of Eskimos—in the fantasy, we are laughing. When an Eskimo says, "Do you want to laugh with my wife?" he is offering her to the guest to sleep with.

You're in my head as somebody who can make affirmations and laugh—I don't mean at outrageous puns—I mean at the quirks of my behavior. You don't make more of them or less of them, they just are. I'm sorry I had to be so vigilant with Mum.

And I'm blocking, saying that you are also cradling my crotch—my penis—with one hand and the rest of my body with the other. And that feels a lot better than having my old Mum, who didn't like peters. Now I see myself as an angry boy with short socks and pants, and I'm scraping my leg against the crack in the pavement and also against her legs. If I make a hole in her legs, it will bleed dark, menstrual blood.

Next session:

He: I dreamt some people arrived, pleasant, offered me a university position I wanted. They respected me.

I'm having a fantasy in which I'm little. Young enough to climb around my mother, who isn't my mother. She is solid and big and sitting down—we are both naked. I'm climbing all over her front and back. I'm sitting on the back of the chair—tumbling down her, going by her breasts, rubbing by her breasts, laughing with glee—I'm conscious of my bare bottom, undiapered, but it's okay. Now I can sit on her lap and pee, and it's okay. She's not horror stricken—she starts to laugh too. And if she holds me up, she holds me in front of her, does not put me aside, and she holds me over the potty and I'm having a bowel movement and it's okay.

And now it's you, and you are dressed in a nice green-and-brown, and it's okay, and the potty has a blue rim on it.

I: You want to know that you'd be wanted as a nice kid to have, bowel movement and all.

He: It wasn't nice to be around my Mum much of the time [weeps]. At the moment, I feel it's autumn, but it's spring—an explanation of analysis . . . I'm 56 years old and going through the spring.

The following week:

> He: I'm climbing back on your lap. I'm smaller, and I say to you, "What do we talk about now?" I'm changing into a ventriloquist's dummy, and you have control—I now keep drawing myself back to myself.
>
> I: So in giving in to the wish to climb back on the lap, you become a dummy.
>
> He: If you have your hand in the small of my back—in my innards, my innards in your hands—then you can also lift your hand and put me down. You can put me on the floor and humiliate me.
>
> I: And how do I do that?
>
> He: You can flick my penis out of the way. The penis is dangerous, and it can get me into trouble.
>
> Now I'm standing in front of you, stamping my foot saying, "But I'm not a dummy," and you say, "You're right, you're not." If I give in to Mum, I'm a dummy. I hear my Dad saying, "Dummy up." Helpful advice from Dad about how to survive in front of Mum, but it didn't work for him.
>
> I want to relax on your lap and to have a gentle hand on me, to play with the finger of the hand. The hand has a gold ring, so it must be my married mother. No, maybe married to me.
>
> I will get down and look around.
>
> I: You will get down when *you* want to, not be put down.
>
> He: Yeah, not out of fear that you are saying, "You are getting too heavy," but I'm ready to get down and look around because being on your lap gets me ready to look around.
>
> Then I had a vision of our walking hand in hand. I am two and five and 10. I see us walking from behind, but that's me and Dad walking. I sing with my Dad, "She was so good and so kind to me, and so was all of the family." Dad and I are bicycling.

Over the next period of time, conflicts about the life of the penis were focal:

> He: I remember in high school having a few beers and going in the backyard and peeing up the hedges—a certain joy in peeing that way, moving my penis from side to side, making the water dance, feeling good in the world and making a pee.
>
> I went to the cockloft once under the ceiling. There was a dollhouse no one was allowed to play with and there was a gilded photo of Grandfather with weskit and coat and a smaller one of Grandmother, with a frilly blouse and so on. And I went up there one day and masturbated all over it deliberately, That was the worst thing I could possibly do. I thought, see, nothing happened—God

didn't strike me down, the house didn't fall down—and I got away with it. Said fuck you to my ancestors, to my Mum, that way and had sex with my mother that way. It was angry sex because she wouldn't take me into her arms or lap or receive me any other way.

I: You have an important insight about angry sex—in your aloneness—when you wanted to defile what you couldn't have. You felt your sex was dirty, and you were going to share that wealth! But it was sad you felt so unwelcome!

He: Sad for her and for me. I flash back to the prize day at school, and I was so worried about getting an erection while walking to the stage to get my prize that I tied my penis to my leg. The couch seems molded to me. It feels right and very personal. [He then has a fantasy of his father and me, playfully tossing him from arms to arms, between us, standing close to each other.]

In spite of his rage at Mother, during this period of the analysis he also tolerated some compassionate understanding of the dynamics of her constraints.

3. To Create in the Gap

Dr. K's defensive use of denial was often buffered by his creative capacities to fill in the gap in what he wished for with hope and imagination. We had talked about this propensity when it came up, but he didn't quite believe he did it. I had told him some weeks ahead that I would be absent for two sessions, but he had made no allusions the previous week to my being away. Toward the end of the hour on Friday, I asked, "How are you feeling about analysis being just two times next week?"

He: [Sounding startled] What? Did you tell me?
I: Yes.
He: I did put in my book—I left out the green circles [that stand for analysis] for the rest of the week and must have noticed they were missing later, so I just filled them in. How am I feeling? We have a lot of work to do. I better just stay the night. I'm shocked. [He is racked with laughter going downstairs. Upstairs, I can't help dissolving into laughter too.]

The following Monday:

He: In fact, it's just five days but seems like a long time. And I will miss you. I wonder if I'm angry at you because I now associate you with the Wicked Witch of the West. You're important protection, confidant, friend, and you are going off with my father.

I: I'm glad you can picture your anger at me, my witchiness, deserting you with your father. From last time, we have the question of what your painful feelings are around the time gap. Your reaction to my being away is your creative filling in the gap as you have creatively filled many gaps—and undoing the gap. And the question is about what is so painful in the gap.

He: The gaps feel like a hard core of me. You are by my side inside me. So my survival is—only my backbone is holding me up. There's not that much to tell, But I'm not telling you out of spite. What's the point of telling you of the jumble in my head when you are going away? And you are doing that by choice. But the greatest gap is a feeling of friendship and intimacy. With you I discover what's behind this skin that feels like it's out to here when I'm with you. There is more of me when I'm with you.

Whenever my mother was angry, she walked away. So the gap is also a loneliness, a new loneliness—and who is here to tell if you are not here—and it's worse because you are tellable to. *And the worst part of childhood was that we didn't talk.* So I'm grieving you're going Thursday and Friday. What now comes to mind . . . I have a checklist of people who can fill the gap, but not really—they can just cover it over.

I think of Rilke's two lovers who look into each other's eyes, hiding their *Los*—"loss"—their fate. I don't want to take as my fate being lonely. I know I've been opening up to people more and in a different way, expecting more kindness and friendship, giving trust. So I didn't want to cross it out in the book, to cross out the meaning, and say, "No analysis." Filling in the gap is magical thinking, the other side of step on a crack, break your mother's back. Maybe you'll get run over by a tram. Whoa! My Dad's truck is making a screeching noise.

4. My Penis, My Self . . . and . . . Goodbye, Pouch

He: I had a dream Friday night while visiting Pam and Beth. Someone said to me, maybe Pam, "You've lost a lot of weight; that can only be done by taking off a kangaroo pouch." And I was glad—it sounded very healthy. My association to kangaroo pouch was that I was becoming less codependent, carrying fewer other people around—so it sounded like a healthy weight loss. Then I thought back to the conversation here about my giving birth to myself, needing to do that. There's some integral change in me that I don't have to be my own Mother and Father any more.

I: Yes . . . and in the dream, Pam was the messenger.

He: I think with her I was her father, but always more mother than
      father—needed to be both. The kangaroo pouch I lost—I don't
      need it because I have a penis now, it's mine, it's here. Maybe
      sometimes it's fallen off; I've taken it off and hidden it. The
      kangaroo bag—is shedding like skin. I'm not comfortable with it
      any more. I don't want to care for people that way any more. My
      kangaroo-bearing days are over, I hope. At the office, everyone
      asks, "Are you losing a lot of weight?" I laugh and say, "No, but I'm
      getting taller." [Actually, he has lost 20 pounds over the last six
      months, and will lose 10 more.]
          Part of me is angry at Joan for not using imaginative parenting
      with Pam and Beth based on inventing something that wasn't
      there, wasn't there for me either.
I: The gap is an ouch in the pouch? [I regretted having indulged in
      playing with the words here.]
He: [Laughs] Yes, I help people see their strengths too.
I: That too you wanted from your mother, who also hadn't had it
      from anyone. You felt she couldn't see your imaginative possibili-
      ties—but also the you leading with your penis, part of your
      exuberant wish to have her. You felt she didn't want to see that.
He: Another thought I've had: I don't have to take my penis off to have
      babies, I don't need a pouch, my penis is mine. Several times today,
      I've thought to myself, you are feeling an organic unity with your
      penis. My penis, my self!

A different session (10-120):

He: Association is—how the pouch is going, gone, and how actually it
      changes the shape of my penis. Without the overhang, it's more
      trim and beautiful—it's not my shit, not stuff I've excreted!

Next session:

He: I want to go sit with my Dad and hold his hands and tell him that
      I've been glad over the years to see my hands grow more and more
      like his. Peaceful hands, strong, maybe cracked and rough but
      always gentle.

5. Gloria, Gloria, I Want to Sleep with Queen Victoria

During this period of the analysis, he sought to bridge his rift between
phallic sexuality and "lovemaking" with a more fully object-related
awareness:

He: The car I'm driving has a front left puncture. I see myself getting out into another car, convertible, light blue. The top is down. What am I singing? "I want to drive with a blonde in a big black car." It's in my head in my Dad's voice. I associate to another song from Dad: "Gloria, Gloria, I want to sleep with Queen Victoria!"

I remember in the early days of my marriage waking up during the night incredibly horny and finding Joan holding my penis. Now it's a terrible thought of having my penis in one person and looking into the eyes of another—not literally, but because there has been some disjunction in me. Both of us were broken in some way—me broken in some way, from the girls in the hut—I associate the night watchman egging them on with my Dad not protecting me with my mother.

I am longing for real lovemaking, which is talking and looking into each other's eyes.

The next day:

He: Now I'm pushing away from a fantasy of our facing each other clothed and having intercourse and looking into each other's eyes at the same time. Why am I pushing off the fantasy? Because Queen Victoria wouldn't be amused! How could my parents have sex? If she rejected me, how could she have sex with him? He's smaller!

At this point, some competitive issues with men in authority came to the fore—he provoked his boss to chastise him, he remembered times of feeling guilty about wanting to hit his father, and so forth.

6. In a Family Tree (A New Triad)

We are now arriving at the events that introduced this chapter.

In the next few months, Dr. K becomes involved with Meg, a woman new to his office. The love relationship becomes serious. She is in the process of separating from her husband. Her six-year-old daughter, Jill, often comes to the office with mother, where there are others as well, but she is drawn especially to Scott, who engages her comfortably in playing, drawing, telling stories, and so on. Within months, she tells her mother, "I think Scott likes me better than Daddy does. He listens to me 'til he knows what I mean!" In the analysis, this period is characterized by several themes in a triad:

1. *Seeing his parents as a unit for the first time, content with each other and fading in importance to him; feeling less anger at his mother.*

He: I think of myself as a benevolent child today, not the kicking one. Feel so much less resentment toward my Mum. I phoned my parents *together, not separately*—and I think I felt your grinning presence. Mum said, "Its really great to have each other, because my bad eyesight—I can't go out without him." I picture Mum and Dad actually enjoying each other, waiting for the exciting part of the day—which is when Meals on Wheels comes by, and they can see what they have for dessert. I felt so warm about the two of them. That's a new thought. At 56, can I be finally getting over some oedipal stuff?

2. *Viewing the sexual and love relationship with Meg as the basis for a collaborative rather than competitive parental unit.*

He: Watching her walk down the street, there is a sort of visceral clutch that's genital. My testicles and penis—a strange feeling, a good one, a sort of attachment different from a sexual desire, different from lust, but with lust in it. I have a strong sense of integrity for Meg, for what is important between us. We said that, if there are things about each other that annoy us, let's *talk about it*. She has said, "I'm my own person, know what I want. I didn't think I would meet it, and I think I've met it in you."

Their lovemaking is passionate.

He: Such lust and comfort and trust . . . what's new is I'm not performing, and I don't mean just the athletic context. I'm not orchestrating—we are dancing, but nobody is leading because we are both leading, we can switch off with each other. Our relationship is a state of mind, not parts of bodies. I feel loved, and loving her feels different. When she reached her arm along my penis and cradled my testicles, I realized there was no apprehension—that's completely new. It was not a category—no worry that she would squeeze or pinch or hurt. And my erection, my penis, felt wonderful, like I didn't know I wanted that experience. Made me want to cry. It's a different road I'm taking, and I'm swimming it. And it's fun to be a parent as a parental unit. It's not coincidental that I can think of two people as parents. In the past, I felt at odds with the other parent. Both Joan and Ellen had problems being close to their kids, so I was closer, had to be better—but always a competition with them. I don't feel that with Meg—we feel complementary to each other.

3. *Responding to Jill's conflicts by gently affirming that there is now a vibrant parental unit—a triad in which she belongs with generational*

continuity. In this way, Dr. K communicates an alternative to the step-child's fears about the inevitability of externally imposed disruptions in loving.

To illustrate, I end with a recent session in which he sits in a family tree. The session begins with his referring to his and Jill's having made a tradition of walking in the park before supper.

He: She teeters, on the wall edge of the pathway, as Jill the Magnificent—making me at times the lion, at times the crocodile. Then there is the lion that she masters. She seems concerned about his teeth and puts stones in his mouth. *This comfort in making new traditions may be the essence of being a stepfather—different from fathering. I feel like a competent parent and useful mate at the same moment.*

An image of myself sitting with Meg on the bough of a tree . . . We have our feet on the ground, and Jill is playing around. A new family—with soup around the table, holding hands and saying Grace. An image of the family with a future. Now getting off the branch and having a picnic like older parents. Then very much older—Meg wrapping a blanket around my legs when Jill is off in college, and Pam and Beth come back. Do they come back? I don't know. A family has to do with being able to talk about anything, with being together and being apart, with changing and accommodating.

Since my parents have faded more in the background, have become more sepia-colored in the photograph, I'm feeling on top, as though my parents were dead in some way. Dad is deaf as a post and says the aerial needs replacing on the TV. But it's not the TV—his hearing aid needs a new battery, which he refuses to get. He wants peace more than sound now.

The family has me in it, in a parental unit, with a spouse who can be my woman, a real woman to me.

An analogy to my sitting on the branch is Christopher Robin watching Pooh Bear, Kanga, and Roo. Sometimes the branch is on an elevator going up and getting a different perspective, and I am relaxed because I feel much less need to control things, to be all things. More security, more trust in me, more trust in the world—less influence of my mother.

I: She's not on top any more. I traveled from the branch rising on the elevator—for perspective—to your childhood fantasy that you could levitate above the garden wall in order to be above your mother's influence.

He: A second layer . . . The apple tree I'm sitting on is in Ohio [where the first marriage took place]. The third layer is the Garden of

Eden, the Tree of *Erkentness*—not Knowledge—*I mean recognition, a deeper bringing to knowledge for the first time, like analysis. No, the analogy to analysis got mixed up, because analysis is like that, but not sinful. I'm sitting in the Tree of Analysis, the beginning of a Family Tree.*

I: [I feel moved. Unfortunately, I say something trite to cover my feeling.] That sounds like a right-side-up tree, unlike the upside-down trees in the question of your childhood. [He had felt "different" as a child—a child forever pondering questions such as, "I wonder if all the trees are upside-down?"]

He: That was my discomfort with me—a neurotic tree.

Dr. K's tree is still bearing unexpected fruits, as yet unnamed. He knows that creative hope, as a defense against depressive gaps, may have rushed his commitment to Meg and Jill—postponing rather than replacing further developments, and these remain to be seen. But he connects his tree—which had roots in his childhood musings about the true nature and position of trees, coloring some of his imagery in brown and green—to the generative reach of his "deeper bringing to knowledge," a creativity now unlinked to gender attributes, a home for continuity of the self in more direct relation to the people who matter to him. The tree, perhaps, sprouted in the wellspring of his determined resilience.

Incest

Incest

What Is It, and How Did It Come to Be?

Moisy Shopper

One cannot write a book about stepparenting without a chapter on incest.[1] In actuality and statistically, sexual relations between stepfathers and their stepdaughters is an occupational hazard for both (Russell, 1984a, b; Sariola and Uutela, 1996).[2] The onset of puberty and feminine attractiveness, coupled with the revival of oedipal interest in the mother's spouse, will often be accompanied by a budding sexual seductiveness. The stepdaughter is now a woman in her own right and a very attractive and desirable conquest to a discerning stepfather. Not only does she resemble the woman he has recently married but she has the attractive inexperience of a virgin. For some stepfathers, intercourse with their stepdaughters may also be related to their feelings and fantasies about their former wives' current husbands, that is, the relationship of their own adolescent daughters and their new stepfathers.

While stepfather–stepdaughter incest is more common, the blending of two biological families also harbors the seeds of stepsibling incest, for here, too, there is an absence of consanguinity compounded by a preponderance of intimacy and extended contact of two adolescents living in the same confined space of their shared home. Although stepmother–stepson incest is rare by comparison, it can be a natural consequence of the family dynamics, as portrayed by Eugene O'Neill in his play *Desire Under the Elms*. Confronted with the oedipal hubris of the father, one of his sons finds an outlet for both his love and aggression through the development

---

[1] Or so I thought until I found Pasley and Ihinger-Tallman (1987) who are the coeditors of 13 chapters dealing with a variety of sociological issues in "theory, research and practice concerning stepparenting." The following words are not to be found in their index: *abuse, incest, sex* (or any compound having sex as its first word), *sexual abuse,* or *stepparent incest*. The list of references, however, is quite extensive. I counted 200 citations from Ag to Gl with the total references comprising 28 pages of the book. As Simon (1992) points out, Fenichel's (1945) grand opus had the entry "Incest—see Oedipus Complex."

[2] Sariola and Uutela found that the incidence of stepfather–stepdaughter incest is 16 times greater than father–daughter. Of interest, Finnish law does not criminalize sexual step relations as incest, nor are acts short of intercourse considered incest. Instead, abuse statutes are used with punishments varying from a fine to 10 years maximum.

of a relationship with his stepmother, a new bride more his own age than that of his father. The offspring of their illicit union is killed, in part the price paid by the violation of the strongest incest taboo, that of mother-son. In this instance, the taboo is attenuated by its being the stepparent-stepchild relationship, that is, one of affinity (marriage) rather than consanguinity.[3]

Definitions

It would be useful to our discussion to understand the definition of incest and how laws, clergy, and culture have participated in creating the conditions that currently exist. In affinity relationships, there is a kinship outside biological lines of inheritance, that is, one that is arranged by the family or the participants and is recognized by law and/or custom. Thus, the mother's brother is an uncle by consanguinity, whereas the mother's brother's wife is an aunt by affinity. A stepparent-stepchild relationship is a kinship by affinity, there being no genetic inheritance involved. The term *consanguinity* refers to a relationship where there are shared genes between the two individuals, that is, ancestors and blood relatives in common. Consanguineous relatives come in various *degrees* (brother-sister and parent-child would be considered first degree). Biological aunt/uncle and niece/nephew would be considered second degree, while first cousins would be considered third degree as would be great-grandparent and great-grandchild. The grandparent would be a "linear" kinsman while the cousins are "collateral" ones. Anthropological research has shown, however, that different cultures void certain biological distinctions by referring to disparate kinship relationships by a common name.

There are also "fictive" relationships, which, although free of biological kinship and affinity through marriage, nevertheless enter into some incest taboo systems of prohibited relationships. A fictive relationship would be that of a godparent to a godchild, a relationship often included in the incest taboo. Other fictive relationships would be that of "blood brother" and of a foster child living in a foster family. For reasons to be discussed later, the further away the relation from a consanguineous one, the more attenuated the incest taboo.

---

[3]The same change from the biological (consanguineous) mother to the affinity relationship of a stepmother occurs in Fredrich Schiller's classic *Don Carlos* wherein his mother dies in childbirth, his stepmother is his former fiancée, and he is eventually killed by his enemy, his father. This variant of the incest theme is discussed at great length by Otto Rank, who considers it a prototypical variant of the incest theme (Rank, 1912).

Views of Church and Law

Since much American law is derived from English common law and English legal precedents, I'll review some of their history of incest. The ecclesiastical courts dealt with incest issues until 1857, when the Matrimonial Causes Act was enacted that defined the nature of the prohibited degrees within which sexual relations are prohibited. Prior to that time, the church (and the law treatises that followed) defined the various degrees of affinity (i.e., by marriage, adoption, etc.) and consanguinity (i.e., blood relations) to the third degree. When published in 1563, the Act was adopted into the canons of the Church of England, given royal approval in 1603, and was required to be posted in each parish. In addition, the English Book of Common Prayer, as part of its contents, detailed thirty specific people (relationships) a man is not supposed to marry and another thirty for the woman.

After Henry VIII had broken from the Catholic Church, he had little specific church doctrine to support his wish to divorce Anne Boleyn, but had to rely on the common customs, which saw treason and adultery as a crime. Fearing these would be insufficient for the divorce, he added the crime of incest. Namely, it was alleged that Anne had incited her brother, George Boleyn, to violate her. Both were beheaded in 1536. Henry himself was the descendent of a consanguineous line mixed since the offspring of Charles the Bald. Henry had married his brother's widow, Catherine, and thought of marrying off his illegitimate son, the Duke of Richmond, with his half sister, Mary. With this historical background, is it any wonder that the common folk would need some specific canon guidance in matters of prohibited unions?

It was not until the Punishment of Incest Act in 1908 that the crime was given a punishment. However, the pressing issue of allowing a husband to marry with his dead wife's sister started in 1842 but was not resolved until 1907, when such marriage was legalized. The opposition to this change was based on the affinity issue. If affinity was no longer a bar to marriage, it would impair the "unity of the husband and wife which lay at the heart of the English kinship system and (which) justified treating affinity like consanguinity" (Wolfram, 1983, p. 310). To include all the affinal relatives to the prohibited degrees suggested would have created the crime of incest in many instances where it previously did not exist. However, the 1907 act defined consanguineal incest to everyone's satisfaction.

In the United States every state has codified incest as an offense and has forbidden marriage between certain specified relatives. In 1793, "Incest was a crime grounded in principles of morality, property, and the laws governing inheritance. By the end of this century, the crime had been transformed into a crime against the person: a very personal kind of sexual assault against the body, usually of a child" (Bienen, 1998, p. 1504). Bienen also notes, and I would agree, that "incest cases are in the middle of the battlefield of sexual politics" (1998, p. 1502). In tracing the development of state statutes, Bienen (1998) notes that many of the prohibited marriage and cohabitation laws "were rooted in part in prohibitions against inbreeding. (However) the fear of inbreeding does not explain the inclusion of step relationships or distant in-laws" (p. 1531). What was prosecuted was the incest between fathers and their minor daughters.[4] However, in a tortured reasoning that makes sense only to those versed in the law, the father's defense attorney argued that the proof of the girl's nonconsent was decisive in proving the innocence of the offending father. As late as 1974, the highest court of criminal appeals in Texas held that females under the statutory age of consent could nonetheless be "consenting accomplices" to sexual acts with their fathers or stepfathers. The notion that incest was committed by consenting adults was transformed into the idea that an underage daughter was an accomplice to the "crime" and therefore the father should be acquitted (Bienen, 1998, p. 1538). The issue of the daughter's being below the age of consent, that is, statutory rape, was not considered by the court. In short, Texas tried to either excuse the offender or deny the offense.

Similarly, the Utah Supreme Court (1978) overturned a jury verdict and held that a 16-year-old adopted stepdaughter was an accomplice to the incest offense and had consented to sexual intercourse. Incest was redefined as a *forcible* offense and even though the stepdaughter was under 16 at the time it started, the Court assumed consent and, thus, the stepfather was provided with a complete defense. When the grandparents of the stepdaughter filed a civil action, they were awarded general and punitive damages for the incest, the first such reported award (Elkington v. Faust 618 P.2d at 39 [Utah 1980] [No. 16298]).

Other countries felt that incest was not a matter for the law but for morals and religion. For some commentators, the current status of English law (1986) allows for the marriage of first cousins (1/4 shared genes), but bars in-law and steprelationship marriages. France has no incest laws but would prosecute the father's sexual relations with his daughter (step, adopted, etc.) as crimes of assault and/or abuse of power. Affinity would be an irrelevant issue in these situations. In Italy, once unification took place in 1861, a uniform legal code was necessary; however, the divergence between legal thinking and social happening was enormous. While the incest statutes spoke of relations between two consenting adults each with the capacity to accept or reject the situation, for the common people,

---

[4]The issue of consent, whether between adults or between an adult and a child, should be a nonissue. Thus, the absence of consent was not an element of the offense.

incest meant the relations between adults and minors, that is, where there is an abuse of authority with the victim unable to express either consent or refusal. In practice what resulted was not just a silence about the offense but secrecy by those who knew and blindness by those who do not want to know. Italian law is in essential agreement with the thinking of a dysfunctional family in that the offense to "family morals" occurs only when secrecy is broken and a public scandal ensues. Only then does incest become legally subject to prosecution.

Morton (1988), commenting in the British *New Law Journal*, raises the question whether consenting sexual relations between an adult brother and sister who had never known each other in childhood should be prosecuted. The then-current Incest Act of 1908 was felt to have come about by a moral crusade designed to stamp out the immorality of the underclass and the rural and urban poor. Of the 1500 cases of incest reported in 1981, six went to court. Morton believes that there are sufficient sanctions (other than incest statutes) available to charge the fathers, stepfathers, and so on who have sexual relations with their daughters. Morton advocates a system such as exists in France, Sweden, and Denmark which makes the "abuse of authority" the punishable crime, and as such would apply to a teacher, coach, and so on as well. In the struggle to define incest, we see that there have been many attempts, both clerical and legal, but there is little uniformity of opinion as to what constitutes a prohibited relationship. Even when there is agreement within a specific country or group, are incest laws necessary or can infractions be more effectively criminalized under the "abuse of power" statutes?

The Redefinition of Incest Under
Rape Reform Statutes

Prior to the rape reform legislation of the 1970s, few states defined incest as sexual intercourse between the father and daughter preferring to reserve the term more for the adult–adult prohibited categories. When confronted with an adult–child sexual intercourse, the prosecutor would have a choice of charging the parent under the traditional incest statutes, or under the traditional statutory rape statutes, or as a form of child abuse. Not only was there duplication and unclarity of the law but the language of the law tended to be moralistic, using terms like *lewd, lascivious, infamous, unchaste, seductive, immoral*, and so on. The new laws replaced the language of morality with the language of medicine, referring explicitly to sexual acts and anatomy. Michigan (1998) was the first to pass rape reform statutes that redefined incest as an offense if the person committing it were over the age of 13 and under the age of 16 and that person was penetrated or had sexual contact with an adult of the household, a relative, or a person in a position of authority. Much of the impetus for the rape reform legislation was fueled by feminist theory and the woman's movement. In a sense, there was no longer a crime of incest since sex relations between consenting adults over the age of 16 was no longer criminalized. The language of the laws were gender-free so that offenses applied equally to heterosexual and homosexual relations. Very clearly, any sexual contact within or outside the family with a child under 13 was defined as criminal. Furthermore, the offense did not necessitate sexual penetration but referred more broadly to any sexual contact. Perhaps the most far-reaching change was the phrase "position of authority," since the prohibited contact was no longer confined to family members, but would extend to anyone who assumed, even temporarily, an *in loco parentis* role. This would include a stepfather, mother's live-in boyfriend, a grandparent, a teacher, a coach, or even the clergy. Clearly stated in these changes is that child sexual abuse, similar to rape, is an assaultive crime. The harm was not solely to be seen in terms of loss of virginity or innocence, but the harm is to the psychological well-being of the person and to the integrity and autonomy of the individual with both short- and long-term consequences. The law in its social role as protector of children was now in a position to do so when the adults would not or could not do so.

Evaluating Reports of Incest

The incidence of incest cannot be ascertained from the statistics of reported cases since only a percentage of cases are reported and only a percentage of those are considered valid or confirmed by the investigating agency. On the other hand, those who have been incest victims may for periods of time not recall the events (Williams and Finkelhor, 1995). Other reports of incest arise out of acrimonious divorce and child custody battles (Mikkelson, Gutheil, and Emens, 1992). One parent, often the mother, brings allegations of sexual contact between the child and the father/stepfather, with the sought-for result being a loss and/or infringement of the latter's custodial and visitation rights. Under these circumstances, a child may be subjected to considerable emotional pressure and be suggestible enough to create credible allegations of parental sexual abuse. Evaluation of these allegations often necessitates a forensic expert well versed in child development and family dynamics, conscious and unconscious. In some instances, the validity or falsity of the allegations becomes obvious. In other cases, even a thorough work-up produces equivocal results, or two different experts each retained by the opposing parties come to opposite conclusions (Shopper, 1991; Nurcombe and Unützer, 1991). The mass hysteria involving sexual abuse at daycare facilities has not only shown the falseness of many children's allegations but demonstrated how readily young children can have reality events suggested and inculcated into them, not just by parents but by overzealous poorly trained "therapists" (Shopper, 1992). Another difficult situation to evaluate is when a person who is overtly psychotic, or has lapses in reality testing as may occur in borderline patients, makes allegations of incest against family members. Is this to be seen as a symptom of a disturbed sense of reality, or is it to be viewed as an etiological factor in their emotional impairment? In any event, one cannot automatically invalidate a patient's allegations of incest as simply another delusion of the psychosis. As Niederland (1959) has demonstrated, even the most bizarre delusions, such as those of the psychotic German jurist Daniel Schreber whose memoirs were analyzed by Freud (1911), have a distinct nucleus of reality in the patient's past childhood experiences.

Further confusing the field is the issue of repressed memory, which in turn has its roots in the history of Freud's (1896) thinking, namely his initial belief that the origin of hysteria was rooted in his female patient's early seduction by the father. Later, he viewed the etiology as residing not in actual events but in the woman's fantasies of incestuous seduction. As a result of this changed theoretical orientation, many feminists reviled psychoanalytic theory as the enemy. Freud was seen as denying the reality of a woman's incestuous experiences. If incest was indeed a reality, the woman was a victim and to fail to validate that reality adds another level of victimization. If it is only a fantasy, however, then the woman is victimizing another. Yet it is not an either/or situation. Many men and women do have and have had oedipal fantasies about their parents, often unconscious fantasies that are accessible in the course of analytic treatment. Similarly, many women and fewer men have been the victims of incestuous sexual abuse. They are not mutually exclusive conditions. The issue of repressed memory is summarized from a legal standpoint by Haldsworth (1998) and from a psychoanalytic standpoint by Brennis (1997).

This emphasis on the "repressed memory" has led to further complexities and mischief, as when a poorly trained/overzealous therapist concludes very early in the therapeutic contact (within the first few sessions) that the patient is a victim of intrafamilial incest. The ensuing therapeutic efforts focus on "recovering the memories" of the abuse, a focus offering a fertile field for a therapist's suggestion and inculcation. This is then followed by accusing the alleged perpetrator, often bringing suit legally, and demanding that the perpetrator acknowledge the incest and apologize with remorse. As a result, many parents were falsely accused and subsequently alienated from their children since parental guilt, not innocence, was assumed. Proving something did not happen made defense difficult. The decisions of judges and juries were often based on estimates of credibility of each witness with sympathies, at least initially, being with the victimized child.

In response to this "recovered memory therapy," the False Memory Syndrome Foundation came into existence in 1992 to expose these therapists, to support a legal defense of accused parents with psychological and psychiatric expert opinions, to raise funds for publication and dissemination of information about recovered memory therapy, to track court cases where the estranged accused parents sued the hospitals and therapists for damages, and to act as a support group for those victimized by these "false memory" therapists. Here too, there was an overreaction and all psychiatric treatment was condemned as potentially dangerous. Legislation was introduced mandating that all these dangers were to be specifically and explicitly enumerated prior to treatment, and the patient was to provide "informed consent" for a treatment that now sounded more harmful than beneficial. Fortunately, many legislatures ignored these "informed consent" statutes, reasoning that the existing standards of practice and existing remedies sufficed. Many (Champagne, 1996) feel that the FMS Foundation has become antitherapy, antifeminist, and more political than scientific, despite a distinguished group of scientists on their advisory board.

The Incest Barrier, Familial Bonding, and Desexualization of Intimacy

As has so often happened in history, our narcissism as *Homo sapiens* leads us to underestimate the abilities and social organization of animals. So, too, Freud when he assumed that animals in the wild had no barriers to incest, the corollary being that it was a unique point in the evolution of society and civilization when the incest taboo came into being. Freud (1913) postulated his theory of the primal horde and as a clinician postulated that all children have incestuous impulses that are repressed into the unconscious. Biological research cited by Erickson (1993) has found that incest is rare throughout the animal kingdom. Further, it is suggested that close proximity during the early formative years may be needed for the development of the incest taboo in animals. This observation may dovetail with the observations on the mating patterns of kibbutz children raised in the Children's Houses by nonfamilial metapelets (governesses). An Israeli anthropologist, Joseph Shepher (1983), found not a single marriage in which the couple had been raised in the same peer group from ages 0–6 (N = 2769). However, eight marriages were from a peer group of ages 6–12, and nine marriages from an adolescent peer group. While there is neither a biological nor affinity relationship between the kibbutz children raised in this communal type of child rearing, the communal living, in and of itself, created a psychological bond between them making them "psychological siblings" (to paraphrase a concept of the "psychological parent," a term coined in a different context by Goldstein, Solnit, and Freud, 1973).

Erickson finds new validity to Westermark's (1894) idea that close early childhood proximity creates an innate aversion to later sexual intercourse.

Erickson notes that his familial bond hypothesis seems to be in apparent conflict with Freud's concept of the universality of the Oedipus conflict. Erickson suggests that adequate bonding may be "an essential precursor and stimulus for healthy progression through the oedipal period" (p. 415). Consequently, in reviewing those factors enhancing the likelihood of incest, our first look would be at early impaired bonding between child and parent, such as might occur when the father is absent from the home, or the father is uninvolved in his daughter's early rearing. To the extent that most of the stepfather's involvement in the life of his stepdaughter often comes after the first five years of life, the incestuous taboo is correspondingly decreased and incestuous activity more likely. Theoretically, this lack of participation in the daughter's early child rearing predisposes the daughter (as well as the stepfather) to an incestuous relationship. Williams and Finkelhor (1995), while in theoretical agreement, strike a note of caution when they emphasize the complexity of the issue and the incompleteness of the research. However, when we speak of the father's involvement in the early child rearing, we are simply speaking of a statistical correlation but not of the process by which incestuous taboos are formed. I would suggest that we need to consider the process, what I would call the *desexualization of intimacy*. Whether it be mother or father participating in the early routine childcare, a great deal of sensual stimulation of the child is entailed and I would suggest of the parent as well.[5] Body, genitals, buttocks, and skin are handled and caressed, the entire body is dressed, rocked, and, in certain ways, made love to. However sensuous this may be, in the average expected household, it is not experienced as sexual but as loving nurturance. I believe that this desexualization of the loving and sensual care of the young child is what distinguishes altruistic object-related nurturance from use of the child as a sexual self-object. The parent–child intimacy, closeness, and body contact are loving but nonsexual.[6] As the child gets older, physical intimacy, as well as

---

[5]In some instances, mothers are either afraid or terminate prematurely the nursing of their infant when they cannot "desexualize" the stimulation and arousal often felt while nursing. For these mothers nursing becomes a sexualized, that is, "sexy," experience and interferes with their image of themselves as a nurturing mother. Similarly, the bouncy, rough-and-tumble play that fathers often engage in with toddlers may cause an erection, which might be interpreted as a sign of (perverse/pedophilic) sexual excitement. If the physical contact and mutual stimulation cannot be desexualized, the father may be reluctant to engage in further physical play with the child.

[6]There are times when the child clearly experiences the mother's ministrations as sexual, as might be seen by overt masturbation, erections, genital exhibitionism

physical contact, diminishes. Although still loving and affectionate, the relationship with the school-aged child becomes in certain ways more physically distant. The onset of puberty awakens both parents to the sexual maturity of their no longer sexually innocent child. The average "good enough" father becomes more circumspect about physical contact with his daughter. He may admire her budding good looks and developing body but he maintains a fatherly quiet appreciation and a fatherly respectful distance. It is during adolescence that the capacity for desexualization of the loving relationship between father and daughter is put to the test. His early involvement in her childcare is the stable foundation for the *continued desexualization* of their relationship during her adolescence and which must withstand the stresses and temptations of an affectionate and loving father–daughter relationship. The stepfather who has not had this early foundation of desexualized nurturing experiences may find it difficult to desexualize his affectionate feelings toward his stepdaughter. It is as though he has to learn desexualization *de novo*. Some stepfathers manage fairly well since the parental models of their childhood provides them with the core identifications for a nonsexualized affectionate relationship. Other stepfathers, lacking desexualized stabilizing parental models, compounded by an absence of participation in their stepdaughter's early childcare, are more vulnerable and liable to succumb to incestuous temptations.

Erickson, Walbek, and Seely (1987) note, from their own experience and that of the literature, that stepfathers may sexually molest their own stepchildren, but will not molest their own children who also live in the home. When stepparent incest occurs, it is often within one or two years of the marriage, that is, "without time for the development of affectionate relationships with stepchildren that might serve to counterbalance the impulse for sexual abuse" (p. 355).

Wallerstein and Blakeslee (1989) note that "the presence of a stepfather can raise the difficult issue of a thinner incest barrier"; "in a remarried family, adults seem less prepared to cope with an adolescent girl's sexual development"; and between the stepfather and his stepdaughter "there is a higher potential for generating sexual interest and excitement" (p. 249).

In the intact family, parental sexuality is practiced discreetly and with little fanfare. With divorce, dating, weddings, and remarriage, the illusion

---

to the parent, and so on. The "good enough" parent does not respond sexually to the child but will help the child rechannel the excitement or use defensive measures to contain the excitement. While "Little Hans" (Freud, 1909) contains prime examples of overt sexual excitement, his mother, it is reported, encouraged and stimulated him sexually for her own narcissistic purposes. Unfortunately for Little Hans, her nurturance and caretaking behavior was infiltrated by her own sexual needs.

of parental celibacy is much harder, if not impossible, to maintain. As a result, there is more sexual excitement, curiosity, and awareness concerning the sexual life of the remarried parents. From the adolescent's standpoint this, too, leads to a "thinning" of the incest barrier, which if too "thin" may be rendered nonexistent by the stepdaughter–stepfather couple.

Concomitant with a father's desexualization processes is a similar one in the adolescent. I have postulated that a normal adolescent developmental stage entails the creation of a defensive "illusion of parental celibacy" (Shopper, 1998). In essence, the adolescent believes that sexuality is the province of adolescents and young adults, and certainly not of those as old as her parents. This belief serves to negate the reality of her parents as active, alive, and enjoying sexuality. This desexualization of the father serves the defensive function of removing him as a sexual object.

In summary, I have tried to put "incest" into our "index," into our thinking, and into our concerns for stepparent families.

References

Bienen, L. B. (1998), Defining incest. *Northwestern Univ. Law Rev.*, 1501, Summer.

Brennis, C. B. (1997), *Recovered Memories of Trauma: Transferring the Present to the Past*. Madison, CT: International Universities Press.

Champagne, R. (1996), *The Politics of Survivorship*. New York: New York University Press.

Erickson, M. T. (1993), Rethinking Oedipus: An evolutionary perspective of incest avoidance. *Amer. J. Psychiat.*, 150:411–416.

Erickson, W. D., Walbek, N. H. & Seely, R. K. (1987), The life histories and psychological profiles of fifty-nine stepfathers. *Bull. Amer. Acad. Psychiat. Law*, 15:349–357.

Fenichel, O. (1945), *The Psychoanalytic Theory of Neurosis*. New York: Norton.

Freud, S. (1896), The aetiology of hysteria. *Standard Edition*, 3:191–221. London: Hogarth Press, 1955.

_____ (1909), Analysis of a phobia in a five-year-old boy. *Standard Edition*, 10:3–147. London: Hogarth Press, 1955.

_____ (1911), Psycho-analytical notes on an autobiographical account of a case of paranoia. *Standard Edition*, 12:9–82. London: Hogarth Press, 1958.

_____ (1913), Totem and taboo. *Standard Edition*, 13:1–161. London: Hogarth Press, 1955.

Goldstein, J., Solnit, A. J. & Freud, A. (1973), *Beyond the Best Interests of the Child*. New York: Free Press.

Haldsworth, L. (1998), Is it repressed memory with relayed recall, or is it false memory syndrome? The controversy and its potential legal implications. *Law & Psychol. Rev.*, 22:103–129.

Mikkelson, E. J., Gutheil, T. G. & Emens, M. (1992), False sexual abuse allegations by children and adolescents: Contextual factors and clinical subtypes. *Amer. J. Psychother.*, 46:556–570.

Morton, J. (1988), The Incest Act of 1908: Was it ever relevant? [Comment]. *Brit. New Law J.*, January 29, pp. 59–60.

Niederland, W. (1959), Schreber: Father and son. *Psychoanal. Quart.*, 28:151–169.

Nurcombe, B. & Unützer, J. (1991), The ritual abuse of children: Clinical features and diagnostic reasoning. *J. Amer. Acad. Child Adol. Psychiat.*, 30:272–276.

Pasley, K. & Ihinger-Tallman, M., eds. (1987), *Remarriage and Stepparenting: Current Research and Theory.* New York: Guilford Press.

Rank, O. (1912), *The Incest Theme in Literature and Legend,* trans. G. C. Richter. Baltimore, MD: Johns Hopkins University Press, 1992.

Russell, D. E. H. (1984a), The prevalence and seriousness of incestuous abuse: Stepfathers vs. biological fathers. *Child Abuse & Neglect,* 8:15–22.

––––––– (1984b), *Sexual Exploitation: Rape, Child Sexual Abuse, and Workplace Harassment.* Beverly Hills, CA: Sage Publications.

Sariola, H. & Uutela, A. (1996), The prevalence and context of incest abuse in Finland. *Child Abuse & Neglect,* 20:843–850.

Shepher, J. (1983), *Incest: A Biosocial View.* New York: Academic Press.

Shopper, M. (1991), Ritual abuse of children [Letter to editor]. *J. Amer. Acad. Child Adol. Psychiat.*, 30:1023–1024.

––––––– (1992), Created reality and false allegations of abuse: Experiences from sex abuse trials. Presented to the Michigan Psychoanalytic Society.

––––––– (1998), The illusion of parental celibacy. Presented to the St. Louis Child Analytic Study Group, St. Louis, MO.

Simon, B. (1992), Incest—see under Oedipus complex: The history of an error in psychoanalysis. *J. Amer. Psychoanal. Assn.*, 40:955–988.

Utah Supreme Court, State v. Faust, 588 P. 2d 170 (Utah 1978).

Wallerstein, J. S. & Blakeslee, S. (1989), *Second Chances: Men, Women and Children a Decade After Divorce.* New York: Ticknor & Fields.

Westermark, E. (1894), *The History of Human Marriage.* London: Macmillan.

Williams, L. M. & Finkelhor, D. (1995), Paternal care-giving and incest: Test of a biosocial model. *Amer. J. Orthopsychiat.*, 65:101–113.

Wolfram, S. (1983), Eugenics and the punishment of Incest Act 1908. *Criminal Law Rev.*, May, pp. 308–316.

Oedipal Reenactments
with Stepmother and Stepfather
Incest and Splitting of the Superego
Léon Wurmser

"I See a Brilliant Golden Dagger Above My Chest"

A few months into his analysis, 30-year-old scientist Reinhold stated, "When I learned my girlfriend might be pregnant I got enraged but then almost immediately felt relief. I thought I deserve to be punished. Then, I thought you would tell me I am not working hard enough. I hoped to find redemption with you, but imagine you would ridicule me . . . that I am just confused. Now I see the image of a brilliant golden dagger above my chest. When things get too bad the dagger will fall down and pierce me. Its blade is cross-shaped and so is the hilt."

I thought of all this as an expression of a momentary sadomasochistic transference. From the beginning of treatment, I had recognized the severity and archaical nature of Reinhold's judgment as the scorn he fears from me had accompanied us like a shadow. I had become a harshly condemning judge, a brutal authority, whose absolution and love he craved with consummate sincerity. One of the important aspects of this superego transference was his attempt to appease these archaic images by idealizing me and sharing the world of ideals with me.

My patient is a tall, attractive, strong man with an open, trusting, and honest face. His eyes are very myopic contributing to a dreamy expression. He sought treatment because of his repeating a unique pattern in every intimate relationship with a woman. Inescapably, he reported, intimacy soon changed into hellish torment and victimhood. In his current relation, his girlfriend kept accusing him of not loving her enough, whereupon he desperately and eventually furiously tried to justify and defend himself. Typically such an encounter would end in intense suicidal and homicidal despair. Yet he felt incapable of separating and described the relationship as: "We cannot be with each other, and we cannot be without each other." He reminded me of the words of another of my patients in similar circumstances: "Torment me, but don't abandon me."

His life history provides a dramatic background to this repetition compulsion. As the oldest of four children, he witnessed a marriage that had been "bad from early times." His childhood had been marked by mother's repeated suicide attempts and multiple hospitalizations. He reconstructed

231

she had had children mostly to bind her husband to her in order to block his liaison with another woman. The family had lived overseas where father had been a university professor. When the patient was six years old, his parents separated and were divorced. When mother was about to return to the United States with her four children, it was decided that Reinhold would stay overseas with his father as a continued link between the parents. At the last moment, he was exchanged for his younger brother. The switch came so abruptly his clothes were left behind. Some years later his brother followed. In his mind, his overseas father remained a luminous, heroic figure, whom he had lost only because he had not been good enough. Even after he learned father had married one of his former students, he yearned deeply for a reunion.

In contrast, mother was regarded as utterly incompetent and contempt-ible: "I remember how my mother shamed me in my childhood in ways I didn't deserve. She would threaten to kill herself and would drive away saying: 'You children are better off without me.' She would not come back until deep into the night. I was deeply ashamed to have such a mother, so unable to be human."

A few years later she married a minister who drank heavily and was capable of considerable brutality. Eventually, this led to fist-fights between stepfather and either Reinhold or his brother. He felt these fights were so savage as to be close to murderous (the patient shot over the head of his stepfather). Reinhold saw himself more and more in the role of protector, a rescuer of his younger siblings including a stepbrother from the mother's remarriage. This youngest and most vulnerable brother evoked particular compassion and protectiveness. When an adolescent, Reinhold joined a fundamentalist Christian sect. By the age of 21, he decided to return to his father who now lived in an Arab country. The relationship to his stepmother, Maya, was immediately marked by a sense of familiarity, trust, and intimacy. In her he found the nurturing, loving, competent mother he never had had. But such intimacy and nurturing soon entailed more and more physical contact. Allegedly, they were mostly initiated by her: "She would come into my bed and put my hand on her breast, saying with pity, 'You have never touched the breast of a woman.' She manipulated me through humiliation, at least that was what I felt: If I didn't touch her breast I would be an incomplete man, a 'nerd.'" In the past he had rebuffed sexual closeness to girls of his own age. Now he was so "smitten" by his stepmother, he responded passionately to her advances. He rationalized she was seeking consolation and expected him to compensate for the deficiencies in her usually inebriated husband.

"For a long time I was grateful to her for having introduced me to sexuality. Once in her bedroom with my hands on her breast, my father suddenly appeared. I hastily pulled back, ashamed he could have seen me. Even now, in talking about it, I feel ashamed. Maya, in front of the entire family, also shamed my father by announcing he wanted her sexually, or that she wished he had affairs with other women in order to make him more interesting. She ruled my father by shaming him, and she attempted to do the same with me."

He described how seemingly playful encounters eventually led to his ejaculating into her vagina. This happened under the bedcovers but it was in the presence of his two stepsisters and his brother, watching TV in the same room. His stepmother later denied the full extent and meaning of this event. Yet he felt overwhelmed by guilt and shame. Somehow he felt his moral base had been shattered, and not long after he decided to return to the States.

He quickly tried to apply what he had learned about sex by aggressively approaching an old girlfriend. He was decisively rebuffed. "Even years later I felt humiliated by this and felt the need to keep apologizing to her." It was a double, a self-contradictory shame. With his stepmother, he had been ashamed that he was still a virgin and sexually inexperienced. With his previous girlfriend, he was ashamed that he had been so obtrusive sexually. This may be considered a form of intrasystemic superego conflict (conflict *within* the system superego).

A few year later, he married a very gifted and professionally successful woman. In a repetition of the earlier sequence with Maya, she too was disappointed he had not been more experienced sexually and kept pushing him to engage in extramarital affairs. But she also claimed the same rights for herself. He resisted these entreaties and would explode in jealous rage. Eventually, he took the same right but it turned out to mean the end of their marriage. In his mind it was the second time his moral base had been destroyed.

Although very successful in his studies and later research endeavors, he always had to fight intense anxiety. At the beginning of his employment by a university, he spent hours hiding in panic and shame in the basement of the institution.

"Taming the Tigress"

He reported a steadily recurring fantasy: He would climb into a tiger pit and tame a tigress with his bare hands. Then he would soothe her and make her his friend. Thus he could change terror and horror to something beautiful—magically transforming the tigress into a loving mother. Immediately, the picture changed: his associations led to an image where he would have to pull out his eyes. The connection of this image of conquest, self-punishment, and symbolic castration to Oedipus eluded him.

In the broader context of his family history we realize he had truly nearly slain his stepfather and really slept with his stepmother. This is an almost perfect real reenactment of the literal oedipal conflict. The oedipal wish fulfilled was immediately followed by other terrifying fantasies. "Having mother for myself, and then she has to die. I saw my wish fulfilled twice—first with my own mother, when she left my father, and then with my stepmother after she married my father. But both times they built a barrier against my father, so that I am forever separated from him. . . . I am so overwhelmed by guilt. . . . I can never ask him for forgiveness."

The pattern of love with sexual victory over his father-rival linked to unforgivable guilt, killing, and self-torment was repeated in every intimate relationship to a woman. The masochistic aspects of the outcome of these intimate relationships included his continuous self-torment he reported. He was quite aware of the connection between his sensed loss of moral base and the oedipal implications.

Yet as his analysis unfolded we encountered the expected deeper layers: He compared his dependence on his depressive, demanding girlfriend to a drug addict's on heroin. At times his fear of giving her up was overwhelming and death appeared to be the lesser evil. Yet, the alternatives tormented him as he fluctuated between intolerable anguish and pain with her and "absolute loneliness" without her. He realized he had vested the absolute hope for a more meaningful relationship in her. It was a matter of totality: "If I lose her, I lose everything."

This was a precise repetition of his early relationship with his mother. She was either withdrawn into herself in a depressive state or interacting with him (or his father) in a cruelly rejecting or seductively clinging way. Thus, what was decisive at the preoedipal core was a relationship of torment alternating with deadly isolation. With such a bond, attachment is characterized by the totality of absolute dependency.

In one session I referred to Ibsens's *Wild Duck*, in connection with his own dilemma about pulling away the veil of lies hiding his dreadful secrets, especially from his father and the risk of destroying a "life's lie— livsløgnen." My patient was so impressed he bought and then systematically read all of Ibsen's realistic dramas. He was able to use their symbolism quite effectively in his concurrent self-analysis in the interval between sessions. In that he had moved far away, we had arranged to meet once a week for two hours in the evening and two hours the following morning, an arrangement that lasted for a period of about two years. During this time he came to understand his masochistic relationship to his partner as the restoration of the *dilemma between a tormentingly symbiotic bond and fear of deadly abandonment*. He repeated these masochistic patterns in the renewed hope to bring this bondage under his control, "to tame the tigress and make her my friend," to dissolve the dilemma. And yet, the outcome threatened to be just the opposite. As he learned in Ibsen's last play, *When We Dead Awaken*, separation can be a form of dying and union may lead to a kind of mutual killing, to dying together.

Thus, in addition to the oedipal situation noted above, was a masochistic pattern we could understand as derived from the preoedipal conflict of separation-individuation versus love and merger.

"The Bastion of Good and His Moral Base"

Reinhold had always conceived of himself as a "bastion of good." Indeed, he had been seen and treated by most people as a form of a savior or healer. "I wear many masks—the pillar of goodness, the tower of strength and a student of literature. Yet they are parts of my true self, not only weapons and defense. But, behind the walls of that fortress burn intense desires for revenge."

Rage was never far from consciousness, nor was it always barred from erupting. More deeply hidden, then, were primitive strivings of *murderous rivalry* against siblings and father. An astonishing connection emerged: Prior to the separation of his parents, he had become aware his father had started a secret liaison with his later, second wife. Perhaps he had seen them kiss, but he felt he had to keep this big secret to himself. He also noticed his father had been actively encouraging an intimate liaison between his wife and his best friend, a clergyman. The patient considered this was to create an alibi, an excuse for his own indiscretions.

When he was 20, Reinhold tried at one of his father's rare visits to inquire about the events preceding the divorce. His father rebuffed him coldly saying it was none of his business. Reinhold was so enraged he hit the sofa he was sitting on. It was not long after this confrontation, he decided to go to the Near East and join what he told himself was "the ideal family"—his father and the same woman he had seen in his childhood. But then he entered the secret and forbidden liaison with his stepmother. On two occasions, his life centered upon secrets, the first a secret kept from his mother connected to a betrayal by his father, the second time a secret withheld from his father in regard to a betrayal against him. It was a kind of reversal but also a revenge which erected a barrier between him and both his parents which could never be removed—"secret means separation," he added.

Let us consider the nature of this reversal further. Instead of being a *jealous outsider*, the excluded third (as at the age of five), a position reaffirmed and deepened by the later rebuff by father (at the age of 20), he then deceives his father and places him in the position of the jealous and excluded third—and with the very same woman! In his words: "The truth is this: the only woman who could have satisfied my wish for revenge on my father was *his* wife. Yet, it was a lifelong desire for my father. The whole thing of my affair with her consisted of revenge on him. . . . I was so sick that I wished my father would die just to have her for myself. The anger against him was itself the result of my enormously intensive desire for him. . . . A very deep love, yet love that hurt. . . . It was not only revenge against him, but *desire for him*—only that she responded, and he didn't." This is another level of conflict—the negative version of the Oedipus complex.

Thus, his particularly significant inner danger is "jealousy" from many sources, each one reinforcing the other. This compound jealousy is never completely and successfully repressed. It may be covered over by reaction formation such as unbounded generosity and readiness to sacrifice for others. His "heroic" involvement is consistently in behalf of those who suffer, especially his siblings and parents. Over time his jealousy found new sources. However, it was clear during the analysis that he would sometimes turn the other into the excluded third and then suffer masochistically their jealous revenge. This repressed conflict is continued under a cloak of idealization by the compounding of projection, reversal, externalization, and turning against the self.

The "Delicate Conscience" and the "Robust Conscience"

Reinhold's conscience has always been overbearing. In an earlier poem he wrote: "The hidden sword cut far into the heart, severing the dreams of life from unknown reality."

He retained a fear of me as an overly idealized, always to be appeased, and somehow ever threatening authority. I believe this reflects his narcissistic-masochistic transference, an anxiety induced by his own conscience by the incessant hammering of shame and guilt. He talked about the masochistic relations in Kafka's "Metamorphosis" and their dehumanizing aspects which he compared with his own devastating needs for punishment. He came to understand how his compulsive evocation of rejection and struggle for forgiveness was related to the depth of his double-edged guilt because of incest—in his own words: "The guilt of keeping such a secret from father . . . the guilt about revealing the secret to him." His conscience was also riven by steadily recurring conflicts of loyalty, that is, in regard to the marital conflicts of friends or in scientific competitive events, just as it had been earlier between his two mothers and between his mother and father. "The smallest infraction of perfect performance ends in a terrible metamorphosis, a dehumanization, just as it did for Gregor Samsa. It is real guilt which deprives me of my humanity." But he added, "Shame must always be dehumanizing and crushing. My obsession with beautiful women is my attempt to dehumanize them—as a revenge for feeling they dehumanized me. I look at a beautiful woman until I discover a flaw and then I discard her. If I do not find a flaw I make an effort to conquer her until there is a hint of affection. With that I have succeeded in dehumanizing her."

He was particularly impressed by a passage in Ibsen's *The Lady from the Sea*. Bolette Wangel says about her stepmother Ellida: "There is so very much that this one does not *see*. Or what she perhaps does not *want* to see—or she does not *care about* it." Reinhold called it at first "soul lie," then we coined the term *soul blindness*. He also observed that the "pleasurable self-torment" of Solness (in Ibsen's *Masterbuilder Solness*) tries to alleviate a "burden of unconscious and unintended guilt".

This analysis of conscience in *Masterbuilder Solness* (and reexperienced by the patient) revealed two forms of conscience opposed to each other: one conscience submitted to the overwhelming power of duty while the other gave a fair hearing to the right to having a "joy of life" and a new pride, the right to pleasure, power, and creative self-expression. Yet this new conscience very rapidly turns into one that wants to place itself "beyond good and evil." Hilde Wangel, a child who (in the earlier drama *The Lady from the Sea*) had "not been seen" by her father and stepmother, had not been recognized with her individual needs and yearnings, returns now, in *Masterbuilder Solness,* as a gloriously rebellious, anarchical woman of dreams and wild mountains. She invites and tempts the oppressed architect Solness to cast off his severe, duty-burdened conscience and to replace it with a new, free conscience, one rapaciously daring, like a bird of prey. When he responds by evoking his "duty," she protests: "Oh, I can't stand that nasty, horrid word!"

"Why not?"

"Because it sounds so cold and sharp and prickly. Duty, duty, duty [plikt, plikt, plikt]! Don't you think so, too? That it seems to sting you? . . . What I'm wondering is whether you weren't born with rather a sickly conscience."

"What the devil's that?"

"I mean your conscience is actually very fragile. Sort of delicate. Won't stand up to things. Can't bear much weight."

"Hmm! What should one's conscience be like then, may I ask?"

"In your case I should want to see a conscience that was . . . well, thoroughly robust."

Reinhold was reflecting on this and saw his own conscience similarly split. In externalized form, especially in love relationships and transference it seemingly consisted of two figures fighting against each other. One figure represented an archaic conscience that functioned as a draconian protective power, guarding against all oedipal and preoedipal transgressions by brutal, radical, and ruthless force. It was a conscience founded on *extreme guilt*. Its opponent was a "free" or "robust" conscience, seemingly shameless and chasing after unbounded power, pleasure, and creativity, and guided by an ideal of strength, resembling Nietzsche's value philosophy "beyond good and evil." It was a conscience set up to guard against *any shame*. In Ibsen's metaphors, Reinhold resonates to the conflict between the "dizzy, delicate, weak conscience" and the "robust, strong, free, proud conscience." Yet in treatment there emerges a third form mediating between those two: that of a rationally weighing authority serving the deeper justice of equal rights and mutuality, one which could be symbolized by the great lawgiver Solon. Thus we encounter three superego types coexisting and combatting each other: Drakon, Nietzsche, and Solon (or Solomon). My patient was frightened of the first and tried to transform me into the second but gradually found in the treatment the third.

The treatment became, largely due to the great geographic distance, more and more sporadic and ended after about seven years (530 sessions). His relationship to his wife had lost much of its narcissistic and sadomasochistic qualities. Professionally he had become very successful.

"Reluctant but Necessary Rape" in the Life of a Tween

Stanley H. Cath

I n the past, the years from preteens to teens (circa 10–12) were considered by developmental theorists a part of a relatively quiescent time, the
so-called latency period. In America's demanding and racing culture, all
too many overstimulated preteens mature so quickly that they face many
of the challenges usually encountered in the adolescent phase of life. In a
recent media article, these precocious youngsters were euphemistically
described as "tweens." While the article focused on the sparkling, creative
contributions bright and articulate youngsters may make, I felt it minimized
the internal, more difficult tasks of processing and modulating premature
endeavor and sexual excitements under the aegis of the particular nurturing but parting environment in which at least half of them live.

Even at best, the predominant memories of how life seemed to most
precocious youngsters I have known or treated have been deeply colored
by feelings of lonely alienation if not deadness, often described subjectively as "I'm bored." The label of tween might be new, but this psychological profile of a young, alienated person engaged in a search for aliveness
strangely resonates with a lovely, sad, wrinkled face of one of my older
patients of yore. Indeed, I thought of her as a stellar tween.

Often emotionally unattended by a set of high-living, reconstituted
parents in Hollywood of the 1930s, a 10-year-old girl turned to an older
stepbrother for comfort in bed almost every lonely night for many years.
This obviously near-incestuous relationship was quickly eroticized. In the
analytic retrospective of my very much alive and still remarkably attractive
patient, this need for soothing by sexual stimulation was described as
"reluctant but necessary rape." I was deeply impressed and pondered long
and hard on this paradox of partial admission of collusion and a partial
denial of the reality of just being a victim. Superficially adjusted, this inner
paradox remained her secret.

My associations led to remembering another paradox, namely how
difficult it has been for me as a so-called expert witness to have any idea
at times who really did what to whom or who was most eager or reluctant.
In my third ear it had often seemed, just as in this case, that most everyone
was threatened and instinctively searching for a safe harbor. But this
attitude raises many questions. What was necessary and exactly how does
rape change its meaning when it is reluctantly needed? Are "loose boundaries between sibs" an accurate appraisal of the desperate search for

coherency and belonging by the terrified participants? And how does all of this change when we learn that this particular "necessary rape" had been prefigured by "real" incestuous experiences with *both* step and biological fathers? While I was awed by the consistency of "boundary crossings" recreated in the adult world of this aged tween, I could not help but return to the importance of such a series of misattunements to the dilemma of true and false accusations. I wondered how many times had such a set of affective imagos been transferred to the many (reluctant?) therapists she alleged had been misled into believing their physical love would comfort her. Could such a complex concept as necessary but reluctant rape be heuristically useful in legal proceedings focused on boundary crossing? Although my patient throughout her long life had engaged in many campaigns against unfairness and had been quite litigious at times, revealingly this had not included any of her "too eager therapists." Was this because on some deep level her compassion was informed by the necessity of her seductiveness? I'm not entirely convinced on the basis of a single case, but it opens up a new way of thinking about such "trauma."

Over time I learned more about the genesis of her "very active sex life as a younger person," to which she added coyly, "well, still somewhat." Her mother was remembered as a "beautiful but spacey woman."

"My alcoholic, bipolar stepfather when lit [drunk] didn't know any boundaries. I would wait for him to come home roaring drunk . . . he'd get into my bed . . . and do his thing . . . that was with his hands . . . so can you believe, I ran to my older stepbrother for protection . . . his son . . . and you see what became of that!"

To set an even earlier stage, family stories documented how irresponsible her hard-drinking, unstable, antiestablishment, biological father had been. In the first half of the 20th century, all her parents, like many others, "paraded around in the nude and believed in free love." Her first remembered dreams were of "finding a good man for myself and my mother." By 18, as a runaway, she found a mate but a man of a different faith from a similarly deprived and traumatized background. This "bad choice" irrevocably separated her from mother, father, and stepfather. She did link her hyperaroused attachment to both brother and stepfather to severe maternal deprivation: "I blame my mother for being such an empty-headed flirt. . . . I knew the cook more than I knew her . . . so what could I do? I became even more of a flirt myself." Despite her tumultuous adolescence, she finished college and started a career as a creative musician. But after becoming pregnant at 20, she lost her "adoring audiences because I didn't know better . . . I was not cut out to be a mother . . . I didn't know how!"

All through her life she made few women friends, only those who admired her independent spirit and musical skills. Early into the music appreciation craze, she found a myriad of social anchorages in the groups she led. But her more intimate life centered on the acquisition of abusive men, consciously designed to support her lifestyle through the eventual redistribution of their wealth after divorce or death. But her seemingly highly sophisticated, erotic, artistic world contained and concealed similar subtle, hostile means of extracting envy while asserting independence from those who had failed to appreciate her. This pattern recapitulated the nature of her quest for a maternal bond. In a sense, we came to think of this form of exploitation as "everyone loses and every soul, especially *men's*, would be reluctantly raped." By midlife, both of her children, who also had been raised by nannies, were estranged from her as well as from a series of stepfathers. Even though financially secure, she felt irresistibly drawn toward new conquests. We reconstructed fathers without boundaries and a stepbrother without restraints had something to do with her inordinately high coefficient of interpersonal distrust of both men and women as well as the inordinate but hostile, rape-like intensity of her sexual attachments.

In more ordinary circumstances, a stepfather has a golden opportunity to help a tween or teen modulate (set limits to) either endeavor or sexual excitement, a process so well delineated by Tessman (1982) in her "Note on the Father's Contribution to the Daughter's Way of Loving and Working."

Despite ongoing conflicts with their "ex," many nonresidential fathers can be there when the pains and pleasures discovered at the crossroads of adolescence test all that has been built theretofore. When a male presence is missing, most "single" female parents hope some male, be he paramour, stepfather, or therapist, may fill some of the needs of their tweens, that is, to achieve a reasonable degree of protective self-regulation along with selective empathic assertiveness in the gratification of elemental sexual needs. Tweens and teens of rupturing families are more likely bewildered by the revenge-filled interactions observed between parting parents alongside the sometimes passionate overt courting behavior of parents as lovers. They may lack the transgenerational gift of appropriately modulated, albeit fluctuating but long term passionate interaction.

Reference

Tessman, L. H. (1982), Note on the father's contribution to the daughter's way of loving and working. In: *Father and Child: Developmental and Clinical Perspectives*, ed. S. H. Cath, A. R. Gurwitt & J. M. Ross. Boston: Little Brown.

Cultural, Social, and Gender Implications

Uncounted Stepfamilies

Remarried Fathers and Their Wives

Jamie K. Keshet

Remarried couples in which the husband has children from a previous marriage and the wife is in her first marriage are generally considered stepfamilies only if one of the children makes his or her primary residence in the couple's home. Most research and writing on stepfamilies excludes stepmother-only families because there are far fewer custodial fathers than residential mothers. Stepfamilies in which both adults have children from previous marriages are studied more frequently (Hetherington and Jodl, 1994; Bray and Kelly, 1998).

These remarried couples in which the stepchildren have their primary home with their mother may be considered childless couples by their friends and relatives; after all, the children only "visit." To the fathers and stepmothers, however, the connection with the husband's children is a major factor in the couple's consciousness and in many practical decisions they make. For example, they may be committed to living within a short distance of the children's home with their mother. When the father has joint physical custody, these couples may have children living in their home half the time.

Even when children live on the other side of the country and visit for two weeks a year, the couple thinks of them at holidays and birthdays, the couple's finances are affected by child support payments, and many occasions remind the father and his wife of his absent children. As one divorced father explained to me, "I am *not* a part-time father. I may spend only part of my time with my children, but I am their father every minute of every day. I hate it when people call me a part-time father."

Visiting stepfamilies are like portable stages in which the props are packed away when the children are not present. When the children arrive, the household transforms itself into a family. This is made concrete by the way space in the house is used. One stepmother transforms her home office to a bedroom when her stepdaughters visit. Another stepmother steels herself as she goes up the driveway to see her stepchildren's clothes and books all over the hallway on the day they have arrived.

A national survey of school-aged children found that approximately 34 percent of the children in grades kindergarten through 12 have fathers who do not live with them. Seventy-five percent of these children had contact with their father in the previous year (Nord, Brimhall, and West, 1997).

About 20 percent of the children of divorced parents move their primary residence, most often during adolescence (Bray and Kelly, 1998). When a child makes his primary residence with his father and stepmother, the history of their relationship during the years of visitation is an important basis for the new structures needed to parent a child on a more constant basis and for the possibility of deepening the child–parent–stepparent connections.

These nonresidential stepfamilies contain structural elements which contribute to stresses in the couple system. Repeatedly making the transition from interacting as a childless couple to parenting in a stepfamily takes a toll on the individuals and the marriage. For many people parenting in short intervals is not as satisfying as parenting over a longer period of time. Neither the childless state or the visiting state feels stable.

In my clinical work with remarried couples, a majority of the couples have been those in which only the husband had children. When couples in which both partners have children from previous marriages come to therapy, about half of them designate problems with the husband's children as the reason for seeking help.

This chapter explores the systemic elements and gender role expectations which create difficulties for these particular remarried couples. Not every couple in this situation will experience these problems or will need therapy to solve them. The material and observations are based on the author's work with primarily self-referred white, middle- and upper-income couples. The conclusions may not be applicable to other populations.

Family Structure and Interpersonal Dynamics

Imbalance of Relational Ties

Minifamily Structure. When a divorced father has an ongoing relationship with his children, he remains part of a family system which includes himself, his former wife, and their children. He and his children form a *minifamily,* a part of a divorced family which functions as a family unit but is not a complete family (Keshet, 1987). As a minifamily the father and children share traditions, old pains, jokes, secrets, and history. The history of the father–child(ren) minifamily is longer than that of the couple's relationship and is likely to include memories of happy times as a nuclear family with the former wife.

As the minifamily forms its identity in the period between the divorce and the remarriage, children and fathers often become closer to each other. One of the few benefits to children of divorce is spending time alone with each parent doing child-centered activities. Most children are reluctant to lose this new status. Moreover, children of divorce, more than other children, tend to resist change. A child who has recently had to accept the reality and consequences of a parental divorce is not eager to move on to the changes required by a parental remarriage. The child, not seeing the parent as a whole person who needs adult companionship, is puzzled by and often resentful of the father's desire to be with a new partner; after all, in the child's words: "He has me." Children rarely see the need for a stepparent in the household.

The father's membership in this minifamily and the stepmother's status as an outsider create difficulties for both, which are further exacerbated by the different perceptions of the husband and wife as well as the gender role expectations of our society for men and women in families.

The stepmother is usually acutely aware that she is not a member of the father–child minifamily. Unlike a woman who has children of her own, she has no corresponding minifamily. Being excluded from the father–child minifamily also flies in the face of two major expectations of many first-time wives: (1) that they will share most aspects of family life with their husbands and (2) that, as women, they will be caretakers of children and should be able immediately to assume a motherly role toward their husbands' children.

Expectations for Marriage. Women tend to give relationships and closeness in those relationships more priority in their lives than men do. Women who are married for the first time may have unrealistically high expectations of their marital relationships. Remarried couples interviewed by Furstenberg and Spanier (1984) reported that in their second marriages romance was less important than the ability to work things out together.

A woman who is in her first marriage may value romance more than her husband who is in a second marriage. The first-married woman is likely to care more about the wedding ceremony, time alone together as a couple, and other romantic rituals than her husband does. One recently married woman reported that she and her husband had been very enthusiastic about planning their wedding and honeymoon. When the woman overheard her husband telling his brother that actually he was doing it all "for her" she was devastated.

The opportunities for romance are definitely limited when children are present. The husband's children may come to be seen by the wife as the sole cause of dissatisfaction with the relationship, becoming the symbol for what is lacking in her marriage. Common complaints of stepmothers in these couples are that their husbands will not leave their children with babysitters for a night out together, that their husbands give more physical attention to their children than to their wives, that the children have free access to the couple's bedroom which reduces privacy and intimacy, and that the children's needs come first in planning vacations and time away.

Problems of Exclusion. Even when the father is genuinely trying to include his new wife in family activities with his children and when she is willing to join them, the style or shared history of the father–child minifamily may make it difficult for this inclusion to come about quickly or smoothly. One stepmother simply could not tolerate the noise and commotion of her husband and three sons when they played rough and tumble games together. Another stepmother had to remain on the beginner's slope while her husband and stepdaughters skied on the more difficult ones. She did not consider skiing a "family activity."

A husband may think his new wife dislikes his children if she is hesitant to join in when everyone is together. He may feel unsupported or criticized by her at just those times when she herself is feeling excluded and ignored.

Sometimes the remarks of the father and children, which refer to their past as a nuclear family, bring up happy memories for them and simultaneously remind the stepmother that she is a newcomer. For example, a father compliments his daughter on her swimming. She says, "Yes, remember how I used to swim when you and Mommy took me to the beach? I'm much better now." This remark reminds the stepmother that there was a time when the third member of the family was "Mommy." When her husband tells his new wife about his first marriage, he may stress how he and his first wife did not get along, but now she is confronted with the reality that the first marriage also held some happy family moments.

The difference in perspective between husband and wife also contributes to different evaluations of time which they spend with the children. One father described a wonderful Sunday in which his new wife and his two sons went swimming together at a local pool. "I had all the people I love the most in the world with me. We were outdoors, doing something we all like to do. It was great." He was shocked to find that his wife had not considered the day great. She felt that he spent more time with his children than with her and that she could not get close either to him or to the children when they were together.

Roles of the Adults in Nonresidential Stepfamilies

The Stepmother's Role and Relationship with the Children. A stepmother's experience or interest in caring for children are not the primary factors which influence how much she will care for the children and how close she will feel toward them. The distance between the stepmother and stepchildren is determined by the complex relationships among the members of the father–child minifamily, the stepmother, and the children's biological mother (Seltzer, 1994). In turn, the stepmother–stepchild relationship often has a profound effect on marital satisfaction.

Gender and Biological Models. A family system assigns different roles to different individuals. In some of these stepfamilies, biological ties are the primary principle by which the roles are assigned: the father is the primary provider of care and nurturance for his children, continuing the role he had in the parent–child minifamily. In other stepfamilies the roles are divided according to traditional gender roles in our society. The stepmother, because she is a woman, becomes the primary caregiver for the children. Of course, many families use gender roles at times and biological roles at others.

In research on stepfamilies with biological mothers and stepfathers, Bray and Kelly (1998) distinguish two forms of stepfamily organization. *Neotraditional* families, in their terms, are stepfamilies which come to resemble nuclear families in the ways in which the adults share responsibility for the children. *Matriarchal* families are those in which the mother maintains authority about how the children are reared and is their primary nurturer.

The stepmother couples who distribute roles on gender lines resemble Bray's neotraditional families. The couples in which the father is the primary parent are similar to the matriarchal families because the biological parent takes charge. However, differences arise since a matriarchal family is in accord with our cultural norms whereas a family with the father as the primary caregiver is not.

Role Distribution by Gender. Frequently a remarried father expects his wife, because she is a woman, to move into the role of primary nurturer of children and to know how to enact this role. The stepmother often assumes this role to please her husband, to fulfill societal expectations, or to make the family's life easier. The wife and husband take the roles which are traditionally assigned to a woman and a man.

Financial considerations often lead to this arrangement. Typically the husband in the household has greater earning power than his wife. The family may suffer more financially if he has to miss work to pick up the children from school or he may need to spend part of his weekend working.

However, the husband's expectations that his wife will share the work of caring for the children do not necessarily mean that he includes her in decision making around children's schedules or routines. Many stepmothers don't insist on being part of the decision making, although they are resentful when they are not included. Some stepmothers complain that they feel like live-in childcare personnel or their stepchildren's personal maids. It is nearly impossible for them to initiate routines in which the children share in the household chores without the cooperation of the children's father. When these stepmothers complain to their husbands about the children's behavior, they do not always receive support from their husbands. If the stepmother dwells on her difficulties in parenting the stepchildren or the frustrations of having the children present, she opens herself to statements such as "You can't handle children. I'm not sure we should have a child together."

In one family, Dan, the father of two adolescent children, prided himself on sharing responsibility with his new wife Mary. When one of the children would approach him with a question such as "Can you pay for me to go on a ski trip with my class?" or "How late can I stay out tonight?" he would simply say "Ask Mary." Although he thought, by redirecting their questions to Mary, he was showing the children that he respected her and indicating that they should also respect her, his approach did not result in successful stepparenting. Mary often felt unprepared for these teenage dilemmas and responded according to the way her parents had raised her as a child. The children resented Mary's sudden entrance into the family in an authority position and often argued with her. When she and they then approached Dan for his opinion, he often felt Mary's responses were too harsh and gave the children a different answer. Mary then felt unsupported and the children saw that they could move in between their father and stepmother.

Who Is in Charge? Many stepmothers report that their relationships with their stepchildren are better when their husbands are not present. Some of these stepmothers are experienced in working with children in other settings, come from large families, or have a way of befriending children. However, the closeness that exists between them when they are alone changes when the father-husband returns. The child and stepmother have often both been missing his company and when he is present they may compete for his attention. As long as the stepmother is the only adult present, the child is likely to respect her authority. When the father arrives, however, there is an implicit shift in authority, perhaps among all family members.

The child may defy his stepmother upon his father's return in order to register anger at the father's absence and show where his major loyalty lies. To be happy with the stepmother in front of someone else may also feel like an act of disloyalty to the child's biological mother. Therefore the child may become sullen or surly with the stepmother in front of her father.

Role Distribution by Biological Ties. Some fathers unconsciously restrict the closeness between their new wives and the children in order to preserve the special intimacy of the father–child minifamily, for example, by insisting that only he read bedtime stories, care for hurts, or have private, heart-to-heart talks with the children. At the same time he may expect his wife to help out with the physical upkeep of the home by cooking, shopping, cleaning, or doing laundry for the children. While he expects her to care for them in his absence, he undermines the closeness between her and the children when he is present. One father, for example, who left his six-year-old son with his wife while he worked on alternate Saturdays would nonetheless insist on preparing the boy's meals on the days when he was home saying "I know just how he likes it." These fathers claim they do so to give the children "continuity" or to fulfill the divorce agreement to care for the children at certain times.

Some stepmothers cooperate with this pattern to please their husbands. They may be impressed and pleased to have a husband who is a competent and involved father. Other stepmothers are just not that interested in children. These couples use biological ties to determine distribution of child-rearing tasks even when gender determines the division of household tasks.

The stepmother whose interactions with her stepchildren are limited can rarely get any of the "goodies" of being with children. They don't often hug her, sit on her lap, tell her their secrets or ask her for help. Some women who expect the stepmother role to be more encompassing feel genuine pain in not being allowed to give as much and as well as they want to.

When a stepmother is not welcome to participate, she may feel both excluded and exploited at those times when her husband is caring for his children. If she chooses to clean up the kitchen (including her stepchild's mess), for example, while her husband puts the child to bed, hoping to spend some time together in the later part of the evening, she may feel that she is left with only the dirty work.

If the father is willing to share more of the quality time with the children with his new wife, and leads the children in opening up the boundary of the parent–child minifamily, the stepmother can develop her own relationship with the stepchildren.

Other Influences on the Stepmother–Stepchild Relationship

Children's Ages and Attitudes. The children's ages, attitudes, and behaviors also have an impact on their relationship with their stepmother. On the whole, younger children seem to adjust to a new adult more easily than adolescents or preadolescents. Younger children are more dependent upon adult care, accustomed to doing things planned by adults and to "playing" rather than being included in adult conversations. Distributing roles by gender may be easier to do with younger children who need more constant care and so will complain less about being cared for by their stepmother.

In contrast, older children, more discriminating about the care they receive from adults, resist their stepparents more because they are less in need of adult care. They wish to be included in conversations and decision making.

Stepmothers, very sensitive to the way the children respond to them, are eager to form good relationships with their husband's children, both to please their husbands and to have the satisfaction of being an important person in a child's life. Despite their efforts they voice a sense of despair when they feel rejected in their parental roles. Several factors contribute to their reactions.

Inexperienced stepmothers may take children's moods and inconsistencies as personal failures and rejections. For example, a stepmother may not recognize that her five-year-old stepdaughter is too hungry and cranky to play a board game at five o'clock in the afternoon and concludes that the child doesn't like her.

Stepmothers may consider the child's statements to be enduring opinions and attitudes rather than expressions of momentary feelings. An angry stepdaughter may yell that she is never going shopping with her stepmother again. Whereas a biological parent would, hopefully, regard this remark as a sign of some immediate upset, a sensitive stepmother might take it as a definitive statement about shopping and never offer another invitation. Literal and longlasting interpretation of children's statements can lead to difficulties between the members of the couple. The father may feel that the stepmother's refusal to help him out by taking his daughter shopping is childish and stubborn. He does not understand how painful it would be for the stepmother to extend another invitation and risk being rejected again. If the stepmother is not willing to try again, however, she may never discover that the child would be happy to go shopping with her and may miss enjoyable opportunities.

Even a stepchild who is not determined to reject a stepmother may not be inclined to be polite or friendly to her. After all, she is a stranger who has moved into his house, is sleeping in his father's bed, and using his family car. This lack of welcoming on the child's part is hurtful to the stepparent and the parent.

Sometimes stepmothers are hurt because the children do not show them recognition or appreciation. For example, some stepmothers are insulted when their stepchildren come to breakfast without saying hello to them, do not greet them when they walk into the house, do not thank them for meals or for rides, or are critical of their cooking. Most parents do not expect their children to express their appreciation. The parent receives some satisfaction merely in knowing that he has provided a good meal for his child or a ride to soccer practice. He sees the child's taking him for granted as a sign of security. However, the stepparent, lacking a deep bond with her stepchildren, does not feel the same satisfaction in knowing they have made it to practice or eaten lunch. Since she is less secure she wants more recognition of her role in the child's life. When her husband can understand her point of view and offer appreciation for the ways in which she is nurturing his children and helping him, the step-mother can feel satisfied without the children's recognition. The father can also be helpful by supervising the preparation of gifts and cards for his second wife so that she is duly honored on holidays and her birthday.

A stepmother's rejection by her stepchildren may lead her to question not only her role in the family, but her sense of herself as a woman and criticize herself because she has not "won over" her stepchildren and is not accepted and cherished by them.

In fact, most stepmothers have ambivalent feelings about their stepchil-dren. A woman who is trying to acknowledge only her loving positive feelings toward the children and to deny her angry and resentful feelings would be open to unconsciously projecting her negative feelings onto them. Most children will supply the stepmother with a few negative behaviors which she can then regard as proof of her projection that she is not loved and not loving.

The Former Spouse. The children's biological mother, the ex-wife of their father, exerts an influence on the relationship between stepmother and stepchildren. Most children are naturally loyal to both of their biologi-cal parents after a divorce. A child who feels the stepmother is moving into territory which "rightfully" belongs to her mother may become angry and resentful. For example, a child who knows that Mommy is home alone may not understand why Daddy is taking this other lady out to dinner when her mother would so much like to go out with them. A child may become enraged when the father takes his second wife on the special vacation which the divorced mother had always dreamed about.

Loyalty to the biological mother makes it difficult for children to accept even the best of stepmothers (see Solomon, this volume). The child may express this loyalty by withdrawing from the stepmother, by criticizing her (especially her cooking), by rejecting care from the stepmother, or by talking incessantly about the biological mother in the stepmother's pres-ence. Most stepmothers are likely to respond negatively to these behaviors. One of the most difficult patterns occurs when a child becomes closer to a stepmother—accepting care, having fun together, or showing affection. All of a sudden the child seems to realize what is happening and pulls back, recognizing disloyalty to his biological mother. A stepmother may be especially distressed when this happens because it seemed like everything was going so well. She rarely understands that, just because it was "going so well," the child felt conflicted and needed to pull away.

Some children cope with this conflict by showing their loyalty to their mothers in their stepmothers' presence. One little boy had to start each weekend visit with his father and stepmother by making a gift or card for his mother. Once this was done and the gift put in a safe place, he was able to enjoy his weekend. A 10-year-old girl showed her loyalty to her mother by outwardly rejecting the stepmother's offers of care, but taking feminine items like lipstick and hair spray from her stepmother's bureau without asking.

Children's loyalty to their biological mothers is a universal phenomenon. In some families, the biological mother deliberately undermines the potential relationship between her children and her ex-husband's new wife. For example, a divorced mother may fear that this new woman will steal her children as she has "stolen" her husband. A former wife who has been especially hurt by the divorce, or is having extreme difficulties as a single parent, may want her children to take care of her emotionally. A mother in this situation may outwardly criticize the stepmother to the extent of calling her a "bitch" or a "whore," even before very young children. She may tell the children that this woman has caused the divorce. One mother told her young children that Daddy's new wife had made them sell their house and move to an apartment.

Mothers who attempt to turn their children against their stepmothers may also try to ignore the stepmother's existence and rights. They tend to call and hang up if the stepmother rather than the ex-husband answers the phone. They will not say hello to the stepmother if both are present at a child's event and will not allow the children to speak about the stepmother.

Socialization. A stepmother's struggle with her feelings about her stepchildren may be complicated by her socialization as a woman. Girls have been traditionally taught from childhood that they will be mommies someday; they are given dolls as children, may have been expected to babysit as teenagers, and are looked at askance if they choose not to have children as adults. Even a woman who has resisted the role of wife and mother in our culture has internalized some of these expectations about herself as a woman. Many of the stepmothers in these families are quite successful in the work world by the time they marry. Nonetheless, a stepmother's self-esteem can be strongly shaken by her difficulties with her stepchildren and her inability to feel total and unambivalent love for them.

A remarried father is also likely to criticize his new wife if she does not love and care for his children as he does. One such father told me that the only reason he was coming for counseling was that "my wife doesn't love my children." The father often finds it hard to understand why it is difficult for his wife to love his children as he does because they are his. He often thinks that love can be accomplished by an act of will or that his wife should love his children as an extension of loving him.

A remarried father has an easier life if his children and his new wife like each other. If they do not get along, he feels torn between them. If his children and wife are not close, the father has the difficult and unfamiliar responsibility of tending to two different minifamilies within the family—a couple minifamily and a parent–child minifamily. The man may experience this responsibility as overwhelming and assume that, if only his wife, the culturally designated relationship expert, would apply herself to loving his children, he could breathe more easily.

In summary, the relationship between stepmother and stepchild is influenced by the attitudes, expectations, and behavior of both the remarried father and the stepmother, by the ages and attitudes of the stepchildren and by the attitude and behavior of the children's biological mother.

Benefits of the Nonresidential Stepfamily

Spending time with his father and stepmother can be an important part of a child's development. The nonresidential stepfamily can provide the child with additional role models, enriching experiences, different ways of problem solving, and a sense of continuity with his father. Either distribution of the parenting roles between the father and stepmother can result in a successful nonresidential stepfamily.

Research on the impact of parental involvement in children's schools, for example, indicates that participation by a nonresidential father in school activities can have a significant impact on the child's performance and enjoyment of school (Nord et al., 1997). Stepmothers often support fathers being involved in children's activities and frequently keep track of the dates of the children's sports events or back-to-school nights. A man who feels uncomfortable showing up alone at a school event where he will see his ex-wife and, possibly, her new husband, may be more at ease if he arrives with his new woman friend or wife.

Impact on the Remarried Couple System

In the first few years of the remarriage the new couple system is especially vulnerable. Conflict and distress may develop easily as a result of difficulties between the stepmother and stepchildren. Both husbands and wives may be disappointed when relations between the stepmother and stepchildren are strained and they often disagree about the appropriate role for the stepmother. The husband may feel so connected to his children that he feels criticized by his wife's criticisms of the children and rejected by her distance from them. He may feel that she has failed him as a wife because she cannot create family harmony. The wife is likely to feel that her happiness comes second to the children's well-being, thus feeling resentment and jealousy. The more her husband criticizes her for not getting along with them, the more likely she is to experience his children as an obstacle to her marriage.

Relationship with the Former Spouse. The husband's former wife can also interfere with the couple's relationship. Her phone calls, in particular, seem intrusive as there is probably no right time for a former wife to call her ex-husband at home. In the first few years of remarriage conflict about the former spouse is usually at its worst. The interactions between divorced spouses tend to be more fiery and emotional when the divorce is not far behind them. The emotion aroused by a call from an ex-wife may be anger, sadness, or confusion. The second wife is likely to be jealous that another woman can arouse these emotions in her husband. The ex-wife's demands for help with the children, finances, or house impact the new couple. The husband cannot often respond without consulting his new wife.

In most divorces, the husbands fare better than the wives financially (Weitzman, 1985). Nonetheless, the second wife is rarely in a position to be compassionate toward her husband's former mate. She sees the requests for increased childcare or money for special expenses as funds depleted from her household. In some remarriages the husband's funds are so tied up in supporting his children and former wife that the new wife is required to use her income to support the couple or to pay for vacations or extras for them. In one such family the second wife had a baby a year after the remarriage. Although she had always wanted to stay home with a baby she and her husband could not afford to live on his income after he paid his alimony and child support. Therefore, she resentfully arranged childcare for her child and kept working.

More common and often more upsetting than requests for money are the requests from former wives for rearranging time with the children. These requests are often very reasonable in the context of shared parenting but are deemed unreasonable to a woman who has never been a parent. For example, a divorced mother asks her ex-husband to return the children from their weekend visit at 8 P.M. on Sunday rather than 4 P.M. to accommodate special plans of hers. She considers this a favor from her ex-husband and also an opportunity for him to spend more time with his children. The ex-husband may look forward to more time with his children and agree willingly to this change. The second wife, however, may feel that this four-hour extension deprives her of the one "adults only" meal of the weekend and the one evening when she and her husband could be alone together. She views this as a big imposition because time alone with her husband is a scarce resource. This couple time often provides the intimacy and continuity which refuel her emotionally for dealing with the difficult role of stepmother. These very different apperceptions lead to arguments in which the husband accuses the wife of being jealous of his children and the wife considers her husband to be controlled by his former spouse.

The triangle of mother–father–stepmother is made more difficult because the mother and stepmother rarely communicate directly with each other. There is no opportunity for them to defuse anger or to see the other's point of view. The stepmother is not also a biological mother and the biological mother is not a stepmother. The lack of shared roles makes it more difficult for them to understand the other's perspective. The more angry and hurt the mother is the less open she is to recognizing the stepmother as a person in her children's life. In some of the worst situations, these mothers attribute the marital breakup to an affair between the stepmother and ex-husband, even if this relationship began after the couple was physically separated.

Gender Roles and Community Expectations

The larger community also tends to assume that stepmothers are in charge of childcare in the family. Parents of the children's friends, for example, may talk to the stepmother about children's activities. One divorced father become discouraged when he tried calling teenage babysitters; the teenagers parents were suspicious of a man calling their daughters. When another father and stepmother took his young children to a family wedding in another state, the husband's relatives referred all questions about the children to her rather than to her husband, although he had packed their clothes at their mother's house and was generally in charge of them at home.

School and mental health professionals may assume that the stepmother should be contacted about the children because she is a woman. When one stepmother complained about difficulties in caring for her sick stepchild, a counselor at a local mental health center provided information about coping with the child. The counselor did not ask if the stepmother resented taking time off from work to care for the child or ask the child's father why he was not staying home with his sick child.

An "Ours" Baby

Another typical dilemma in remarried couples is whether or not to have a child together. The most common disagreement occurs when the husband does not want another child and the wife wants a child of her own. The husband sees having a baby as going back to the stage of changing diapers and waking up in the middle of the night with a crying baby. He looks forward to having his children become independent so that he can relax or travel without considering children's needs. The wife is likely to look forward to the experience of becoming a biological mother. She knows that her stepchildren do not fill the same place in her life as her own child would and she wants that special connection which she sees her husband and children sharing.

Sometimes a man claims that he does not want more children because he thinks his wife will have as many problems with a new baby as she has with her stepchildren. He does not understand that his wife will feel differently about a child which is theirs together than she does about his child from his former marriage, and she will be more comfortable with a child whom she has raised from birth. By stating that the issue is his wife's role performance, the husband may avoid recognizing his own guilty feelings about his divorce or his parenting. He may not want his children to have to share him with a new baby or may not want to share his second wife with a child.

Clinical Implications

A remarried couple seeking therapy may be having both stepfamily and marital problems. They may be having difficulty in managing and operating their stepfamily. They may feel isolated from extended family and friends who do not understand what they are experiencing. Moreover, the stepfamily structural issues may be compounded by the particular problems of the children.

As a couple, they may have problems in their communication, intimacy, or ability to work as a team. They may come from very different backgrounds which make it harder for them to be understanding and compassionate. Since they are older than most couples in first marriages, they may each be more "set" in their ways.

The couple problems can make it more difficult for them to solve the problems of the stepfamily. It is tempting for the therapist to begin by doing marital therapy. However, the members of a remarried couple often need to address the stepfamily issues and find practical solutions before they can accept the need for the couples therapy. If they are fearful of recognizing the problems in the marriage they may be able to focus on the problems with the children and former spouse more easily. If, in the beginning stages of therapy, the couple can make some changes in the way the stepfamily functions they may feel more successful as a couple and gain confidence to work on their other issues. If the difficulties between the husband and wife interfere with carrying out any of the initial family changes, the therapist can point out the necessity of addressing the marital issues in order to improve the stepfamily functioning.

Family Model

In working out the roles of the adults in the stepfamily, the couple may be attempting to use a model in which roles are distributed by gender or a model in which roles are distributed according to biological ties. Problems arise from the attempt to apply either model too strictly.

Both gender roles and biological ties have to be considered in creating stepfamily roles. The special relationship which the father and children have formed in their minifamily and the history which they share cannot be ignored when the remarriage takes place. But some changes must be made or the stepmother will continue to be excluded. She won't be able to make her unique contributions to the stepfamily and the father will be too engaged with his children to free up some time and energy for the couple.

In the beginning of the relationship, the first job of the stepmother is to help the father to be a better parent. She can do this by offering him feedback and guidance, by giving him support for taking a difficult stand with the children, or suggesting he loosen up with them. Even if she barely talks to the children, if she helps her husband to be a good parent, she has contributed to the well-being of the family.

The children are most likely to accept the stepmother if she initially acts more like an aunt or a counselor than another parent. She can slowly build her authority in the family by supporting her husband's rules. Problems often arise when the stepmother tries to take on a parental role too soon. When the stepmother is solely in charge of children, if she cares for them frequently while their father is working, for example, he has to be very clear with the children that he wants them to listen to her.

The therapist can become a consultant to the couple who are discovering and forming roles which work for them. The children's ages, the amount of time the children spend with the couple, the adults' work needs, and the personalities of the family members must be taken into account. The couple can be prepared to expect changes in roles and closeness among family members as children develop. Similar changes take place in nuclear families as members mature.

Developing a unique family model is an opportunity for the husband and wife to liberate themselves from roles which are dictated either by gender or by biology. There is no task that one can assume should be done by a stepmother rather than a father. One father may want to do the shopping and cooking; another may do these tasks only when urged to by his wife. One stepmother may enjoy shooting baskets with her stepchildren and another may teach them to make omelets.

In the process of creating the model by which the adults will interact with the children, the couple can also learn to express their needs and preferences, to negotiate with each other, to give each other support for learning new behaviors, and to work together as a team.

Most of these structural changes may be done with the couple by themselves and do not require the children to attend therapy sessions. The couple can experience their competence in making changes at home.

Accepting Differences

The husband and wife in a remarried couple are likely to have different goals, different experiences of the same family events and different points of view about the problems in their family. The therapist's role is often to encourage the couple to express and recognize their differences rather than try to see things the same way. Understanding each other's perspectives can move the couple away from blaming each other for their problems. Seeing these differences also helps the couple members to know and respect each other as individuals and to feel compassion for one another.

Often the husband and wife are both ambivalent about some aspect of the children's behavior but get stuck in a confrontation with each member expressing only one side. One young stepmother was annoyed when her preschool stepdaughter had frequent colds and had to stay home rather than go to daycare. When she expressed her frustration her husband was effusive in his sympathy for his child. Then the next time the biological mother called to say the child was sick and needed to stay with them, the stepmother said, "Poor Katy. She's been so ill this winter." Her husband then responded, "Yeah, and it always seems to happen on our days. I'm getting tired of rearranging my schedule." In this conversation they had each expressed the other side of their ambivalence.

Family-of-Origin Work

In the course of working on the stepfamily issues it can become apparent that the stepfamily structure is replicating some patterns from one of the partner's childhood. For example, a stepmother who is having difficulties may have been the parentified child in her family of origin. Now she is again placed in the situation of caring for another person's children without full authority. Recognizing these patterns gives the stepmother an opportunity to work on issues from that earlier time in her life, either within the couple's therapy or by herself.

Limits to Resolving Stepfamily Problems

One of the realities of living in a stepfamily is that the remarried couple do not have as much control over the children's lives as they would in a nuclear family. In many couples where the husband is the parent, his children live primarily in another household with their mother.

The therapist is often limited by these realities as well. Sometimes the biological mother will not give permission for the children to attend therapy. Her influence on the children is not within the boundaries of the therapy as it is not within the boundaries of the stepfamily. The therapist often feels the same frustration that the couple feel. He or she can help the couple to set realistic goals within the limitations of their power.

Summary

A clinician working with a remarried couple can help them to accept the realities of their situation and to recognize the differences between the stepfamily and the nuclear family. Therapy can provide a setting in which problem solving and structural changes take place. When problems within the couple system or individual patterns going back to previous life experiences arise from the stepfamily work, these can be addressed. The most creative task of therapy with these particular remarried couples is to work out a role division within the family which respects and challenges both the biological ties of the father and children and the gender roles for which men and women have been socialized.

References

Bray, J. H. & Kelly, J. (1998), *Stepfamilies: Love, Marriage, and Parenting in the First Decade*. New York: Broadway Books.

Furstenberg, F. F. & Spanier, G. B. (1984), *Recycling the Family*. Beverly Hills, CA: Sage Publications.

Hetherington, E. M. & Jodl, K. M. (1994), Stepfamilies as settings for child development. In: *Stepfamilies: Who Benefits? Who Does Not?* ed. A. Booth & J. Dunn. Hillsdale, NJ: Lawrence Erlbaum Associates, pp. 55–80.

Keshet, J. K. (1987), *Love and Power in the Stepfamily*. New York: McGraw-Hill.

Nord, C. W., Brimhall, D. & West, J. (1997), *Fathers' Involvement in Their Children's Schools* (NCES 98-091). National Center for Education Statistics, U.S. Department of Education, Office of Educational Research and Improvement.

Seltzer, J. A. (1994), Intergenerational ties in adulthood and childhood experience. In: *Stepfamilies: Who Benefits? Who Does Not?* ed. A. Booth & J. Dunn. Hillsdale, NJ: Lawrence Erlbaum Associates, pp. 153–163.

Weitzman, L. J. (1985), *The Divorce Revolution*. New York: Free Press.

Birthlands, Steplands, and Adopted Lands

The Immigrant's Tryst with Psychogeographic Maps and Territories

Purnima Mehta

I was born and raised in Kampala, Uganda, while it was a British protectorate. Hence, I became a British subject, but of Indian origin, since my parents were immigrants from the subcontinent of India. I subsequently became an exile at the age of 16 years under Idi Amin's regime, living both in Britain and India before immigrating to the United States 16 years ago with a resident alien visa, the well-known green card. I am writing this chapter soon after obtaining my U.S. citizenship. I am no longer a stepchild but have adapted to and been adopted by the United States. Finally, I can say that I am a citizen of a country. It is a developmental milestone. With this personal background and interest in psychological issues of immigrants, I am sensitized to the relationship of the person to his birth land, the nuances of attachment and the changing relationship to the land one immigrates to, resides in, and then begins to belong to and own.

Immigration is essentially a geographic displacement whether near, far, temporary, permanent, voluntary, or involuntary. Environment has a deep impact on the human psyche. One chooses habitats in order to feel connected and experiences a profound sense of disconnectedness in new surroundings. V. S. Naipaul (1987) describes this experience eloquently:

> After all my time in England, I still had that nervousness in a new place, that rawness of response, still felt myself to be in the other man's country, felt my strangeness, my solitude. And every excursion into a new part of the country—what for others might have been an adventure—was for me like tearing at an old scab.

The purpose of this chapter is to discuss and elaborate the reactions and relationship of the immigrant to his birthland and land of immigration, which parallels the relationship of the child to his biological parents, stepparent, or adoptive parents. I hope that such an inquiry can enrich our understanding of a patient's experiences on immigration and the process of integrating his or her identity.

Birthlands

The birthland is often referred to as the motherland or fatherland, denoting its capacity to provide and nurture. Many travelers ceremoniously kiss the earth of the land in which they arrive. Immigrants often feel that leaving their old land, and land of birth, is leaving behind their source of support and nourishment. The land of birth confers a powerful status on the person, that is, that they have a birthright akin to that toward a biological parent—deep, unshakable, and permanent. Qualities are assigned to the land of birth. This has particularly been emphasized in my patients as they describe the Ganges River in the Indian subcontinent. This river is considered to be the holiest river, with its name implying "sacredness." It is considered pure, despite visible signs of blatant pollution, and people flock to the river for pilgrimage—both the healthy and the dying—so that their souls might be liberated. It is supposed to have healing powers, show the road to salvation, and transport one to liberation. Many Hindu families keep some of its water in a container. Similar descriptions are provided about the land, its powerful capacity to provide, forgive, and be fertile. These sentiments have deep significance in a patient's material, with some very significant omnipotent fantasies about the land in which one resides.

The land of birth connects one deeply and provides a sense of belonging that is imperishable. In this context, I will reflect on some personal material related to the Ugandan exodus of 1972, and to my return to my birthland after a 25-year period of exile.

Migration in itself is a painful and complex process needing much work and resolution of conflicts brought on by moving from one country to another. Hence, exile would have all the similar experiences which, of course, are much more intense, heart-wrenching, and, sometimes, unresolvable. It can sometimes come close to soul murder. Shengold (1989) describes soul murder as a certain category of traumatic experience when there is repeated and chronic overstimulation or emotional deprivation, deliberately brought about by another individual. The repeated and chronic traumatic experiences sustained over time can leave people scarred, disoriented, immobilized, and depressed in many aspects of their life. As Shengold further states, the *cold indifference* and *destructive hatred* that reign are what make people as recipients of the soul murder doubt the evidence of all senses and memory. It is not easy to peer into the pictures of this hell. The listener is often inclined to seek a defense against the terrible intensity of these stories, stories of helpless people under the tyranny of monstrous rulers.

Freud (1920) defined psychic trauma as a "breach in the protective shield against stimuli" (p. 28). A number of people asked him what "protective shield" meant. Freud (1924) could only hint at an answer: The protective shield, he said, was a discontinuous mode of functioning, a discontinuity that lay at the base of the concept "time" (p. 231). Somehow, "time" formed a foundation for Freud's idea of a protective shield. But the inventor of psychoanalysis would go no further with this answer. In her book, *Too Scared to Cry*, Terr (1990) has attempted at least to update this language. She states:

> Fitting a frightened event into time, either personal time or work time, helps a person to cope with that event. Seeing, furthermore, how sequences of events work together and how long events will last also helps prevent any flooding of the psyche. Feeling rhythms, in addition, helps maintain a person's sense of balance. If all these time awarenesses fail, however, to prevent a person from becoming traumatized, the person's time sense will undergo some damage. This damage will show, just as the flood lines on the walls of the Venetian churches show. As a stimulus barrier, time functions both as a protection against damage and as a marker of the damage [p. 149].

Taking all these points into consideration, one needs to consider the idea of the exile's sense of time, his inability to gauge as to when he will return, under what circumstances he will return, and whether the protective shield becomes permanently compromised.

The mainstay of the problem of the exiled is that he must leave his home without so much as a goodbye to friends and family. Ferlosio (1983) established that goodbye is in the strictest sense a ritual. It establishes protective borders. Departure is the border that divides the state of union between two people—the one who leaves and the one who stays behind—from the state of separation. As the dividing line between presence and absence, departure creates the tension of belief that we will meet again and the tension of fear that we will never meet again. The traveler believes that not bidding farewell brings on a sense of uneasiness, apprehension, and a tremendous sense of anxiety. He often tries to compensate for the missing goodbye later, by using the telephone to exchange the messages "thank goodness you are okay and thank goodness you called." To hear the other's voice has a calming, repertory effect. A goodbye places a protective shield around the frontier that is crossed by the departure. It is a protection that implies the hope of seeing each other again and yet also contains the fear of never seeing each other again. When misfortune strikes, such as an exile and an exodus of the proportion that took place in Uganda, and of course, the African slavery and the Jewish Holocaust, goodbyes are the first thing one clings to with all one's heart and soul in an attempt to understand and accept the tragedy of separation. The rite of farewell virtually stamps the incomprehensible with a watermark that locates and orients one during a critical moment. The first thing consciousness needs to know is where is it now, where is it going? The rite of farewell is a marking device that clearly fixes a border between what has been called from time immemorial "the land of the living and the land of the dead" (Grinberg and Grinberg, 1989).

It is clear that the exiled are not able to exercise the protective rite of bidding farewell. Most often they are forced to leave precipitously, and under brutal conditions, without a chance to explain, stand up for themselves, and take the time to absorb the abrupt termination.

> In addition to other anxieties, they carry the anxiety of not having said their goodbye, which makes them feel that they're suspended in the space between the land of the dead and of the living. At the deepest level, all the loved ones they could not say goodbye to and whom they fear they will not see again become transformed into the dead. They feel that they also have become dead to others and hence cannot achieve a satisfactory separation [Grinberg and Grinberg, 1989].

The term *exile* is used to indicate involuntary departures as well as the transplanted, displaced, and stateless persons. It was initially associated with the Athenians, who banished certain citizens for political reasons. Today, of all the problems stemming from civil war and violent upheavals around the world, exile is one of the most serious. It isolates important sectors of the population from national life, forcing them to adjust to unwanted, hurtful, frustrating situations.

In this context, though, there is a proposal that these kinds of conditions lead to a distortion or inability to be nostalgic. I wish to extend this idea further, that sometimes no nostalgia is possible. Having considered the aforementioned factors of the interruption of an adequate, mature form of goodbye that has been violated, I propose that what will happen is a "hunger for memory" rather than a defense against nostalgia. Parts of the mind, as Shengold (1989) says in *Soul Murder*, were sequestered due to traumatic departures. The question is, does the return to the land of exile help heal the sequestered aspect, or does it allow it to remain with some sense of permanence and solidarity? Does grieving become possible under such circumstances? Detachment is imperative. It seems that, sometimes, traumatic exile can be linked to the childhood loss of an important object. Reactions have included unconscious and sometimes conscious denial of the reality of the parent's death, rigid screening out of all affective responses connected with the parent's death, marked increase in identification with an idealization of the dead parent, decrease in self-esteem, and unconscious fantasies of an ongoing relationship or reunion with the dead parent (Miller, 1971). Because of the nature and suddenness of such trauma, it is difficult for the exile to take into account the finalities of what has taken place. Here, the issue of time becomes crucial. There was no time for leave-taking. There was no time for preparing or anticipating. Hence, the mind or psyche is permanently suspended in disbelief and this disbelief probably accounts for "memory hunger." Hence, when people are not able to recollect the land or the landscape or the memories of the land they left behind, it may not be masking a defense against nostalgia so much as an absence of memory created by traumatic circumstances. Has this been suppressed or has it been denied? Or has it been left in psychic vacuum? I suspect the latter. The repetition compulsion does become effective, as has been described in Edgar Allan Poe's history, where he was burdened with the death of his mother at a very young age. His relationships with women were marked by his need to have and destroy those relationships over time again and again in order to witness the death. One wonders whether the exiled would have a similar experience of having to leave a place repeatedly in order to master the trauma of exile. There have been experiences of many Ugandans who have been interviewed at a later date. Some have described a life of continued depression, lack of spontaneity, and inability to find in a new society the ability to recreate partially the old familiar environment.

The exile's settlement in the new country was many-faceted. He or she did not actually travel. They fled or were expelled. The feelings of bitterness, resentfulness, or frustration may be faced with denial of the present, which then becomes an imprisonment in a past mythologized life (converted into the "only thing worthwhile"). The future represented by the illusion of being able to return home—the more the illusion is nourished, the greater the impossibility of acting on it.

Contrary to the poisoning of the nostalgia, oftentimes, the rejection from exiles' home country leaves behind a sense of hatred toward the country that expelled them and is projected onto the new country that has received them. Thus, as they see the new country as their salvation, others simultaneously see it as the cause of all their troubles, while idealizing their original country with never-ending nostalgia. The situation is similar to children who are adopted. Their new parents relieve their suffering temporarily, especially because they are finding somebody who will listen. Subsequently, the adoptive parent is also destroyed. Hatred is a two-edged sword. It is a viable stimulus if it can be controlled and cautiously exercised, but it is a dangerous, destructive weapon when out of control. It can attack the person's sanity and can destroy the sources of hope that have been established. That hope is irrecoverable. I suggest that it is this irrecoverable hope that leads to "memory hunger." Working through the pain and frustration of loss under circumstances of turmoil, trauma, and abrupt rejection creates a different reality and acceptance. In the case of the Uganda exodus, the reception was filled with hostility, anger, and resentment on the part of the Britons. The experience of the exiled was intermingled with hopes for the new land and the loss of the homeland. There is no chance for nostalgia. Instead a deep-rooted feeling of "absence of memory" exists. This can best be described in Benedetti's (1982) novel, *Primavera con una Esquina Rota* ("Spring with the Corner Torn Off"):

> I say you have to start by taking control of the streets, the corners, the skies, the cafes, the sun and more important, the shade. When you feel that a street is not foreign to you only then does the street stop looking at you like you're a foreigner. People don't understand this kind of homesickness. It is almost impossible to understand this homesickness.

I will present some personal recollections of having visited Uganda, my homeland, recently after 25 years of exile. Returning home is a psychic effort, accepting many changes in a relatively short length of time. To love, the possibility of return, even in a voluntary migration, is filled with the experience of an exciting trip. This feeling is related to the inner conviction that one's roots are safe in the land of one's birth. The person may be far from home and from his loved ones but he does not feel uprooted. The parts of him contained in the home left behind would still be there. On preplanned return, one discovers abandoned objects that have a calming influence because of the established time limit for being away. However, the return to the home of exile may be more complicated and has certain specific phases that I will describe as I undertook by trip back to Uganda.

My return, which had been anticipated for eight to 10 weeks, took place under unusual and less than optimal circumstances. However, despite the days of anguish and internal turmoil that might have clouded the experience, I will best describe some of the outstanding features of the return that may contribute to our psychodynamic understanding of the problem of traumatic migrations—a severance from birthlands.

Phase I

It appears that I did not reminisce about Uganda in the past 25 years. I would not necessarily think that it was a poisoning of nostalgia or a defense against it, as much as a memory hunger that left me sometimes spontaneously reacting to landscapes that were similar to Uganda—with an awe and joy that connected me in some ways to the tropics in which I grew up.

Phase II

When the plans were finalized—I owe this to Dr. Afaf Mahfouz, who helped me plan and arrange this trip with the help of the NGO Conference of the United Nations that she was going to lead—there was a sense of disbelief and a terrible fear that the return home would not occur. This fear I must say persisted until two weeks before the departure. I imagined that this must have been partly the persistent fear that the return would be impossible or another sudden uprooting such as occurred at the time of exile (a form of "flashback") might occur in the midst of anticipation and planning.

Phase III

A few weeks before, as I began to read about Uganda for the first time, I experienced profound crying. Many fears emerged, particularly of my home being nonexistent, more sensitive issues of general domination and control, susceptibility to feelings of helplessness, and a sense of internal destabilization combined with an anxiety that was linked to fears of destruction, and ultimately, a fear of returning and wondering what I would find. A week before the visit, I found myself experiencing a heightened sensitivity to destability. A friend whom I talked to shortly before my departure wondered if I was hectically preparing to return to Uganda. I said, "I have not packed yet." In fact, I felt that I was returning home and would be taken care of. For the first time, I began recollecting roads and sights to be visited in more detail, and an anticipation of landing at Entebbe airport. The apprehension and excitement increased and a powerful wish to embrace, smell, and touch Uganda concretely was beginning to permeate my mind. I talked to an acquaintance who had recently visited Uganda. He indicated that Uganda was being revived and a deep sense of relief overtook me. The central idea of the destruction and devastation still persisted in my mind, combined with a sense of relief that I would not be visiting a wasteland, but a land of plenty. There was a slow, very cautious recovery of some painful childhood memories, but I still could not think about pleasant memories. Finally, I had my first dream a week before departure, related to the actual departure and traumatic exile memory. It was a long delayed effort to master partially the days around the exile.

The last 24 to 48 hours before leaving for Uganda was a tumultuous time. I experienced some freedom and elation, more energy and excitement, and anticipation of being able to reunite with Uganda. A few hours before leaving for Uganda, more pleasant and joyful memories began to emerge. I think this can be explained by what Grinberg and Grinberg call, in one word, "radiance." This is more typical in returns home when there is voluntary migration, where the unconscious hostility of those who have been left behind has done no irreparable harm. At the time of the reunion, those who have been left behind have forgiven us for abandoning them and made clear that they have not forgotten us and love us still. In the case of returning home under circumstances of exile, however, the fears of persecution permeate to a greater extent the joyful recovery of memories. There is nobody to receive.

Phase IV

As I began to both fear and look forward to being able to touch my homeland, and as the plane landed, I was filled with an enormous sense of stability, strength, and courage, which I think will persist as life goes on. This stability was the ability to go back to my roots, touch the land that gave birth to me, and be able to make reconnections and continuity in time that had been denied for 25 years. As I landed in Uganda, this sense of exhilaration was one of the most memorable times. Subsequently, I was able to spend a week in Uganda with recovering memories, feelings of sadness, and grief, some of it heart-wrenching. It was difficult to cry. However, there was an enormous sense of pleasure at seeing Uganda revive. Certainly, Uganda had become symbolic for the Africans, and so it must be and remain so. I visited the hospital where my parents worked, the schools that were now filled with African children, and the Indian temples. The paradox lay in both the permanence and impermanence of sites I visited.

Before the end of the trip, I was able to visit my birth home, which had been seized at the time of our flight from the country. As I went from room to room, I was filled with a sense of awe—the awe that the house was still there. The old dining table from 25 years ago remained. Inanimate objects remained permanent. Inanimate objects cannot be destroyed. The finding of the dining table permitted me to feel that life had gone on in Uganda, that things had both remained and not remained—some were destroyed, some were there. The memories of my family having dinner together remained.

One of the most beautiful sights for me as a testimony to recovery was at the United Nations Conference. Women took on a leadership role and were dressed in gorgeous, colorful native costumes. They took an active role, talking freely about women's rights. This is in direct contradiction to the role I saw women playing as I was growing up, particularly the African women who were subjugated to roles of servanthood combined with a lack of literacy. A striking fact was that local people did not mention Idi Amin's name. This might be a desire to deny or discover part of their own traumatic past.

Phase V

One final transient experience was that of wanting to come back and live in Uganda, and of contributing to the growth of Uganda more actively.

This idea persisted for a few days on return. My psyche began to get flooded with childhood memories, both pleasant and unpleasant. A sense of integration began to take place. A part that had been sequestered will, I think, always remain. Sometimes soul murder may be irreversible and unforgivable. When devoid of vengeance, the psychic pain can bring a sense of justice to the human mind. I believe that this might be the case. The memory hunger was receding, filled with some sense of hope, loss, sadness, and grief. I was able to take a piece of furniture from my old home, served as a transitional object, linking me to my birthland.

Finally, as psychoanalysts, we need to consider how one comes to peace with trauma. We talk of survival, but not transcendence. We talk of resolution of Oedipus complex and separation-individuation, transitions into latency and adulthood, but the concept of peace lacks sorely in our literature. While we consider the conflictual aspects of trauma, migrations, soul murders, executions, and the holocaust—traumas that leave people in much despair and helplessness—how and when does inner peace prevail? Inner peace is much more than a nostalgic clouding. It is an adult concern. It is a yearning that can moderate mature lives, and an important force, whereby we feel that our days and years can bring to fruition the truest, deepest seed in us. It is a call from the center of us. Hence, peace does not come completely from having grieved the dead. It comes from the knowledge that there is death ahead of us. Reconnections to the past help acknowledge the reality of both the present and future. Hence, while the human traits of language, intelligence, and knowledge are somewhat superfluously useful, the actual consciousness of the reality of dissolution, cessation, nonbeing, and death of animate objects humbles us, becoming central to our clinical work. It provides a psychic space above and beyond the nostalgic cloud, which in it can serve as a maladaptive regressive defense against living and subsequent death.

I hope that this conveys some aspects of one's connection, disconnection, and reconnections with the birthland. Many exiled are commonly called refugees. A *refugee* is not just a person who has been displaced and has lost all or most of his possessions. In fact, a *refugee* is most akin to a child whose ties have been severed with *biological* parents for various reasons—leaving him or her helpless, devoid of initiative, somebody on whom any kind of charity and brutality can be practiced, somebody who is in a vulnerable position and ensured a totally malleable creature.

Rushdie (1989) in his famous novel *Satanic Verses* describes the experience of exile, a forced disconnection from one's biological birthland:

Exile is a soulless country. In exile, the furniture is ugly, expensive, all bought at the same time in the same store and in too much of a hurry: shiny silver sofas with fins like old Buick DeSotos Oldmobiles, glass-fronted bookcases containing not books but clippings files. In exile the shower goes scalding hot whenever anybody turns on a kitchen tap, so that when the Iman goes to bathe, his entire retinue must remember not to fill a kettle or rinse a dirty plate. When the Iman goes to the toilet, his disciples leap scalded from the shower. In exile no food is ever cooked; the dark-spectacled bodyguards go out for take-away. In exile all attempts to put down roots look like treason: they are admissions of defeat [p. 208].

Steplands

I use this term to describe the relationship of an immigrant to his new country upon migration. In the United States, a clear distinction is made between *resident alien* and citizenship. The primary manifest difference is that of voting rights. A psychodynamic exploration reveals very similar aspects of relatedness as described in relationships in stepfamilies.

The resident alien status simultaneously depicts the contradictory feelings inherent in the stepchild's relationship to his parent. On the one hand, while a sense of belonging is implied in the *resident* status, a sense of not belonging is strongly implied in the *alien* status. This paradoxical double self-representation gives rise to a constant sense of vacillation of one's rights, ownership, belonging, and familiarity.

Landau-Stanton, Griffiths, and Mason (1985) have worked with many immigrating families and they believe that the integration of stepfamilies is similar to the acculturation process that occurs when a family immigrates from one culture to another. Visher and Visher (1996) make a strong case for three basic experiences in stepfamily integration—the lack of a sense of belonging, the need for control and cultivating familiarity. Collins (1988) has described the following principles in stepparenting:

1. Care can be as important as love.
2. Understanding is important.
3. Stepfamilies are not inferior imitations of biological families.
4. Stepparents are not necessarily parents.
5. Personal relationships can hurt, but they can also heal.
6. Guilt can damage the health of the household.
7. Comparisons are odious.
8. Myths and superstitions have no place in a modern stepfamily.
9. Human emotions are seldom straightforward.
10. Parents are not emotional caddies [pp. 19–20].

I (Mehta, 1998) have described the struggles of immigrant parents, the developmental tasks of second-generation immigrant children, and the negotiation of the third space. The psychic meaning and significance of this experience is present between children and their parents, just as in stepfamilies, that is, some members of the family have arrived from someplace else. The wish for a birth identity similar to those of other family members serves to obliterate the third space. Despite their similiar skin color, children become aware of the difference in their birthplace from that of their parents based on different accents, and the parents' lack of knowledge of local culture, compounded by their nostalgic experiences of their birthland. I have described the concept of core and acquired identity; that is, the child born in the United States has a core identity of being American, while the acquired identity (step identity) rests on that of the immigrant parents. In reverse, the parents' core identity is deeply tied to their birthland, while the acquired (i.e., step) identity is American. Hence, there is a basic difference between first-generation immigrants and their second-generation children that distinguishes both at the most manifest and latent level: their birth countries are different. The birth country both betrays and legitimizes an individual in a powerful way. The narcissistic injury is profound when parents experience rivalry with their children, who are the "biological" children of America, while the parents are akin to stepchildren. Elsewhere I have referred to the parents as adopted, but I think a distinction between stepchild and adopted child is necessary. This often manifests itself in the abrupt legal transition between resident alien status and U.S. citizenship. U.S. citizenship apparently confers a "superior status," the assurance that you will be protected in most circumstances. Resident alien status is viewed as an inferior imitation of U.S. citizenship, much as the stepchild feels inferior to the biological child.

This experience is akin to Collins's (1988) description of the stepfamily ties. He states that while human kinship binds human beings together and is central to the core in a biological family system, human beings develop other ties that get emphasized in stepfamilies. An understanding of this can enhance our listening to patients attempting to define their ties with their stepland on immigrating. It is precisely these ties that can lead to vacillating cathexis to their land of immigration and subsequent utilization of this to imbed further neurotic conflict. Many exasperated children of immigrant parents tell their deeply conflicted parents: "Now live with your choice to come to the United States. You asked for it." However, understanding Collins's description of the nature of ties in stepfamilies could lead to a more empathic understanding of the unverbalized feelings of the immigrants toward their stepland. Collins (1988) believes that stepfamilies are held together by moral rather than emotional factors and that the taken-for-granted affection in biological families is not the primary mode of caretaking. Instead, stepfamilies are based on a decision to care for someone else's children. This has strong moral overtones because it embodies assumptions about obligations to other people. Collins (1988) states that "they have voluntarily entered into a commitment to children, which is a commitment of supreme moral stature," and that "this probably means loyalty, a human quality of great importance, which allows one to develop and sustain mutual obligations under the most adverse circumstances" (p. 28). I believe this requires mature object relatedness, a deeper commitment with greater sacrifice and flexibility and a willingness to give more than can be received. Immigrants have the same task. They cannot hope to feel the patriotic fervor for their adopted land, but one hopes they will learn to care for their new country with loyalty. Huge losses sustained on migrating further complicate this task, and I believe it takes several years for an integration of the identity of immigrants to their new land. Sometimes it might take a couple of generations to feel a sense of ownership and cohesiveness. Meanwhile, one of the conflicts between children and their immigrant parents can be understood by emphasizing the nature of ties with the land and culture at large—kinship versus loyalty. One is emotional and the other moral. It demands a sense of responsibility that is above and beyond that generated by biological ties. It involves care—a conscientious and thoughtful relationship with the new land and culture in the absence of natural and spontaneous affection and love. The demands on the psyche can be high, but the rewards great—for internal growth, development, and sustenance, a simultaneous loss and growth.

In *Diario de un Emigrante* ("Diary of an Immigrant"), Delibres (1980) describes Lorenzo's immigration from Spain to Chile. It is a testimony to the space that exists between the cathexis to the birthland and the new land:

> We docked in Buenos Aires and from there took the train to Santiago. By that time I was a little stunned and it occurred to me, seeing more people thronging in those streets than I had ever seen before, that five million people could walk past my nose and I wouldn't find one familiar face; and then it occurred to me that this was worse than being in the desert, and I had a feeling, like being sad about everything, and I couldn't stop. I started to remember my house, the block, and the cluster of buildings, and I said to Anita, I wonder what the old folks are doing right now, and what time it is over there.

Adopted Lands

To *adopt* means "to take and treat as a child, giving a title to the rights of a child" (*Webster's Dictionary*, 1992). Grinberg and Grinberg (1989) "refer to the place of residence of persons whose lives and activities occur either temporarily or permanently somewhere outside their native country as their 'adopted country.'" While this helps emphasize the anxiety of unwantedness inherent in the adoption and immigrant experience, a sharper distinction between the dynamics of stepparenting and adoption might be useful. Although stepparenting still maintains the tie to the biological parent, adoption essentially severs this tie. The gaining of U.S. citizenship is a separate process worthy of attention. It requires relinquishment of rights of citizenship to other countries. In stepfamilies, dual loyalty is exercised to varying degrees. On the other hand, relinquishment remains a key experience in adoption. The relinquishment of legal and protective rights to the country of origin heightens the reunion desire. This is similar to the reunion wish in the adopted. The wish to return permanently to the land of origin becomes powerfully fueled as one gains more stability and permanence in the new country. (Jews at the Passover service have a phrase, "Next year in Jerusalem," a return to the Biblical homeland after the diaspora.)

Divakaruni, a South Asian writer, describes eloquently in her book *The Mistress of Spices* (1998) her reactions on seeing an American flag. The nostalgic experience was powerful as she spoke of her love for America over the 20 years she has lived here. She describes the freedom, amazement, and gratitude she felt as she became part of the American culture and told her three-year-old American-born son about the American flag. However, she reflects:

> There was something else I needed to say, something important about the complexities of culture and allegiance and patriotism and ancestry, how they change and yet do not change, but I didn't have the words for it. I thought about what it had meant for me to be Indian, and what it meant for my children to be American. I thought of the great gap—mental as much as geographic—that my moving to this country had created between the generations of my family: my mother, who lives in a little Indian village, myself, balanced between two continents, and my children, whose primary ties will always be to the Bay area. But I believe all immigrant parents go through them at some time or other, when they must weigh the gains of what they have given their American children against the losses. And then will my children ever fit into this country in the way a person of European background can? Many people will look at them and always see foreigners.

Alternate pessimism and optimism (past/future, hope/loss) highlight this experience. The vacillations of these affects are present in every human experience. However, major life events, traumas, early losses, immigrations, stepfamilies, and adoption lead to a greater challenge to the ego and maybe a more frequent or intense vacillation of these affects. The reunion fantasy with the birthland is also an idealized fantasy, for it is never glorious, wonderful, and perfect. In fact it is just another immigration, sometimes even more complicated. In this context, I would like to note that it is common practice for young Indian couples to immigrate without their young children or babies who they leave in the care of grandparents with the idea that they will call for them or eventually return to India. On exploring this with one of my patients, it became clear that the guilt of leaving, both the country and family, was so acute, that the baby, under rationalized reasons served as a sacrifice (a replacement for leaving parents). Of course, the consequences of early separation were far reaching for the child and parents. This helps to demonstrate the depth of feelings and conflict related to immigration. One patient who returned to India wrote to me:

> We moved from the USA back to India thinking we wanted to settle here permanently. However my daughter is *very* disappointed that we are not going back to the USA. I kind of feel guilty. We are seriously contemplating returning to the USA. Our children's happiness is probably the most important factor. They need to return to the land that gave birth to them.

As psychoanalysts, we need to be well aware that psychoanalysis is an imported culture. Many psychoanalysts were immigrants to this country. However, the study of immigration and one's relationship to America is a more recent endeavor. I believe that one of the primary reasons is that immigration involves a narcissistic injury and hence it brings issues of shame, idealization, loss, and devaluation. Our ability to think about these issues by understanding relatedness in biological parenting, stepparenting, and adoptive parenting can, one hopes, permit us to become more deeply attuned and empathic to ourselves and our patients who might range from a first-generation to a fourth-generation immigrant. I believe it is fitting to end with Freud's (1938) experience of his immigration to England:

> The triumphant feeling of liberation is mingled too strongly with mourning; for one had still very much loved the prison from which one has been released. I came to Vienna as a child of four years from a small town in Moravia. After seventy-eight years including more than half a century of strenuous work, I had to leave my home, saw the scientific society I had founded dissolved, our institute destroyed, our printing press (Verlap) taken over by the invaders, the books I had published confiscated and reduced to ashes, my children expelled from their professions. Don't you think the columns of your special number might rather be reserved for the utterances of non-Jewish people less personally involved than myself? In this connection my

mind gets hold of an old French saying: "Le bruit est pour le fat, la plainte est pour le sol" [The noise is for the pretentious, the complaint falls to the ground].

References

Benedetti, M. (1982), *Primavera con una Esquina Rota* [Spring with the Corner Torn Off]. Madrid: Alfaguara.

Collins, S. (1988), *Stepparents and Their Children*. London: Souvenir Press.

Delibres, M. (1980), *Diario de un Emigrante* [Diary of an Immigrant]. Barcelona: Destino.

Divakaruni, C. B. (1998), *The Mistress of Spices*. New York: Doubleday.

Freud, S. (1920), Beyond the pleasure principle. *Standard Edition*, 18:7–64. London: Hogarth Press, 1955.

———— (1924), A note upon the "mystic writing pad." *Standard Edition*, 19: 225–232. London: Hogarth Press, 1961.

———— (1938), Letter to the editor. *Time and Tide*, 26. Manuscript Division, Library of Congress, Washington, DC.

Grinberg, L. & Grinberg, R. (1989), *Psychoanalytic Perspectives on Migration and Exile*. New Haven, CT: Yale University Press.

Landau-Stanton, J. K., Griffiths, J. G. & Mason, G. (1985), The extended family in transition: Clinical implications. In: *The International Book of Family Therapy*, ed. F. Kaslow. New York: Brunner/Mazel.

Mehta, P. (1998), The emergence, conflicts, and integration of the bicultural self. In: *The Colors of Childhood*, ed. S. Akhtar & S. Kramer. Northvale, NJ: Aronson.

Miller, J. (1971), Children's reactions to the death of a parent: A review of the psychoanalytic literature. *J. Amer. Psychoanal. Assn.*, 19:697–719.

Naipaul, V. S. (1987), *The Enigma of Arrival*. New York: Vintage Books.

Rushdie, S. (1989), *Satanic Verses*. New York: Viking Penguin.

Shengold, L. (1989), *Soul Murder*. New Haven, CT: Yale University Press.

Terr, L. (1990), *Too Scared to Cry*. New York: Basic Books.

The Stepfather in Sophocles' *Electra*

Melvin R. Lansky

I

In the vast array of relationships portrayed in Western literature, there is a surprising dearth of attention to the stepfather–stepchild relationship, particularly the stepfather in relation to a stepchild or stepchildren actually living with him and their mother.

Two distinguished exceptions to this general observation are, of course, Claudius in *Hamlet* and Aegisthus in the Orestes plays of Aeschylus, Sophocles, and Euripides. Of the Greek tragedies, however, only the *Electra* of Sophocles portrays the situation of the stepchild actually living with the mother and the stepfather. A third instance might be Jesus living with Mary and her husband Joseph, though this story is from scripture, not from literature per se, and it is questionable to view Joseph as stepfather in the usual sense when the Deity is the father. I shall return briefly to the question of Jesus in section VII.

It is not easy to surmise why there should be so few great works dealing with stepfathers and stepchildren since the predicament is by no means rare, the conflicts are intense, and the potential for literary substance seemingly as great as in other types of relationships that are more abundantly represented. The feeling so commonly felt by stepchildren about the stepfather situation—of betrayal and abandonment by mother, of idealization of, attachment to, and desertion by the father, and the loyalty conflicts posed by the stepfather's presence and his union with mother, the potential for splitting and displacement onto the stepfather of ambivalence toward either parent—all have their counterpart in other types of relationships that have a much greater prevalence in great works of literature. I shall conjecture below that the paucity of works on the stepfather may be related, in part, to shame conflicts stirred up in a very special way by the stepfather situation.

In this chapter, I will pursue both a general examination of Sophocles' play and a specific focus on the stepchild–stepfather relationship. I attempt both because I believe that the play, considered in and of itself, highlights features of the dynamics of unacknowledged shame in relation to rage, family conflict, mourning, and helplessness that in turn shed light on certain widespread dynamics that underlie the stepchild's perception of the stepfather in ways that deal with the child's ambivalence towards both parents and attempt to cope with quite specific shame conflicts that

arise when the mother is viewed as betraying, abandoning, and danger-
ously lustful.

I will be assuming that the specific circumstances of the play and of its
characters are not set arbitrarily. As with the operations of the dream work
in dream symbols, the royal status of the family, the public significance of
regicide, the actual murder of both parents and the stepfather are not
arbitrary circumstances in a story involving a stepfather. They are elaborations of unconscious fantasies put forward by the poet that resonate with
the deep unconscious sense of the significance of the familial events: that
the status of the parents is royal; that anger leads to murder, that privately
felt shame is public scandal and disgrace; that the mother's union with
the stepfather betokens complete disenfranchisement of the child; and
that passive and depressed preoccupation with family upheaval is permanently and hopelessly damaging.

Before I turn to these issues in the play itself, I will provide some
background for the *Electra*, its context, and its critics.

II

Tragic drama deals with the family (Simon, 1988). The tragedians who
flourished in fifth century B.C.E. Athens provided some of the most
inspired portrayals of familial relationships ever preserved in great literature. Themes of matricide (the Orestes plays), filicide (*Medea*), patricide
(*Oedipus Tyrannus*), murder by siblings (*Seven Against Thebes*), sibling
bonds (*Antigone*), and incest (*Oedipus Tyrannus, Hippolytus*) are explored
with great insight and intensity.

The Orestes plays are concerned primarily with the issue of matricide.
The role of the stepfather appears in the context of that larger theme.
Aegisthus, lover of Clytemnestra, with whom he conspires to kill her
husband, Agamemnon, is the stepfather who appears in the Orestes plays
of the three great tragedians. The frame tale is complex and nuanced
(Graves, 1955). Every character in the Orestes plays has good reasons to
feel vengeful and also to worry in turn that he or she may be the recipient
of the vengeance of others. Aegisthus himself was the son of Thyestes, son
of Pelops. Thyestes was the brother of Atreus, who was the father of
Agamemnon and Menelaus. Thyestes seduced Atreus' wife and usurped
the throne of Mycenae from Atreus. Atreus regained the throne and, to
avenge himself on Thyestes, invited him to Mycenae with a promise of
amnesty and half the throne, only to serve him a meal that contained parts
of Thyestes' sons, who had been slain, cut up, and cooked. Later, Thyestes
ravished his own daughter and impregnated her. Atreus, not knowing who
the daughter was or that she was pregnant, married her and raised the son,
Aegisthus, as his own. He sent Aegisthus, when a very young child, to kill

the visiting Thyestes, but the plot was foiled, Thyestes identified himself, and the young Aegisthus was sent to kill Atreus. He did so, that is, killed his own stepfather, placing his father on the throne. Thyestes was later driven out of Mycenae by Atreus' son, Agamemnon, who took the throne.

Agamemnon, commander-in-chief of the Greek army, spent 10 years in Troy to destroy the city and bring back Helen, the wife of his brother, Menelaus, and sister of his wife, Clytemnestra, after Helen had run off with the Trojan prince Paris. As the Greek fleet was about to set sail from Aulis for Troy, Agamemnon offended the goddess Artemis. An oracle revealed that no wind would arise to take the Greek fleet to Troy or back to Greece unless Agamemnon sacrificed his daughter, Iphigenia, to Artemis. Agamemnon's wife, Clytemnestra, enraged by the attention devoted to her reprobate sister and by the murder of her daughter and seduced by Aegisthus, murdered Agamemnon on his return from Troy and married Aegisthus, who took the throne. By the quick action of Clytemnestra's daughter Electra, Agamemnon's son Orestes escaped and was placed in the hands of a tutor who raised him in the land of Phocis until he was old enough to return for revenge. Aegisthus and Clytemnestra reigned seven years in Mycenae, forbidding their daughters Electra and Chrysothemis from marrying for fear that their sons would take vengeance on them, and fearing the return of Orestes to take revenge and to claim his father's throne.

Sophocles' *Electra* takes place on the day that Orestes arrives in Mycenae following Apollo's orders to return and take vengeance by stealth and without an army.

III

The argument of the play is as follows: The prologue is in two parts. In the first part, Orestes, his comrade Pylades, and the tutor who had originally taken him from Electra arrived in Mycenae after Apollo's oracle had told Orestes to return for revenge by stealth. Orestes sends the tutor to the palace with the story that he, Orestes, has been killed in an athletic contest in Phocis. Orestes and Pylades go with libations to Agamemnon's grave. As they leave, they hear Electra's plaintive cries within.

Electra appears onstage alone, lamenting the death of Agamemnon seven years previously, vowing revenge, praying for Orestes' return and proclaiming that her mourning will never cease. The chorus of women of Mycenae appear and sympathetically ask why she mourns so long. After her refusal to do otherwise, the chorus points out that her sister Chrysothemis lives more sensibly, acknowledging the power of Aegisthus and Clytemnestra. Electra responds to their entreaties by saying that marriage and childbearing have passed her up. She rails against Aegisthus.

In the first episode, Electra's sister Chrysothemis appears to beseech Electra to stop her reproaches and visible wailing because Clytemnestra and Aegisthus plan to lock her away in a cave if she does not cease berating them. Electra defiantly welcomes such a punishment. Chrysothemis then says that she is on her way to Agamemnon's grave with an offering from Clytemnestra who had been frightened by a dream about Agamemnon that made her fear that Orestes would return. Electra pleads with Chrysothemis not to put offerings of an enemy on their father's grave. Chrysothemis agrees and takes tokens from Electra to be put on the grave instead. The chorus, encouraged by Electra's reaction to the dream, foresees revenge.

The second episode begins with Clytemnestra's entrance on the way to a prayer to Apollo. She reproaches Electra for being outside the palace and for disgracing and berating her mother publicly. She defends the murder of Agamemnon as justified by his murder of Iphigenia. Electra responds to her argument carefully, point for point, then flies into a rage at Clytemnestra, reproaching her for sleeping with Aegisthus, having more children, and driving out Agamemnon's children. She flaunts Orestes' eventual return. Clytemnestra threatens retaliation when Aegisthus returns and prays to Apollo for protection against hateful children, and implicitly offers a prayer for Orestes' death. At this point, the tutor enters with the news that Orestes has been killed in an accident in an athletic competition in Phocis. He has been cremated and his remains put into an urn that will soon arrive in Mycenae. Clytemnestra voices mixed feelings of relief and grief. Electra is devastated. As Clytemnestra and the tutor leave, she tells the chorus that she first lost Agamemnon and then Orestes and now has no wish for life.

The third episode begins with Chrysothemis' hasty return from Agamemnon's grave with the news that a lock of hair and other offerings found on the grave make it certain that Orestes has returned. Electra silences her with the news that Orestes has been killed. She proposes to Chrysothemis that the two sisters themselves kill Clytemnestra and Aegisthus. Chrysothemis replies that they are women, not men, and must coexist with those that have the power. The chorus agrees. Electra reviles her sister for cowardice and vows to assassinate the royal couple herself. Chrysothemis leaves as the chorus extols Electra's nobility.

In the fourth episode, the still-disguised Orestes appears, telling Electra that he has arrived with Orestes' remains. Electra takes the urn, and her protestations of grief and mourning so move Orestes that, after ascertaining that the women in the chorus can be trusted, reveals himself to his sister. Their reunion is joyful but interrupted by the tutor who reprimands them for losing time. Orestes and the tutor take the urn inside the palace where Clytemnestra is alone. Electra, with the chorus, prays to Apollo for success, while the chorus chants of impending vengeance. Electra, watching for Aegisthus' return, hears Clytemnestra cry out and herself cries out vengefully as the cries of the dying Clytemnestra reach her. Orestes returns as Aegisthus is seen approaching the palace. Aegisthus demands to see the Phocians and hear the news directly. He is told that the body has been brought and demands that it be displayed publicly as a reminder to those who would defy his rule. Clytemnestra's shrouded body is brought to him. He asks Orestes to draw the covers but is told that uncovering the body is his duty. He uncovers the dead Clytemnestra's head, recoils in horror and realizes that he has been trapped by Orestes. He asks for a chance to speak, but Electra flies into a vengeful rage, urging Orestes to kill him and fling his body out without burial. Orestes orders Aegisthus into the palace to be slain in the same room in which he and Clytemnestra slew Agamemnon. The chorus praises the freedom won by the day's deeds.

IV

Sophocles' treatment of the myth differs in emphasis from that of Homer, Aeschylus, or Euripides. Homer treats the matricide per se more or less nonchalantly as an unavoidable and obligatory act of vengeance performed by Orestes on his father's murderers. In contrast, Aeschylus' great trilogy, *The Oresteia*, concentrates heavily on the issue of matricide, the madness of Orestes, and his pursuit by the Furies (Erinyes) after Clytemnestra is killed. In *The Libation Bearers*, the second play of the trilogy, Electra is more or less Orestes' accomplice, playing a secondary role. Aegisthus' death precedes that of Clytemnestra and is morally unimportant, certainly in comparison with the matricide. In Euripides' *Electra*, matricide is emphasized and very much reviled, but Electra has been put in an unconsummated marriage and does not live in the palace. The relationship to Aegisthus as stepfather is not developed.

From the point of view of the stepfather, Sophocles' *Electra* has more in common with *Hamlet* than it does with Aeschylus' *Libation Bearers* or Euripides' *Electra*. Indeed, the comparisons are striking: both are offspring of a murdered king. In both cases, the murderer was a near relative of the father. The murderer subsequently married the mother, who seemed to have lost all regard for the slain father. In both cases, the mother's lust for the stepfather is incomprehensible since the stepfather does not measure up to the father. Both Electra and Hamlet are disinherited (Hamlet did not succeed his father as king), both live with the stepfather and mother after the marriage, both mourn in ways that cause consternation and embarrassment to the family and the outside world. Both are admonished for excessive and conspicuous public mourning. In both cases, their reproaches and defiance are so burdensome that they are to be sent away. Both specifically reproach their mothers for their loathsome sexual union with the stepfather. Both regard the stepfather as unmanly, cowardly, and inept. Both exist in states of paralyzed plans for revenge. This paralysis extends to their ambitions and desires and seems incomprehensible to others. Both are finally involved in killing the stepfather. In both cases, the mother is killed also. I shall return to the significance of these special circumstances below.

A good deal of classical criticism is spent discussing the issue of matricide in Sophocles' *Electra* and the question of why it is that little, if any, attention in Sophocles' play is devoted to the Furies, the forces of revenge that follow the matricide—that is, to whether or not Sophocles is morally indifferent to the issue of matricide, as is Homer; is horrified, as are Aeschylus and Euripides; or is merely opaque (Sheppard, 1918, 1927a, b; Winnington-Ingram, 1954; Kells, 1973). Electra's unnatural attachment to and mourning for Agamemnon is, of course, a defining feature of the play. Stevens (1978) and others emphasize her permanent loss of self-respect, her shame, her guilt and her degradation. Dale (1969) emphasizes her unnatural hate for Clytemnestra as well. Linforth (1963) notes that despite excessive mourning and protestation, nowhere does Electra proclaim actual love for Agamemnon whom she hardly knew before he left for the Trojan War. Kirkwood (1942), stressing the importance of the reversal of order of killing of Clytemnestra and Aegisthus in Sophocles' *Electra* from that of Aeschylus' *Libation Bearers*, stresses that the hatred of Clytemnestra outweighs that of Aegisthus and that the death of Clytemnestra is the true climax of the play. Woodward (1964, 1965), in two important papers, stresses the dialectical relationship between Orestes and Electra, Orestes being free-ranging, athletic, professional, business-like, and characterized by action, and Electra homebound, unambitious, poverty stricken, spiteful, treated like a slave, and irreparably lost in emotion.

Among psychoanalytic thinkers, Freud repudiated Jung's attempt to analogize Electra's attachment to Agamemnon as the female counterpart of the male Oedipus complex. Freud (1931) argued that the male and female situations were simply not symmetrical: "We have an impression here that what we have said about the Oedipus Complex applies with complete strictness to the male child only and that we are right in rejecting the term 'Electra complex' which seeks to emphasize the analogy between the attitudes of the two sexes" (pp. 228–229). Details of this controversy are beyond the scope of this discussion.

The Orestes plays are insightfully discussed by Doris Bernstein (1993) in her consideration of female development and the Oedipus complex. Bernstein stresses the helplessness of the female predicament vis-à-vis both parents compared to that of the male predicament, which is resolvable by identification. I am in complete agreement with Bernstein's analysis as far as it goes. She does not, however, stress the issue of stepfather and stepchild.

V

The play so well illustrates the predicament of the fantasied or actual perception of the stepfather by the stepchild that I will turn first to the phenomenology of the play for some of the features exaggerated in Electra herself and, in counterpoint, understated in her siblings. Then I will highlight the stepchild's experience of the stepfather.

1. Most prominent at the forefront, of course, is the excessive mourning that has become the signature feature of the Electra myth. Her father is idealized and her attachment to him an unremitting and public preoccupation that is embarrassing to her family.

> And again the house of my misery
> my bed is witness to my all-night sorrowing
> dirges for my unhappy father.
> Him in the land of the foreigner
> no murderous God of battles entertained.
> But my mother and the man who shared her bed,
> Aegisthus, split his head with a murderous ax,
> like woodsmen with an oak tree.
> For all this no pity was given him,
> by any but me, no pity for your death,
> father, so pitiful, so cruel.
> [Lines 93–102]

Yet she barely voices real love for Agamemnon, nor did she presumably know him very well. He left for the Trojan War when she was only a child, killed her sister in sacrifice, and returned 10 years later parading his concubine Cassandra through the house publicly, only to be slain shortly thereafter by Clytemnestra and Aegisthus. He is nonetheless idealized and Aegisthus denigrated; that is, the split paternal imago serves to defend against Electra's ambivalence toward Agamemnon himself. The same split is seen in *Hamlet*, where the comparison of the older Hamlet to his brother Claudius is: "So excellent a king, that was to this / Hyperion to a satyr" (*Hamlet*, I, ii, lines 139–140).

2. The father is experienced as having been killed. This killing was a direct result of an illicit preexisting sexual union between mother and future stepfather who is also father's near kinsman. Mother's incomprehensible and uncontrolled lust is an essential ingredient of the conspiracy to kill father. Furthermore, mother's attraction to stepfather remains enigmatic and is blamed on her excessive lustiness and on the seductiveness of the stepfather.

all ye who look upon those who die unjustly,
all ye who look upon the theft of a wife's love,
come all and help take vengeance for my father,
for my father's murder!
[Lines 113–116]

Although Gertrude is not specifically involved in her husband's murder, a similar situation is of course true in *Hamlet*. He reproaches his mother:

O shame, where is thy blush? Rebellious hell,
If thou canst mutine in a matron's bones,
To flaming youth let virtue be as wax
And melt in her own fire. Proclaim no shame
When the compulsive ardor gives the charge,
Since frost itself as actively doth burn,
And reason panders will.
[*Hamlet*, III, iv, lines 83–98]

3. The attachment to and mourning for the father has a powerful and public impact on the family. It stands as an ongoing reproach that shames the new parental couple and broadcasts not merely the child's misery but also a chronically defiant stance that proclaims the wretchedness, rejection, and persecuted status of the stepchild, while at the same time entrenching Electra's alienation at home even deeper.

Shameful death that my father saw
dealt him by the hands of the two,
hands that took my own life captive,
betrayed, destroyed me utterly.
For these deeds may God in his greatness,
the Olympian one, grant punishment to match them.
And may they have no profit of their glory
who brought these actions to accomplishment.
[Lines 205–212]

Here Electra's life of helplessness and defiance is contrasted to Orestes' action-oriented existence.

I have awaited him always
sadly, unweariedly,
till I'm past childbearing,
till I am past marriage,
always to my own ruin.
Wet with tears, I endure

an unending doom of misfortune.
But he has forgotten
what he has suffered, what he has known.
What message comes from him to me
that is not again belied?
Yes, he is always longing to come,
but he does not choose to come, for all his longing.
[Lines 164–172]

Electra is also contrasted with her sister Chrysothemis, who tries to make a reasonable adaptation to the circumstances she likes no better than does Electra. Chrysothemis nonetheless adapts herself to the realities of power in the family. She admonishes Electra:

Will you never learn, in all this time,
not to give way to your empty anger?
Yet this much I know, and know my own heart, too,
that I am sick at what I see, so that
if I had strength, I would let them know how I feel.
But under pain of punishment, I think,
I must make my voyage with lowered sails,
that I may not seem to do something and then prove
ineffectual. But justice, justice,
is not on my side but on yours. If I am
to live and not as a prisoner, I must
in all things listen to my lords.
[Lines 330–340]

4. There is a pronounced lack of involvement with ambition, desire, or the outside world. Electra has no desires except for Orestes' return and for revenge. She has not married and has no children. (The word *electra* may have been intended as wordplay on *alectra*—"unmarried.") Unlike Orestes, who seeks not revenge for its own sake but restoration of his lands and his kingdom, Electra is preoccupied only with mourning and revenge and, by implication, a sense of irreparable damage to herself.

This helpless, preoccupied, shame-filled, depressed state is in sharp contrast to that of the action-oriented Orestes and that of the adaptable Chrysothemis. Electra represents not merely one possible resolution of the stepfather predicament but the unconscious sense of rejection, damage, and defeat that must be faced by stepchildren generally no matter what the specific resolution of their intrapsychic conflicts. Electra feels not simply grief for her father and resentment for her stepfather but also, in some fundamental and permanent way helpless, powerless, disinherited, and filled with shame.

For my part, I
will never cease my dirges and sorrowful laments,
as long as I have eyes to see
the twinkling light of the stars and this daylight.
So long, like a nightingale, robbed of her young,
here before the doors of what was my father's house
I shall cry out my sorrow for all the world to hear.
[Lines 103–109]

The same situation is present in *Hamlet*, even though he has been named as Claudius' successor.

5. Electra lives under the threat of retaliation. In the play, as in real-life familial situations, the matter is complex since her feeling of persecution and her actual mistreatment may, in some sense, be seen as reactive to her hostility, provocativeness, and relentless posture of humiliating reproach to the mother and stepfather. In the play, we are told that both Electra and her sister are in fact kept down and prohibited from marrying. Chrysothemis quietly acquiesces and enjoys the material advantages of being a princess. Provocative Electra, however, is dressed in rags and confined to the palace. She is oblivious not only to the impact of her provocations but also to the consequences. Warned by Chrysothemis of plans to lock her in a cave, she is unfazed:

You shall live out your life in an underground cave
and there bewail sorrows of the world outside.
With this in mind, reflect. And do not blame me
later when you are suffering.
Now is a good time to take thought.

Electra
So this is what they have decided to do with me.

Chrysothemis
Yes, this exactly, when Aegisthus comes home.

Electra
As far as this goes, let him come home soon.

Chrysothemis
Why such a prayer for evil, my poor darling?

Electra
That he may come—if he will do what you say.

Chrysothemis
Hoping that *what* may happen you? Are you crazy?

Electra
That I may get away from you all, as far as I can.

Chrysothemis
Have you no care of this, your present life?

Electra
Mine is indeed a fine life, to be envied.

Chrysothemis
It might be, if you could learn common sense.

Electra
Do not teach me falseness to those I love.

Chrysothemis
That, that is not what I teach, but to yield to authority.

Electra
Practice your flattery. This is not my way.

Chrysothemis
It is a good thing, though, not to fall through stupidity.

Electra
I shall fall, if I must, revenging my father.
[Lines 382–399]

6. There is overt rage at the mother and horror and humiliation at the sexual union with the stepfather that is voiced impulsively and vehemently.

Women, I am ashamed if I appear
to you too much the mourner with constant dirges.
What I do, I must do. Pardon me. I ask you
how else would any well-bred girl behave
that saw her father's wrongs, as I have seen these,
by day and night, always, on the increase
and never a check?
First there's my mother, yes, my mother, now become
all hatred. Then in the house I live with those

who murdered my father. I am their subject, and
whether I eat or go without depends
on them.
　　What sort of days do you imagine
I spend, watching Aegisthus sitting
on my father's throne, watching him wear
my father's self-same robes, watching him
at the hearth where he killed him, pouring libations?
Watching the ultimate act of insult,
my father's murderer in my father's bed
with my wretched mother—if mother I should call her,
this woman that sleeps with him.
She is so daring that she paramours
this foul, polluted creature and fears no Fury.
[Lines 254–276]

7. Electra's, then, is a life of chronic narcissistic rage, vengefulness, and depression. To understand this, we must look beyond the manifest issues of mourning and mistreatment to the chronic, unremitting sense of having been cheated, damaged, cast away from special status and irreparably wounded that she has carried with her for years and that she will continue to carry with her after the revenge and restoration of Orestes to power (Stevens, 1978). Electra's is a sense, then, not just of bereavement but of inner damage and permanent, irreparable, narcissistic wounding. (Kells, 1973, makes a similar point.) It is to the nature of this wounding and sense of shame that I shall now turn.

VI

Electra's central manifest preoccupations are her attachment to her father and her hatred of her stepfather. The split paternal imago is at the forefront of her consciousness. Her central and most devastating conflicts, however, are with her mother (Kirkwood, 1942; Dale, 1969; Cairns, 1993). The play, after all, is a play on the by then signature theme of matricide so intimately associated with the Orestes plays of Aeschylus and Euripides.[1] Step-parricide is a subordinate theme. Electra's rage-filled envy at her mother's sexuality and her feeling that her mother has betrayed the family by a sexual union with the stepfather has been elegantly pointed out by Doris Bernstein (1993). Electra can scarcely talk

---

[1]Aeschylus' *Oresteia* antedates Sophocles' play by decades. Euripides' *Electra* was also performed earlier.

to her mother or about Aegisthus to anyone without fulminating about Clytemnestra's sexual union with Aegisthus.

Electra's attack on the couple is truly envious, not simply jealous. She feels, from her mother, abandonment and betrayal that have resulted in irreparable damage and an inner sense of unresolvable shame. That this betrayal of father and children resulted from mother's uncontrolled and continuing lust for the stepfather escalates the envy and shame to intolerable proportions. Electra must deal not only with the sexuality of a loving father in phase-appropriate, primal scene conflicts, she has the added burdens, felt perhaps to some extent by all young stepchildren living with mother and stepfather, of dealing with the fantasy regarding the mother in relationship to her children (in the play, of course, these circumstances are realities), of the mother's rejection of her and the father's children (Clytemnestra had, Electra presumed, planned to murder Orestes before Electra sent him off with the tutor); the mother's abandonment of her maternal functioning and of responsiveness to the children's need for mothering; her murder of the father and her future begetting of more favored children with the stepfather.

To these, of course, must be added the intensification of conflicts that have to do with comparisons and competition with the mother as a sexual person or as a mother. Electra, as do many stepchildren, faces these comparisons and competitions with a sense of inner damage, shame, and neediness that has resulted from the very betrayal of her mother-rival. Electra sees her mother, governed, in her view, by unbridled and ruthless lust, go from her rightful sexual partner, Agamemnon, to Aegisthus, oblivious of the consequences of this to the family. She faces normal primal scene conflicts and oedipal conflicts with the added and powerful dimension that the anxiety, shame, rage and, later, guilt are not offset by the fact that this sexual union takes place between two loving parents who are loving and beloved by the children of their union. The stepfather qua seducer of mother and murderer of father is not merely a set of dramaturgic circumstances common to Sophocles' *Electra* and Shakespeare's *Hamlet*. That fantasy resonates with the virtually ubiquitous unconscious (or conscious) anxiety of stepchildren regarding stepfathers and ignites and escalates already existing anxiety having to do with the primal scene. The sense of having value as an important and beloved product of the parents' sexual union becomes eroded as do other sustaining fantasies about the child's own origins. These conflicts escalate to the point at which an unmanageable amount of anticipatory anxiety, depression, guilt, and especially shame are generated.

Electra also competes with her mother as the mother of Orestes. During the period of time that Electra is deceived about Orestes' death, in the fourth episode, the disguised Orestes lets her mourn for the urn which presumably contains his ashes. She laments:

Alas for my nursing of old days,
so constant—all for nothing—which I gave you;
my joy was in the trouble of it. For never
were you your mother's love as much as mine.
None was your nurse but I within that household.
[Lines 1144–1148]

Electra, though competitive with her mother as mothering person, is nonetheless made ashamed of her need for her mother, by the absence of her father, by the loss of her status, by the exposure of her vulnerabilities and helplessness, by her unmarried and unmarriageable status, and by her uncontrollable verbal attacks on her mother. She has developed an unremitting view of herself as damaged, disempowered, rageful, uncontrolled, and destined never to have a sexual partner or children. This shameful view of herself inflames and escalates when the awareness of her stepfather and his sexual union with her mother come to consciousness. This happens most dramatically in the play in the second episode, the only one between mother and daughter. After a calm and effective rebuttal of Clytemnestra's justifications for murdering Agamemnon (lines 558–553), Electra bursts into a rage about Clytemnestra's relationship with Aegisthus.

No. Think if the whole is not a mere excuse.
Please tell me for what cause you now commit
the ugliest of acts—in sleeping with him,
the murderer with whom you first conspired
to kill my father, and breed children to him, and
your former honorable children born
of honorable wedlock you drive out.
What grounds for praise shall I find in this? Will you say
that this, too, is retribution for your daughter?
If you say it, still your act is scandalous.
It isn't decent to marry with your enemies
even for a daughter's sake.
[Lines 583–600]

The outburst itself fills her with more shame after her mother's reproach.

Clytemnestra
What need have I of thought in her regard
who so insults her mother, when a grown woman?
Don't you think she will go to any length, so shameless
as she is?

Electra
You may be sure I am ashamed,
although you do not think it. I know why
I act so wrongly, so unlike myself.
The hate you feel for me and what you do
compel me against my will to act as I do.
For ugly deeds are taught by ugly deeds.
[Lines 612–621]

So the cycle continues: Electra's need for her mother as maternal gives rise to shame as does her self-conscious comparison with her mother as a sexual woman. These sources generate shame, the awareness of which is also humiliating. The shame is bypassed and turns into rage (Lewis, 1971), loss of control in verbal attack, and consequent guilt and more shame. The net result is a feeling of shameful, disenfranchised, anxious, angry confusion, and volatility. The safest compromise formations are her idealized attachments to men: her father in the form of pathological mourning and her brother in the anticipation of future revenge, together with a savage and provocative hatred of her stepfather. But these very compromise formations voiced publicly and defiantly are experienced as hostile and shaming by Clytemnestra and Aegisthus who are thus provoked to more anxiety and hostility and the escalation continues. Electra's status as a loving and beloved child of her mother is even further eroded by these escalating cycles of shame to rage to provocation to guilt and fear and uncertainty of the bond to her mother.

In the play, and in the unconscious fantasy of countless stepchildren, these conflicts escalate to the point of complete isolation, even in the presence of the love of her sister and the chorus. Sophocles has rendered this escalation brilliantly by the movement of the play. The first stasimon shows Electra in caring connection with the chorus. In the first episode, she combatively prevails over her somewhat loving and still-loved sister, who agrees not to take Clytemnestra's offering to her father's grave. Hostilities explode in the second episode with escalating anger between mother and daughter being interrupted by the tutor's arrival and announcement of Orestes' death. Electra is now cut off from her mother, her stepfather, and her brother. In the third episode, endeavoring to convince her sister to conspire to kill Clytemnestra and Aegisthus, she reaches a stage of complete isolation.

This isolation appears superficially to have been broken when Orestes reveals himself to her and the pair accomplish their act of revenge, but Sophocles develops the last part of the play in such a way that Electra's isolation continues. It is Orestes who acts. He kills Clytemnestra inside the palace with vituperative cries from Electra onstage. She has been sent as a sentry to watch for Aegisthus. There is an empty quality to the revenge for Electra. Orestes has taken revenge and has throne, lands, and family restored to him. He is a man of action. It is on this basis that some have questioned whether or not the play should be called a tragedy, but it is a tragedy indeed. We are left with an empty, hollow, unsatisfied sense that, for Electra, the act of revenge does not solve a problem in the way that it does for Orestes. He has never had an emotional bond with Clytemnestra or Aegisthus in the intimate way that Electra has. He has gotten back the throne, his lands and restoration of the loving bond with the one family member to whom he was really close, Electra. She, on the other hand, has become a person so consumed with a sense of shame and damage, bitterness and vengefulness, that she does not even participate in the act of vengeance (Kitto, 1961). She is on the sidelines crying out vengefully. When Clytemnestra within the palace is struck by Orestes, Electra cries out, "If you have strength—again!" (line 1417). Later, when Aegisthus is surprised by Orestes, he pleads for a chance to speak, but Electra cries out vengefully.

Aegisthus
This is my end then. Let me say one word.

Electra
Not one, not one word more,
I beg you, brother. Do not draw out the talking.
When men are in the middle of trouble, when one
is on the point of death, how can time matter?
Kill him as quickly as you can. And killing
throw him out to find such burial as suits him
out of our sights. This is the only thing
that can bring me redemption from
all my past sufferings.
[Lines 1483–1490]

The killings of Clytemnestra and Aegisthus do not resolve her difficulties. She remains filled with a sense of inner damage, unworthiness, and shame. This is her tragedy.

I believe that it is for this reason that Sophocles downplayed the role of the Furies (Erinyes) in his version of the Electra story. The Furies represent guilt. Aeschylus, the consummate poet of guilt, gives great prominence to the struggle of matricidal Orestes with the avenging Furies. Orestes has performed matricide. This is a destructive *action* and destructive actions, however justified they may be, give rise to guilt. Electra's tragedy is not a tragedy of action or of guilt. It is a tragedy of inner destruction by the sense of being damaged, vengeful, and ashamed. Deprived of both her father and her mother when she needs them, she is also deprived of an identity as a sexual woman. Whereas the act of matricide is restorative (albeit guilt-producing), for Orestes, it is a vengeful verbal outburst, not an actual act, for Electra. Nor do the actual murders of Clytemnestra and Aegisthus solve a problem for Electra in the way that they do for Orestes. She remains damaged, vengeful, and ashamed. Sophocles, downplaying the role of the Furies, evidences neither Homeric offhandedness nor implicit condonement of matricide. His dramaturgy evidences his deep understanding of his heroine's overarching sense of permanent damage and shame. To emphasize the Erinyes would be to miss the point. Guilt and the Furies pertain to the child and stepchild who comes from afar to commit an action that gives rise to the guilt—not the child or stepchild who remained at home, who rages verbally rather than acts, and who remains filled with shame.

VII

I return briefly and speculatively to two issues raised earlier—the question of the paucity of representations of the stepchild–stepfather predicament in Western literature and of the question of Jesus as stepchild. I believe that both of these issues have to do with the intensity of shame conflicts over primal scene anxieties and the erosion of fantasies concerning the child's special origin in the parents' sexual union that are evoked by the child's perception of the intrusion of the stepfather.

As Sophocles' *Electra* and Shakespeare's *Hamlet* so brilliantly illustrate, the stepfather's presence to the dependent child living in the home signifies not only betrayal and abandonment by the mother at a time of intense dependency and need, they also provide a fantasy of real attribution of the cause of that betrayal and abandonment to the mother's destructive lust and the stepfather's seductiveness. Whereas in optimal development, fantasies about the mother's sexuality and the primal scene are offset by the child's feelings of specialness and being loved by both parents in the sexual pairing, in the stepfather situation, anxieties about the couple's sexuality escalates as does the dramatic sense of shame experienced by the child feeling denied the sense of specialness and feeling excluded from the sexual doings of his or her parents. The child's fantasied elaborations concerning the stepfather's impact show up in the specific circumstances of both Sophocles' *Electra* and Shakespeare's *Hamlet*, that the father was killed by the sexual couple (and so the child is in danger of being disposed of also); that the mother betrayed and abandoned her mothering functions for the child; that the child has no more special status with the new couple and might be replaced by children of that union. (For a discussion of the significance of the primal scene in *Hamlet*, see Cavell, 1987.) That the actual response to the child is also colored by the couple's fear, shame, and anger at the child's attacks of humiliated fury or reproachful idealization of the father makes the topic so overpowering and the conflicts so interrelated that perhaps only a Sophocles or a Shakespeare could really manage them in all their complexity and intensity.

Perhaps consideration of the same type of conflict portrayed with a much different resolution is conveyed in the story of Jesus. He is not the product of a sexual union. The conception of Jesus is an intimate part of the power of the story. Primal scene anxiety is not aroused because there has been no maternal intercourse. The father is idealized but remains a presence. The stepfather Joseph is a nonsexual consort, not a persecutory sexual partner. Primal scene anxiety is absent because there is no primal scene. The Savior is not a product of a sexual union, and the stepfather's role is not a sexual one and not one opposed to the father or to the status to the child. The stepfather has not replaced the father, the father is not experienced as abandoning or murdered, and the stepfather has not replaced/murdered the father. Anxiety is not high and a split paternal imago is not required to preserve the image of one good parent.

VIII

I have tried to demonstrate that a close reading of Sophocles' *Electra* reveals many of the deep anxieties of the stepchild about the presence of the stepfather. Despite the surface prominence of intense attachment to the absent or dead father and the resentment of the stepfather, the dominant conflicts are those with the mother and especially the mother, seen as betraying and abandoning her children, disposing of or killing the father, and preferring sexual union with the stepfather to the security and satisfaction of her children. Since these basic anxieties about the mother and her sexuality are not offset by feeling lovingly toward and loved by the marital couple, anxieties and shame–rage cycles escalate to the point of a chronic inner state of depressed and shameful helplessness. Sophocles' masterpiece illustrates these issues brilliantly and the tragic resolution of the play points strongly to shame and the sense of inner damage rather than guilt over destruction as the true source of the stepchild's tragedy.

References

Bernstein, D. (1993), *Female Identity Conflict in Clinical Practice*. Northvale, NJ: Aronson.

Cairns, D. L. (1993), *Aidos*. Oxford, England: Clarendon Press.

Cavell, S. (1987), Hamlet's burden of proof. In: *Disowning Knowledge in Six Plays of Shakespeare*. Cambridge, England: Cambridge University Press, pp. 179–191.

Dale, A. M. (1969), The *Electra* of Sophocles. *Collected Papers*. Cambridge, England: Cambridge University Press, pp. 221–229.

Graves, R. (1955), *The Greek Myths*. Baltimore, MD: Penguin.

Freud, S. (1931), Female sexuality. *Standard Edition*, 21:223–243. London: Hogarth Press, 1961.

Kells, J. H., ed. (1973), *Sophocles' Electra*. Cambridge, England: Cambridge University Press, pp. 1–19.

Kirkwood, G. M. (1942), Structural features of Sophocles' *Electra*. *Trans. Amer. Philol. Assn.*, 73:86–95.

Kitto, H. D. F. (1961), *Greek Tragedy*, 3rd ed. London: Routledge.

Lewis, H. B. (1971), *Shame and Guilt in Neurosis*. New York: International Universities Press.

Linforth, I. M. (1963), Electra's day in the tragedies of Sophocles. *Univ. Calif. Publ. Classic. Philol.*, 19:89–126.

Sheppard, J. T. (1918), The tragedy of Electra according to Sophocles. *Classics Quart.*, 49:80–88.

_____ (1927a), Electra: A defense of Sophocles. *Classic. Rev.*, 41:2–9.

_____ (1927b), Electra again. *Classic. Rev.*, 41:163–165.

Simon, B. (1988), *Tragic Drama and the Family*. New Haven, CT: Yale University Press.

Sophocles. *Electra*, trans. D. Grene. *The Complete Greek Tragedies*, Vol. IV. New York: Modern Library, 1957.

Stevens, P. T. (1978), Sophocles' *Electra*: Doom or triumph. *Greece and Rome*, 25:111–120.

Winnington-Ingram, R. P. (1954), The *Electra* of Sophocles: Prolegomena to an interpretation. *Proc. Cambridge Philol. Soc.*, 83:20–27.

Woodward, T. M. (1964), *Electra* by Sophocles: The dialectical design. *Harvard Stud. Classic. Philol.*, 68:163–205.

_____ (1965), *Electra* by Sophocles: The dialectical design (Part II). *Harvard Stud. Classic. Philol.*, 70:195–233.

Forensic Issues

Legal Rights of Stepparents

A Concept in Development

Moisy Shopper

Traditionally the stepparent in the courtroom has fared little better than the stepparent in the fairy tale ("Hansel and Gretel," "Cinderella"). Both have been stereotyped and regarded in the most negative of terms and variously considered to be legally nonexistent, that is, they have no standing in court.[1] It is the aim of this chapter to clarify the legal assumptions and sources that created this nadir of legal rights for the stepparent. With persistent legal and psychological challenges to these antiquated but tradition-entrenched legal doctrines, there has been a slow but significant evolution of stepparent rights. Since family law issues are for the most part left to each state's legislature to develop, state laws and case material will vary from jurisdiction to jurisdiction. While each legislature and court system has the autonomy to pass and interpret its own unique laws, legislators and judges are aware of and often influenced by events in other states. Nevertheless, there may be vast differences, even in adjacent states. With the demise of the traditional nuclear family, that is, one parent married to another parent of the opposite sex for their first and only marriage, all states are confronted with issues of children in divorced, remarried, and often divorced-again families. Whether a state recognizes same-sex marriage as a legal entity, these same-sex (as well as opposite sex) marriages occur without legal recognition, such as in the common-law marriage. In addition, federal and constitutional issues have affected all 50 states. With the recognition that our highly mobile population moves from state to state, the creation of some measure of nationwide uniformity and coherence in matters concerning children would be an advantage.[2] Many mental health professionals having little knowledge of family law, and fearful of gaining any, would prefer to avoid the legal involvements and intrusions that threaten the confidentiality of ongoing therapy and often encourage the therapist to become an advocate for one side of an acrimonious family dispute. Accordingly, I assume the reader to

---

[1] "Standing" is a legal term referring to the right to prosecute or to state a claim.

[2] In 1994, a new Uniform Adoption Act was overwhelmingly approved for transmission to the legislatures of the 50 states by the National Conference of Commissioners of Uniform State Laws. The stated goal of the Act is the maintenance of a child's ties to those "who are committed to, and capable of, parenting them" (from the Uniform Adoption Act, Prefatory Note, at 3).

have a somewhat negative preconception of legal involvement. It is hoped that it will be counterbalanced by a desire to increase one's knowledge so as to make reasonably informed judgments on highly emotional issues which have long-term ramifications for everyone: children, parents, and stepparents.

The Traditional View

The "parental rights doctrine" is a basic assumption of law. It states that in custody disputes between a child's biological parents and all others (including those who might be considered the "psychological parent"), the child's best interest lies in being raised by a "fit" biological parent. Furthermore, there is an implicit assumption that "fitness" exists in the biological parent; therefore, it does not have to be proven to the court. The burden of proof is on those who question the biological parent's fitness. At the other end of the legal continuum is the more recent concept of the "psychological parent" carefully enunciated by the psychoanalysts, Goldstein, Anna Freud, and Solnit (1973). The psychological parent is one who may be either a biological parent or an adoptive, step, foster, or common-law parent, who cares for the child on a day-to-day basis, over time, and so fulfills the child's need for emotional and physical nurturing. This person is considered by the child to fulfill the role of the parent and is considered by the child to be his or her parent. The subtleties and realities of the psychological parent's *legal* status may not be apparent nor considered by the child. What is considered is the reality, that this is a person who has "actually acted as a parent, who has assumed the responsibilities of a parent, who has formed a parent–child relationship with the child—and whom the child perceives and relates to as a parent" (Lowe, 1996, pp. 379–425). From a strictly legal standpoint this concept can be faulted since its roots are in social science rather than law, and it lacks obvious, legally measurable landmarks. In addition, expert testimony may often be required to ascertain whether a certain individual claiming to have "psychological parent" status, is indeed such a parent. The most controversial aspect is that it deliberately brushes aside the common-law traditional landmarks of biological kinship (blood ties) and legal kinship (marriage). To their credit, many legislators and judges have struggled to bring the law's traditional, accumulated precedents into harmony with the changing shapes of the American family and with the many nonlegal sources of established knowledge, including psychoanalysis and child development.

The following case illustrates an "extreme" form of a family unit, "extreme" in the sense of nonrecognition by civil law, the legal problems entailed in achieving unanimity of definition of a "parent," the supremacy of biological ties, and finally the need for parental autonomy outbalancing the need for considering the "best interest of the child."

Case Example. A lesbian couple shared a home and all expenses. They decided on parenthood and arranged for the artificial insemination of one of the women. When the child was two years and four months of age the couple "divorced" with the biological mother retaining custody of the child. Visitation with the noncustodial parent continued for the next three years. Then the biological mother bought out her former partner's share of the house, restricted visitation, and finally forbade all contact between the child and the former partner. The latter then sued for renewed visitation.

The majority opinion held that under the existing law the former partner did not qualify under the term "parent" and therefore had no standing. The biological mother, being fit, had the right to determine with whom her child associated, since to do otherwise would interfere with the parent's right to custody and control. The former partner had claimed that she was a "de facto" parent and should be viewed as such "by estoppel." The dissenting opinion noted that the majority's hard-line interpretation of the term "parent" would quickly exclude all others who were not in a biological or legal relationship with the child: stepparents, common-law relationships, and so forth. The dissenting judge also noted that the majority opinion prevents the court from even considering the "best interest of the child" and does damage to the maintenance of bonds already established with the noncustodial parent (Weisberg and Appleton, 1991). Whether a lesbian parent, stepparent, or grandparent[3] wishes visitation, the legal issues are identical: not being the biological parent, does one have "standing" in court as a "psychological parent", or to put it differently, does the child have the right to maintain the psychological parent–child relationship and does that adult have corresponding rights?

The Limits of Biological Kinship

When legally convenient, biological kinship has been ignored by the law, since to do otherwise would muddy kinship and inheritance issues beyond recognition. It is a legal assumption that a child born to a legally married couple is the child of that marriage, that is, the husband is assumed to be the biological and genetic father of that child. In some instances, not only is this not the case, but it is known by both husband and wife, often the husband knowing before delivery. In other couples this constitutes the mother's marital secret, coming to light only under duress or when parents are being typed for an organ donation for their child, or as part of a genetic

---

[3]All states now permit grandparents to petition for visitation.

counseling investigation. While the law is pleased with its "child of the marriage" criterion, in actuality in the above-mentioned situations, we have an actual stepparent who, without the formality of an adoption and without the recognition or acknowledgment of his nonbiological status, nevertheless is considered the legal parent. In other instances where it is acknowledged that the husband is not the father of the child (as with artificial insemination by unknown donor sperm), many attorneys advise the father to formally adopt the child to codify and clarify everyone's legal status.

The phrase "child of the marriage" is commonly used by state legislatures in wording state laws concerning divorce, custody, and visitation. Until recently such wording was taken literally so that a stepparent had no standing in a divorce and custody hearing since the relevant laws applied only to the "children of the marriage." This meant that the stepparent was not an interested (a term to be taken in its legal sense) party and therefore had no standing in court to bring claim for custody or visitation. Many states have changed their legislative phraseology to avoid this unintended consequence.

The problem with the Parental Rights Assumption is that it places greater emphasis on the biological connections than on the actual physical and psychological ones, often to the detriment of the young child. For example, until 1972 when the U.S. Supreme Court ruled otherwise, the parental rights doctrine was used to remove children placed with adopting parents when the biological father, whose consent for the adoption was not sought, now wished to state his claim to his biological child, regardless of the time the child has spent in the adoptive home and regardless of the psychological parent–child relationship that had been established. In 1972, the U.S. Supreme Court ruled in *Stanley*[4] that not all biological fathers are equal. There are those who manifest "parenting behavior" by involvement in the woman's pregnancy, delivery, and neonatal period. The Court reasoned that since he acknowledges the child to be his, is concerned and involved with the child, and is willing to assume some measure of responsibility for the child, the biological father can assert a claim that he has the right to consent or withhold consent for adoption. Other biological fathers who give no such indication, forfeit the right to veto a proposed adoption. The Court made clear in *Lehr*[5] that the "mere existence of a biological link" between the unwed father and his child does not entitle him to constitutional protection of his property right to his child. The "rights of the parents are a counterpart of the responsibilities they have assumed."

---

[4]*Stanley v. Illinois*, 405 U.S. 645,651 (1972).
[5]*Lehr v. Robertson*, 463 U.S. 248 (1983).

The parental rights doctrine furnishes the legal underpinning for those laws and practices involved in "family preservation." In the past, when a social agency was confronted with a dysfunctional family (severe alcohol and drug use and child sexual and physical abuse and neglect), these vulnerable and traumatized children were often placed with foster families, many of whom were eager to adopt the child. Such adoption, even when subsidized by the state, would still be economically advantageous to the state, to say nothing about the psychological benefit to the child. With the current emphasis on family preservation, the social agencies are obligated to make a "reasonable effort" at family reunification. In effect this means the expenditure of considerable time and money attempting to rehabilitate the family unit. In the meantime the time clock ticks, the child grows older, and languishes in the limbo of perpetual foster care while the attorneys and court argue how the term "reasonable efforts" should be defined and whether social service has lived up to its legal mandate. I have seen several years elapse before social services could convince the court that their staff has done everything they could, offered all the services available, offered the parent(s) many opportunities and second chances and now they could document everything for the court in their quest for a termination of parental rights. I have been appalled by the inevitability of failure of social services, since they did not or could not utilize experts to assess if the court's limited resources and superficial behavioral therapeutic techniques and "contracts" with the parent(s) could indeed accomplish the job of family reunification. While the social agency's pressure produced snippets of adequate behavior, renewed promises and "contracts" for more adequate parenting, in fact, over time the parent proves to be incapable of sustained adequate parenting. In order to overcome the traditional legal view that a mother's blood ties, and property rights of the biological father to a child are almost a constitutional guarantee, the agency's documentation must be extensive and conclusive. Only then will extremely reluctant judges order a termination of parental rights, particularly so since there is a certain finality to the order and it goes counter to our cherished ideal of innate mother–child love (Williams, 1996). However, the termination of parental rights does free the child for adoption and for the possibility of a stable loving family.

The court is not the only obstacle to adoption. At times, it is the biological parent. Even though the biological parent may do little financially or emotionally for the child, and may not even care about the child, it is still a major emotional hurdle for that parent to consent to a termination of parental rights (in other words, forever) and thus free the child to be adopted by others. For the biological parent intrapsychically, the consent may represent a massive loss for the biological parent. Loss in these parents may have special conscious and unconscious meanings for the parent and may not be well tolerated. In addition, motives of malice, hatred, control, and power against the former spouse or against the stepparent, may determine the biological parent's refusal. In a sense, it is the classic case of whether the parent will do what is best for the child out of love for the child even though it may not be best for the parent.[6] Often this is too much to ask of a parent for whom the biological tie to the child may be all they can give to or take from of the child emotionally. As a result of the biological parent's refusal to terminate voluntarily their parental rights, the stepparent is rendered legally helpless. The child(ren) are in an extremely vulnerable position since their relationship with the stepparent is without legal protection or recognition. In case of the spouse's death, the stepparent may not even be allowed visitation, much less legal custody.

Case Example. When the two boys were ages one and a half and three years, their mother divorced their alcoholic abusive father. Within two years she married an educated artistic furniture executive and settled in the more avant garde neighborhood of a large city where her boys attended a large suburban school. The biological father sought assistance from his evangelical fundamentalist church and from A.A., married an ex-alcoholic, and settled in a small rural community. Although the distance between the father's residence and mother's residence was only a one-hour drive, the educational, social, religious, and cultural distances between them were huge. The biological father did not visit or otherwise communicate with his sons. He, his wife, and his new children attended church several times a week and lived their lives within the confines of their small rural community.

The stepfather was referred to as "father" or "dad" and was the only father they knew. When the two boys were 11 and 12½ years of age, their mother developed cancer and died within six months. The biological father's attorney obtained a writ of *habeus corpus* (i.e., to produce the children in court) and the children walked out of court with their biological father and stepmother. The writ took precedence over any motion filed by the stepfather's attorney for the stepfather to have custody or visitation. The parental rights doctrine prevailed and the stepfather had at that time (1982) no standing in court. Fortunately, the maternal grandmother was given visitation rights and the stepfather piggy-backed his visitation on hers. The psychological trauma to the children of the multiple losses, that

---

[6]This is the classic legend of King Solomon who, when confronted by two women, each claiming to be the mother of a child, ordered that the child be cut in half. The real mother of the child renounced her parental claim out of love for the child and so saved her child. This test of love was determinative to King Solomon in pronouncing his judgment.

is, of mother's death, loss of stepfather, their home, and the entire school and community of friends, was unrecognized and unaddressed by the court.

Often, the stepparent cannot adopt the child to become the legally recognized parent. Yet from the child's perception, the stepparent, over time, functions as the parent and becomes the child's "psychological parent." Some legal scholars have found a legal theory that serves to give recognition to the psychological parent by invoking an already existent legal concept, namely, *in loco parentis.*

Child Support and Stepparents and *In Loco Parentis*

Common law recognizes an obligation of the parents to support their children, namely, that by begetting them they incur a voluntary obligation to support them (Blackstone commentaries, paragraph 447). Traditionally this referred to the father. With more women in the workforce outside the home, support obligations have become gender neutral.[7] A stepparent gains recognition by the concept of *in loco parentis,* in that the stepparent "stands in place" of the parent and assumes voluntarily financial and other parental obligations. Since the status of *in loco parentis* is voluntary and can be terminated unilaterally at any time, the child cannot enforce support obligations. As a result, the stepchild's future financial security is open to the whims of the stepparent and is totally unprotected by law.

The Obligations of the Stepparent

The common-law tradition is that the stepparent is under no obligation to support the stepchildren either during the marriage or after its dissolution. However, several states have imposed a financial responsibility on the stepparent once the child has been received into the family. Some states rely on the concept of *in loco parentis* where the stepparent simply does that which a parent would do for the child. Once the "in loco" changes through a divorce, the stepparent is relieved of all responsibilities. Whether the stepparent's financial status should be taken into account in determining the biological parent's postdivorce level of financial support, is an open legal question and therefore is settled on a case-by-case basis.

---

[7]Orr v. Orr, 440 U.S. 268, 278–283 (1979) ruled that husbands-only alimony obligations violate the equal protection clause of the U.S. Constitution.

There are some subcultures that view parenting as a community responsibility. This has been documented by an anthropologist, Carol Stack (1974), who found that "child-keeping" by relatives and friends created parental bonds, rights, and obligations recognized by the community. They may be coterminous with the rights of the biological mother or she may even by excluded. Under certain social conditions communal child rearing may be adaptive for the child since the community intentionally creates multiple parental figures. The loss of one or more of these is not the disaster it would be in the nuclear family. However, recognition by the community is neither recognized nor respected legally in a system that does not recognize the existence of shared parental responsibility and cooperative childrearing.

The concept of *in loco parentis* has served some jurisdictions as a legal basis for awarding visitation between a stepparent and the child, without specifically relying on the "best interest of the child" concept. The latter is often regarded by the law as a nebulous concept since a variety of factors and circumstances need to be evaluated and factored into the final result. Nevertheless, it may be that the trial judge, influenced by "best interest" considerations, stretches the *in loco parentis* doctrine to give the stepparent standing in court. Having achieved standing, the stepparent is treated as a parent and then the case can be heard on its merits.

About one half of the states now have provisions for granting custody to third parties, that is, other than the biological parents. Almost all, however, have a presumption that the biological parents should receive priority. To gain custody, third parties have to prove that the biological parent is "unfit." This too is a nebulous term, open to many interpretations not the least of which is the reigning moral standards of the judge and the community. Proving "unfitness" is an uphill battle, requiring ample legal access and funding, and whatever the outcome, liable to increase the acrimony between the competing parties.

The Challenge of the Concept: The Psychological Parent

Obviously, the earlier in the child's development the stepparent enters the child's life, all things being equal, the stronger will be the psychological bonds between them. There are many other factors that can either weaken or strengthen the child–stepparent bonds. The biological parents, the stepparent, and the child all contribute variables that will influence the strength of these bonds. Such bonds tend to endure even after the stepparent and biological parent dissolve their legal bonds. However, the *in loco parentis* status ends with the legal termination of that marriage. As a result, there is no legal recognition or standing for the enduring relationship between the child(ren) and the stepparent.

The Least Detrimental Alternative and Its Rebuttal

The Family Law Section of the American Bar Association (August 1991) has proposed a model act that takes a two-tiered approach to the issue of postdivorce visitation, namely, whether the stepparent is to have standing in court and whether visitation is in the child's best interest. The stepparent will have standing if he has acted *in loco parentis*. The "best interest of the child" factor must be supported by a "clear and convincing" standard of proof, one somewhat higher than the usual "preponderance of evidence" standard. Similarly awarding custody to the stepparent rather than to the biological parent would require a finding of "unfit" for the latter and a "clear and convincing" standard of evidence indicating that the child's best interest resides with the stepparent.

These legal considerations approach the concepts promulgated by Goldstein, Freud, and Solnit. Let me briefly review the major paradigm advocated by *Beyond the Best Interests of the Child*. The authors argue that child custody decisions should have as their paramount interest the psychological well-being of the child. The law must ensure that the child will be a part of a family that will provide material and emotional nurturance and growth. An important factor is the child's need for the continuity of relationships. Goldstein et al. take the child's perspective that ignores the legal and biological relationship, in preference to the person who provides day-to-day hands-on care as the "psychological parent." They assume that ruptures in the continuity of relationship between the child and the psychological parent are detrimental. Decisions regarding children should take into account the child's sense of time which is vastly different from the court's sense of time. Further, it is their belief that the law is unable to control or supervise interpersonal relationships, is poor at long-range prediction in those relationships, and contend that the law can do little more than acknowledge and affirm a relationship or disrupt it. Accordingly, their standard is not the "best interest of the child," but the "least detrimental alternative."

While these guidelines seem clear-cut, in actuality, there may be conflicts between the guidelines as pointed out in Batt's discussion of *Painter v. Bannister*.[8] When the mother and daughter were killed in an auto accident, Painter, the father, was too distraught to keep his five-year-old son, who was sent to live with his maternal grandparents and with whom

---

[8]Not only does Batt come to a different opinion in the case , but he offers a point-by-point critique of Goldstein, Freud, and Solnit's least detrimental alternative and suggests that there are alternative psychoanalytic theories (Erikson, Lifton, Bateson, Kohut, etc.) which are "less reductionistic, closed and negativist" than "classical orthodox psychoanalysis" advanced by A. Freud (p. 674).

he made an attachment so close that they became his psychological parents. Two years later the father remarried and wished to have his son live with him. The Iowa Supreme Court held that the continuity of the son's relationship with his grandparents should not be disrupted. The court was influenced by expert opinion utilizing concepts from Goldstein, Freud, and Solnit. However, as Batt points out, the expert and the court did not address the child's five-year history of attachment to the father and the disruption of that relationship. Batt offers another paradigm, namely placement with the person who is most emphatically attuned to the child's developmental phase needs. "In particular cases, it might be appropriate to modify the custody decree as the child moves from one stage to another stage . . . courts should not hesitate to change custody, at any time, if a shift would maximize the best interests position of the child" (p. 685). While purporting to be sensitive to the child's shifting and changing developmental needs, I believe Batt is almost totally insensitive to issues of continuity of care, the disruptive effect of geographic moves, the disruptive effect of changes in caretakers, to say little of the more complex issues of the transference of the affects, expectations, and attachments from a past relationship to a current one.

There are many parents who, when divorced from the child(ren)'s stepparent, would prefer that no visitation take place between the stepparent and the child(ren), even if (and in some cases *especially* if) there is a clearly discernable relationship and bond between the two. The stepparent may even have become a "psychological parent" during the time of the marriage. The stepparent may wish to assert visitation rights even over the former spouse's objection. It may be argued, as Abraham (1997) does, that to force a custodial parent to have visitation with the stepparent "not only appears to be detrimental to the best interest of the child, but also an unconstitutional violation of family privacy rights" (p. 125). The child is placed in a loyalty conflict and may readily become the pawn in the continuing postdivorce fighting and conflict. A stepparent has the potential to interfere continuously in the relationship between the child and parent. Abraham seeks support from several U.S. Supreme Court opinions holding that "the right to raise one's children is a fundamental liberty interest protected by the Fourteenth Amendment to the Constitution." Since a single parent with child(ren) is considered a family, and thus entitled to family privacy and autonomy, and if the parent is the best guardian of the child's best interests, stepparent visitation ordered over the parent's objection, is deemed both legally and psychologically unwise and runs counter to the best interest of the child. Abraham believes the best interest of the child would be served if there was an enduring and close bond between the child and the stepparent that should not be disrupted and that the stepparent continue to stand *in loco parentis* by offering continued financial support to the child.

In view of the possible harm to the child resulting from forced stepparent visitation, Abraham suggests that an examination of the "integrity" of the stepparent's willingness to financially support the child would serve to dissuade a frivolous or malicious request for visitation. Further she suggests that the stepparent should have stood in loco parentis during the marriage. This would not only solidify the stepparent's standing to petition for visitation, but would also carry legal impact since the stepparent prior to the divorce assumed the responsibilities of parenthood. With the postdivorce assumption of financial responsibilities, the stepparent was entitled to the benefits, that is, visitation. Abraham recognizes the need for the child to have a continuing relationship with a stepparent, postdivorce, but alerts us to the need to have statutory safeguards to prevent stepparents from "improperly interfering with the lives of their former spouses and stepchildren" (p. 131).

Summary

At the time of the dissolution of a marriage the courts and legislatures need to recognize the stepparent who has been in loco parentis as having standing to be a party to custody and visitation disputes. While some stepparent petitions for custody/visitation may be maliciously motivated with intent to harass, the case should be heard on its merits notwithstanding the parental rights doctrine and constitutionally protected rights to family autonomy and privacy. In some circumstances continued financial support by the stepparent may be ordered, not as a test of integrity of the stepparent's intentions but as an additional way of cementing the child–stepparent relationship as well as the stepparent continuing in loco parentis. As case law and legislatures address these issues and courts wrestle with the conflicting values, I predict the legal situation of the stepparent will continue to improve, state by state, decision by decision. However, the legal situation of the stepparent when the spouse dies is very tenuous. The surviving biological parent can readily assert his or her right to the child and in some instances may prevail to prevent the stepparent form having visitation. These instances highlight the need for the courts to consider the child's welfare their primary concern, that is, over that of the parents be they, step or biological. Many courts are willing to do this but may be constrained by the wording of current statues, existing case law, and the traditional baggage of legal presumptions and the common law from which they have evolved.

References

Abraham, D. L. (1997), *California's Stepparent Visitation Statute: For the Welfare of the Child, or a Court-Opened Door to Legally Interfere with Parental*

Autonomy: Where Are the Constitutional Safeguards? 7 S. Cal. Rev. L. &
Women's Stud., 125.
Blackstone, W. (1902), *Commentaries on the Laws of England*, ed. W. D. Lewis.
Philadelphia, PA: Rees Welsh, Book 1, Chapter 16, p. 447.
Goldstein, J., Freud, A. & Solnit, A. J. (1973), *Beyond the Best Interests of the Child.*
New York: Free Press.
Lowe, A. D. (1996), Parents and strangers: The Uniform Adoption Act revisits the
Parental Rights Doctrine. *Fam. Law Quart.*, 30:379–425.
Stack, C. (1974), *All Our Kin: Strategies for Survival in a Black Community.* New
York: Harper & Row.
Weisberg, D. K. & Appleton, S. F. (1991), *Modern Family Law: Alison D.* New
York: Aspen Law and Business Publishers.
Williams, C. C. (1996), *Juvenile Proceeding, Parental Rights: Provide Guidance for*
Reunification or Termination of Parental Rights. 13 GA. St. U.L. Rev., 91,
November.

Some Forensic, Financial, and Transference Considerations

A Stepdaughter as "Family Brick"

Stanley H. Cath

Geriatric clinicians often encounter multiple levels of incompetence with fluctuating states of lucidity in their older patients. With the impending or actual death of one member of "reconstituted" couples, conflicting interests among heirs may lead to very differing lay opinions as to testamentary competency of the parent with complex legal and financial sequellae. In this highly charged atmosphere, all forms of transference run rampant. In John Grisham's novel *Testament* (1999), Troy, a multibillionaire, from a suicide's grave uses his final "willpower" to exact revenge on his widows and despised heirs of his three legitimate marriages. Troy shocks all of them when he leaves the bulk of his estate to his unknown, illegitimate daughter, the child of a secret liaison from his past, working as a missionary in the remote jungles of South America. His duplicity in enriching someone who does not want his money succeeds in further driving wedges of confused hate into his families and their multiple attorneys.

I have heard many similar but less dramatic accounts depicting the sardonic, comic-tragedies of adult children, stepchildren, and caretakers who struggle to influence the distribution or redistribution of money during their elders' final years. Envy and greed are readily projected onto outsiders, adopted or stepchildren. These highly charged decisions may reflect the darker issues of late life, intergenerational responsibilities such as an heir's obligations to make the sacrifices his long-lived parent may expect or require.

In modern times, caring for children and the aged has been delegated in varying measure to "hired hands" with indeterminate training and skills. Just under the surface of these late-life negotiations I have found many silent reflections such as, "Who and what was I to this powerful figure? What does he or she deserve? Did we really like each other? Of what value am I compared to the others? How much did I owe to him or to her? What are my legal rights?" And, most relevant to this study, "Whose responsibility is he (or she) anyway?"

Because so many elders are forced to turn to strangers for safe anchorage in their final storms, often children and stepchildren feel silently accused of not having loved the elder enough and may overreact by becoming inordinately solicitous. Should the elder give any indication of rewriting his will, especially to include nonrelated caretakers, universities, or charities, "a testamentary crisis" is almost inevitable. As in the Grisham novel, whenever an estate seems threatened or placed in legal limbo for an indeterminate time, family coherency is threatened. Inventories of worthiness, assumed relatedness, and old rivalries are likely reactivated. Accusations of irresponsibility fly back and forth along projective paths as everyone's behavior and motives are questioned. Consanguineous heirs confronted by newly discovered claims, by either alien beneficiaries or charitable organizations, understandably become territorial and litigious.

As a geriatric psychiatrist, I have learned that it is not unusual for elderly people to deeply attach themselves to "strangers" who nurse them and tend to their needs. My countertransference leans toward a rather sympathetic identification with the elder and the hired hand in the same way most psychiatrists have identified with the less able, the vulnerable infirm, and the very young. One stepson, taken aback by a new will, described his "repeated encounters with the law at extraordinary costs, especially because my stepbrother and I were absolutely certain my stepfather Paul had been taken in by his neighbor, imagine . . . to give everything to her!"

Paul's motive was clear. He needed to be touched or visited as an essential antidote to empty loneliness. In his words, "All I ask for is someone to knock on my door and listen to me grouse!"

While true gratitude may be a part of such a late-life, newfound friendship, more idealized images of each other are easily sustained, even in the face of family opposition, precisely because the new relationship lacks the transference residues of disappointed expectations. Indeed, the family side of the supportive relationship has been bitterly described by other ignored elders as, "one good friend is worth seven children!"

In training programs, I have often encountered "hired hands" with strong professional aspirations, pleading to be acknowledged by other staff or families as compassionate companions if not healing associates. Not surprisingly, they also expect to be appropriately rewarded. Are these fantasies much different than the motives of many therapists of whatever discipline or school of thought? The vignette below will illustrate the complexities of attachments among a middle-aged caretaker, an immigrant widow with grown children, and her elderly employer, his spouse, and biological and stepped children.

Mary had come into a stepfamily's life to care for Walter's third wife, Babs, at their home on the Cape. This arrangement had lasted for seven years before a nursing home for Babs became a necessity. Even before her confinement to an Alzheimer's unit, Babs had become combative and emotionally unavailable to her "old curmudgeon" husband. Shy socially, even if a bear at home, he had turned to Mary for basic attention and affection. The "blood offspring" lived in various places in the Midwest, and, until dementia took its toll, had had rare contact with their progenitors and their caretakers. A stepdaughter living in a nearby city had been my main contact.

Over the years the open closeness between Walter and Mary had become an anathema to both the biological and stepfamilies. Even though none of them had ever discussed the matter with Walter or the doctors involved, they all told me "mother knew something was going on." Secretly, I doubted this, and serendipitously I learned what was going on from one of the daughter's projections of guilt over neglecting her mother and father. In her own words, "I should have called more. That *girlfriend* had been hired to care for mother and could not possibly do her job well and care for father too. She surely made herself at home in *our* house."

The stepchildren and children had formed an "unholy alliance" to explore their legal rights. Fearing a new will might be in the works, they uncharacteristically formed a representative group and consulted an attorney to find out "if father was in his right mind." The family physician and the attorney agreed that "Walter seemed fine at the time of writing of his last will," so this channel was closed. In some family correspondence, it was learned some of the biological offspring had not wanted their overcontrolling mother in their homes because "she would disrupt our lives!" When they found they had no legal right to see Walter's will while Walter was alive, they openly accused Mary of being a gold-digger. It was never clear who was or was not mining gold, but in my view everyone was, each for unique reasons.

My advice to the family to proceed patiently and not rock the boat until we understood more allowed Mary to "stay on out of loyalty." She did not deny her affection for Walter, but protested that her care was divided equally. Every time I visited the home, Mary would cry at the unfairness of it all and cite her altruism by delineating how much of her income had been sent to Ireland where her mother and two grown sons still lived. While Mary may well have been expecting to be remembered in Walter's will, she was deeply hurt by the children and stepchildren completely negating her positive contributions. She knew that, combined with Walter's successful business, her presence had allowed all the children to maintain their lifestyles uninterruptedly (as in *Testament*).

Some of the biological children had been prone to phone the nursing home, enraged about some medical matter, or, after Babs became more resistive to nursing care, "a black-and-blue issue." Embarrassed after finding out Babs had resisted and assaulted her aides, they would turn on and dehumanize Mary. "She's not too bright and is only interested in a cushy job!" After several family meetings including teleconferences, these trends were moderated. It was conceded that "Dad was as good as he had ever been, quite chipper!" His happiest times were those he spent with Mary. We refocused on the shared family pain of watching someone lose personhood while wondering about the implications for one's own future. It was acknowledged that Mary's presence had lessened the demands on the distal family, especially during periods of intermittent brain failure. Then the burden had fallen on the proximal stepdaughter, who now became known as the "family brick."

A deep sense of gratitude for Mary's honest caretaking gradually replaced her gold-digger image. At one point I asked if there was anything to change in Mary's pattern of turning first to the stepdaughter for both advice and support and the stepdaughter turning to the medical staff. Was this what all of them wanted her to do and if not, why not? Silence! Everyone realized all major decisions had been left in Mary's hands through default and she, in turn, turned to the "brick" and the "brick" to me, and it was best that it remain that way.

Along the way, we learned that Mary had been a stepchild herself, had always felt excluded, and had felt guilty about leaving her children to be raised by their grandmother. From that point on she was indeed humanized.

The issue of legal proceedings faded away. Two years later Walter was hospitalized with cardiac failure. The family was terrified that, on Walter's discharge from hospital, they would be asked "to take him in and tolerate his irascibility the way Mary does." Walter soon died and Mary was left an uncontested sum of money.

Forensic and Therapeutic Issues in Stepparent Adoptions

A Psychoanalytic Perspective

Harold J. Bursztajn and Rachel R. Boersma

Stepparenting continues to increase rapidly. Thus, Visher and Visher (1998) state: "Estimating from recent divorce and remarriage figures, it appears that there are approximately 1300 new stepfamilies formed every day in the United States, and demographers are predicting that, by the year 2010, there will be more stepfamilies in the United States than any other type of family."

At the same time, so do disputes in family law. For example, the issue of what rights "natural" parents have versus what rights other "stakeholders" have in relationship to children remains an area of flux. While the latest Supreme Court decision (*Troxel v. Granville*, 2000) seems to emphasize the priority of "natural" parents' rights (by way of overturning a Washington state law as being overly broad in denying a mother's desire to limit the grandparents' visitation rights subsequent to the child's father's suicide), this Supreme Court decision is more accurately read as an expression of the justices' sentiments to protect the nuclear family (e.g., a grieving widow and child) from state intrusion and mandates. In fact, on a local level, although there is a great deal of individual variation when it comes to child custody and visitation, judges tend to continue to rely on mental health professionals' opinions to make decisions on a case-by-case basis guided by the "best-interest-of-the-child" standard.

At the same time, there is an accelerating pace of change in the role of mental health professionals who consult regarding stepparent adoption and stepparent related custody issues. These changes are influenced by the changing standard for expert opinion and testimony in the wake of a series of Supreme Court decisions beginning with *Daubert* (1993, p. 444).

The changing standards for forensic mental health evaluation are the result of the last decade's emphasis on judges' roles as gatekeepers to keep out "junk science." Beginning with the decisions of *Daubert v. Merrel Dow* (1993), *General Electric v. Joiner* (1997), and *Kumho Tire v. Carmichael* (1999), judges have felt increasingly empowered to ask that experts go beyond *ipse dixit*, that is, "it is because I say so," to explain the reliability of the method by which their opinion comes to be formulated as well as to demonstrate how its content is relevant to the question at hand. While these developments first arose in the context of product liability litigation, the atmosphere of increasing scrutiny of expert opinion has permeated the judicial system. Even in family court, with its relatively compartmentalized judiciary, there is an ongoing change in atmosphere. For example, where previously judges would automatically follow the recommendations of the court-appointed mental health professionals, there is now an increasingly open mindedness in regards to contrary but better substantiated opinions by mental health experts who are not in the employ of the court system.

Case Example of a Pre- and Post-*Daubert* Stepparent Fitness-to-Adopt Evaluation

Ms. K, a middle-aged stepmother, was described as "borderline" and unfit to maintain custody by the court-appointed evaluator, when she and her husband divorced. Contrary to well established forensic guidelines, the court-appointed evaluator was also the therapist to whom the father had brought the child for "therapy", in the midst of divorce proceedings. Although Ms. K had, five years previously, adopted the now 10-year-old girl, the evaluator opined that the child's natural father, whom Ms. K was divorcing, ought to maintain custody. That conclusion was based primarily on the examiner's observations regarding Ms. K's anger, accusatory tone, and defensiveness during his initial exam of her. The judge's initial negative ruling reflected the court-appointed evaluator's recommendation.

Subsequently, Ms. K was reexamined by one of the authors (HB). While a degree of dissociation and hyperarousal was noted on examining Ms. K, such symptoms were only evoked when her relationship with her ex-husband was being explored. That relationship had been independently documented to be physically abusive. Her symptoms included irritability throughout the legal process, culminating in courtroom outbursts, and defensiveness when being forensically examined. At the same time, her symptoms were primarily manifest in the context of reminders of her relationship with her husband. While such symptoms could occasionally be intrusive and disruptive in social contexts, they were manageable via the patient's use of a well-developed capacity for insight. Moreover, her social function outside of her engagement with the legal process was adoptive and mature. Medical and psychosocial history, examination, and subsequent psychological testing (MMPI-2, Rorschach), while indicating a likelihood of symptoms consistent with a diagnosis of Posttraumatic Stress Disorder, did not support the court-appointed examiner's concluding opinion that Ms. K was suffering from a Borderline Personality Disorder. Reports from teachers and parent–child observations did not show the severe impairment of parental capacity, which the initial examiner had attributed to the patient. There were a variety of omissions, biased assumptions, and leaps of reasoning in the court-appointed examiner's report and opinion that were in conflict with published guidelines and practice parameters for child custody evaluation (National Interdisciplinary Colloquium on Child Custody, 1998a, b).

Subsequent to the author expert's (HB) well-referenced critique of the court-appointed evaluator's report, a decision was made by the stepmother's attorney to appeal the original ruling. Although such requests are rarely granted, the expert's affidavit, which recapitulated the deficiencies in the court-appointed evaluator's methods, and reasoning were sufficient to grant the appeal. Upon rehearing, the earlier decision was reversed, and the adoptive (step) mother was granted joint custody with the child's natural father.

The Forensic Context: Stepparent Adoption

Although the above case composite reflects an extreme, it is indicative of how even family-court judges are increasingly influenced by the Supreme Court's mandate of intellectual rigor in expert testimony. In view of the above, it is now more important than ever to proceed thoughtfully to evaluate a stepparent's capability as a parent even during the initial adoption proceedings. A careful initial evaluation can set the stage for a successful adoption, which can survive even the turmoil of those marriages that end in bitter divorce.

A forensic context that commonly arises in second marriages is that of stepparent adoption. While important in itself, a deep understanding of the issues raised by stepparent adoption can also serve as an entrée to the complexities of stepparenting and the additional complexities when adoption and custody issues are raised. A concise and useful statement of how most states view the nature and purpose of adoption is given in Schetky and Benedek (1992): "Adoption is the legal proceeding in which a person takes another person into the relation of child and thereby acquires the rights and incurs the responsibilities of parents in respect of such other person" (New York State Domestic Relations Law Sec. 110, p. 170).

While such a definition is prima facia clear, to the extent that the rights and responsibilities of parents are by no means universally agreed upon, it leaves a great deal of room for ambiguity and state-to-state variation. A more universal principle is the standard of the "best-interest-of-the-child." Such a standard is widely accepted as the metaprinciple in judicial determination of custodial decisions and may also be relied upon to resolve conflicts and ambiguities as to what adoption means in a given state in a specific case. While the courts give appropriate weight to the noncustodial, biological parent's custodial claim, however, the "best-interest" standard weakens this biological claim to the extent of that parent's unobstructed failure to act as such. (For further review of this issue, see MGL c.210 s.3;

regulations of the Office of Child Care Services [OCCS]—formerly the Office for Children 102 CMR 5.01.)

In order for a stepparent to be allowed to adopt a spouse's child, the other biological parent, if living, must either surrender parental rights voluntarily or have these rights terminated secondary to cause, such as, abandonment or child abuse. Abandonment is typically defined as a lack of meaningful contact or provision of financial support for a year. The biological parents often contest stepparent adoptions and thus custody issues all too often come into play. There are a variety of dynamic factors which increase the likelihood of such custody contests, ranging from unresolved grief to envy, and a variety of unresolved multiple family systems issues harking back to earlier dyadic and triadic conflicts of the participants' own childhoods. For this and other reasons, the adopting stepparent and partner should prepare carefully for their assessment. According to Smith (1993), "A home study will be conducted which will look at the interaction between the child and adopting parent, the home life of the couple and other issues concerning the child's welfare" (p. 57).

The area of stepparent adoption is still in flux. For example, recently the Massachusetts legislature amended the adoption statute. Effective July 1, 1999, the Courts will recognize Post-Placement Contact Agreements under certain legally defined circumstances. A termination of parental rights decree may recognize an agreement for postadoption contact between or among a minor to be adopted, the birth parents and the prospective adoption parents. The court issuing the adoption decree must also approve this same agreement. The court's applicable standard is that the agreement be in the best interest of the child, that the terms of the agreement be fair and reasonable, and that all parties undertake the agreement voluntarily. It is useful to know however, that failure by any party to perform in accordance with such an agreement will not affect the validity of the adoption. Under Massachusetts's law, the Post-Placement Contact Agreement is incorporated but not merged in the adoption decree, thereby allowing a party to the agreement to seek remedy for the other party's failure to adhere to the terms of the agreement via a civil action. It is still too early to predict whether such a structure will address one potential reason for postadoption litigation.

This recent statutory amendment in Massachusetts, the likelihood of other states legislating similar concepts, and the prospect of ongoing uncertainty, supports the importance of further exploration with the prospective parents in a therapeutic context separate from the forensic evaluation. The possibility of such an agreement being sought by a biological parent may complicate the decision making of a potential stepparent concerning his or her ability to manage feelings, intensifying when and if such contact is to take place. This exploration can be best undertaken in individual therapy and the results of such a discussion reviewed in the couple's therapy. However, many couples can only afford one therapy. In any case, separately from any therapist, the forensic evaluator needs to assess the parent's understanding of the potential consequences of adoption, the risks, benefits, and alternatives to adoption. The treating clinician and the forensic evaluator both have roles in the process of stepparent adoption, but they are separate and distinct roles. From a psychoanalytic perspective, it is essential to respect the boundary between treatment and evaluation. This is accomplished by referring the stepparent for a forensic psychiatric evaluation whenever the medicolegal issue of "fitness" arises.

Psychoanalytically oriented practitioners are familiar with the multiple reasons for maintaining such a clear boundary (Goldstein et al., 1986, p. 79; Bursztajn, Scherr, and Brodsky, 1994, pp. 611–635; Strasburger, Gutheil, and Brodsky, 1997, pp. 451–454). In essence, the objective, distanced stance of the evaluator is incompatible with the subjective, empathic perspective of the therapist. The nature of the questioning and investigation undertaken by a therapist acting as a forensic evaluator may undermine the therapeutic alliance existing between the therapist and the patient. Additionally, a violation of confidentiality would occur when a therapist or evaluator reports on the patient in court. Indeed, attempting to combine the two roles entails a conflict of interest, since the clinician's duty is to serve the patient while the evaluator is retained to formulate an objective opinion in keeping with the ever increasing emphasis on "reliability" after the 1993 Supreme Court *Daubert* decision (*The Psychiatric Clinics of North America* and ethical effective testimony). Forensic evaluation needs to be guided by a striving for objectivity free from preconceptions and biases. For example, Case, Lin, and McLanahan (1999) state:

> Remarriage is not the panacea it was once thought to be. Children who grow up in two-parent families consisting of a biological parent and a stepparent have outcomes very similar to children who grow up with only one parent, and worse than children who are raised by both of their biological parents. . . . One explanation is that stepparents are less altruistic and, indeed, may be quite hostile toward nonbiological children. According to the theory of parental solicitude, such feelings are rooted in psychological mechanisms that have evolved over time through the process of natural selection [pp. 234–235].

Taken to an extreme, this view can be misconstrued, as in the popular bias that stepparents lack such parental solicitude. This easily becomes the overly simplified belief that when parents are related biologically to their children, they have a genetically driven ability to care for and nurture them. In actuality, no reliable or relevant data exists to support such a theory. For example, a relationship with the child based primarily upon fulfilling the potential parent's narcissistic needs is not grounded in solicitude. In view of the increasing emphasis on expert testimony going *beyond ipse dixit* in the post-*Daubert* era, (*Daubert v. Merrell Dow Pharmaceuticals*, 1993; *General Electric Co. v. Joiner*, 1997; *Kumho Tire Co. Ltd. v. Carmichael*, 1999) an expert's opinion cannot simply be based on theories or assumptions, such as "natural is best," but instead must include a comprehensive review and analysis of the available biopsychosocial data, references, and case-specific reasoning relevant to fitness-to-parent or custody.

Given the actual complexities inherent in individual variability, remaining impartial as to which parent is best for the child, is a must during the course of a forensic evaluation. In the actual examination of a stepparent wishing to adopt his or her partner's child and the review and analysis of corroborated data, the examiner must be attuned to those parental characteristics that demonstrate a focus on the best interests of the child. An example might be a stepmother who is able to support the child's efforts to maintain an internalized image of his or her biological mother without being unduly threatened or hurt. A stepmother who supports the child's desire to have photographs of the biological mother on display can be demonstrating both parental solicitude and acting in the child's best interest by being empathic about the child's loss. Additionally, the stepmother may be indicating an understanding of and comfort with the developmental needs of the child. A potential adoptive stepparent must be able to become attached to the child and focus on the child's needs.

The Psychoanalytically Informed Forensic Psychiatric Evaluation

A forensic psychiatric evaluation is indicated when the adoption agency questions the "fitness" of the stepparent to adopt (still a reflex reaction in some agencies) or when a custody dispute is anticipated or arises between the stepparent and biological parent. In view of the growing recognition of the rights of stepparents, as detailed above, what was once a fait accompli in a custody battle between a stepparent and a biological parent now has become a genuinely contested issue on today's more level playing field. Nonetheless, residual prejudice against stepparents makes it essential to have an evaluation applying the same standard to stepparents as to biological parents. Psychoanalytically trained forensic examiners will be more aware of their own potential prejudices and make diagnostic use of his countertransference feelings as well as the implicit prejudice that may exist in some legal arenas.

Common stigmas against stepparents exist in many segments of our society. Visher and Visher (1998) state:

> Stepfamilies receive little attention from the media, from educators, and from many segments of society, including public policy makers and the legal system. Unfortunately, this doesn't come under the heading of "benign neglect." When they are noticed, remarriage families are often described in terms that are even less complimentary than they are in the fairy tales of Cinderella and Snow White [p. 446].

Such social stigmas can readily validate examiner–examinee dyad specific countertransference driven biases in the therapist such as in our case example. The initial examiner, sensitive to the accusatory tone of the examinee, all too quickly labeled her as Borderline. According to Schetky and Devoe (1992), countertransference issues may be activated by child custody conflicts reminiscent of a therapist's need to take sides with one of his or her own parents during childhood, or anger over an absentee or abusive parent. A child being considered for adoption may have experienced physical, sexual and/or emotional trauma, and the resulting countertransference issues originating in the therapist's own personal traumatic experiences need acknowledgment and awareness. Moreover, an examiner striving for perfection or acceptance may react to an angry, accusatory parent by defensively saying, "I am good, it is the accusing parent whose examination behavior is not only obnoxious but of necessity reflects a character flaw and fundamental impairment to parent." The more likely way to avoid having one's interests unfairly biased by an examiner's unexplored prejudices is to retain a psychoanalytically informed forensic examiner who through his own earlier therapeutic experiences has "explored" himself.

It is important to keep in mind that neither parents nor stepparents need to be perfect. If the evaluation's focus is on the issue of fitness to parent or termination of parental rights, the forensic examiner may inquire about areas detailed in Schetky and Benedek (1992), where the use of the word *parent* may be understood as stepparent. Areas to be examined include:

1. Are the parents currently able to meet the child's needs?
2. What is the parent's current level of functioning, and does this represent an arrest in development or regression?
3. Is the parent's condition treatable, and, if so, is the parent motivated to change and willing to accept therapy?
4. What is the parent's record with respect to following through on recommendations for treatment?

5. If the parent is treatable, will treatment improve the parent sufficiently to meet the child's needs within the child's time perspective? (A child's time perspective differs from both an adult's and a legal perspective. A child's developmental needs may be adversely impacted by a delay while a caregiver is seeking treatment.)
6. What is the impact of the parent's pathology or conduct on the child, and what ameliorating factors might be present such as the protection and nurturance of a spouse or grandparent?
7. Does the child have special needs or problems that require exceptional parenting skills?
8. Why does the parent want to adopt? [p. 173]

With an initial caveat against countertransference biased interpretation, or approaching the evaluation in a cookbook fashion, the above questions are a useful guide for forensic evaluation. At the same time, additional caveats worthy of consideration include awareness of evaluator's potential overemphasis on parental compliance, godlike certainty and self-serving claims of Olympian authority. Other potential pitfalls include a confirmation bias so that first impressions become ultimate conclusions, an overemphasis on protection and undervaluing of nurturance, a readiness to assume the worst when accusations of child sexual abuse emerge in the context of divorce and custody disputes, and a failure to consider the impact of an extended forensic evaluation and protracted legal proceedings on the child's and each parent's welfare and the future of the child's relationship with each parent.

Only by keeping such potential pitfalls in mind can existing guidelines be translated into acceptable practice standards. Thus, the American Academy of Child and Adolescent Psychiatry (1997) has established a set of guidelines entitled *Practice Parameters for Child Custody Evaluation*. Although these are not fitness guidelines, this document details some necessary elements of the forensic evaluation including the referral process, structuring an evaluation, interviewing of parents, interviewing the child or children, joint sessions with the parents and child or children, the value of interviewing others and those areas which should be addressed in the forensic evaluator's written report. Further discussion of courtroom testimony is also discussed and the reader is referred to that document for further detail. Consideration of all of these areas and adherence to the guidelines should facilitate determination of a parent or stepparent's fitness to parent and act in the best interests of the child. These parameters need to be supplemented by a psychoanalytically informed interpretation of data.

Other special issues that deserve to be considered at more length in the psychoanalytically informed forensic psychiatric examination of the adopting stepparent include the all too common allegations of child sexual abuse. While these often arise in the context of custody battles, they also occur in contested adoptions. Such allegations need to be thoroughly investigated without bias or preconceived notions. Although automatic denial or dismissal of such allegations needs to be avoided, so does the common tendency to accept allegations as proven facts, without skepticism. Differential diagnosis has to include false allegations, influenced by parental coercion or suggestion, misattribution, a child seeking to please a parent's or examiner's stated or implicit expectations, an expression of the child's desires and needs, conscious or unconscious fantasies, as well as actual child abuse.

Recent social trends have increased the number of same-sex couples desiring adoption. While the issues detailed here including avoidance of countertransference-motivated bias, are pertinent to same-sex couples, their unique issues are beyond the scope of this chapter.

The Role of Couples Therapy

From a clinical perspective, psychoanalytically informed couples therapy can be very helpful for a decision that a stepparent should adopt the partner's child. Lebow, Walsh, and Rolland (1999) describe both divorce and remarriage as transitional processes characterized by complex relationship networks. The associated stresses of these complexities result in a divorce rate of nearly 60% among remarried couples, highest among those with children from former unions (p. 238). Couples therapy with a psychoanalytically trained practitioner will facilitate their exploration of unstated or understated wishes, expectations, and meanings they have about their union, allowing them to understand more fully what will be superimposed on their parenting role. This discussion and the resulting insights may help the couple to delve more deeply into themselves when confronted with the many questions about their reasons for desiring adoption. It also prepares the couple for a high level of communication and cooperation in problem solving in the midst of complexity and uncertainty. Such preparation is crucial in reducing the risk of subsequent impasses and the consequences of yet another divorce. There are numerous questions that need to be explored in the course of such couples therapy. Their discussion should include examination of the process arriving at a "good decision" to adopt. These needs and desires will be grounded in culturally driven mores about how one makes a decision as well as unconscious over identification with family of origin styles of decision making. The psychoanalytically trained therapist can help the couple explore and distinguish between the two. It is important to keep in mind that in any complex personal decision, individual values and life goals have to be considered (Bursztajn, Gutheil, and Cummins, 1987). Overt motives may shield more covert ones. Motives to be considered should include any peer group influence (e.g., "everyone has kids"), the voluntariness of such a decision by both partners ("I want to adopt my stepdaughter for my husband to be happy"), the impact such a decision to adopt may have on extended families (e.g., what about the stepgrandparent?) and an agreement on whether the extended families should be involved at all in the decision making. If other individuals are allowed involvement, then the extent of their involvement should be mutually discussed and agreed upon by all concerned. This is best done beforehand.

A psychoanalytically trained therapist will be able to facilitate each individual's examination of inherently conflicting wishes and desires. For example, a stepmother wishing to adopt the child of her husband may harbor a fantasy that her husband will stay home more. Initially, she may not be cognizant of this underlying fantasy, but with discussion and support from a psychoanalytically trained therapist, she may be able to recognize and discuss with her husband her underlying sense of abandonment. By the same token, adoption decisions driven by unconscious guilt or conflict of one or both partners will often end badly. For example, warning signs include a desire for adoption driven by a stepfather's feelings that he needs to compensate for "taking" the child's mother away from the child, thereby providing the child with a substitute for the "lost" parent. By helping to make the unconscious influences conscious as well as bearable, a therapist can support a couple's maturation.

While it can also be helpful to explore issues raised by a potential adoption process, perhaps in individual therapy, it is also important to note that these areas are not solely the domain of individual therapy. Attitudinal and dispositional queries that are first discussed in individual therapy and any issues that are difficult to answer or that generate conflicting responses may become useful areas to explore in couples therapy. Often unconsciously shared fantasies that define the couples' relationship, for example, the fantasy to be the "perfect parents" to compensate for the partner's own early childhood deprivation may be particularly open to exploration leading to resolution in the context of couples therapy.

Another area which may be most usefully explored in couples therapy is the multiple meanings and fantasies which may be associated with financial arrangements relevant to adoption. The meaning of financial responsibility for a child or additional children needs to be considered with an emphasis on the commitment until the child's maturity granted by an adoption decree. Emotional responsibility for a child is integral to the adoption process, and a minimum expectation by both parties of 18 years of care must be set. Having a child might necessitate a move to a location better suited to child rearing, especially if a child has special needs, talents, or disabilities. A final area, which may be distasteful for partners still grieving for the end of their previous marriages to contemplate, is consideration of the stepparent assuming financial responsibility for the stepchild, now adopted child, should the remarriage end. Written agreements, tactfully presented, can be reassuring. An experienced therapist must direct and support consideration of this issue in the context of Visher and Visher's (1998) statement: "The most recent data for the United States predicts that 45% of children born during the 1990s will experience the divorce of their parents before they are 18 years of age" (p. 444).

The Role of Individual Therapy

Of significant concern is the impact that parenting has on the lifestyle of both the individual and the couple. Marriage to a custodial parent of a child results in two new relationships instantaneously. The nine months of pregnancy allow the partners to fantasize about a future-parenting role and to embrace gradually the role of parent. Because, this is unavailable in a stepparent adoption process, it is critical that each partner have some opportunity to explore the same issues. Individual therapy with a psychoanalytically trained therapist can support the process of creating a fresh child-sensitive perspective for child rearing. There may often be more than one level of individual meaning to a variety of prima facie interpersonal questions. For example, a difference in opinion over what age to send a child to nursery school can be shadowed by the parents' own residual issues around childhood separation and experienced deprivation.

An individual's free time, privacy, and social life may be compromised by parenting of a child, regardless of the age of the child. Contact with stepchildren may stimulate erotic feelings and fantasies in a stepparent not used to parenting. A stepparent's ability to tolerate such feelings without becoming seductive, abusive, or overwhelmed with guilt, withdrawing, and becoming neglectful is crucial to explore.

It will be imperative for the individual therapist to be nonjudgmental and maintain neutrality. This includes monitoring the therapist's own countertransference in order to support the exploration of negative feelings about such activities and child companionship. Presenting the positive feelings only may be the inclination of the would-be adopting parent. A psychoanalytically inclined therapist, however, can help the individual express and bear repressed and unconscious ambivalence and uncertainty (Reiser et al., 1987).

A discussion of the qualities of parental love and its many manifestations, with exploration of the concept of parental love in the context of each partner's family of origin, can be undertaken by a therapist who does not shy away from "love" as an area worthy of exploration. How easily an individual feels and expresses love to others, particularly children, can be talked about.

A parent may have unexplored and unconscious ideals and expectations about the outcomes of raising a child. Whether a child ultimately resembles either or both of the parents in the realm of interests, values, and goals may be useful to examine, as would discussion of the potential impact on either or both parents if the child is different from the parents, or is disappointing to the parents. Again, countertransference driven avoidance of such exploration, or a failure to be aware of such elements in the patient's transference to the therapist, has to be carefully considered. Helping a couple address their own, often-unconscious insecurities and unresolved separation and narcissistic issues can free each member of the family to develop in an authentic yet convivial and harmonious manner. For example, when largely repressed fears of abandonment are addressed, counterphobic detachment from spouse and child can be resolved. The adopted child may not feel "good enough" by virtue of having the biological parent agree to the adoption. Such feelings may be worked through when the adopted parent or stepparent can respond to the (adopted or step) child's insecurities, free of their own, often unconscious, attitudes of perfectionism and self-righteousness. Of critical importance for discussion prior to accepting the decision to adopt is whether either individual places upon the child an expectation to fulfill that individual's need for happiness.

Implicit expectations placed upon each of the parents by their families of origin to provide companionship and support for their own elderly parents need also to be considered. Open discussion between the partners of such an expectation being placed upon their adopted child needs to occur, but can only occur if each of the parents is aware of his or her own previously unconscious models, conflicts, and guilt. Finally, how an individual would handle feelings of subsequent regret after the fact, for having made a "poor" decision to adopt, needs exploration. The impact of such regrets on the individual, the couple, and the child should be considered. This should be undertaken and guided by the therapist regardless of any vehement denial, expressed by either partner, that such post hoc feelings of regret would never occur. With some prospective parents, much of the above exploration may need to wait postadoption, given individual differences in needs and coping mechanisms.

Conclusion

Clearly, many issues exist for all parties to a stepparent adoption. A forensic psychiatric evaluation with a psychoanalytically trained examiner will facilitate thorough assessment of motives, attitudes, prejudices, and areas of ambivalence that can exist during the stepparent adoption process. In light of the current forecast of the number of stepfamilies predicted for the new millennium and the complexities of stepparent adoption, the inclusion of the psychoanalytically trained forensic examiner, separate from the treating clinicians, is likely to improve both process and outcome for families and their children. While distinct, such an evaluation can also be a useful prelude or complement to ongoing psychoanalytically informed psychotherapy. Otherwise, ordinary regret can all too easily turn to pathological grief. Due to this, what might have been otherwise, can all too easily become the gold standard by which the present becomes devalued, the future dominated by the past, and change and growth become frozen in time past (Modell, 1990).

References

Bursztajn, H. J. & Brodsky, A. (1998), Ethical and effective testimony during direct examination and cross-examination post-*Daubert*. In: *The Mental Health Practitioner and the Law*, ed. L. Lifson & R. Simon. Cambridge, MA: Harvard University Press, pp. 262–280.

_____ Gutheil, T. G. & Cummins, B. (1987), Conflict and synthesis: The comparative anatomy of ethical and clinical decision making. In: *Divided Staffs, Divided Selves*, ed. S. J. Reiser, H. J. Bursztajn, P. S. Appelbaum & T. G. Gutheil. Cambridge, England: Cambridge University Press.

_____ Scherr, A. E. & Brodsky, A. (1994), The rebirth of forensic psychiatry in light of recent historical trends in criminal responsibility. In: *The Psychiatric Clinics of North America*, ed. S. Romm & R. S. Friedman. Philadelphia, PA: Saunders, 17:611–635.

Case, A., Lin, I. F. & McLanahan, S. (1999), Household resource allocation in stepfamilies: Darwin reflects on the plight of Cinderella. *Amer. Econ. Rev.,* 89:234–239.

Daubert v. Merrell Dow Pharmaceuticals 509 US 579 (1993).

Galatzer-Levy, R. M. & Kraus, L., eds. (1999), *The Scientific Basis of Child Custody Decisions*. New York: Wiley.

General Electric Co. v. Joiner 522 US 136 (1997).

Goldstein, J., Freud, A., Solnit, A. J. & Goldstein, S. (1986), *In the Best Interests of the Child*. New York: Free Press.

Kumho Tire Co. Ltd. v. Carmichael 119 D. Ct. 1167 (1999).

Lebow, J., Walsh, F. & Rolland, J. (1999), The remarriage family in custody evaluation. In: *The Scientific Basis of Child Custody Decisions*, ed. R. M. Galatzer-Levy & L. Kraus. New York: Wiley, pp. 236–256.

Modell, A. H. (1990), *Other Times, Other Realities: Toward a Theory of Psychoanalytic Treatment*. Cambridge, MA: Harvard University Press.

National Interdisciplinary Colloquium on Child Custody (1998a), Evaluating mental health expert advice and testimony: Questions about objectivity. In: *Legal and Mental Health Perspectives on Child Custody Law: A Deskbook for Judges*. New York: West Group, pp. 371–378.

_____ (1998b), General rules governing custody adjudication. In: *Legal and Mental Health Perspectives on Child Custody Law: A Deskbook for Judges*. New York: West Group, pp. 21–35.

Reiser, S. J., Bursztajn, H. J., Appelbaum, P. S. & Gutheil, T. G. (1987), *Divided Staffs, Divided Selves: A Case Approach to Mental Health Ethics*. Cambridge, England: Cambridge University Press.

Schetky, D. H. (1992). Termination of parental rights. In: *Clinical Handbook of Child Psychiatry and the Law*, ed. D. H. Schetky & E. P. Benedek. Baltimore, MD: Williams & Wilkins, pp. 162–181.

_____ & Devoe, L. (1992), Countertransference issues in forensic child psychiatry. In: *Clinical Handbook of Child Psychiatry and the Law*, ed. D. H. Schetky & E. P. Benedek. Baltimore, MD: Williams & Wilkins, pp. 230–245.

Smith, W. J. (1993), *You, Your Family and the Law: A Legal Guide for Today's Families*. Washington, DC: HALT, Inc.

Strasburger, L. H., Gutheil, T. G. & Brodsky, A. (1997), On wearing two hats: Role conflict in serving as both psychotherapist and expert witness. *Amer. J. Psychiat.*, 154:448–456.

Troxel, et vir Petitioners v. Tommie Granville (No. 99-138) 137 Wash. 2d 1, 969 P. 2d 21 (2000).

Visher, E. R. & Visher, J. S. (1998), Stepparents. *Fam. & Conciliation Courts Rev.*, 36:444–452.

Work Group on Quality Issues (1997), Practice parameters for child custody evaluation. *J. Amer. Acad. Child & Adol. Psychiat.*, 36(10 Suppl):57S–68S.

Epilogue

The Therapeutic Importance of "Recognition Processes" in Attachment, Detachment, and Reattachment Experiences

Stanley H. Cath and Moisy Shopper

We touch one another, bond and break,
drift away on force fields we don't understand.
—J. Winterson (1994)

W hen repeated disappointments become the inevitable destiny of lovers, we must ask what is known about the origins and fate of such "force fields." In this regard, we would paraphrase Freud's observations on the etiology of hysteria: namely, stepfamilies also suffer from a surfeit of painful reminiscences of being unrecognized. In people who split apart, their history is consistently narrated with a growing sense of surprise about the lack of knowledge they had of each other in the past and with what distortions they regard each other in the present.

To the authors of the chapters in this book, however, no such set of disillusioning or humiliating memories generated by splitting up or reattaching have fully captured the massive destabilization and scarring experienced by so many of our adult and child patients. Of course there is the fundamental loss of a very meaningful person and his or her unique, once beloved ways of being and being with. Instead of a storehouse of supportive imagos of a *loving* spouse, mother, father, grands, and/or extended family members, the affective residue of the relationships reported by divorcees and their offspring usually encompasses a mysterious mixture of *hate,* rage, shame, confusion, self-doubt, and depression. From these accounts of love turned to hate, it would seem such emotional turmoil has never been experienced in such depth before and is hardly to be forgotten lifelong (Wallerstein, 2000). Still, in every post-breakup inventory some of the regrets center on "agency," that is, how much traumatic disillusionments are the consequences of immature personal choices or naïve, wishful thinking. We listen to misleading euphemisms like "love is blind," almost universally tempered by the paradox, "I should have known better."

With much gratitude for the editorial assistance of Dr. Phyllis Cath and Dr. Erik Gann.

331

Some find solace in the oversimplified rationalization that they loved not wisely but too well. When children are involved, the focus may move to self-accusations that usually include failing to be a good enough parent, even when the divorce was appropriate, well justified, and reflected true concern for the vulnerable young.

Over time, the authors have been increasingly convinced that these ostensible reasons often conceal more than they reveal. Grief over the loss of the image of a once beloved spouse even when augmented by disappointment in the idealized self seems to lack sufficient explanatory power to account for the depth of these force fields. In that most of these ruptures take place in midlife when the trauma of such unimaginable chaos in the life-lived so far may seem quite enough to dampen or destroy hope for more positive relationships in the life remaining, the setting and time to make important contributions (Cath, 1965, pp. 25–26).

There are many motivations to rather quickly reestablish various forms of attachments. In some, the imperative toward reengagement may be to restore self-care by finding a significant other as soon as possible. In another cohort, often therapists by nature or vocation, the healing power of giving care to others or to others' children may quickly restore a sense of worth and dignity. In still others a very strong motivation is the urgency of finding another to share in the care of the children from the first marriage.[1] While these factors may propel toward the rapid reconstruction of new attachments, they may also conspire to seal off prematurely needed self-exploration. For a select few, statistics tell us, life in such new "family settings" works out well. But the same statistics inform us this is not the case for the majority who try marriage again. We would conjecture this is more likely in those in whom grief seems frozen and whose lack of sufficient insight into mostly unconscious, negative force fields are still operative. Unconscious templates continue to interfere in their best attempts to seek a more fulfilling, less conflicted life. This brings us to some therapeutic considerations.

In the past decade, psychoanalytic theory about these templates has been in the process of a major reformulation stimulated by three rich sources of data:

1. Better informed clinical material from within its own analytic borders.
2. Neuroscience: the linking of genetic predisposition (the development and organization of the immature brain), the earliest recurring, comforting/chaotic, dyadic and triadic experiences in the first three years of life, and psychological disturbances later in life (Fonagy, 2000).

---

[1] A cartoon in the *New Yorker* magazine (February 28, 2001) portrays a man kneeling before a woman proposing, "Emily, I want you to be the woman who picks out a nanny for my children."

3. Most relevant to this essay, direct observations of how infants of various temperaments become securely or insecurely attached to a series of caretakers, kin and nonkin, in a pattern likely to be repeated in various interpersonal constellations all along the life span.

Enriched by this perspective, we believe the heuristic value of this book is enhanced by the stress placed by many of our authors on the appropriateness of the long-term psychotherapeutic approach to the complexities of reconstructing families. Our thinking owes much to the seminal contributions of Louis Sander and many infant researchers on the earliest origins, nature, and derailments of human attachment in the domain of how we learn to be with, idealize, and depend on kin and nonkin as children and later as adults. Marriage and especially parenthood changes people and their unmet needs in ways they do not seem to know but sense desperately. Shakespeare clearly recognized this paradox: "There lives within the very flame of love / A kind of wick or snuff that will abate it."

Falling out of love or being disappointed in aspirations as an adult challenges the accumulated, convicted experience of knowing the rightness of the fit, of what was wanted or needed and found missing, or possibly only just dreamed of in the past. All these factors have an impact on how a person responds to and copes with what is available in the present and what is to be hoped for in the future. At a point of despair of finding the life they anticipated, most divorcees, their children, and *many therapists* still are likely to minimize or deny that subconscious templates have been established long ago in their earliest attachment dyads and triads. Some are convinced a misplaced trust was simply shattered by a frustrating mismatch, an abandoning mother or a "deadbeat dad," and that the "agency" of each participant plays a minimal role in where they find themselves to be. This may be true for some in that after a temporary, possibly disorganized period of self-protective isolation or recalibration of goals, they may be quite successful with a different mate. Yet in describing second marriages, we are likely to hear of that same, deep, puzzling sense of not knowing what was real or why. To be sure, the less fortunate also ponder on the interaction between themselves and their environment as well as how their unconscious may have distorted or sabotaged their perceptions of past partners. Outside of pointing to these individual variations, is there anything more to be said about the usual earthquake quality to the rupture of intimate bonds so poetically described at the beginning of this epilogue?

We attempt to address this puzzle with data from those who came for therapy complaining of not knowing what was real and confused as to how much to rely on using their own intuitive intentionality in safely loving again. We offer three guidelines found especially helpful.

The first is the importance of communicating to the patient, sometimes by the way one listens, the therapist's acknowledgment of the subjective impact on *each* individual in the family system of the lost imago of a once-idealized source of self- and family integrity. In pointing to the importance of the miscarriage of having been recognized and loved by a now ambivalently regarded spouse and family, we have been guided by Sander's work highlighting this basic phenomenon in infants. In our opinion, his findings around separation and derailed dialogues are clearly echoed in the explicatory language of hatred heard around divorce. We listen but may not appreciate the significance of complaints of "not being known . . . I thought he [or she] knew me . . . I found I did not know him [or her] . . . everyone else knew . . . where was I?" This pattern of feeling unknown or mysteriously unknowing may have even impelled toward therapy, but usually is accompanied by a unique variant on resistance to self-exploration, "What happened is not knowable!" Statistics reaffirm this may be true for some as the problematic pattern of how one is and how one shares life with others is so often blindly reiterated with step-figures in the even more painful derailments so likely in reconstituted settings.

For those not familiar with these theoretical concepts (Sander, 1995, 2000a, b), a word of explanation as to why they are so helpful here may be in order. Sander applied the concept of "matched specificities" between two systems attuned to each other, to the infant and its caretakers at the very beginning of human awareness. "Matching" implies repeated moments of mutual understanding between two states of consciousness, such as between lovers, husbands and wives, steps, and so on. We suggest the loss of a shared protective family imago is as significant in the life of disappointed lovers as in their children, especially in so-called dysfunctional families. Unwittingly, all lovers intermittently call on some of these basic anlagen of attachment in matchmaking or in cohabiting in order to anchor themselves in time and space. Each encounter becomes a part of each couple's historical identity, an internal representation hard to erase. Sometimes people are predisposed to "reknow" themselves only through nonkin. This deeply engrained part of their composite identity may have been reiteratively threatened by the experiences of not being known or rejected by kin and plays a part in object choice, be it in marriage, affairs, or in the various forms of more cautious cohabitations that may precede or follow divorce. These highly charged affect-memory streams have their own sexual characteristics and may be supercharged by real or imagined infidelities by partners.

This brings us to a second consideration: namely, to suggest that it is helpful for therapists to be more attuned to selected valences of their empathic stance when listening to the narratives of high-intensity marital conflicts. Under the sway of their personal background to various degrees, it is sometimes impossible to avoid identifying with either partner or with the children as "victims" and to share the wished-for solutions (Cath, 1982). It has been productive to share an understanding of how alienating and disorganizing it can be for *all* who lose their family structure to feel unanchored and misunderstood during the usually prolonged splitting up of a family. The therapist's tendency is to drift into a secretly hostile countertransference toward a nonresidential or an abusive parent. This nonverbal behavior may capture, convey, and explore negative affects but preclude those that stood under the former attachment, especially when the patient is feeling deeply exhausted and betrayed yet guilty over vindictiveness. In taking this seemingly obvious corrective stance, our tone may be as important as the content of what is discussed, and if it works will minimize the residential parent's demand on the children to match the hatred of the now missing or despised spouse. If in tune, this facilitates a much needed but still feared therapeutic alliance. By acknowledging the puzzling, inordinately disillusioned, depleted state in the family, we avoid alienating those who feel overwhelmed or secretly disappointed *in themselves* as well as in their partner. Many report feeling betrayed by therapists who could not resist taking sides. In the words of one patient, her therapist "did not seem to feel what I've been through, how hard I loved . . . and just did not understand what I had lost! I didn't just want to blame someone else . . . I knew better!" In this group of patients, we can minimize iatrogenic trauma by focusing on the need for affirmative recognition of the couple's best efforts and allowing a free flow of the ambivalences engendered by unknown force fields.

Our third consideration also centers on a transference and countertransference issue. Most therapists consciously abhor divorce no matter how appropriate they think it might be. We know of no study on the countertransference impact of a therapist's personal marital status on his dealings with his patient's splitting up, having affairs, reattaching, or refusing to ever get involved with the opposite sex again. But, in supervision and case seminars, it is obvious that many therapists and analysts have responded with hardly concealed discomfort and distance when either patients' or colleagues' conflicts led to separations, divorces, custody battles, or major attempts to restructure life's basic anchorages. We have observed how often their overall discomfort led to inappropriate activity and was reinforced by sociocultural values as well as by specific instabilities (blind spots?) in their own intimate relationships. Furthermore, most therapists with strong rescue fantasies have difficulty with the transferences of patients who have learned not to trust previous therapists and come to us quite reluctant to emotionally engage with, become dependent on, or feel grateful to anyone ever again. Match the inner state of these "ungrateful patients" (Gabbard, 1998) who need affirmation-vindication but can give little in return with most therapists' need for their kind of recognition feedback (that they are well-intended rescuers and doing their very best) and we find a mirror phenomenon in the mutual hunger for best-self appreciation. In this setting an accompanying urge toward self-exposure may inexplicably emerge. At the root of silent affect needs of therapists are the same precursors of attachment security and self-coherency that operate in our patients and may contribute to the increased danger of boundary crossings. We share a unique history of the rise and fall of attachment-recognition experiences and we cope as best we can. Listening to a patient's vivid narrative may mirror part of our own dilemmas to various degrees, but this shared ground can facilitate a more rapid therapeutic alliance and much productive work.

In this essay, we have elected to draw attention to one outstandingly painful, experience-near, leading edge of anxiety, namely, the disorganizing phenomenon of feeling unknown by someone previously regarded as intimately knowing the deepest, the darkest, and the best sides of one's self. In particularly predisposed more insecurely attached people, including some therapists, this sequence may lead to a subjective triad of despair:

1. An untested depth of narcissistic dys-equilibrium never experienced before.
2. A reactivated, dreaded anticipation of the uncertain, unanchored future.
3. A sense of ongoing strain, requiring much intensive intrapsychic reorganization to survive.

In this extraordinarily rapidly changing world, our countertransference deserves special monitoring when working with detaching and reattaching couples and children.

References

Cath, S. H. (1965), Some dynamics of the middle and later years. In: *Geriatric Psychiatry: Grief, Loss and Emotional Disorders in the Aging Process*. New York: International Universities Press, pp. 25–26.

_____ (1982), Divorce and the child: The father question hour. In: *Father and Child: Developmental and Clinical Perspectives*, ed. S. H. Cath, A. R. Gurwitt & J. M. Ross. Boston: Little Brown, pp. 467–479.

Fonagy, P. (2000), The development of psychopathology from infancy to adulthood. Plenary session at the World Association for Infant Mental Health Congress, Montréal.

Gabbard, G. (1998), The ungrateful patient. Presented at meeting of the Massachusetts Institute of Psychoanalysis, Boston.

Sander, L. (1995), Identity and the experience of specificity in a process of recognition. *Psychoanal. Dial.*, 5:579–593.

_____ (2000a), In honor of Louis Sander [Special issue]. *Infant Ment. Health J.*, 21:1–2.

_____ (2000b), Where are we going in the field of infant mental health? [Special issue] *Infant Ment. Health J.*, 5.
Wallerstein, J. S. (2000), *The Unexpected Legacy of Divorce*. New York: Hyperion.
Winterson, J. (1994), *Written on the Body*. New York: Knopf.

Index